Microsoft®
MS-DOS®
Programmer's Reference

Written, edited, and produced by
Microsoft Corporation

Distributed by Microsoft Press

The Official Reference Manual for MS-DOS Programming

Microsoft
P R E S S

PUBLISHED BY
Microsoft Press
A Division of Microsoft Corporation
One Microsoft Way, Redmond, Washington 98052-6399

Copyright © 1991 Microsoft Corporation.

Library of Congress Cataloging-in-Publication Data

MS-DOS programmer's reference : version 5.0 / Microsoft Corporation.
    p. cm.
  Includes index.
  ISBN 1-55615-329-5
  1. MS-DOS (Computer operating system) I. Microsoft.
QA76.76.O63M745 1991
005.4'46--dc20   91-8992
                                                    CIP
Printed and bound in the United States of America.

1 2 3 4 5 6 7 8 9 MLML 6 5 4 3 2 1

Distributed to the book trade in Canada by Macmillan of Canada, a division of Canada Publishing Corporation.

Distributed to the book trade outside the United States and Canada by Penguin Books Ltd.

Penguin Books Ltd., Harmondsworth, Middlesex, England
Penguin Books Australia Ltd., Ringwood, Victoria, Australia
Penguin Books N.Z. Ltd., 182-190 Wairau Road, Auckland 10, New Zealand

British Cataloging-in-Publication Data available.

Document No. SY0766b-R50-0691

Contents

Chapter 9 Device Drivers

Introduction

1.1 About This Manual

This manual describes the system functions, interrupts, and structures of the Microsoft® MS-DOS® operating system. These features enable MS-DOS programs to use the operating system to carry out tasks such as reading from and writing to files; allocating memory; starting other programs; and using the keyboard, screen, and communications ports.

Topics include overviews of the MS-DOS system functions; a comprehensive reference to the system functions, interrupts, and structures; an explanation of device drivers; and a description of the function interfaces for MS-DOS extensions, such as print spooling, national language support, and task switching.

MS-DOS system functions, interrupts, and structures are designed to be used in assembly-language programs or in assembly-language modules that can be incorporated in C, Pascal, and other high-level-language programs. Therefore, to get the most from this manual, readers should be familiar with the architecture of the 8086 family of microprocessors and have some experience programming in assembly language for the 8086 microprocessor.

Although this manual presents the basic concepts and tasks associated with the system functions, it is not intended to teach programming in the MS-DOS environment. The manual does not provide detailed information about interfaces that are features of a given computer, device adapter, or software extension. For additional resources about MS-DOS and related topics, see Section 1.5, "Further Reading."

1.2 Organization of the Manual

The *MS-DOS Programmer's Reference* consists of nine chapters and three appendixes.

This chapter, "Introduction," shows how to use the manual and provides a brief description of conventions used to present information.

Chapter 2, "Overview of MS-DOS," discusses system features, functions, components, and organization. It also presents a simple MS-DOS program, elaborates the importance of device independence and cooperation as characteristics of MS-DOS programs, and offers programming guidelines.

Chapter 3, "File System," describes the MS-DOS file system, particularly as it relates to disk drives and similar storage devices.

Chapter 4, "Character Input and Output," presents the MS-DOS character devices, such as the system console and communications ports, and describes the system functions used to access these devices.

Chapter 5, "Program Management," defines the resources that are available when programs first start, explains how programs load and run other programs, and shows the proper method for terminating a program. This chapter also describes the format of MS-DOS program files and explains how MS-DOS loads these files and transfers control to them.

Chapter 6, "National Language Support," presents the features of MS-DOS that provide support for foreign-language markets, such as country information, keyboard layouts, and code pages.

Chapter 7, "Interrupts," provides information about software interrupts that a program can use to request services from the operating system and from extensions to the operating system.

Chapter 8, "Interrupt 21h Functions," describes the MS-DOS system functions available through Interrupt 21h. The functions are listed in numeric order according to the number used to call the function.

Chapter 9, "Device Drivers," describes the format of MS-DOS device drivers. It explains how MS-DOS uses device drivers to provide an interface between the operating-system kernel and hardware devices.

Appendix A, "Code Pages," contains code-page tables for the six code pages included with MS-DOS.

Appendix B, "Extended Key Codes," lists the keys and key combinations that generate the extended key codes MS-DOS retrieves when reading from the keyboard.

Appendix C, "Error Values," lists the error values returned by MS-DOS system functions.

1.3 How to Use This Manual

The manual is designed to provide quick access to the syntax and usage of each MS-DOS system function, interrupt, and structure. This section describes the information presented on each reference page. A reference page has the following format:

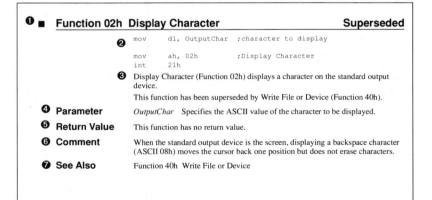

These are the elements shown:

1   The function, interrupt, or structure name. For any function that has been superseded, the word "Superseded" appears to the far right of the function name.

2   The function, interrupt, or structure syntax. The syntax specifies each parameter (or field). It also gives the register that each parameter must be copied to. Comments to the right briefly describe the purpose of each parameter (or field).

3   A description of the function, interrupt, or structure, including its purpose and details of operation. This section may include any special consideration for the function, such as whether the function has been superseded.

4   A full description of each parameter (or field), including permitted values and related structures.

5   A description of the return value or values, including possible error values.

6   A description of special considerations related to use of the function, interrupt, or structure in a program.

7   A list of related functions, interrupts, and structures.

1.4 Notational Conventions

The following notational conventions are used throughout this manual:

Convention	Description
bold	Bold type is used for keywords—for example, the names of commands and of structures and their fields. These names are spelled exactly as they should appear in source programs.
italic	Italic type is used to indicate the name of an argument; this name must be replaced by an actual argument. Italic type is also used to show emphasis in text.
`monospace`	Monospace type is used for syntax and code examples that are provided to illustrate system calls and to show the format of data structures.
FULL CAPITALS	Full capital letters are used for filenames and paths, structure names, and constants.
SMALL CAPITALS	Small capital letters are used for the names of keys and key combinations.

1.5 Further Reading

Following are two of the books that readers may find useful:

Microsoft MS-DOS User's Guide and Reference
MS-DOS Extensions, Ray Duncan, General Editor, for Addison-Wesley

The following books are available from Microsoft Press:

Advanced MS-DOS Programming, 2d ed, by Ray Duncan
Managing Memory with DOS 5, by Dan Gookin
The MS-DOS Encyclopedia, Ray Duncan, General Editor
The Programmer's PC Sourcebook, 2d ed, by Thom Hogan
Programmer's Quick Reference: MS-DOS Extensions, by Ray Duncan
Programmer's Quick Reference: MS-DOS Functions, by Ray Duncan

For more information about references available on the 8086 family of micro-processors, call (800) 548–4725 or write to Intel Literature Sales, P.O. Box 58130, Santa Clara, CA 95052–8130.

Readers who are interested in learning more about the technical details of a computer, device adapter, or software extension should contact that product's manufacturer for additional books and pamphlets.

Overview of MS-DOS

2.1 Introduction

This chapter provides a brief overview of MS-DOS and MS-DOS programs. In particular, it describes the following:

- MS-DOS programming interface
- MS-DOS features
- Programs and device drivers
- Programming guidelines
- System configuration

2.2 MS-DOS Programming Interface: System Functions

MS-DOS provides general, device-independent access to the resources of a computer. The typical MS-DOS computer is a personal or laptop computer based on the 8086 family of microprocessors. The computer operates in real mode and provides devices for mass storage and for input and output—devices such as disk drives, keyboard, screen, and parallel and serial ports.

From a programmer's perspective, the heart of MS-DOS is its system functions, which provide access to the computer's devices and to a wide range of other services, from memory management to national language support.

Programs that use MS-DOS system functions are device-independent—that is, they need no device-specific code to use a given device. Instead, they rely on MS-DOS and its device drivers to handle all device-specific operations.

Even though the number and capabilities of MS-DOS system functions grow with each new version, programs written for the current version can often run with earlier versions as well. A program should always check the version of MS-DOS with which it is running and use this information to determine which MS-DOS features and system functions it can use.

2.3 MS-DOS Features

Programs use MS-DOS system functions to allocate memory, load programs, read from and write to files and devices, connect to a network, and so on.

Programs that use MS-DOS system functions have access to the following features of MS-DOS:

- File system: The MS-DOS file system consists of the files, directories, and supporting data structures on the disks of the computer. Although MS-DOS controls the file system, programs can create, read from, write to, and delete files and directories. The primary supporting data structure for the file system is the file allocation table (FAT). Programs do not access the FAT directly. Instead, MS-DOS manages all the details of the operations on files, including updating the FAT as files are created and modified.

- Character devices: Character devices process data one byte (one character) at a time. Examples of character devices are the computer's keyboard, screen, and serial and parallel ports. Programs can open, read from, and write to character devices by using the same functions as they use for accessing files. Devices have logical names, such as CON and PRN, that programs use to open them. Programs can set operating modes for character devices by using input-and-output-control (IOCTL) functions.

- Program execution: Although MS-DOS is a single-tasking operating system—that is, it runs only one program at a time—programs can load and run other programs. While one program runs, the program that started it is temporarily suspended. MS-DOS ensures that adequate memory and other resources are available to each program.

- Memory management: When it starts a program, MS-DOS allocates memory for program code and data and copies the program file from the storage medium into memory. Programs can free unneeded memory or allocate additional memory while they run. MS-DOS organizes memory in blocks of one or more paragraphs (a paragraph is 16 bytes).

- Networks: A network enables programs running on one computer to use the drives and devices of other computers. Programs can make connections to network drives and devices and then access files and character devices to open, read from, and write to the network drives and devices.

- National language support: National language support permits programs to adapt themselves for operation in a variety of national markets. Programs use country information to prepare the characters and formats for date, time, currency, and other information they display; they use code pages to display and print characters that are language-specific or country-specific.

- Interrupt handling: Programs can install custom interrupt handlers to carry out special processing while they run. For example, a program can install a CTRL+C handler that replaces the default action when the user presses the CTRL+C key combination.

- Task-switcher notifications: Programs can add themselves to the notification chain of the MS-DOS task switcher. Programs that are sensitive to task switches, such as communication programs that must respond immediately to asynchronous input, add themselves to the chain to control when and under what conditions task switching occurs.

2.4 MS-DOS Programs and Device Drivers

MS-DOS supports a broad range of programs—from simple, text-based programs like More to sophisticated, interactive programs like MS-DOS Shell. The MS-DOS system functions provide a comprehensive set of services that satisfy the needs of most programs. Furthermore, programs that require additional features, such as access to custom devices, can enhance MS-DOS by using device drivers. Device drivers extend the capabilities of MS-DOS without requiring changes to the MS-DOS system functions.

2.4.1 MS-DOS Programs

MS-DOS recognizes two program types: .COM and .EXE. A .COM program, sometimes called a "tiny model" program, consists of code, data, and a stack, in a single segment. Such programs typically have a single purpose: carrying out a task and terminating. On the other hand, an .EXE program is usually large and has code and data in separate segments. In fact, an .EXE program can have any number of segments, the combined size of which is limited only by system memory. An .EXE program can be loaded anywhere in memory. MS-DOS adjusts any segment addresses in code and data when it loads the program.

2.4.1.1 A Simple MS-DOS Program

MS-DOS programs can use system functions to carry out their work. Programs call the system functions by using the **int** instruction and specifying Interrupt 21h. For this reason, many MS-DOS programs are written in assembly language or in a mixture of assembly language and a high-level language such as C.

When a program issues an interrupt, execution control transfers to the MS-DOS routine that handles system-function requests. MS-DOS installs this routine at system startup.

The following sample program shows how system functions are called. The program writes the message "Hello, MS-DOS!" to the screen and then terminates immediately.

```
title 'Sample Program'
.model small

.data
String      db 'Hello, MS-DOS!', 13, 10
StringLen   equ $ - String

.code

Start:

        mov     bx, 1                   ;handle of file or device
        mov     cx, StringLen           ;maximum number of bytes to write
        mov     ax, seg String
        mov     ds, ax
        mov     dx, offset String       ;ds:dx points to buffer containing data

        mov     ah, 40h                 ;Write File or Device
        int     21h

        mov     al, 0                   ;program-defined return value

        mov     ah, 4Ch                 ;End Program
        int     21h

.stack  256

        end Start
```

This program calls two system functions: Write File or Device (Interrupt 21h Function 40h) and End Program (Interrupt 21h Function 4Ch).

Write File or Device writes the message. It requires a file or device handle in the BX register; the length of the string, in bytes, in the CX register; the address of the string in the DS:DX registers; and the function number, 40h, in the AH register. In this example, the program uses the standard-output device handle (1), which is supplied by COMMAND.COM when it starts the program. Unless the user redirects output, the program can use the standard-output device handle to write to the screen.

End Program terminates the program and returns control to COMMAND.COM. Every MS-DOS program must terminate by using a system function such as End Program.

2.4.1.2 Terminate-and-Stay-Resident Programs

Although most programs offer their services to users only while the programs are running, MS-DOS allows programs to offer their services even after they terminate. Such programs are called terminate-and-stay-resident programs (TSRs). These programs receive execution control through hardware or software interrupts, such as the interrupt generated by pressing the SHIFT+PRINT SCREEN key combination. The interrupt temporarily suspends the program that is currently running and lets the TSR carry out work. When the TSR has completed its task, it reactivates the suspended program by returning control to it.

Many MS-DOS programs are TSRs—for example, Nlsfunc, Keyb, Share, and Doskey. MS-DOS uses these programs to provide extended capabilities in areas such as national language support and file sharing.

2.4.2 Device Drivers

Programs that need access to custom devices need device drivers. A device driver consists of a pair of routines that handle input and output for a given device. Device drivers are similar to TSRs in that they do not run on their own. Instead, MS-DOS calls the device driver's routines whenever the system needs access to the device. The driver then carries out whatever device-specific operations are required to read from or write to the device, passing information about the operation to MS-DOS.

Most computers and custom devices provide device-support routines in read-only memory (ROM). These routines are collectively called the ROM BIOS (ROM basic input/output system). The ROM BIOS tests and initializes the devices and provides service routines that device drivers can use to read from or write to the devices.

Occasionally, the ROM BIOS for a given device may not be adequate for a program's needs. In such cases, the ROM BIOS for that device can be replaced with a special TSR called a hardware support program. Such a program provides low-level support for an interrupt-driven device. It installs an interrupt service routine that handles interrupts generated by the device. Hardware support programs also define an interface that device drivers or programs can use to retrieve input and send output. Although such programs use some features of MS-DOS, they are extremely device-dependent.

2.5 Programming Guidelines

Two general characteristics enable MS-DOS programs to operate on various computers and to avoid corruption of code and data: device independence and cooperation. The next two sections present guidelines for writing programs that use these characteristics effectively.

2.5.1 Device-Independent Programs

Programs written to use specific devices or to run under a specific version of MS-DOS may not run successfully on all computers. To ensure device independence, programmers should use the following guidelines:

- Avoid direct calls to ROM BIOS routines. Although most computers provide a ROM BIOS, there is no guarantee that all ROM BIOSs are 100-percent compatible.

- Avoid direct access to devices. Programs that improve their performance by accessing devices directly cannot be guaranteed to run successfully on all MS-DOS computers. For example, a program that writes to video memory will work only on computers that have the same or compatible video adapters. Programs should rely on device drivers to access devices.

- Avoid using "undocumented" features. System functions, interrupts, and structures that are internal to MS-DOS are subject to change at any time. Programs that use these undocumented features cannot be guaranteed to run with future versions of MS-DOS.

- Check the MS-DOS version number before using a version's features. Since users may attempt to run programs with older versions of MS-DOS, programs that use features of the latest version should use the system function that retrieves the MS-DOS version number. If the versions do not match, a program can avoid using the features or terminate.

- Check the original equipment manufacturer (OEM) version number before using OEM features. Many computer manufacturers adapt MS-DOS for their own computers and in the process may provide additional features that take advantage of the hardware. Although programs can use these additional features, they should use the system function that retrieves the OEM version number before proceeding.

2.5.2 Cooperative Programs

To prevent corruption of code and data, MS-DOS programs must run cooperatively. To ensure cooperation, programmers should use the following guidelines:

- Use only the memory and resources owned by the program. Since MS-DOS provides no memory protection, it cannot prevent a program from writing to memory it does not own. Unfortunately, writing to memory owned by MS-DOS, by device drivers, or by other programs can corrupt code or data and cause the system to fail.

■ Check for invalid pointers and out-of-bounds indexes. Programs must check the addresses they use, to prevent unintentionally writing to unallocated memory. In particular, programs must not write to memory beyond the end of any allocated block, since doing so may destroy data belonging to another program or corrupt structures MS-DOS uses to manage memory.

■ Do not leave interrupts disabled. Programs should not disable interrupts unless they need to carry out operations that must not be interrupted, such as changing the stack registers. If a program disables interrupts, it should complete the task and reenable the interrupts as quickly as possible.

■ Do not switch the operating mode of the central processing unit (CPU). MS-DOS runs in real mode. Programs that switch to other modes, such as protected mode, effectively disable MS-DOS.

2.6 System Configuration

The system configuration defines limits for certain MS-DOS resources and affects how much memory MS-DOS allocates to support these resources. The system configuration is set by commands in the MS-DOS configuration file, CONFIG.SYS. For programs with special needs, the user may need to add or modify one or more commands.

The following is a list of the configuration commands that may affect programs:

Command	Comments
buffers	Sets the number of file buffers. More buffers can improve performance of programs that repeatedly open the same files or files in the same directories. Disk-caching programs, such as SMARTDrive, can also be used to speed access to files.
country	Sets the current country code. Programs that modify their output for different national markets should require the user to specify this command.
device	Installs a device driver. Programs that require device drivers must direct the user to supply an appropriate **device** or **devicehigh** command.
dos	Specifies whether MS-DOS is to relocate to the high memory area (HMA) and whether MS-DOS is to make upper memory blocks (UMBs) available to programs. Programs that either need more memory or can improve performance with additional memory should recommend this command.
fcbs	Sets the number of file control blocks (FCBs) a program can have open at one time. This setting is useful for programs that use FCBs.

Command	Comments
files	Sets the maximum number of files that may be open at any one time. Programs that open many files or run child programs that open their own files should direct the user to set an appropriate maximum.
install	Loads a terminate-and-stay-resident program (a TSR). A program that must run as a TSR can recommend that the user install it by using this command.
lastdrive	Sets the maximum number of drives MS-DOS permits access to. Programs that connect to many network drives may need to direct the user to set an appropriate maximum.
stacks	Specifies the size and number of stacks used for hardware interrupts. This command is useful for hardware support programs that install interrupt service routines for selected interrupts, especially if the service routines require large amounts of stack space.

For more information about these commands, see the *Microsoft MS-DOS User's Guide and Reference.*

Chapter

3

File System

3.1 Introduction

The MS-DOS file system consists of files, directories, and supporting data structures on a permanent storage device of the computer. MS-DOS controls the file system but allows programs to access it through system functions. This chapter describes these functions and explains the file-system data structures.

3.2 Names and Paths

Each drive, file, and directory has a name. Drive names consist of a single letter (A through Z) followed by a colon (:). File and directory names can have up to eight characters, optionally followed by a period (.) and an extension of up to three characters.

Names and extensions can contain letters, digits, and any of the characters in the following set:

```
! # $ % ^ & ( ) - _ { } ~
```

MS-DOS does not distinguish between uppercase and lowercase letters in filenames and extensions. In other words, the filenames abc and ABC are the same. Although extended ASCII characters (characters with values greater than 127) are also permitted in names, programs should avoid them, since the meanings of the extended characters may differ with different code pages. If a program requires extended characters in names (for example, to spell foreign-language names accurately), the program should use code page 850 to generate the names.

Functions that search for files by pattern accept wildcards in filenames. The MS-DOS wildcards are the asterisk (*) and the question mark (?). The asterisk matches any combination of characters in a name, and the question mark matches any single character.

A path is a combination of a drive name and a directory name that together uniquely specify a directory, or a combination of a drive name, a directory name, and a filename that together uniquely specify a file. The following are valid paths:

```
a:\sample\abc.txt    ;full path specifying a file
a:\sample            ;full path specifying a directory
\sample\abc.txt      ;partial path, assumes current drive
a:abc.txt            ;partial path, assumes current directory
abc.txt              ;partial path, assumes current drive and directory
..\abc.txt           ;partial path, relative to the parent directory
```

Programs use full paths to make an unambiguous reference to a file, and partial paths to let the system construct a full path based on the current drive, the current directory, or both. A path, excluding drive name, must not exceed 64 characters. This rule also applies to full paths that MS-DOS constructs from partial paths.

A network name identifies a resource, such as a drive, file, or device, that is available to a program when network software is installed. The name consists of at least a computer name and a share name; it may also include a path. The computer name uniquely identifies the network server owning the resource, and the share name identifies the resource. If a path is given, it uniquely identifies a directory or file on a network drive.

Network names have the following forms:

```
\\server1\datafiles                  ;network drive
\\computer2\laser                    ;network printer
\\server1\datafiles\readme.txt       ;file on network drive
\\server1\datafiles\log\june91.txt   ;file in path on network drive
```

Programs use network drive and printer names to connect to network resources; they use network filenames to open or create files or directories on network drives.

3.3 Logical Drives

MS-DOS creates one or more logical drives that map to the physical drives of a computer. Programs access logical drives by using a single set of MS-DOS functions, regardless of the type of hardware used by the physical drives.

A computer can have up to 26 logical drives. MS-DOS assigns each drive a unique number, sequentially from 1 through 26 (or from 0 through 25 for the Interrupt 21h functions Set Default Drive and Get Default Drive). The drive numbers correspond to the drive letters used in paths: drive 1 corresponds to drive A, drive 2 to drive B, and so on.

Drive 0 corresponds to the default drive—that is, the drive MS-DOS uses whenever a program supplies a path that does not explicitly specify a drive. When MS-DOS first starts, the default drive is the same as the drive from which the system files were loaded (the startup drive). A program can determine the default drive by using Get Default Drive (Interrupt 21h Function 19h) to obtain the drive number. A program can set the default drive by using Set Default Drive (Interrupt 21h Function 0Eh). A program can determine the startup drive by using Get Startup Drive (Interrupt 21h Function 3305h). On a ROM-based version of MS-DOS, there may be no startup drive; in this case, Get Startup Drive returns the number of the drive containing the CONFIG.SYS file.

Set Default Drive also returns the number of logical drives available. Since few computers have a full set of 26 drives, programs that present a list of available drives to the user must determine which drives are valid. If the CONFIG.SYS file contains a **lastdrive** command, Set Default Drive returns either the number of logical drives for the computer or the number of drives specified by **lastdrive**, whichever is larger. The **lastdrive** command is typically used to prepare extra drive numbers for use with network connections or commands such as **subst**. The extra drive numbers are not valid until a connection to a physical drive is established.

A program can check a logical drive to determine whether it has a corresponding physical drive by using Is Drive Remote (Interrupt 21h Function 4409h). If the logical drive is valid, Is Drive Remote clears the carry flag. Otherwise, the function sets the carry flag and returns 000Fh (ERROR_INVALID_DRIVE). For valid drives, Is Drive Remote also returns the device-attribute value and sets bit 12 if the drive is remote (for example, if it represents a network connection) or is a nonstandard file system (for example, CD-ROM).

Although a program may have determined that a drive is valid, the file system associated with the drive may still be inaccessible. For example, drives with removable media may have an open disk-drive door or no tape mounted on a tape drive. If a program attempts to access a drive under these or similar conditions, the system may prompt the user with an "Abort, Retry, or Fail?" message; if the user selects Abort or Fail, the program terminates immediately. If it is important to prevent the user from terminating the program at this point, the program may need to replace Critical-Error Handler (Interrupt 24h) with a customized handler that receives control whenever drive errors, such as an open drive door, occur. For more information about Critical-Error Handler, see Chapter 7, "Interrupts."

MS-DOS usually reserves the first two logical drives for floppy disk drives. On computers that have only one floppy disk drive, the second logical drive is often treated as an alias for the first. In this case, Is Drive Remote specifies the first and second logical drives as valid drives, even though they share the same physical drive. A program can determine whether two or more logical drives share a physical drive by using Get Logical Drive Map (Interrupt 21h Function 440Eh). This function clears the carry flag and returns a nonzero drive number in the AL register if the drive has aliases. This drive number specifies which logical drive is currently being used to access the physical drive. If a program attempts to access the physical drive by using another logical drive, the system prompts the user with an "Insert diskette for drive..." message. A program can avoid this problem by first using Set Logical Drive Map (Interrupt 21h Function 440Fh) to change the logical drive that is to be used to access the physical drive.

If the file system is accessible, a program can determine how much space is available in the file system by using Get Disk Free Space (Interrupt 21h Function 36h). The function returns the total number of clusters in the file system and the number of available clusters. (A cluster is the smallest amount of space that MS-DOS will allocate for a file or directory.) Get Disk Free Space also returns the number of bytes per sector and the number of sectors per cluster, so the program can compute the total number of bytes currently available in the file system. A program can also use Get Disk Free Space to determine whether a logical drive has a corresponding physical drive. If there is no corresponding physical drive, the function returns 0FFFFh.

3.3.1 Removable-Media Drives

Many programs use removable media, such as disks and tapes, to store data. A program can determine whether a drive supports removable media by using Does Device Use Removable Media (Interrupt 21h Function 4408h). If the specified drive supports removable media, the function clears the carry flag and returns zero in the AX register.

To help distinguish one removable disk or tape from another, the **format** command creates a unique identifier for each volume (for example, each disk or tape) as it formats the volume. Programs can also create their own unique identifiers by using Set Media ID (Interrupt 21h Function 440Dh Minor Code 46h) to set the volume label, volume serial number, and file-system type. A program can retrieve this information by using Get Media ID (Interrupt 21h Function 440Dh Minor Code 66h). (A volume label consists of up to 11 characters of the same type used in filenames.)

Since the user can change the volume in a removable-media drive at any time, programs that read from or write to removable media need ways to prevent inadvertently reading from or writing to the wrong volume. Some drives have change-line capability that helps MS-DOS automatically detect media changes and prompt the user to insert the proper volume so that read and write operations can be completed. A program can determine whether a drive has change-line capability by examining the **dpDevAttr** field in the **DEVICEPARAMS** structure returned by Get Device Parameters (Interrupt 21h Function 440Dh Minor Code 60h). This field also specifies whether the drive supports removable media. (For a full description of the **DEVICEPARAMS** structure, see Section 3.7, "Structures.") If a drive does not have change-line capability, MS-DOS checks for the proper volume before read and write operations. To ensure that data is not lost when a disk is removed, a program may also need to direct MS-DOS to write all data immediately to the volume (that is, *commit* the file).

3.4 Directories

MS-DOS arranges and stores file-system contents in directories. Every file system has at least one directory, called the root directory, and may have additional directories either in the root directory or ordered hierarchically below it. The contents of each directory are described in individual directory entries. MS-DOS strictly controls the format and content of directories.

The root directory is always the topmost directory. MS-DOS creates the root directory when it formats the storage medium. The root directory can hold information for only a fixed number of files or other directories, and the number cannot be changed without reformatting the medium. A program can identify this limit by examining the **dpRootDirEnts** field in the **DEVICEPARAMS** structure returned by Get Device Parameters (Interrupt 21h Function 440Dh Minor Code 60h). This field specifies the maximum number of root-directory entries for the medium.

MS-DOS keeps track of a current directory for each logical drive. The current directory is the default directory MS-DOS uses whenever a program specifies a file without giving a full path. A program can identify the current directory for a drive by using Get Current Directory (Interrupt 21h Function 47h). It can set the current directory for a drive by using Change Current Directory (Interrupt 21h Function 3Bh). Note that changing the current directory for a drive does not change the current drive.

A program can generate a complete list of the directories on a given drive (the directory tree) by using Find First File (Interrupt 21h Function 4Eh) and Find Next File (Interrupt 21h Function 4Fh). If the program specifies the attribute ATTR_DIRECTORY when it calls these functions, they return information about directories as well as files. To generate a complete tree, the program must start the search in the root directory and recursively search each directory it finds.

3.4.1 Directory Management

A program can use Create Directory (Interrupt 21h Function 39h) to add new directories within the current directory, or within other directories if the full path required to specify the new directory does not exceed 64 characters. Unlike the root directory, the new directory is limited only by the amount of space available on the medium, not by a fixed number of entries. MS-DOS initially allocates only a single cluster for the directory, allocating additional clusters only when they are needed.

Every directory except the root directory has two entries when it is created. The first entry specifies the directory itself, and the second entry specifies its parent directory—the directory that contains it. These entries use the special directory names . (an ASCII period) and .. (two ASCII periods), respectively. Programs can use these "names" to form partial paths.

Each directory has attributes that specify the type of access programs have to it. Programs set these attributes by using Set File Attributes (Interrupt 21h Function 4301h). The most common attributes, hidden and system, are often set to prevent users from displaying the directory with the **dir** command. A directory can also be made read-only, although this attribute does not prevent the deletion of the directory or its files. A program can retrieve a directory's attributes by using Get File Attributes (Interrupt 21h Function 4300h)

A program can rename a directory by using Rename File (Interrupt 21h Function 56h), but the new name must not cause the full path for the directory to exceed 64 characters. The program must check the path length, since MS-DOS does not.

A program deletes a directory by using Remove Directory (Interrupt 21h Function 3Ah). A directory cannot be deleted unless it is empty—that is, contains no files or other directories.

3.5 Files

MS-DOS gives programs access to files in the file system. Programs can read from and write to existing files, as well as create new ones.

Files can contain any amount of data, up to the limits of the storage medium. (Since MS-DOS stores the size of a file as a 31-bit number, the theoretical maximum for file size is 2 gigabytes.) MS-DOS stores a file's data in the order the program writes the data, so the meaning and format of the data are entirely up to the program.

Apart from its contents, every file has a name (possibly with an extension), access attributes, and an associated date and time. This information is stored in the file's directory entry, not in the file itself.

3.5.1 File Management

A program can create a new file by using Create File with Handle (Interrupt 21h Function 3Ch). This function creates a file, gives it the specified name, places it in the specified directory on the specified drive (or in the current directory on the current drive, if a path is not given), and returns a handle for the file. The new file is initially empty (that is, it contains zero bytes), but it is opened for both reading and writing, so the program can write to it by using Write File or Device (Interrupt 21h Function 40h) and then read from it by using Read File or Device (Interrupt 21h Function 3Fh).

When a program creates a file, it sets file attributes that specify the type of access programs have to the file. These attributes can be any of the following:

Attribute	Description
ATTR_READONLY (01h)	Specifies a read-only file. Programs cannot write to the file.
ATTR_HIDDEN (02h)	Specifies a hidden file. System commands such as **dir** do not list the file. Functions such as Find First File and Find Next File (Interrupt 21h Functions 4Eh and 4Fh) do not return information about the file unless the search specifies this attribute.
ATTR_SYSTEM (04h)	Specifies a system file. This attribute is usually reserved for system files such as IO.SYS and MSDOS.SYS. This has the same effect as ATTR_HIDDEN and, when applied to program files, prevents COMMAND.COM from finding and running the files.
ATTR_ARCHIVE (20h)	Specifies a file that is new or has been modified. The system automatically sets this attribute when the file is created or written to. The attribute does not affect access to the file but gives programs a quick way to check for potential changes to the file contents.

A file is a normal file (ATTR_NORMAL) if it has no other attributes. Programs have full access to normal files.

Note that, even if the program specifies the read-only attribute, a new file is always opened for both reading and writing, so that the program can write to the initially empty file. The read-only attribute does not take effect until after the file is closed for the first time.

A program can determine a file's attributes by using Get File Attributes (Interrupt 21h Function 4300h), and it can change them by using Set File Attributes (Interrupt 21h Function 4301h).

A program can retrieve a file's date and time by using Get File Date and Time (Interrupt 21h Function 5700h). MS-DOS initially sets the date and time when a file is created and updates them when a program writes to the file. A program can change the date and time for a file by using Set File Date and Time (Interrupt 21h Function 5701h).

A program can retrieve the name, attributes, time, date, and size of one or more files by using Find First File (Interrupt 21h Function 4Eh) and Find Next File (Interrupt 21h Function 4Fh). These functions search for files having names and attributes that match values supplied by the program. If the functions find files that match, they return information for the files in a **FILEINFO** structure. (For a full description of the **FILEINFO** structure, see Section 3.9, "Structures.") If the name supplied by the program contains wildcards, the functions return information about all files that match the patterns. Wildcard searches are iterative—that is, the program calls Find First File and then repeatedly calls Find Next File until all files matching the name and attributes have been found. Both Find First File and Find Next File copy the file information to the buffer pointed to by the disk transfer address (DTA). By default, MS-DOS sets the DTA to point to the last 128 bytes of the program segment prefix (PSP). (For information about the PSP, see Chapter 5, "Program Management.") If this default buffer is not adequate, the program can change the DTA by using Set Disk Transfer Address (Interrupt 21h Function 1Ah). A program can retrieve the current DTA by using Get Disk Transfer Address (Interrupt 21h Function 2Fh).

A program can rename a file by using Rename File (Interrupt 21h Function 56h). This function replaces the name and extension in the directory entry with a new name and extension. All other information remains unchanged.

A program can also use Rename File to move files. If the program supplies a new path for the file, the function moves the file's directory entry from the old directory to the new one. However, the function cannot move a file from one drive to another.

A program can delete a file by using Delete File (Interrupt 21h Function 41h). This function frees any space on the drive that has been allocated for the file and marks the file's directory entry as deleted.

3.5.2 File Input and Output

Most MS-DOS programs carry out file operations through file-handle functions that use a unique 16-bit value, called a handle, to identify a file. The program receives a file handle when it opens or creates a file and uses the handle with subsequent functions to read from, write to, or carry out other operations on the file.

Programs can open existing files by using Open File with Handle (Interrupt 21h Function 3Dh). The program supplies a filename (or full path) and the type of file access required: read-only, write-only, or read-and-write. The function opens the file and returns a handle for reading from, writing to, and closing the file.

A program can read from a file opened for read access by using Read File or Device (Interrupt 21h Function 3Fh). Similarly, a program can write to a file opened for write access by using Write File or Device (Interrupt 21h Function 40h). When a program reads from or writes to a file, it specifies the number of bytes of data to be read or written and supplies the address of the buffer that contains or receives the data. A program can continue to read from a file until it reaches the end of the file; it can continue to write to a file until the file system has no more space available.

Every open file has a file pointer that specifies the next byte to read from the file or the next position to receive a byte written to the file. When a file is opened or created, the file pointer is set to zero, the beginning of the file. As a program reads from or writes to the file, the system moves the file pointer by the number of bytes read or written. When a program has read all bytes in a file, the file pointer moves to the end of the file and no further reading is possible. When a program writes to a file, the system writes over existing data unless the file pointer is at the end of the file, in which case the system appends the new data to the file and moves the file pointer to the new end of the file.

A program can move the file pointer by using Move File Pointer (Interrupt 21h Function 42h). The program must specify the amount to move and where to move from (beginning of file, end of file, or current position). The function moves the pointer and returns its new position relative to the beginning of the file.

When the number of bytes between the file pointer and the end of the file are fewer than the program requests, MS-DOS reads only to the end of the file. For example, if a program requests 512 bytes but only 250 bytes remain between the file pointer and the end of the file, only those 250 bytes are read. Read File or Device returns the number of bytes read, so that the program can determine how many bytes in its buffer are valid. Similarly, Write File or Device returns the number of bytes written, which may be fewer than requested if writing that number of bytes would exceed the maximum file size or if all available space on the storage medium has been used before the write operation is complete.

A program can truncate an existing file to zero bytes by using Create File with Handle and specifying the name of the existing file. (If the existing file is already open, however, Create File with Handle simply creates an additional handle for it.) To avoid unintentionally destroying existing files when creating new ones, a program should use Create New File (Interrupt 21h Function 5Bh), which returns an error value if the new filename matches an existing filename.

Programs often use temporary files for short-term storage and delete the files when no longer needed. A program can create temporary files with unique names by specifying a path for Create Temporary File (Interrupt 21h Function 5Ah), which then creates a file having a name that does not conflict with the name of any other file in that path.

Programs should close files when they are no longer needed. Leaving files open can cause loss or corruption of data if a system fails. A program can close a file by using Close File with Handle (Interrupt 21h Function 3Eh). If the program changed the file, MS-DOS updates the file's time and date and sets the archive attribute. MS-DOS closes any open files when a program terminates.

3.5.3 Internal File Buffers

By default, MS-DOS collects data in internal file buffers before writing it to a drive. This improves system performance by reducing the number of times MS-DOS accesses the drive hardware. MS-DOS usually holds the data from a write operation until the buffer is filled or the program closes the file. While held in a buffer, data is inaccessible to the program.

If necessary, a program can transfer a file's written data to a drive immediately by using Commit File (Interrupt 21h Function 68h). If a program must ensure that data written to a file is always committed to the drive immediately, it can open or create the file by using Extended Open/Create (Interrupt 21h Function 6Ch) and specifying the OPEN_FLAGS_COMMIT option. This option causes MS-DOS to commit the file after each write operation, without individual calls to Commit File.

A program can commit the data in all internal file buffers in one step by using Reset Drive (Interrupt 21h Function 0Dh). This function is typically used by CTRL+C Handler (Interrupt 23h) to ensure that the contents of all open files are updated before the program terminates. Note, however, that this function does not update the directory entries for the files, so changes to time, date, and file size may not be recorded.

3.5.4 File Handles

By default, MS-DOS imposes a system-wide limit of 8 on the number of file handles available for all programs. This means that current programs (whether running or suspended) can have no more than eight open files among them. MS-DOS automatically opens three devices (CON, PRN, AUX) as standard devices. Since the standard devices always remain open, the number of available open files is always 3 less than the system limit. If more files are needed, the user can set a new limit (up to 255) by using the **files** command in the CONFIG.SYS file.

MS-DOS also imposes a limit of 20 on the number of file handles available for individual programs. Since most programs inherit copies of the standard-device handles, the number of available handles is always 5 less than the program limit. (Although MS-DOS opens only three standard devices, the program inherits 5 handles to access them.) If more handles are needed, a program can increase its own limit by using Set Maximum Handle Count (Interrupt 21h Function 67h). Increasing the number of available handles does not increase the maximum number of open files. Alternatively, the program can close one or more of the standard devices and free the handles for other files.

A program can open the same file more than once, receiving a unique handle each time. The program can use any of the handles to access the file. For file management, some of the information maintained by the system for each handle is shared by all handles. For example, no matter how many handles exist for a given file, the file never has more than one file pointer. This means a program cannot access different parts of the file at the same time, because moving the file pointer by using one handle also moves it for all other handles.

3.6 Network Drives

A program can access the files and directories on a network drive by connecting to the drive using Make Network Connection (Interrupt 21h Function 5F03h). This function associates a drive name with the network drive, permitting the program to use the network drive as a logical drive. A program can connect to a network drive only if the network is running. To determine whether the network is running, a program can use Get Machine Name (Interrupt 21h Function 5E00h). This function returns an error value if the network is not running.

To connect to a network drive, a program must supply the drive's network name, which consists of a computer name and a share name. The computer name uniquely identifies the network server owning the drive, and the share name identifies the drive. A program creates a network name by combining the computer and share names as a zero-terminated ASCII string with the form shown in the following example:

```
NetworkDrive    DB '\\SERVER\FILES',0,0
```

If the network drive is password-protected, the program must supply the password, as shown in the following example:

```
NetworkDrive    DB '\\SERVER\FILES',0,'PaSsWoRd',0
```

The drive name the program provides must be the name of one of the available drives identified by using Set Default Drive (Interrupt 21h Function 0Eh). If the specified drive is valid (that is, if it has a corresponding physical drive), the physical drive is temporarily inaccessible while the drive name is associated with the network drive.

After a network connection is made, a program can use functions such as Get Disk Free Space (Interrupt 21h Function 36h) to retrieve information about the network drive, and it can open or create files and directories on the network drive, as long as the network grants read-and-write permission.

Once a program connects to a network drive, the connection is a global resource until the drive is explicitly disconnected. A program can check for existing network connections by using Is Drive Remote (Interrupt 21h Function 4409h). This function sets bit 12 in the DX register if a logical drive is associated with a network drive. A program can retrieve the drive's network name by using Get Assign-List Entry (Interrupt 21h Function 5F02h).

A program can disconnect from a network drive by using Delete Network Connection (Interrupt 21h Function 5F04h) to remove any association between the drive name and the network drive. In general, a program should close and disconnect from any network device it no longer needs.

Some network software may provide other means to connect and disconnect network drives. For more information about network connections, see the applicable network documentation.

3.7 File Sharing

Any program can share its open files with any other program. By default, the system permits programs to open and modify a file even if another program has the file open already. Because unrestricted file sharing can lead to such problems as one program writing over the data another program is trying to read, MS-DOS provides file-sharing modes that restrict access to open files, as well as a file-locking function that enables one program to temporarily deny other programs access to one or more regions (consecutive bytes) of a file.

File-sharing mode determines whether a file can be opened by more than one program at a time. When a program opens a file by using Open File with Handle (Interrupt 21h Function 3Dh), it can set the file-sharing mode to one of the following:

Mode	Description
OPEN_SHARE_COMPATIBILITY (000h)	Allows other programs full access to the file.
OPEN_SHARE_DENYREADWRITE (0010h)	Prevents other programs from opening the file.
OEPN_SHARE_DENYWRITE (0020h)	Permits other programs to open the file for reading but not for writing.
OPEN_SHARE_DENYREAD (0030h)	Permits other programs to open the file for writing but not for reading.
OPEN_SHARE_DENYNONE (0040h)	Permits other programs to open the file for reading and writing, but not for compatibility access.

In general, programs that access files across a network or that leave files open while running child programs should deny other programs access to those files, to prevent unexpected changes to them. Some programs, however, are designed to share their open files and must not deny access to them. These programs can prevent unexpected changes by using Lock/Unlock File (Interrupt 21h Function 5Ch) to lock one or more regions of the file.

When a region is locked, other programs can open the file but cannot access the locked region. Attempting to do so returns a lock-violation error. The program that locks a region can also unlock it by using Lock/Unlock File.

In general, a program that locks regions should unlock them as soon as possible, to keep other programs from waiting unnecessarily. To enhance the performance of programs that lock regions, MS-DOS automatically retries access to a locked region several times before returning the lock-violation error. This reduces the number of times a program must retry access on its own. A program can set the number of retries MS-DOS is to attempt by using Set Sharing Retry Count (Interrupt 21h Function 440Bh).

File-sharing modes and file locking are available on a local computer only if the Share program is loaded. A program can determine whether Share is loaded by using Get SHARE.EXE Installed State (Interrupt 2Fh Function 10h). If Share is loaded, this function clears the carry flag and sets the AL register to 0FFh.

3.8 Low-Level Input and Output

Low-level input and output gives a program access to the individual sectors on a logical drive. (A sector is a drive's smallest storage unit.) This low-level input and output completely bypasses MS-DOS file-system control and enables a program to directly manipulate the data structures that support the file system. Programs that read and write sectors do so at their own risk.

3.8.1 Device Parameters

Programs that read and write sectors need device-parameter information to avoid corrupting the medium. A program can retrieve a logical drive's device parameters by using Get Device Parameters (Interrupt 21h Function 440Dh Minor Code 60h). These parameters, returned in the form of a **DEVICEPARAMS** structure, specify such information as the total number of sectors on the medium and the sizes of the file-system data structures. The **DEVICEPARAMS** structure has the following form:

```
DEVICEPARAMS        STRUC
        dpSpecFunc      db    ?    ;special functions
        dpDevType       db    ?    ;device type
        dpDevAttr       dw    ?    ;device attributes
        dpCylinders     dw    ?    ;number of cylinders
        dpMediaType     db    ?    ;media type
                                   ;Start of BIOS parameter block (BPB)
        dpBytesPerSec   dw    ?    ;bytes per sector
        dpSecPerClust   db    ?    ;sectors per cluster
        dpResSectors    dw    ?    ;number of reserved sectors
        dpFATs          db    ?    ;number of file allocation tables
        dpRootDirEnts   dw    ?    ;number of root-directory entries
        dpSectors       dw    ?    ;total number of sectors
        dpMedia         db    ?    ;media descriptor
        dpFATsecs       dw    ?    ;number of sectors per FAT
        dpSecPerTrack   dw    ?    ;sectors per track
        dpHeads         dw    ?    ;number of heads
        dpHiddenSecs    dd    ?    ;number of hidden sectors
        dpHugeSectors   dd    ?    ;number of sectors if dpSectors = 0
                                   ;End of BIOS parameter block (BPB)
DEVICEPARAMS        ENDS
```

For a full description of the **DEVICEPARAMS** structure, see Section 3.9, "Structures."

A program can set the device parameters of a logical drive by using Set Device Parameters (Interrupt 21h Function 440Dh Minor Code 40h). If the physical drive permits a variety of media formats, this function enables the program to select the specific format it requires. For example, a program can set the parameters to format a 360-kilobyte floppy disk in a 1.2-megabyte drive. The following statements define device parameters for several common formats:

```
SS160   DEVICEPARAMS <0,1,2,40,0,512,1,1,2, 64, 320,0feh,1, 8,1,0,0>
SS180   DEVICEPARAMS <0,1,2,40,0,512,1,1,2, 64, 360,0fch,2, 9,1,0,0>
DD320   DEVICEPARAMS <0,1,2,40,0,512,2,1,2,112, 640,0ffh,1, 8,2,0,0>
DD360   DEVICEPARAMS <0,1,2,40,0,512,2,1,2,112, 720,0fdh,1, 9,2,0,0>
SH320   DEVICEPARAMS <0,1,2,80,0,512,2,1,2,112, 640,0fah,1, 8,1,0,0>
DH360   DEVICEPARAMS <0,1,2,80,0,512,2,1,2,112, 720,0fch,2, 9,1,0,0>
DH640   DEVICEPARAMS <0,1,2,80,0,512,2,1,2,112,1280,0fbh,2, 8,2,0,0>
DH720   DEVICEPARAMS <0,1,2,80,0,512,2,1,2,112,1440,0f9h,3, 9,2,0,0>
DH144   DEVICEPARAMS <0,1,2,80,0,512,1,1,2,224,2880,0f0h,9,18,2,0,0>
DH120   DEVICEPARAMS <0,1,2,80,0,512,1,1,2,224,2400,0f0h,7,15,2,0,0>
```

3.8.2 Absolute Disk Read and Write Operations

A program can read one or more sectors from a drive by using Absolute Disk Read (Interrupt 25h). The program must specify a drive number, a pointer to a buffer, a starting-sector number, and the number of sectors to be read. The function copies the specified sectors to a buffer.

A program can write one or more sectors to a drive by using Absolute Disk Write (Interrupt 26h). Programs that write directly to sectors must take care not to corrupt the data MS-DOS uses to maintain the file system. For information about this data, see Section 3.8.4, "Logical-Drive Contents."

Absolute Disk Read and Absolute Disk Write read and write only nonhidden sectors. (Nonhidden sectors are numbered consecutively starting from zero.) This means that neither function can be used on sectors containing partition tables. For information about accessing all sectors of a logical drive, see Section 3.8.3, "Input-and-Output-Control Functions."

3.8.3 Input-and-Output-Control Functions

MS-DOS provides input-and-output-control (IOCTL) functions to read from, write to, and format sectors on drives. The IOCTL functions, like the Absolute Disk Read and Write functions, can access one or more sectors at a time. Unlike the Absolute Disk Read and Write functions, however, the IOCTL functions can read and write hidden sectors, such as those containing partition tables and other file-system data structures.

A program can read and write sectors on a drive by using Read Track on Logical Drive (Interrupt 21h Function 440Dh Minor Code 61h) and Write Track on Logical Drive (Interrupt 21h Function 440Dh Minor Code 41h). These functions require the program to specify the cylinder number, head number, and starting-sector number of the sectors to read or write.

The numbers of cylinders, heads, and sectors are properties of the medium and are specified in its device parameters. For example, the **dpHeads** field in a logical drive's **DEVICEPARAMS** structure returned by the Get Device Parameters function specifies the number of heads for the drive. For a full description of the **DEVICEPARAMS** structure, see Section 3.9, "Structures."

3.8.4 Logical-Drive Contents

A logical drive has the following general format:

Data area	Description
Hidden sectors	Although any logical drive can have hidden sectors, these sectors are usually associated with disks that can be divided into partitions. If a disk has partitions, its first hidden sector contains a table of **PARTENTRY** structures, each specifying the size and location of the physical sectors in a single partition. The table is placed at the end of the sector. For a full description of the **PARTENTRY** structure, see Section 3.9, "Structures."
Reserved sectors	A logical drive can have any number of reserved sectors but usually has only one, called the startup sector. The startup sector contains the MS-DOS startup program and information that defines the size and format of the disk. The sector ends with the startup-sector signature, 0AA55h, stored in the last 2 bytes.

Data area	Description
File allocation table	The file allocation table (FAT) is an array used by MS-DOS to keep track of which clusters on a drive have been allocated for each file or directory. As a program creates a new file or adds to an existing one, the system allocates sectors for that file, writes the data to the given sectors, and keeps track of the allocated sectors by recording them in the FAT. To conserve space and speed up record-keeping, each record in the FAT corresponds to two or more consecutive sectors (called a cluster). The number of sectors in a cluster depends on the type and capacity of the drive but is always a power of 2.

Every logical drive has at least one FAT, and most drives have two, one serving as a backup should sectors containing the other fail. The FAT immediately follows the startup sector and any other reserved sectors. |
| Root directory | Every volume has a root directory with entries that specify the volume's name, files, and other directories. |
| File and directory space | All remaining space in the volume is reserved for files and additional directories. |

Depending on the number of clusters on the drive, the FAT consists of an array of either 12-bit or 16-bit entries. Drives with more than 4086 clusters have a 16-bit FAT; those with 4086 or fewer clusters have a 12-bit FAT.

The first two entries in a FAT (3 bytes for a 12-bit FAT and 4 bytes for a 16-bit FAT) are reserved. In most versions of MS-DOS, the first byte contains the media descriptor (the same descriptor provided in the **DEVICEPARAMS** structure) and the additional reserved bytes are set to 0FFh.

Each FAT entry represents a corresponding cluster on the drive. If the cluster is part of a file or directory, the entry contains either a marker specifying the cluster as the last in that file or directory, or an index pointing to the next cluster in the file or directory. If a cluster is not part of a file or directory, the entry contains a value indicating the cluster's status. The following table shows possible FAT entry values. The digit in parentheses represents the additional 4 bits of a 16-bit entry.

Value	Meaning
(0)000h	Available cluster.
(0)002h-(F)FEFh	Index of entry for the next cluster in the file or directory. Note that (0)001h does not appear in a FAT, since that value corresponds to the FAT's second reserved entry. Index numbering is based on the beginning of the FAT.

Value	Meaning
(F)FF0h-(F)FF6h	Reserved; do not use.
(F)FF7h	Bad sector in cluster; do not use cluster.
(F)FF8h-(F)FFFh	Last cluster of file or directory.

Each file and directory consists of one or more clusters, each cluster represented by a single entry in the FAT. The **deStartCluster** field in the **DIRENTRY** structure corresponding to the file or directory specifies the index of the first FAT entry for the file or directory. (For a full description of the **DIRENTRY** structure, see Section 3.9, "Structures.") This entry contains 0(F)FFFh if there are no further FAT entries for that file or directory, or it contains the index of the next FAT entry for the file or directory. For example, the following segment of a 16-bit FAT shows the FAT entries for a file consisting of four clusters:

```
        .
        .
        .

    dw  0003h   ; Cluster 2 points to cluster 3
    dw  0005h   ; Cluster 3 points to cluster 5
    dw  0FFF7h  ; Cluster 4 contains a bad sector
    dw  0006h   ; Cluster 5 points to cluster 6
    dw  0FFFFh  ; Cluster 6 is the last cluster for the file
    dw  0       ; Clusters 7,8 and 9 are available
    dw  0
    dw  0
        .
        .
        .
```

3.9 Structures

This section describes the structures MS-DOS uses in the system functions that support file systems.

■ BOOTSECTOR

```
BOOTSECTOR   STRUC
    bsJump              db  3 dup(?)          ;E9 XX XX or EB XX 90
    bsOemName           db  '????????'        ;OEM name and version
                                              ;Start of BIOS parameter block
    bsBytesPerSec       dw  ?                 ;bytes per sector
    bsSecPerClust       db  ?                 ;sectors per cluster
    bsResSectors        dw  ?                 ;number of reserved sectors
    bsFATs              db  ?                 ;number of file allocation tables
    bsRootDirEnts       dw  ?                 ;number of root-directory entries
    bsSectors           dw  ?                 ;total number of sectors
    bsMedia             db  ?                 ;media descriptor
    bsFATsecs           dw  ?                 ;number of sectors per FAT
    bsSecPerTrack       dw  ?                 ;sectors per track
    bsHeads             dw  ?                 ;number of heads
    bsHiddenSecs        dd  ?                 ;number of hidden sectors
    bsHugeSectors       dd  ?                 ;number of sectors if bsSectors = O
                                              ;End of BIOS parameter block
    bsDriveNumber       db  ?                 ;drive number (8Oh)
    bsReserved1         db  ?                 ;reserved
    bsBootSignature     db  ?                 ;extended boot signature (29h)
    bsVolumeID          dd  ?                 ;volume ID number
    bsVolumeLabel       db  11 dup(?)         ;volume label
    bsFileSysType       db  8 dup(?)          ;file-system type
BOOTSECTOR   ENDS
```

The **BOOTSECTOR** structure contains information about the disk (or other storage medium) for a particular drive. The structure appears at the beginning of the first sector (the boot, or startup, sector) of the disk.

Fields

bsJump   Contains a jump instruction to the bootstrap routine, which loads the operating system from the drive.

bsOemName   Specifies the name of the original equipment manufacturer (OEM) and the manufacturer's version of MS-DOS.

bsBytesPerSec   Specifies the number of bytes per sector.

bsSecPerClust   Specifies the number of sectors in a cluster. The sectors must be consecutive, and the number must be a power of 2.

bsResSectors   Specifies the number of reserved sectors on the drive, beginning with sector 0. Typically, this value is 1 (for the startup sector), unless the disk-drive manufacturer's software reserves additional sectors.

bsFATs   Specifies the number of file allocation tables (FATs) following the reserved sectors. Most versions of MS-DOS maintain one or more copies of the primary FAT and use the extra copies to recover data on the disk if the first FAT is corrupted.

bsRootDirEnts   Specifies the maximum number of entries in the root directory.

bsSectors   Specifies the number of sectors on the drive. If the size of the drive is greater than 32 MB, this field is zero and the number of sectors is specified by the **bsHugeSectors** field.

bsMedia   Specifies the media descriptor, a value that identifies the type of media in a drive. Some device drivers use the media descriptor to determine quickly whether the removable medium in a drive has changed. MS-DOS passes the media descriptor to the device driver so that programs can check the media type. Also, the first byte in the FAT is often (but not always) identical to the media descriptor.

Following is a list of the most commonly used media descriptors and their corresponding media:

Value	Type of medium
0F0h	3.5-inch, 2 sides, 18 sectors/track (1.44 MB); 3.5-inch, 2 sides, 36 sectors/track (2.88 MB); 5.25-inch, 2 sides, 15 sectors/track (1.2 MB). This value is also used to describe other media types.
0F8h	Hard disk, any capacity.
0F9h	3.5-inch, 2 sides, 9 sectors/track, 80 tracks/side (720K); 5.25-inch, 2 sides, 15 sectors/track, 40 tracks/side (1.2 MB).
0FAh	5.25-inch, 1 side, 8 sectors/track, (320K).
0FBh	3.5-inch, 2 sides, 8 sectors/track (640K).
0FCh	5.25-inch, 1 side, 9 sectors/track, 40 tracks/side (180K).
0FDh	5.25-inch, 2 sides, 9 sectors/track, 40 tracks/side (360K). This value is also used for 8-inch disks.
0FEh	5.25-inch, 1 side, 8 sectors/track, 40 tracks/side (160K). This value is also used for 8-inch disks.
0FFh	5.25-inch, 2 sides, 8 sectors/track, 40 tracks/side (320K).

bsFATsecs   Specifies the number of sectors occupied by each FAT.

bsSecPerTrack   Specifies the number of sectors on a single track.

bsHeads   Specifies the number of read/write heads on the drive.

bsHiddenSecs   Specifies the number of hidden sectors on the drive.

bsHugeSectors   Specifies the number of sectors if the **bsSectors** field is zero. This value supports drives larger than 32 MB.

bsDriveNumber   Specifies whether the drive is the first hard disk drive, in which case the value is 80h; otherwise, the value is 00h. This field is used internally by MS-DOS.

bsReserved1   Reserved; do not use.

bsBootSignature   Specifies the extended boot-signature record. This value is 29h.

bsVolumeID   Specifies the volume serial number.

bsVolumeLabel   Specifies the volume label.

bsFileSysType   Specifies the type of file system, given as an 8-byte ASCII string. This field can be one of the following values:

Name	Meaning
FAT12	12-bit FAT
FAT16	16-bit FAT

If the name has fewer than eight characters, space characters (ASCII 20h) fill the remaining bytes in the field.

Comments   The **BOOTSECTOR** structure shares the first sector with the bootstrap routine and the boot-sector signature. The boot-sector signature, stored in the last two bytes of the sector, must be 0AA55h.

■ DEVICEPARAMS

```
DEVICEPARAMS      STRUC
    dpSpecFunc      db   ?    ;special functions
    dpDevType       db   ?    ;device type
    dpDevAttr       dw   ?    ;device attributes
    dpCylinders     dw   ?    ;number of cylinders
    dpMediaType     db   ?    ;media type
                              ;Start of BIOS parameter block (BPB)
    dpBytesPerSec   dw   ?    ;bytes per sector
    dpSecPerClust   db   ?    ;sectors per cluster
    dpResSectors    dw   ?    ;number of reserved sectors
    dpFATs          db   ?    ;number of file allocation tables
    dpRootDirEnts   dw   ?    ;number of root-directory entries
    dpSectors       dw   ?    ;total number of sectors
    dpMedia         db   ?    ;media descriptor
    dpFATsecs       dw   ?    ;number of sectors per FAT
    dpSecPerTrack   dw   ?    ;sectors per track
    dpHeads         dw   ?    ;number of heads
    dpHiddenSecs    dd   ?    ;number of hidden sectors
    dpHugeSectors   dd   ?    ;number of sectors if dpSectors = 0
                              ;End of BIOS parameter block (BPB)
DEVICEPARAMS      ENDS
```

The **DEVICEPARAMS** structure contains device parameters for the medium in a given logical drive.

Fields

dpSpecFunc   Specifies the special function or functions to be carried out by Set Device Parameters (Interrupt 21h Function 440Dh Minor Code 40h). This field can contain some combination of the following values:

Bit	Meaning
0	0 = Use the fields **dpBytesPerSec** through **dpHugeSectors** to set the default BIOS parameter block (BPB) for this device.
	1 = Use the device BPB for all subsequent Build BPB requests.
1	0 = Read all fields.
	1 = Ignore all fields, but read the **TRACKLAYOUT** structure appended to the end of the structure.
2	0 = Do not use.
	1 = The sectors in the track are all the same size, and the sector numbers are in the range 1 through the total number of sectors on the track. This bit should always be set.

All other bits are reserved and must be zero.

dpDevType   Specifies the device type. This field can be one of the following values:

Value	Meaning
00h	320/360K
01h	1.2 MB
02h	720K
03h	8-inch, single-density
04h	8-inch, double-density

Value	Meaning
05h	Hard disk
06h	Tape drive
07h	1.44 MB
08h	2.88 MB
09h	Other

dpDevAttr   Specifies device attributes. This field can contain some combination of the following values:

Bit	Meaning
0	0 = The medium is removable.
	1 = The medium is not removable.
1	0 = Disk change-line is not supported (no door-lock support).
	1 = Disk change-line is supported (door-lock support).

All other bits are reserved and must be zero.

dpCylinders   Specifies the maximum number of cylinders that the physical device can support. This information is set by the device.

dpMediaType   Specifies which medium the drive currently accepts (for drives that accept more than one media type). For a 1.2-MB drive, if bit 0 is clear, it indicates that the drive accepts quad-density, 1.2-MB disks (the default media type); if bit 0 is set, the drive accepts double-density, 320/360K disks.

dpBytesPerSec   Specifies the number of bytes per sector.

dpSecPerClust   Specifies the number of sectors in a cluster. The sectors must be consecutive, and the number must be a power of 2.

dpResSectors   Specifies the number of reserved sectors on the drive, beginning with sector 0. Typically, this value is 1 (for the startup sector), unless the disk-drive manufacturer's software reserves additional sectors.

dpFATs   Specifies the number of file allocation tables (FATs) following the reserved sectors. Most versions of MS-DOS maintain one or more copies of the primary FAT and use the extra copies to recover data on the disk if the first FAT is corrupted.

dpRootDirEnts   Specifies the maximum number of entries in the root directory.

dpSectors   Specifies the number of sectors on the drive. If the size of the drive is greater than 32 MB, this field is set to zero and the number of sectors is specified by the **dpHugeSectors** field.

dpMedia   Specifies the media descriptor, a value that identifies the type of media in a drive. Some device drivers use the media descriptor to determine quickly whether the removable medium in a drive has changed. MS-DOS passes the media descriptor to the device driver so that programs can check the media type. Also, the first byte in the FAT is often (but not always) identical to the media descriptor.

Following is a list of the most commonly used media descriptors and their corresponding media:

Value	Type of medium
0F0h	3.5-inch, 2 sides, 18 sectors/track (1.44 MB); 3.5-inch, 2 sides, 36 sectors/track (2.88 MB); 5.25-inch, 2 sides, 15 sectors/track (1.2 MB). This value is also used to describe other media types.
0F8h	Hard disk, any capacity.
0F9h	3.5-inch, 2 sides, 9 sectors/track, 80 tracks/side (720K); 5.25-inch, 2 sides, 15 sectors/track, 40 tracks/side (1.2 MB).
0FAh	5.25-inch, 1 side, 8 sectors/track, (320K).
0FBh	3.5-inch, 2 sides, 8 sectors/track (640K).
0FCh	5.25-inch, 1 side, 9 sectors/track, 40 tracks/side (180K).
0FDh	5.25-inch, 2 sides, 9 sectors/track, 40 tracks/side (360K). This value is also used for 8-inch disks.
0FEh	5.25-inch, 1 side, 8 sectors/track, 40 tracks/side (160K). This value is also used for 8-inch disks.
0FFh	5.25-inch, 2 sides, 8 sectors/track, 40 tracks/side (320K).

dpFATsecs   Specifies the number of sectors occupied by each FAT.

dpSecPerTrack   Specifies the number of sectors on a single track.

dpHeads   Specifies the number of read/write heads on the drive.

dpHiddenSecs   Specifies the number of hidden sectors on the drive.

dpHugeSectors   Specifies the number of sectors if the **dpSectors** field is zero. This value supports drives larger than 32 MB.

See Also   Interrupt 21h Function 440Dh Minor Code 60h Get Device Parameters
Interrupt 21h Function 440Dh Minor Code 40h Set Device Parameters

■ DIRENTRY

```
DIRENTRY      STRUC
    deName          db  '????????'      ;name
    deExtension     db  '???'           ;extension
    deAttributes    db  ?               ;attributes
    deReserved      db  10  dup(?)       ;reserved
    deTime          dw  ?               ;time
    deDate          dw  ?               ;date
    deStartCluster  dw  ?               ;starting cluster
    deFileSize      dd  ?               ;file size
DIRENTRY      ENDS
```

The **DIRENTRY** structure contains information about a file or directory name, attributes, date, time, and starting cluster.

Fields

deName   Specifies the name of the file or directory. If the file or directory was created by using a name with fewer than eight characters, space characters (ASCII 20h) fill the remaining bytes in the field. The first byte in the field can be a character or one of the following values:

Value	Meaning
00h	The directory entry has never been used. MS-DOS uses this value to limit the length of directory searches.
05h	The first character in the name has the value 0E5h.
2Eh	The directory entry is an alias for this directory or the parent directory. If the remaining bytes are space characters (ASCII 20h), the **deStartCluster** field contains the starting cluster for this directory. If the second byte is also 2Eh (and the remaining bytes are space characters), **deStartCluster** contains the starting cluster number of the parent directory, or zero if the parent is the root directory.
0E5h	The file or directory has been deleted.

deExtension   Specifies the file or directory extension. If the extension has fewer than three characters, space characters (ASCII 20h) fill the remaining bytes in this field.

deAttributes   Specifies the attributes of the file or directory. This field can contain some combination of the following values:

Value	Meaning
ATTR_READONLY (01h)	Specifies a read-only file.
ATTR_HIDDEN (02h)	Specifies a hidden file or directory.
ATTR_SYSTEM (04h)	Specifies a system file or directory.
ATTR_VOLUME (08h)	Specifies a volume label. The directory entry contains no other usable information (except for date and time of creation) and can occur only in the root directory.
ATTR_DIRECTORY (10h)	Specifies a directory.
ATTR_ARCHIVE (20h)	Specifies a file that is new or has been modified.

All other values are reserved. (The two high-order bits are set to zero.)

If no attributes are set, the file is a normal file (ATTR_NORMAL).

deReserved   Reserved; do not use.

deTime   Specifies the time the file or directory was created or last updated. The field has the following form:

Bits	Meaning
0–4	Specifies two-second intervals. Can be a value in the range 0 through 29.
5–10	Specifies minutes. Can be a value in the range 0 through 59.
11–15	Specifies hours. Can be a value in the range 0 through 23.

deDate   Specifies the date the file or directory was created or last updated. The field has the following form:

Bits	Meaning
0–4	Specifies the day. Can be a value in the range 1 through 31.
5–8	Specifies the month. Can be a value in the range 1 through 12.
9–15	Specifies the year, relative to 1980.

deStartCluster   Specifies the starting cluster of the file or directory.

deFileSize   Specifies the size of the file, in bytes.

See Also

Interrupt 21h Function 11h Find First File with FCB
Interrupt 21h Function 12h Find Next File with FCB

■ DISKIO

```
DISKIO  STRUC
    diStartSector   dd  ?   ;sector number to start
    diSectors       dw  ?   ;number of sectors
    diBuffer        dd  ?   ;address of buffer
DISKIO  ENDS
```

The **DISKIO** structure contains information specifying the location and number of sectors to read or write.

Fields

diStartSector   Specifies the number of the first sector to be read or written.

diSectors   Specifies the number of sectors to read or write.

diBuffer   Specifies a 32-bit address (segment:offset) to the buffer that receives the data read or contains the data to write.

Comments

The **DISKIO** structure is used only if the number of sectors on the drive exceeds 65,535.

See Also

Interrupt 25h Absolute Disk Read
Interrupt 26h Absolute Disk Write

■ DPB

```
DPB     STRUC
     dpbDrive        db ?    ;drive number (0 = A, 1 = B, etc.)
     dpbUnit         db ?    ;unit number for driver
     dpbSectorSize   dw ?    ;sector size, in bytes
     dpbClusterMask  db ?    ;sectors per cluster - 1
     dpbClusterShift db ?    ;sectors per cluster, as power of 2
     dpbFirstFAT     dw ?    ;first sector containing FAT
     dpbFATCount     db ?    ;number of FATs
     dpbRootEntries  dw ?    ;number of root-directory entries
     dpbFirstSector  dw ?    ;first sector of first cluster
     dpbMaxCluster   dw ?    ;number of clusters on drive + 1
     dpbFATSize      dw ?    ;number of sectors occupied by FAT
     dpbDirSector    dw ?    ;first sector containing directory
     dpbDriverAddr   dd ?    ;address of device driver
     dpbMedia        db ?    ;media descriptor
     dpbFirstAccess  db ?    ;indicates access to drive
     dpbNextDPB      dd ?    ;address of next drive parameter block
     dpbNextFree     dw ?    ;last allocated cluster
     dpbFreeCnt      dw ?    ;number of free clusters
DPB     ENDS
```

The **DPB** structure contains information about a drive and the medium in the drive.

Fields

dpbDrive   Specifies the drive number (0 = A, 1 = B, and so on).

dpbUnit   Specifies the unit number. The device driver uses the unit number to distinguish the specified drive from the other drives it supports.

dpbSectorSize   Specifies the size of each sector, in bytes.

dpbClusterMask   Specifies one less than the number of sectors per cluster.

dpbClusterShift   Specifies the number of sectors per cluster, expressed as a power of 2.

dpbFirstFAT   Specifies the sector number of the first sector containing the file allocation table (FAT).

dpbFATCount   Specifies the number of FATs.

dpbRootEntries   Specifies the number of entries in the root directory.

dpbFirstSector   Specifies the sector number of the first sector in the first cluster.

dpbMaxCluster   Specifies one more than the maximum number of clusters on the drive.

dpbFATSize   Specifies the number of sectors occupied by each FAT.

dpbDirSector   Specifies the sector number of the first sector containing the root directory.

dpbDriverAddr   Specifies the 32-bit address (segment:offset) of the **DEVICE-HEADER** structure for the device driver supporting the specified drive.

dpbMedia   Specifies the media descriptor for the medium in the specified drive.

dpbFirstAccess   Specifies whether the medium in the drive has been accessed. This field is 0FFh if the medium has not been accessed.

dpbNextDPB   Specifies the 32-bit address (segment:offset) of the next drive parameter block.

dpbNextFree   Specifies the cluster number of the last allocated cluster.

dpbFreeCnt   Specifies the number of free clusters on the medium. This field is 0FFFFh if the number is unknown.

See Also   Interrupt 21h Function 1Fh Get Default DPB
Interrupt 21h Function 32h Get DPB

■ EXTENDEDFCB

```
EXTENDEDFCB    STRUC
    extSignature    db  Offh            ;extended FCB signature
    extReserved     db  5 dup(O)        ;reserved bytes
    extAttribute    db  ?               ;attribute byte
                                        ; file control block (FCB)
    extDriveID      db  ?               ;drive no. (O=default, 1=A, etc.)
    extFileName     db  '????????'      ;filename
    extExtent       db  '???'           ;file extension
    extCurBlockNo   dw  ?               ;current block number
    extRecSize      dw  ?               ;record size
    extFileSize     db  4 dup (?)       ;size of file, in bytes
    extFileDate     dw  ?               ;date file last modified
    extFileTime     dw  ?               ;time file last modified
    extReserved     db  8 dup (?)       ;reserved bytes
    extCurRecNo     db  ?               ;current record number
    extRandomRecNo  db  4 dup (?)       ;random record number
EXTENDEDFCB    ENDS
```

The **EXTENDEDFCB** structure contains a file control block (FCB) and 7 additional bytes, including an attribute byte.

Fields   **extSignature**   Specifies the extended FCB signature. This value must be 0FFh.

extReserved   Reserved; must be zero.

extAttribute   Specifies the attributes of the file or directory. This field can contain some combination of the following values:

Value	Meaning
ATTR_READONLY (01h)	Specifies a read-only file.
ATTR_HIDDEN (02h)	Specifies a hidden file or directory.
ATTR_SYSTEM (04h)	Specifies a system file or directory.
ATTR_VOLUME (08h)	Specifies a volume label. The entry contains no other usable information (except for date and time of creation) and can occur only in the root directory.
ATTR_DIRECTORY (10h)	Specifies a directory.
ATTR_ARCHIVE (20h)	Specifies a file that is new or has been modified.

All other values are reserved. (The two high-order bits are set to zero.)

If no attributes are set, the file is a normal file (ATTR_NORMAL).

extDriveID   Identifies the drive containing the file (0 = default, 1 = A, 2 = B, and so on).

extFileName   Specifies the name of the file. The filename must be padded with space characters (ASCII 20h) if it has fewer than eight characters.

extExtent   Specifies the extension. The extension must be padded with space characters (ASCII 20h) if it has fewer than three characters.

extCurBlockNo   Specifies the current block number, which points to the block that contains the current record. A block is a group of 128 records. This field and the **extCurRecNo** field make up the record pointer. When opening the file, MS-DOS sets this field to zero.

extRecSize   Specifies the size of a logical record, in bytes. MS-DOS sets this field to 128. A program that uses a different record size must fill this field after opening the file.

extFileSize   Specifies the size of the file, in bytes. When opening an existing file, MS-DOS initializes this field from the file's directory entry.

extFileDate   Specifies the date the file was created or last updated. When opening an existing file, MS-DOS initializes this field from the file's directory entry. This 16-bit field has the following form:

Bits	Meaning
0–4	Specifies the day. Can be a value in the range 1 through 31.
5–8	Specifies the month. Can be a value in the range 1 through 12.
9–15	Specifies the year, relative to 1980.

extFileTime   Specifies the time the file was created or last updated. If the file already exists, MS-DOS initializes this field from the file's directory entry when opening the file. This 16-bit field has the following form:

Bits	Meaning
0–4	Specifies two-second intervals. Can be a value in the range 0 through 29.
5–10	Specifies minutes. Can be a value in the range 0 through 59.
11–15	Specifies hours. Can be a value in the range 0 through 23.

extReserved   Reserved; do not use.

extCurRecNo   Specifies the current record number, which points to one of 128 records in the current block. This field and the **extCurBlockNo** field make up the record pointer. MS-DOS does not initialize this field when opening the file. The calling program must set it before performing a sequential read or write operation. This field is maintained by MS-DOS.

extRandomRecNo   Specifies the relative record number for random file access. This field specifies the index of the currently selected record, counting from the beginning of the file. MS-DOS does not initialize this field when opening the file. The calling program must set it before performing a random read or write operation. If the record size is less than 64 bytes, all 4 bytes of this field are used. Otherwise, only the first 3 bytes are used.

See Also

Interrupt 21h Function 11h Find First File with FCB
Interrupt 21h Function 12h Find Next File with FCB

■ EXTHEADER

```
EXTHEADER STRUC
    ehSignature      db 0ffh           ;extended signature
    ehReserved       db 5 dup(0)       ;reserved
    ehSearchAttrs    db ?              ;attribute byte
EXTHEADER ENDS
```

The **EXTHEADER** structure contains attributes for file and directory searches.

Fields

ehSignature   Specifies the extended search-header signature. This value must be 0FFh.

ehReserved   Reserved; must be zero.

ehSearchAttrs   Specifies the attributes used in the search for files and directories. This field can contain some combination of the following values:

Value	Meaning
ATTR_READONLY (01h)	Specifies a read-only file.
ATTR_HIDDEN (02h)	Specifies a hidden file or directory.
ATTR_SYSTEM (04h)	Specifies a system file or directory.
ATTR_VOLUME (08h)	Specifies a volume label. The entry contains no other usable information (except for date and time of creation) and can occur only in the root directory.
ATTR_DIRECTORY (10h)	Specifies a directory.
ATTR_ARCHIVE (20h)	Specifies a file that is new or has been modified.

All other values are reserved. (The two high-order bits are set to zero.)

If no attributes are set, the file is a normal file (ATTR_NORMAL).

See Also

Interrupt 21h Function 11h   Find First File with FCB
Interrupt 21h Function 12h   Find Next File with FCB

■ FCB

```
FCB     STRUC
    fcbDriveID    db  ?            ;drive no. (0=default, 1=A, etc.)
    fcbFileName   db  '????????'   ;filename
    fcbExtent     db  '???'        ;file extension
    fcbCurBlockNo dw  ?            ;current block number
    fcbRecSize    dw  ?            ;record size
    fcbFileSize   db  4 dup (?)    ;size of file in bytes
    fcbFileDate   dw  ?            ;date file last modified
    fcbFileTime   dw  ?            ;time file last modified
    fcbReserved   db  8 dup (?)    ;reserved
    fcbCurRecNo   db  ?            ;current record number
    fcbRandomRecNo db 4 dup (?)    ;random record number
FCB     ENDS
```

The **FCB** structure contains information that identifies a file and its characteristics.

Fields

fcbDriveID   Identifies the drive containing the file (0 = default, 1 = A, 2 = B, and so on).

fcbFileName   Specifies the name of the file. The filename must be padded with space characters (ASCII 20h) if it has fewer than eight characters.

fcbExtent   Specifies the filename extension. The filename extension must be padded with space characters (ASCII 20h) if it has fewer than three characters.

fcbCurBlockNo   Specifies the current block number, which points to the block that contains the current record. A block is a group of 128 records. This field and the **fcbCurRecNo** field make up the record pointer. MS-DOS sets this field to zero when opening the file.

fcbRecSize   Specifies the size of a logical record, in bytes. MS-DOS sets this field to 128. A program that uses a different record size must fill this field after opening the file.

fcbFileSize   Specifies the size of the file, in bytes. When opening an existing file, MS-DOS initializes this field from the file's directory entry.

fcbFileDate   Specifies the date the file was created or last updated. When opening an existing file, MS-DOS initializes this field from the file's directory entry. This 16-bit field has the following form:

Bits	Meaning
0–4	Specifies the day. Can be a value in the range 1 through 31.
5–8	Specifies the month. Can be a value in the range 1 through 12.
9–15	Specifies the year, relative to 1980.

fcbFileTime   Specifies the time the file was created or last updated. If the file already exists, MS-DOS initializes this field from the file's directory entry when opening the file. This 16-bit field has the following form:

Bits	Meaning
0–4	Specifies two-second intervals. Can be a value in the range 0 through 29.
5–10	Specifies minutes. Can be a value in the range 0 through 59.
11–15	Specifies hours. Can be a value in the range 0 through 23.

fcbReserved   Reserved; do not use.

fcbCurRecNo   Specifies the current record number, which points to one of 128 records in the current block. This field and the **fcbCurBlockNo** field make up the record pointer. MS-DOS does not initialize this field when opening the file. The calling program must set it before performing a sequential read or write operation. This field is maintained by MS-DOS.

fcbRandomRecNo   Specifies the relative record number for random file access. This field specifies the index of the currently selected record, counting from the beginning of the file. MS-DOS does not initialize this field when opening the file. The calling program must set it before performing a random read or write operation. If the record size is less than 64 bytes, all 4 bytes of this field are used. Otherwise, only the first 3 bytes are used.

Comments   When opening or creating a file, a program initializes an FCB that contains only the drive number, the filename, and the filename extension. All other fields are zero. MS-DOS fills in the remaining fields, as described in the preceding "Fields" section, once the file is open.

See Also   Interrupt 21h Function 0Fh Open File with FCB
Interrupt 21h Function 10h Close File with FCB
Interrupt 21h Function 11h Find First File with FCB
Interrupt 21h Function 12h Find Next File with FCB
Interrupt 21h Function 13h Delete File with FCB
Interrupt 21h Function 14h Sequential Read
Interrupt 21h Function 15h Sequential Write
Interrupt 21h Function 16h Create File with FCB
Interrupt 21h Function 17h Rename File with FCB
Interrupt 21h Function 1Bh Get Default Drive Data
Interrupt 21h Function 1Ch Get Drive Data
Interrupt 21h Function 21h Random Read
Interrupt 21h Function 22h Random Write
Interrupt 21h Function 23h Get File Size
Interrupt 21h Function 24h Set Random Record Number
Interrupt 21h Function 27h Random Block Read
Interrupt 21h Function 28h Random Block Write
Interrupt 21h Function 29h Parse Filename

■ FILEINFO

```
FILEINFO     STRUC
    fiReserved      db   21 dup (?)    ;reserved
    fiAttribute     db   ?             ;attributes of file found
    fiFileTime      dw   ?             ;time of last write
    fiFileDate      dw   ?             ;date of last write
    fiSize          dd   ?             ;file size
    fiFileName      db   13 dup (?)    ;filename and extension
FILEINFO     ENDS
```

The **FILEINFO** structure contains information about a file or directory name, access attributes, date, and time.

Fields   **fiReserved**   Reserved; do not use.

fiAttribute   Specifies the access attributes of the file or directory. This field can contain some combination of the following values:

Value	Meaning
ATTR_READONLY (01h)	Specifies a read-only file.
ATTR_HIDDEN (02h)	Specifies a hidden file or directory.
ATTR_SYSTEM (04h)	Specifies a system file or directory.
ATTR_VOLUME (08h)	Specifies a volume label. The entry contains no other usable information (except for date and time of creation) and can occur only in the root directory.

Value	Meaning
ATTR_DIRECTORY (10h)	Specifies a directory.
ATTR_ARCHIVE (20h)	Specifies a file that is new or has been modified.

All other values are reserved. (The two high-order bits are set to zero.)

If no attributes are set, the file is a normal file (ATTR_NORMAL).

fiFileTime　Specifies the time the file or directory was created or last updated. The field has the following form:

Bits	Meaning
0–4	Specifies two-second intervals. Can be a value in the range 0 through 29.
5–10	Specifies minutes. Can be a value in the range 0 through 59.
11–15	Specifies hours. Can be a value in the range 0 through 23.

fiFileDate　Specifies the date the file or directory was created or last updated. The field has the following form:

Bits	Meaning
0–4	Specifies the day. Can be a value in the range 1 through 31.
5–8	Specifies the month. Can be a value in the range 1 through 12.
9–15	Specifies the year, relative to 1980.

fiSize　Specifies the size of the file, in bytes.

fiFileName　Specifies the name and extension of the file or directory.

See Also　Interrupt 21h Function 4Eh　Find First File
Interrupt 21h Function 4Fh　Find Next File

■ FVBLOCK

```
FVBLOCK STRUC
    fvSpecFunc    db  0    ;special functions (must be zero)
    fvHead        dw  ?    ;head to format/verify
    fvCylinder    dw  ?    ;cylinder to format/verify
FVBLOCK ENDS
```

The **FVBLOCK** structure specifies the head and cylinder to format or verify.

Fields　**fvSpecFunc**　Must be zero.

fvHead　Specifies the number of the read/write head. The head number is used to determine the track to format or verify.

fvCylinder　Specifies the number of the cylinder. The cylinder number is used to determine the track to format or verify.

See Also　Interrupt 21h Function 440Dh Minor Code 42h　Format Track on Logical Drive
Interrupt 21h Function 440Dh Minor Code 62h　Verify Track on Logical Drive

■ MID

```
MID STRUC
    midInfoLevel   dw  0              ;information level
    midSerialNum   dd  ?              ;serial number
    midVolLabel    db  11 dup (?)     ;ASCII volume label
    midFileSysType db  8 dup (?)      ;file system type
MID ENDS
```

The **MID** structure contains information that uniquely identifies a disk or other storage medium.

Fields

midInfoLevel   Specifies the information level. This field must be zero.

midSerialNum   Specifies the serial number for the medium.

midVolLabel   Specifies the volume label for the medium. If the label has fewer than 11 characters, space characters (ASCII 20h) fill the remaining bytes in this field.

midFileSysType   Specifies the type of file system, given as an 8-byte ASCII string. This field can be one of the following values:

Name	Meaning
FAT12	12-bit file allocation table (FAT)
FAT16	16-bit FAT

If the name has fewer than eight characters, space characters (ASCII 20h) fill the remaining bytes in this field.

See Also

Interrupt 21h Function 440Dh Minor Code 66h Get Media ID
Interrupt 21h Function 440Dh Minor Code 46h Set Media ID

■ PARTENTRY

```
PARTENTRY   STRUC
    peBootable     db ?  ;80h = bootable, 00h = nonbootable
    peBeginHead    db ?  ;beginning head
    peBeginSector  db ?  ;beginning sector
    peBeginCylinder db ? ;beginning cylinder
    peFileSystem   db ?  ;name of file system
    peEndHead      db ?  ;ending head
    peEndSector    db ?  ;ending sector
    peEndCylinder  db ?  ;ending cylinder
    peStartSector  dd ?  ;starting sector (relative to beg. of disk)
    peSectors      dd ?  ;number of sectors in partition
PARTENTRY   ENDS
```

The **PARTENTRY** structure specifies the size and the starting and ending sectors of a partition on a disk that can be partitioned.

Fields

peBootable   Specifies whether the partition is bootable. If this field is 80h, the partition is bootable; if the field is 00h, the partition is not bootable.

peBeginHead   Specifies the head number used to determine the first track in the partition.

peBeginSector   Specifies the number of the first sector in the partition. This sector number is relative to the first track in the partition.

peBeginCylinder   Specifies the cylinder number used to determine the first track in the partition.

peFileSystem   Specifies the type of file system. This field can be one of the following values:

Value	Meaning
00h	Unknown type
01h	12-bit file allocation table (FAT); partition smaller than 10 MB
04h	16-bit FAT; partition smaller than 32 MB
05h	Extended DOS partition
06h	16-bit FAT; partition larger than or equal to 32 MB

Although other values are possible, MS-DOS recognizes only those given.

peEndHead   Specifies the head number used to determine the last track in the partition.

peEndSector   Specifies the number of the last sector in the partition. This sector number is relative to the first track in the partition.

peEndCylinder   Specifies the cylinder number used to determine the last track in the partition.

peStartSector   Specifies the number of the first sector in the partition. This sector number is relative to the beginning of the disk.

peSectors   Specifies the number of sectors in the partition.

Comments   MS-DOS supplies a partition table for every disk that can be partitioned. The table, placed at the end of the first hidden sector on the logical drive, consists of one or more **PARTENTRY** structures.

See Also   Interrupt 21h Function 440Dh Minor Code 41h Write Track on Logical Drive
Interrupt 21h Function 440Dh Minor Code 61h Read Track on Logical Drive

■ RENAMEFCB

```
RENAMEFCB    STRUC
    renDriveID      db  ?              ;drive no. (O=default, 1=A, etc.)
    renOldName      db  '????????'     ;old filename
    renOldExtent    db  '???'          ;old file extension
    renReserved1    db  5 dup(?)       ;reserved
    renNewName      db  '????????'     ;new filename
    renNewExtent    db  '???'          ;new extension
    renReserved2    db  9 dup(?)       ;reserved
RENAMEFCB    ENDS
```

The **RENAMEFCB** structure contains the old and new names for a file that is being renamed.

Fields   **renDriveID**   Specifies the drive number (0 = default, 1 = A, 2 = B, and so on).

renOldName   Specifies the old filename. If the filename has fewer than eight characters, space characters (ASCII 20h) must fill the remaining bytes.

renOldExtent   Specifies the old extension. If the extension has fewer than three characters, space characters must fill the remaining bytes.

renReserved1   Reserved; do not use.

renNewName   Specifies the new filename. If the filename has fewer than eight characters, space characters must fill the remaining bytes.

renNewExtent   Specifies the new extension. If the extension has fewer than three characters, space characters must fill the remaining bytes.

renReserved2   Reserved; do not use.

See Also   Interrupt 21h Function 17h Rename File with FCB

■ RWBLOCK

```
RWBLOCK STRUC
    rwSpecFunc      db  0   ;special functions (must be zero)
    rwHead          dw  ?   ;head to read/write
    rwCylinder      dw  ?   ;cylinder to read/write
    rwFirstSector   dw  ?   ;first sector to read/write
    rwSectors       dw  ?   ;number of sectors to read/write
    rwBuffer        dd  ?   ;address of buffer for read/write data
RWBLOCK ENDS
```

The **RWBLOCK** structure contains information that specifies the sectors that are to be read or written.

Fields   **rwSpecFunc**   Must be zero.

rwHead   Specifies the head number used to determine the track to read from or write to.

rwCylinder   Specifies the cylinder number used to determine the track to read from or write to.

rwFirstSector   Specifies the number of the first sector (relative to the beginning of the track) to read or write.

rwSectors   Specifies the number of sectors to read or write.

rwBuffer   Specifies a 32-bit address (segment:offset) of the buffer that receives the data to read or that contains the data to write.

See Also   Interrupt 21h Function 440Dh Minor Code 61h Read Track on Logical Drive
Interrupt 21h Function 440Dh Minor Code 41h Write Track on Logical Drive

■ TRACKLAYOUT

```
TRACKLAYOUT STRUC
    tklSectors  dw  SECTORS          ;number of sectors on track
    tklNumSize  dd  SECTORS dup(?)    ;array of sector numbers and sizes
TRACKLAYOUT ENDS
```

The **TRACKLAYOUT** structure contains an array of numbers and sizes for the sectors on a track.

Fields

tklSectors   Specifies the number of sectors.

tklSecNumSize   Contains an array of sector numbers and sizes. Each element of the array has the following form:

```
tklSectorNum    dw ?
tklSectorSize   dw ?
```

Field	Description
tklSectorNum	Specifies the number of the sector. Each sector number must be unique and in the range 1 through the the number of sectors specified in **tklSectors**.
tklSectorSize	Specifies the size of the sector, in bytes.

The **tklSectors** field specifies the number of elements in this field.

Comments   All sector sizes must be equal.

See Also   Interrupt 21h Function 440Dh Minor Code 40h Set Device Parameters

Character Input and Output

4.1 Introduction

This chapter provides an overview of MS-DOS character devices and describes the system functions that enable programs to read from, write to, and set the modes for character devices.

4.2 Character Devices

A character device is any device that processes data one byte (one character) at a time. The computer's keyboard, screen, real-time clock, and serial and parallel ports are character devices.

Each character device has a name. MS-DOS uses the following names:

Name	Description
AUX	Auxiliary device, usually a serial communications port.
CLOCK$	Real-time clock.
COM1	First serial communications port. AUX is usually an alias for COM1.
COM2	Second serial communications port.
CON	Keyboard and screen.
LPT1	First parallel printer port. PRN is usually an alias for LPT1.
LPT2	Second parallel printer port.
LPT3	Third parallel printer port.
NUL	"Bit bucket" device that discards all output and provides no input.
PRN	Printer device (also called a list device), usually a parallel communications port.

Programs open character devices by supplying the device names to Open File with Handle (Interrupt 21h Function 3Dh). The functions use the device names much as they use filenames, opening the device and returning a file handle. Once a program has a handle, it can read from, write to, and close the device by using such file-handle functions as Read File or Device (Interrupt 21h Function 3Fh), Write File or Device (Interrupt 21h Function 40h), and Close File with Handle (Interrupt 21h Function 3Eh).

Note   A program cannot create a file with the same filename as a device (such as CON.TXT), regardless of the extension. Attempting to open or create a file with the same name as a device opens the device instead.

4.2.1 Input and Output Modes

Input/output (I/O) modes determine how character devices process input and output. MS-DOS has two I/O modes: ASCII and binary. (These are sometimes called "cooked" and "raw" modes, respectively.)

The chief difference between these two modes is the way in which MS-DOS processes control characters. In ASCII mode, MS-DOS checks for control characters as it processes input or output for a device. If it encounters a control character, it removes the character from the input and carries out its corresponding action, described in the following table:

Control character	Action in ASCII mode
CTRL+C	Passes control to the CTRL+C exception handler. Subsequent actions depend on the current handler; the default handler terminates the program.
CTRL+P	Copies all subsequent input characters, up to the next CTRL+P, to the printer device.
CTRL+S	Suspends further output to the device. The next input character restores output.
CTRL+Z	Marks the end of the file. Subsequent calls to Read File or Device (Interrupt 21h Function 3Fh) return zero bytes.

In binary mode, no action is carried out and control characters remain as input until they are read by a program.

ASCII mode also may affect the way characters are displayed. For example, a screen device expands tab characters to space characters in ASCII mode, but not in binary mode.

By default, the MS-DOS I/O mode is ASCII. A program can determine the current I/O mode for a device by using Get Device Data (Interrupt 21h Function 4400h). This function takes a device handle as a parameter and returns a value indicating the device status. If bit 5 is set, the device is in binary mode. Otherwise, the device is in ASCII mode. Set Device Data (Interrupt 21h Function 4401h) changes the mode for a device.

The I/O mode is a property of the device handle and affects the input and output of only those programs that own the handle.

4.2.2 Keyboard Control

A program opens a keyboard by using Open File with Handle (Interrupt 21h Function 3Dh). This function takes the device name CON and the read-only access parameter and returns a handle for the keyboard. The program uses the handle with Read File or Device (Interrupt 21h Function 3Fh) to read from the keyboard.

In ASCII mode, MS-DOS reads characters from the keyboard and copies the characters to standard output. It checks for control characters as it reads and, if it finds one, carries out the corresponding action. It also checks for the BACK-SPACE key and function keys (such as F1, F2, and F3) and carries out the same editing actions for these keys as it does for COMMAND.COM. It removes the editing-key codes from the input as it carries out the editing action. MS-DOS continues to read characters until it has read the number of characters specified by the program or until the user presses CTRL+Z or ENTER. It translates the ENTER key into a carriage return-linefeed character pair.

In binary mode, MS-DOS reads the exact number of characters requested by the program. It does not copy characters to the screen, nor does it process editing keys and control characters. Instead, it reads all characters as input.

4.2.3 Screen Control

A program opens a screen device by using Open File with Handle (Interrupt 21h Function 3Dh). The function takes the device name CON and returns a handle for the screen device. The program uses the handle with Write File or Device (Interrupt 21h Function 40h) to write to the screen.

In ASCII mode, MS-DOS sends all characters to the screen, checks at the keyboard for control characters as it writes and, if it finds one, carries out its corresponding action. Tab characters (ASCII 09h) are expanded to space characters based on eight-space tab settings. MS-DOS continues to write characters to the screen until it has sent the requested number of characters or reached an end-of-file character (ASCII 1Ah).

In binary mode, MS-DOS writes the exact number of characters requested by the program. It does not process control characters (except the carriage-return and newline characters), expand tab characters, or stop writing at the end-of-file character.

By default, the cursor moves to the right for each new character. It moves down for a linefeed character (ASCII 0Ah) and to the leftmost column for a carriage-return character (ASCII 0Dh). For programs that need more complicated screen control, MS-DOS supplies an installable device driver, ANSI.SYS. This driver processes ANSI escape sequences that control cursor position and display modes such as color display and line wrapping. If ANSI.SYS has been loaded, programs can set the display mode by using Set Display Mode (Interrupt 21h Function 440Ch Minor Code 5Fh) and retrieve the current display mode by using Get Display Mode (Interrupt 21h Function 440Ch Minor Code 7Fh). Both functions require a pointer to a **DISPLAYMODE** structure that specifies the number of colors, columns, and rows available with the display mode.

4.2.4 Printer Control

A program opens a printer by using Open File with Handle (Interrupt 21h Function 3Dh). The function takes the device name PRN and the write-only access parameter and returns a handle to the printer. The program uses this handle with Write File or Device (Interrupt 21h Function 40h) to write to the printer.

If the printer is not present or not ready to receive data, a program that writes to it may hold indefinitely. Before attempting to send data to a printer, a program should use Check Device Output Status (Interrupt 21h Function 4407h) to determine whether the printer is present and ready to receive output.

4.2.5 Auxiliary Device Control

A program can open an auxiliary device for reading and writing by using Open File with Handle (Interrupt 21h Function 3Dh), supplying the device name AUX, and specifying the read-and-write access parameter. The function returns a file handle that the program can use with Read File or Device (Interrupt 21h Function 3Fh) and Write File or Device (Interrupt 21h Function 40h).

If the auxiliary device is not present or not ready to receive or send data, a program that reads or writes to the device may hold indefinitely. Before attempting to read from the auxiliary device, a program should use Check Device Input Status (Interrupt 21h Function 4406h) to determine if the device is present and ready to send input. Similarly, a program should use Check Device Output Status (Interrupt 21h Function 4407h) before attempting to send data to the auxiliary device.

4.2.6 Real-Time Clock Control

Programs can open the clock device for reading and writing. Reading from the clock device always returns three 16-bit values. These values are the low, middle, and high parts of the system time, representing the number of milliseconds elapsed since January 1, 1980. Writing to the clock device overwrites all three values and changes the system time for MS-DOS and all other programs.

To ensure compatibility with future versions of MS-DOS and with other operating environments, programs should avoid accessing the clock device directly. Instead, they should use Get Date (Interrupt 21h Function 2Ah), Set Date (Interrupt 21h Function 2Bh), Get Time (Interrupt 21h Function 2Ch), and Set Time (Interrupt 21h Function 2Dh) to get and set the system time.

4.3 ANSI Escape Sequences

ANSI escape sequences affect output to the screen device, giving programs control of the screen's cursor, colors, and display modes. (An escape sequence is one or more characters preceded by the escape character ASCII 1Bh.) When a program writes an escape sequence to the screen, the screen device translates the sequence into its corresponding action, such as positioning the cursor or changing colors.

The following list summarizes the ANSI escape sequences supported by the ANSI.SYS driver. ANSI escape sequences are available only if this driver has been installed. Parameters shown in *italic* type are ASCII strings representing integers.

Escape sequence	Action
ESC[2J	Clears the entire screen and moves the cursor to upper-left corner (home).
ESC[K	Clears the screen from cursor to end of line.
ESC[*rows*A	Moves the cursor up the specified number of rows without changing the column. If *rows* is omitted, the cursor moves one row.
ESC[*rows*B	Moves the cursor down the specified number of rows without changing the column. If *rows* is omitted, the cursor moves one row.
ESC[*cols*C	Moves the cursor to the right the specified number of columns without changing the row. If *cols* is omitted, the cursor moves one column.
ESC[*cols*D	Moves the cursor to the left the specified number of columns without changing the row. If *cols* is omitted, the cursor moves one column.
ESC[*row;col*H	Moves the cursor to an absolute position. For example, ESC[1;1H moves the cursor to the upper-left corner, and ESC[25;80H moves the cursor to the lower-right corner on a 25-character by 80-character screen. Either *row* or *col* can be omitted.
ESC[s	Saves the current cursor position.
ESC[u	Moves the cursor to the position most recently saved by ESC[s.
ESC[6n	Returns the current cursor position in the format ESC[*row;col*R. A program should read the cursor position from standard input immediately after writing the escape sequence.
ESC[*attr*m	Selects from the character attributes and colors on the next page. If more than one attribute or color is specified, values are separated by semicolons. The ability to display certain attributes and colors depends on the screen device.

Escape sequence	Action	
ESC[*attr*m *(continued)*	**Value**	**Attribute**
	0	No special attributes
	1	High intensity
	2	Low intensity
	3	Italic
	4	Underline
	5	Blinking
	6	Rapid blinking
	7	Reverse video
	8	Invisible (no display)
	Value	**Foreground color**
	30	Black
	31	Red
	32	Green
	33	Yellow
	34	Blue
	35	Magenta
	36	Cyan
	37	White
	Value	**Background color**
	40	Black
	41	Red
	42	Green
	43	Yellow
	44	Blue
	45	Magenta
	46	Cyan
	47	White

Escape sequence	Action
ESC[=*mode*h	Selects one of the following display modes:

Value	Mode
0	40 columns by 25 rows, 16-color text (color burst off)
1	40 columns by 25 rows, 16-color text
2	80 columns by 25 rows, 16-color text (color burst off)
3	80 columns by 25 rows, 16-color text
4	320 pixels by 200 pixels, 4-color graphics
5	320 pixels by 200 pixels, 4-color graphics (color burst off)
6	640 pixels by 200 pixels, 2-color graphics
7	Enable line wrap
14	640 pixels by 200 pixels, 16-color graphics (EGA/VGA, MS-DOS version 4.0 and later)
15	640 pixels by 350 pixels, 2-color graphics (EGA/VGA, MS-DOS version 4.0 and later)
16	640 pixels by 350 pixels, 16-color graphics (EGA/VGA, MS-DOS version 4.0 and later)
17	640 pixels by 480 pixels, 2-color graphics (MCGA/VGA, MS-DOS version 4.0 and later)
18	640 pixels by 480 pixels, 16-color graphics (VGA, MS-DOS version 4.0 and later)
19	320 pixels by 200 pixels, 256-color graphics (MCGA/VGA, MS-DOS version 4.0 and later)

ESC[07l	Disables line wrap.

4.4 Structure

This section provides a complete description of the **DISPLAYMODE** structure.

■ DISPLAYMODE

```
DISPLAYMODE        STRUC
       dmInfoLevel      db  ?    ;information level (must be zero)
       dmReserved1      db  ?    ;reserved
       dmDataLength     dw  ?    ;length of remaining data, in bytes
       dmFlags          dw  ?    ;control flags
       dmMode           db  ?    ;display mode
       dmReserved2      db  ?    ;reserved
       dmColors         dw  ?    ;number of colors
       dmWidth          dw  ?    ;screen width, in pixels
       dmLength         dw  ?    ;screen length, in pixels
       dmColumns        dw  ?    ;columns
       dmRows           dw  ?    ;rows
DISPLAYMODE        ENDS
```

The **DISPLAYMODE** structure contains information about the current display mode of a screen device, such as number of colors, rows, and columns.

Fields

dmInfoLevel   Specifies the information level. This field must be zero.

dmReserved1   Reserved; do not use.

dmDataLength   Specifies the length, in bytes, of the remaining fields in the structure. This field should be 14.

dmFlags   Specifies the control flags. This field is 00h if intensity is off or 01h if intensity is on.

dmMode   Specifies the display mode. This field can be one of the following values:

Value	Meaning
01h	Text mode
02h	Graphics mode

dmReserved2   Reserved; do not use.

dmColors   Specifies the number of colors available.

dmWidth   Specifies the screen width, in pixels. This field is used for graphics mode only.

dmLength   Specifies the screen length, in pixels. This field is used for graphics mode only.

dmColumns   Specifies the number of text columns.

dmRows   Specifies the number of text rows.

Comments   The number and type of display modes for a given screen device depend on the device type and the ANSI.SYS driver. For a list of display modes, see Section 4.3, "ANSI Escape Sequences."

See Also   Function 440Ch Minor Code 5Fh Set Display Mode
Function 440Ch Minor Code 7Fh Get Display Mode

Chapter

5

Program Management

5.1 Introduction

This chapter describes how MS-DOS manages the programs it loads and runs. Topics include programs and their resources, child programs, terminate-and-stay-resident programs (TSRs), overlays, and the .COM and .EXE file formats.

5.2 Programs and Program Resources

When MS-DOS runs a program, it allocates memory for the program code and data and copies the program from its program file into memory. The system then creates additional data defining the program's environment and passes control to the program's entry point—the instruction identified in the program as the first to be executed.

To run a program, the system uses the program's code, static data, stack, allocated memory, open files, and additional data created by the system for the program's use. In addition to this information, the system uses the following resources to run a program:

- Program memory
- Program segment prefix (PSP)
- Environment block
- Command tail
- Standard devices

These resources are described in the following sections.

5.2.1 Program Memory

When loading a program, MS-DOS allocates a certain amount of memory for it, depending on the type of program. For .COM programs, MS-DOS allocates all available memory. For .EXE programs, it allocates all available memory up to the amount requested in the program's file header. If MS-DOS cannot allocate enough memory to load a program, it terminates the request and returns an error value. The minimum amount of memory required for loading depends on the type of program file. For information about loading programs, see Section 5.7, "Program-File Formats."

A program can use any memory allocated for it by the system and can free any extra memory so that it is available for other programs. Programs that will run other programs must free enough memory to load them.

5.2.2 Program Segment Prefix

For each program, MS-DOS builds a 256-byte program segment prefix (PSP) that contains such information about the program's environment as the amount of memory the system allocates for the program, the location of the program's environment block, and the command-line arguments supplied to the program.

MS-DOS places the PSP in the first 256 bytes of memory allocated for the program. The program code and data immediately follow the PSP.

The form of the PSP corresponds to that of the **PSP** structure:

```
PSP      STRUC
         pspInt20            dw ?               ;Int 20h instruction
         pspNextParagraph    dw ?               ;segment addr of next paragraph
                             db ?               ;reserved
         pspDispatcher       db 5 dup(?)        ;long call to MS-DOS
         pspTerminateVector  dd ?               ;Termination Address (Int 22h)
         pspControlCVector   dd ?               ;CTRL+C Handler (Int 23h) addr
         pspCritErrorVector  dd ?               ;Crit-Err Handler (Int 24h) addr
                             dw 11 dup(?)       ;reserved
         pspEnvironment      dw ?               ;segment address of environment
                             dw 23 dup(?)       ;reserved
         pspFCB_1            db 16 dup(?)       ;default FCB #1
         pspFCB_2            db 16 dup(?)       ;default FCB #2
                             dd ?               ;reserved
         pspCommandTail      db 128 dup(?)      ;command tail (also default DTA)
PSP      ENDS
```

For a full description of the **PSP** structure, see Section 5.8, "Structures."

5.2.3 Environment Block

An environment block contains zero-terminated ASCII strings, each of which represents the name and value of an environment variable. Programs use environment variables for information about their operating environment. For example, a program may use the PATH variable to determine which directories to search for programs to run, or it may use the TEMP variable to determine the drive and directory in which to place the temporary files it creates.

Each string in the environment block consists of a name, an equal sign (=), and a value, as in the following example of a typical PATH setting:

```
PATH=C:\DOS;C:\BIN
```

The last string in the block is followed by a null character indicating the end of the environment block (that is, there are two null characters at the end of the block).

The content of a program's environment block is set by the program that starts it. When the command processor, COMMAND.COM, starts a program, its environment block contains at least the COMSPEC and PATH variables: COMSPEC specifies the location of COMMAND.COM, and PATH specifies the possible locations of program files and batch files. This environment block may also contain additional variables set by the user with the **set** command.

5.2.4 Command Tail

The command tail is one or more bytes of ASCII text representing a program's command-line arguments. When starting the program, the user provides the command tail by typing arguments, such as filenames and switches, after the program name. COMMAND.COM copies these arguments to the program as the command tail. Programs that start other programs can also provide command tails.

The command tail has three components: a leading byte that specifies the length of the text, the text itself, and a carriage-return character (ASCII 0Dh) that marks the command tail but is not counted in the length of the text. The following example shows a typical command tail:

```
SampleCommandTail    db 7, " /c dir", 0Dh
```

The text should start with at least one space character (ASCII 20h), since some programs may require a leading space.

5.2.5 Standard Devices

The standard devices are the keyboard, screen, auxiliary device, and printer. The system provides open file handles to these devices when it starts a program, as shown in the following table:

Name	Handle	Default device
Standard input (STDIN)	0	CON
Standard output (STDOUT)	1	CON
Standard error (STDERR)	2	CON
Standard auxiliary (STDAUX)	3	AUX
Standard printer (STDPRN)	4	PRN

A program can use the specified handles in such system functions as Read File or Device (Interrupt 21h Function 3Fh) and Write File or Device (Interrupt 21h Function 40h), to read from and write to the standard devices.

By default, a standard device corresponds to the device specified in the preceding table. However, users can redirect the standard devices, associating one or more of the handles with other character devices or with files. For example, a user can redirect the standard input to a file, so that the program reads input from the file instead of from the keyboard. The program does nothing special to read from the redirected device; it simply uses the standard input handle (now associated with a file) in Read File or Device to read characters from the file.

A program is not notified that a standard device has been redirected. This can lead to problems if the redirection is to a file and the disk has limited space. If the standard output is redirected to a file, Write File or Device fails when the disk becomes full. A program can use Get Device Data (Interrupt 21h Function 4400h) to determine whether a standard-device handle refers to a character device or a file.

A program can set the input/output (I/O) mode of a standard device. This setting has the same effect for a standard device as it does for a device opened explicitly by the program. Note that, since standard devices are shared by all programs, setting the I/O mode affects standard devices for all programs. Before changing the mode of a standard device, a program should use Get Device Data to save the current mode. Before terminating, the program should restore the previous mode by using Set Device Data (Interrupt 21h Function 4401h).

Programs that change the I/O mode of a standard device should also incorporate custom critical-error and CTRL+C interrupt handlers that either restore the I/O mode or prevent unexpected termination. For more information about interrupt handlers, see Chapter 7, "Interrupts."

5.3 Memory Management

MS-DOS manages memory to ensure that all programs have access to the memory they need to run successfully. The system allocates memory for a program during loading, and the program can allocate additional memory as needed, or free any unneeded memory.

5.3.1 Conventional Memory

Programs allocate conventional memory (addresses 0000:0000 through A000:0000) by using Allocate Memory (Interrupt 21h Function 48h). This function searches for a block of memory at least as large as the requested block and returns the segment address of the new block. Since MS-DOS may allocate all available conventional memory when loading a program, Allocate Memory may return error value 0008h (ERROR_NOT_ENOUGH_MEMORY). If so, the BX register contains the size of the largest available block, in paragraphs.

If a program no longer needs the memory it has allocated, it can free the memory by using Free Allocated Memory (Interrupt 21h Function 49h). Once freed, the memory is available to be allocated again by the same program or by other programs. A program can increase or reduce the amount of memory in a block to a specified number of paragraphs by using Set Memory Block Size (Interrupt 21h Function 4Ah).

A program that runs another program (called a child program) often uses Set Memory Block Size to reduce its own size, making more memory available to the child program. In such a case, the parent program passes the segment address of its PSP to the function, along with the new size. However, the parent program must not free the memory containing its own code, data, and stack if subsequent memory allocations will destroy that memory. To avoid this situation, some programs copy their code and data to disk and free all but a small routine that reallocates the freed memory and reloads the code and data when they are needed again.

The current allocation strategy, set by Set Allocation Strategy (Interrupt 21h Function 5801h), determines how Allocate Memory searches for an available block of memory. The search can start from either the beginning or the end of conventional memory and ends upon reaching the first block that satisfies the request or, if none is available, the block that most closely matches the request. The allocation strategy also determines whether the function searches conventional memory or the upper memory area. A program can retrieve the current allocation strategy by using Get Allocation Strategy (Interrupt 21h Function 5800h).

Note   If a program changes the allocation strategy, it should save the original allocation strategy and restore it before terminating.

5.3.2 Upper Memory Blocks

An upper memory block (UMB) is random-access memory (RAM) in the upper memory area that is available for program use. The upper memory area (addresses A000:0000 through FFFF:0000) is reserved primarily for read-only memory (ROM) and memory-mapped devices, but MS-DOS can map RAM to any addresses in this area that are not used by ROM or devices.

A program allocates an upper memory block by using Allocate Memory. Before allocating any memory, however, the program must set an appropriate allocation strategy and link the upper memory area. Just as it does with conventional memory, a program sets the allocation strategy by using Set Allocation Strategy. An allocation strategy such as FIRST_FIT_HIGH (0080h) directs Allocate Memory to search the upper memory area for a memory block and to continue searching in conventional memory if it finds no available block.

Note   If a program changes the allocation strategy to permit allocations from the upper memory area, it *must* save the original allocation strategy and restore it before terminating.

Allocate Memory cannot search the upper memory area unless the area is linked to the rest of system memory. A program can link the upper memory area by using Set Upper-Memory Link (Interrupt 21h Function 5803h), and it can determine whether the area is linked by using Get Upper-Memory Link (Interrupt 21h Function 5802h).

Note   If a program changes the upper-memory link, it should save the original state of the link and restore it before terminating.

A program can use Free Allocated Memory to free any upper memory blocks it no longer needs. It can also use Set Memory Block Size to reduce or increase the size of the allocated block.

If a program was started by using the **loadhigh** command, the system loads that program into memory allocated from the upper memory area. Although a program may be in upper memory, any memory it allocates is subject to the current allocation strategy.

Upper memory blocks are not accessible through MS-DOS system functions unless the **dos=umb** command is included in the CONFIG.SYS file and the HIMEM.SYS driver and memory-management software such as EMM386.EXE are loaded. If **dos=umb** is not specified in CONFIG.SYS but the memory-management software is loaded, programs can access the upper memory area by using direct calls to memory-management software. For information about these direct calls, see Get HIMEM.SYS Entry-Point Address (Interrupt 2Fh Function 4310h).

5.3.3 Memory Arena

MS-DOS keeps track of memory by creating a linked list of the **ARENA** structures that define the sizes and owners of blocks of memory. The **ARENA** structure has the following form:

```
ARENA   STRUC
        arenaSignature   db   ?              ;4dh = valid, 5ah = last
        arenaOwner       dw   ?              ;owner of arena item
        arenaSize        dw   ?              ;size of item, in paragraphs
        arenaReserved    db   3 dup(?)       ;reserved
        arenaName        db   8 dup(?)       ;owner filename
ARENA   ENDS
```

For a full description of the **ARENA** structure, see Section 5.8, "Structures."

When first starting, MS-DOS creates arenas for available memory. It creates additional arenas as needed when it loads programs and device drivers or as programs allocate their own memory. The number, size, and location of the arenas depend on the size of the memory blocks allocated.

Programs must not alter the **ARENA** structures. MS-DOS has no provisions for repairing structures that programs have overwritten or modified. If an **ARENA** structure is altered, functions such as Allocate Memory and Free Allocated Memory fail and return error value 0007h (ERROR_ARENA_TRASHED).

5.3.4 A20-Line Processing

For 80286, 80386, and 80486 computers, the CPU's 21st address line (A20 line) controls access to the extra 64K of address space called the high memory area (HMA). Computer manufacturers often include a circuit to disable the A20 line when the CPU runs in real mode. This ensures that the operating environment is identical to the 8086 environment, in which addresses such as FFFF:0010 wrap back to the beginning of memory. When the A20 line is enabled, however, addresses that would otherwise wrap (that is, addresses in the range FFFF:0010 through FFFF:FFFF) provide access to the HMA.

If a computer provides RAM for the HMA, MS-DOS can enable the A20 line and relocate system code to the HMA, thereby freeing conventional memory for other programs. MS-DOS relocates to the HMA only if the **dos=high** command is in the CONFIG.SYS file and the HIMEM.SYS driver is loaded. This driver provides the code required to enable and disable the A20 line.

To support programs that expect addresses to wrap, MS-DOS disables the A20 line whenever it loads and runs a program. While the A20 line is disabled, MS-DOS in the HMA is not directly accessible, although programs can still call MS-DOS system functions. To accomplish this, MS-DOS redirects all system calls to a "stub" in conventional memory that enables the A20 line and jumps to the requested MS-DOS system function. Once enabled by the stub, the A20 line remains enabled even after the system function returns to the program.

Programs must not use the HMA if MS-DOS has been relocated there. A program can determine whether MS-DOS is in the HMA by using Get MS-DOS Version (Interrupt 21h Function 3306h). This function sets bit 4 in the DH register to 1 if MS-DOS is in the HMA.

5.4 Child Programs

A child program is any MS-DOS program that has been started by another program. While a child program is running, the system temporarily suspends the parent program, returning control to it when the child program terminates. A good example of a parent program is COMMAND.COM, which loads and runs a child program whose name is typed at the command prompt. While the child program is running, the system suspends COMMAND.COM, returning control to it when the child program terminates.

A program loads and runs a child program by using Load and Execute Program (Interrupt 21h Function 4B00h). Once started, the child program can use any MS-DOS system function to carry out its work, but it must terminate by using End Program (Interrupt 21h Function 4Ch). This function frees the child program's memory, closes any open files, and returns control to the parent program. The parent program can then call Get Child-Program Return Value (Interrupt 21h Function 4Dh) to retrieve the child program's return value.

Most parent programs provide their child programs with such information as the environment block, the command tail, and the default file control blocks (FCBs). In addition, parent programs handle the following:

- Parameter block
- Inherited files
- Standard-device redirection
- Return values
- Batch files

When Load and Execute Program returns, the carry flag indicates whether the child program was run. If the carry flag is set, the function failed and the AX register contains an error value indicating the reason for the failure. The parent program can retrieve additional information about the failure by using Get Extended Error (Interrupt 21h Function 59h).

By default, MS-DOS sets a .COM program's stack at the high end of the 64K segment that contains the program. Before reducing its memory allocation, a .COM program must move its stack within the new range of memory to be allocated.

Note   MS-DOS version 2.*x* does not preserve the parent program's registers (except CS:IP). Before calling Load and Execute Program, the parent program must push onto the stack all registers it needs to preserve.

5.4.1 Parameter Block

The parameter block, provided by the parent program, contains the addresses of the environment block, command tail, and default FCBs to be used by the child program. The parent program passes the address of the parameter block to Load and Execute Program.

The form of the parameter block corresponds to the form of the **LOADEXEC** structure:

```
LOADEXEC STRUC
    leEnvironment     dw ?      ;environment-block segment
    leCommandTail     dd ?      ;address of command tail
    leFCB_1           dd ?      ;address of default FCB #1
    leFCB_2           dd ?      ;address of default FCB #2
LOADEXEC ENDS
```

For a full description of the **LOADEXEC** structure, see Section 5.8, "Structures."

The default FCBs for the child program are provided for compatibility with programs designed for earlier versions of MS-DOS. Few programs use the default FCBs for file operations; however, some programs do inspect the contents of the FCBs, so parent programs should create "empty" FCBs when running these programs. An empty FCB consists of 11 bytes containing space characters (ASCII 20h), followed by 5 bytes containing null characters (ASCII 00h), as in the following example:

```
emptyFCB      db 11 dup(20h), 5 dup(00h)
```

An invalid address for a parameter-block item or for the parameter block itself generally does not cause Load and Execute Program to fail. However, if MS-DOS copies invalid data to the child program's PSP, unexpected or improper execution of the child program may result.

5.4.2 Inherited Files

The child program inherits all file handles belonging to the parent program except those opened with the no-inheritance option. These handles identify standard files, disk files, or devices that the parent program has opened. Child-program operations that affect these handles (such as reading or writing to the file) also affect the parent program's file pointers associated with the handles.

So that the parent program can continue to use inherited files, they remain open after the child program terminates. The status of these files—for example, information about file-pointer locations—remains exactly as the child program left it.

5.4.3 Standard-Device Redirection

A parent program can redirect a standard device for the child program by associating the standard-device handle with a new device or file before it starts the child program. To do this, the parent program should follow these steps:

1 Duplicate the standard-device handle by using Duplicate File Handle (Interrupt 21h Function 45h).

2 Save the duplicate handle.

3 Open the new file or device.

4 With the new handle retrieved in step 3, modify the standard-device handle by using Force Duplicate File Handle (Interrupt 21h Function 46h). The standard-device handle should now identify the same file or device as the new handle.

5 Load and run the child program.

A parent program can restore the original standard-device handle by using Force Duplicate File Handle and specifying the duplicate handle saved in step 2.

5.4.4 Program Termination and Return Values

When a child program uses End Program to terminate, MS-DOS closes files that the program opened, frees memory that the program allocated (including the memory occupied by the program code and data), and returns control to the parent program. The child program must restore any interrupt vectors it set before terminating.

A child program can specify a return value when it terminates, and its parent program can inspect the return value when it resumes running by using Get Child-Program Return Value. By convention, a return value of zero indicates success; increasingly large nonzero values indicate increasingly severe errors.

Get Child-Program Return Value places the child program's return value (if any) in the AL register and places one of the following termination-status values in the AH register:

Termination status	Meaning
00h	The child program terminated normally.
01h	The child program terminated because the user pressed CTRL+C.
02h	The child program was terminated by the critical-error handler.
03h	The child program terminated normally and stayed resident.

5.4.5 Batch Files

Programs cannot load and run batch files directly, although they can run them by loading and running COMMAND.COM. To run a batch file, a parent program calls Load and Execute Program, specifying the location of COMMAND.COM (from the COMSPEC variable) and a command tail consisting of the /c switch followed by the name of the batch file. COMMAND.COM runs the batch file and immediately returns control to the parent program when the batch file ends.

5.5 Terminate-and-Stay-Resident Programs

A terminate-and-stay-resident program (often called a TSR) returns control to its parent program without relinquishing the memory that contains its code and data. The TSR program stops running, but its code and data remain in memory to be used by other programs. For information about TSRs, see Chapter 7, "Interrupts."

5.6 Overlays

An overlay is a partial program containing code and data that another program, called the main program, loads and uses as needed. Overlays are useful for large, complex programs that must run in limited memory.

Overlays can be either .COM or .EXE programs and need not have the same format as the main program. To load an overlay, the main program allocates memory for it (MS-DOS does not) and then calls Load Overlay (Interrupt 21h Function 4B03h), specifying a parameter block whose form corresponds to that of the **LOADOVERLAY** structure:

```
LOADOVERLAY STRUC
    loStartSegment      dw ?      ;segment address of overlay's memory
    loRelocationFactor  dw ?      ;relocation factor
LOADOVERLAY ENDS
```

For a full description of the **LOADOVERLAY** structure, see Section 5.8, "Structures."

After loading the overlay, the main program transfers control to it by using a far call. The entry point for the overlay depends on the convention the main program uses. Typically, the entry point is at offset 0000h in the overlay. In any case, the overlay should return control to the main program by using a far return.

The system does not construct a PSP for the overlay; it considers the overlay part of the main program. Any memory the overlay allocates and any files it opens belong to the main program.

5.7 Program-File Formats

The two MS-DOS program-file formats differ in several respects, including structure and memory requirements. The following sections describe each format in detail.

5.7.1 The .COM File Format

A .COM file contains an absolute image of a program—that is, the exact processor instructions and data that must be in memory in order to run the program. MS-DOS loads the .COM program by copying this image directly from the file into memory; it makes no changes.

To load a .COM program, MS-DOS first attempts to allocate memory. Since a .COM program must fit in one 64K segment, the size of the .COM file must not exceed 65,024 bytes (64K minus 256 bytes for a PSP and at least 256 bytes for an initial stack). If MS-DOS cannot allocate enough memory for the program, a PSP, and an initial stack, the attempt fails. Otherwise, MS-DOS allocates as much memory as possible (up to all remaining memory), even though the .COM program itself cannot be greater than 64K. Before attempting to run other programs or allocate additional memory, most .COM programs free any unneeded memory.

After allocating memory, MS-DOS builds a PSP in the first 256 bytes of that memory, setting the AL register to 00h if the first FCB in the PSP contains a valid drive identifier or to 0FFh if it does not. MS-DOS also sets the AH register to 00h or to 0FFh, depending on whether the second FCB contains a valid drive identifier.

After building the PSP, MS-DOS loads the .COM file, starting immediately after the PSP (offset 100h). It sets the SS, DS, and ES registers to the segment address of the PSP and then creates a stack. To create a stack, MS-DOS sets the SP register to 0000h if at least 64K of memory has been allocated; otherwise, it sets the register to two more than the total number of bytes allocated. Finally, it pushes 0000h onto the stack to ensure compatibility for programs designed for very early versions of MS-DOS.

MS-DOS starts the program by transferring control to the instruction at offset 100h. Programmers must ensure that the first instruction in the .COM file is the program's entry point.

Notice that, because the program is loaded at offset 100h, all code and data offsets must be relative to 100h. Assembly-language programmers can ensure this by setting the program's origin to 100h (for example, by using the statement **org 100h** at the beginning of the source program).

5.7.2 The .EXE File Format

An .EXE file contains a file header and a relocatable-program image. The file header contains information that MS-DOS uses when loading the program, such as the size of the program and the initial values of the registers. The file header also points to a relocation table containing a list of pointers to relocatable-segment addresses in the program image.

The form of the file header corresponds to that of the **EXEHEADER** structure:

```
EXEHEADER STRUC
        exSignature     dw  5A4Dh       ;.EXE signature
        exExtraBytes    dw  ?           ;number of bytes in last (partial) page
        exPages         dw  ?           ;number of whole and part pages in file
        exRelocItems    dw  ?           ;number of pointers in relocation table
        exHeaderSize    dw  ?           ;size of header, in paragraphs
        exMinAlloc      dw  ?           ;minimum allocation
        exMaxAlloc      dw  ?           ;maximum allocation
        exInitSS        dw  ?           ;initial ss value
        exInitSP        dw  ?           ;initial sp value
        exCheckSum      dw  ?           ;complemented checksum
        exInitIP        dw  ?           ;initial ip value
        exInitCS        dw  ?           ;initial cs value
        exRelocTable    dw  ?           ;byte offset to relocation table
        exOverlay       dw  ?           ;overlay number
EXEHEADER ENDS
```

For a full description of the **EXEHEADER** structure, see Section 5.8, "Structures."

The program image, which contains the processor code and initialized data for a program, starts immediately after the file header. Its size, in bytes, is equal to the size of the .EXE file minus the size of the file header, which is equal to the value in the **exHeaderSize** field multiplied by 16. MS-DOS loads the .EXE program by copying this image directly from the file into memory and then adjusts the relocatable-segment addresses specified in the relocation table.

The relocation table is an array of relocation pointers, each of which points to a relocatable-segment address in the program image. The **exRelocItems** field in the file header specifies the number of pointers in the array, and the **exRelocTable** field specifies the file offset at which the relocation table starts. Each relocation pointer consists of two 16-bit values: an offset and a segment number.

To load an .EXE program, MS-DOS first reads the file header to determine the .EXE signature and calculate the size of the program image. It then attempts to allocate memory. First, it adds the size of the program image to the size of the PSP and to the amount of memory specified in the **exMinAlloc** field of the **EXEHEADER** structure. If the total exceeds the size of the largest available memory block, MS-DOS stops loading the program and returns an error value. Otherwise, it adds the size of the program image to the size of the PSP and to the amount of memory specified in the **exMaxAlloc** field of the **EXEHEADER** structure. If this second total is less than the size of the largest available memory block, MS-DOS allocates the amount of memory indicated by the calculated total. Otherwise, it allocates the largest possible block of memory.

After allocating memory, MS-DOS determines the segment address, called the start-segment address, at which to load the program image. If the value in both the **exMinAlloc** and **exMaxAlloc** fields is zero, MS-DOS loads the image as high as possible in memory. Otherwise, it loads the image immediately above the area reserved for the PSP.

Next, MS-DOS reads the items in the relocation table and adjusts all segment addresses specified by the relocation pointers. For each pointer in the relocation table, MS-DOS finds the corresponding relocatable-segment address in the program image and adds the start-segment address to it. Once adjusted, the segment addresses point to the segments in memory where the program's code and data are loaded.

Then MS-DOS builds the 256-byte PSP in the lowest part of the allocated memory, setting the AL and AH registers just as it does when loading .COM programs. MS-DOS uses the values in the file header to set the SP and SS registers and adjusts the initial value of the SS register by adding the start-segment address to it. MS-DOS also sets the ES and DS registers to the segment address of the PSP.

Finally, MS-DOS reads the inital CS and IP values from the program's file header, adjusts the CS register value by adding the start-segment address to it, and transfers control to the program at the adjusted address.

5.8 Structures

This section describes the structures MS-DOS uses to load and run programs.

■ ARENA

```
ARENA   STRUC
    arenaSignature  db  ?              ;4dh valid item, 5ah last item
    arenaOwner      dw  ?              ;owner of arena item
    arenaSize       dw  ?              ;size of item, in paragraphs
    arenaReserved   db  3 dup(?)       ;reserved
    arenaName       db  8 dup(?)       ;owner filename
ARENA   ENDS
```

The **ARENA** structure contains information about a block of memory. MS-DOS uses a linked list of these structures to keep track of and manage system memory.

Fields   **arenaSignature**   Specifies whether the structure is valid. This field must contain either 4Dh or 5Ah. The value 5Ah indicates that the structure is the last in the linked list.

arenaOwner   Specifies the owner of the block. This field contains the segment address of the program segment prefix (PSP) for the owning program. It contains zero if the block is not owned.

arenaSize   Specifies the size of the block, in paragraphs. The block starts immediately after the **ARENA** structure.

arenaReserved   Reserved; do not use.

arenaName   Contains a zero-terminated string specifying the filename of the program that owns the memory. If the filename has fewer than eight characters, the remaining characters in this field are not used. Names such as SC and SD are used by MS-DOS to represent system code (programs) and system data, respectively.

Comments   Each **ARENA** structure is followed immediately by a contiguous block of memory. The next **ARENA** structure in the linked list follows the contiguous block. This means the segment address of the next structure in the list is equal to the segment address of the current memory block plus its size.

MS-DOS fills the **arenaName** field for a block of memory when it loads a program into the block. The **ARENA** structures for memory allocated by programs using Allocate Memory (Interrupt 21h Function 48h) are not filled in this way.

See Also   Interrupt 21h Function 48h Allocate Memory

■ ERROR

```
ERROR   STRUC
    errAX       dw  ?   ;ax register
    errBX       dw  ?   ;bx register
    errCX       dw  ?   ;cx register
    errDX       dw  ?   ;dx register
    errSI       dw  ?   ;si register
    errDI       dw  ?   ;di register
    errDS       dw  ?   ;ds register
    errES       dw  ?   ;es register
    errReserved dw  ?   ;reserved 16 bits
    errUID      dw  ?   ;user (computer) ID (O = local computer)
    errPID      dw  ?   ;process ID (O = local process)
ERROR   ENDS
```

The **ERROR** structure contains information about the current error.

Fields   **errAX**   Specifies the error value. For a table of error values, see Appendix C, "Error Values."

errBX   Specifies the error class in the high-order byte and the suggested action in the low-order byte. The error class may be one of the following values:

Value	Meaning
ERRCLASS_OUTRES (01h)	Out of resource, such as storage.
ERRCLASS_TEMPSIT (02h)	Not an error, but a temporary situation that is expected to end, such as a locked region in a file.
ERRCLASS_AUTH (03h)	Authorization problem.
ERRCLASS_INTRN (04h)	Internal error in system.
ERRCLASS_HRDFAIL (05h)	Hardware failure.
ERRCLASS_SYSFAIL (06h)	System software failure not the fault of the active program (caused by missing or incorrect configuration files, for example).
ERRCLASS_APPERR (07h)	Application error.
ERRCLASS_NOTFND (08h)	File or item not found.
ERRCLASS_BADFMT (09h)	File or item with an invalid format or type.
ERRCLASS_LOCKED (0Ah)	Interlocked file or item.
ERRCLASS_MEDIA (0Bh)	Wrong disk in drive, bad spot on disk, or other storage-medium problem.
ERRCLASS_ALREADY (0Ch)	Existing file or item.
ERRCLASS_UNK (0Dh)	Unknown.

The suggested action may be one of the following values:

Value	Meaning
ERRACT_RETRY (01h)	Retry immediately.
ERRACT_DLYRET (02h)	Delay and retry.
ERRACT_USER (03h)	Bad user input—get new values.
ERRACT_ABORT (04h)	Terminate in an orderly manner.
ERRACT_PANIC (05h)	Terminate immediately.
ERRACT_IGNORE (06h)	Ignore the error.
ERRACT_INTRET (07h)	Prompt the user to remove the cause of the error (to change disks, for example) and then retry.

errCX   Specifies the error-location value. This value can be one of the following:

Value	Location
ERRLOC_UNK (01h)	Unknown
ERRLOC_DISK (02h)	Random-access device, such as a disk drive
ERRLOC_NET (03h)	Network
ERRLOC_SERDEV (04h)	Serial device
ERRLOC_MEM (05h)	Memory

errDX   Specifies the DX register contents at the time the error occurred.

errSI   Specifies the SI register contents at the time the error occurred.

errDI   Specifies the DI register contents at the time the error occurred.

errDS   Specifies the DS register contents at the time the error occurred.

errES   Specifies the ES register content at the time the error occurred.

errReserved   Reserved.

errUID   Identifies the computer, for errors that occur on remote computers. If this field is zero, the error occurred on the local computer.

errPID   Identifies the program, for errors that occur on remote computers. If this field is zero, the error occurred in a program on the local computer.

See Also   Interrupt 21h Function 5D0Ah Set Extended Error

■ EXECSTATE

```
EXECSTATE   STRUC
    esReserved  dw ?        ;reserved
    esFlags     dw ?        ;type flags
    esProgName  dd ?        ;points to ASCIIZ string of program name
    esPSP       dw ?        ;PSP segment of the new program
    esStartAddr dd ?        ;starting cs:ip of the new program
    esProgSize  dd ?        ;program size, including PSP
EXECSTATE   ENDS
```

The **EXECSTATE** structure contains information used to prepare a program to be run.

Fields   **esReserved**   Reserved; must be zero.

esFlags   Specifies the execution flags. This value can be a combination of the following values:

Value	Meaning
ES_EXE (0001h)	Program is an .EXE program. If this value is not given, the program is a .COM program.
ES_OVERLAY (0002h)	Program is an overlay.

esProgName   Points to a zero-terminated ASCII string that specifies the name of the program. The string must be a valid MS-DOS filename.

esPSP   Specifies the segment address of the program segment prefix (PSP) for the program.

esStartAddr   Specifies the starting address (initial CS:IP values) for the program.

esProgSize   Specifies the size of the program, in bytes, including the PSP.

See Also   Interrupt 21h Function 4B05h Set Execution State

■ EXEHEADER

```
EXEHEADER STRUC
    exSignature     dw 5A4Dh      ;.EXE signature
    exExtraBytes    dw ?          ;number of bytes in last (partial) page
    exPages         dw ?          ;number of whole and part pages in file
    exRelocItems    dw ?          ;number of pointers in relocation table
    exHeaderSize    dw ?          ;size of header, in paragraphs
    exMinAlloc      dw ?          ;minimum allocation
    exMaxAlloc      dw ?          ;maximum allocation
    exInitSS        dw ?          ;initial ss value
    exInitSP        dw ?          ;initial sp value
    exCheckSum      dw ?          ;complemented checksum
    exInitIP        dw ?          ;initial ip value
    exInitCS        dw ?          ;initial cs value
    exRelocTable    dw ?          ;byte offset to relocation table
    exOverlay       dw ?          ;overlay number
EXEHEADER ENDS
```

The **EXEHEADER** structure contains values that MS-DOS uses when loading a relocatable program—values such as the size of the program and the initial values of the registers.

This structure appears at the beginning of the file header for an .EXE file. The complete .EXE file header consists of this structure and a relocation table. The size of the file header, in paragraphs, is specified by the **exHeaderSize** field.

Fields

exSignature   Specifies the .EXE file signature. This field must be set to 5A4Dh (the ASCII values for the letters M and Z).

exExtraBytes   Specifies the number of bytes in the last (partial) page in the file, as represented by the remainder, if any, when the total number of bytes in the file is divided by 512 (bytes per page).

exPages   Specifies the number of whole and partial pages in the file. Dividing this total number of bytes in the file by 512 (bytes per page) gives the number of whole pages. If the division leaves a remainder, the number of pages is increased by one and the remainder is stored in the **exExtraBytes** field. For example, in a file 513 bytes long, the **exPages** field is 2 and the **exExtraBytes** field is 1.

exRelocItems   Specifies the number of pointers in the relocation table.

exHeaderSize   Specifies the size of the file header, in paragraphs. Since each paragraph has 16 bytes, the file header size is always a multiple of 16.

exMinAlloc   Specifies the minimum amount of extra memory, in paragraphs, required by the program. The extra memory is in addition to the memory required to load the program image. If the values of both **exMinAlloc** and **exMaxAlloc** are zero, the program is loaded as high as possible in memory.

exMaxAlloc   Specifies the maximum amount of extra memory, in paragraphs, requested by the program. If the values of both **exMinAlloc** and **exMaxAlloc** are zero, the program is loaded as high as possible in memory.

exInitSS   Specifies the initial value of the SS register. The value is a relocatable-segment address. MS-DOS adjusts (relocates) this value when loading the program.

exInitSP   Specifies the initial value of the SP register.

exCheckSum   Specifies the checksum of the file. This value is equal to the one's complement (inverse) of the sum of all 16-bit values in the file, excluding this field.

exInitIP   Specifies the initial value of the IP register.

exInitCS   Specifies the initial value of the CS register. This value is a relocatable-segment address. MS-DOS adjusts (relocates) the value when loading the program.

exRelocTable   Specifies the offset, in bytes, from the beginning of the file to the relocation table.

exOverlay   Specifies a value used for overlay management. If this value is zero, the .EXE file contains the main program.

Comments   The **exOverlay** field can be followed by additional information used by the system for overlay management. The content and structure of this information depends on the method of overlay management used by the main program.

See Also   Interrupt 21h Function 4B00h Load and Execute Program
Interrupt 21h Function 4B01h Load Program
Interrupt 21h Function 4B03h Load Overlay

■ LOAD

```
LOAD STRUC
    ldEnvironment    dw  ?    ;environment-block segment
    ldCommandTail    dd  ?    ;address of command tail
    ldFCB_1          dd  ?    ;address of default FCB #1
    ldFCB_2          dd  ?    ;address of default FCB #2
    ldCSIP           dd  ?    ;starting code address
    ldSSSP           dd  ?    ;starting stack address
LOAD ENDS
```

The **LOAD** structure contains addresses of the environment block, command tail, and default file control blocks (FCBs) to be used by the child program.

Fields   **ldEnvironment**   Specifies whether the child program receives a copy of the parent program's environment or a new environment created by the parent program. If this field is zero, the child program receives an exact duplicate of the parent program's environment block. If the field is nonzero, the value entered must be the segment address of a block of memory containing a copy of the new environment for the child program.

ldCommandTail   Specifies a 32-bit address (segment:offset) of the command tail. The system copies the command tail to offset 80h (**pspCommandTail** field) in the program segment prefix (PSP). The command tail must not exceed 128 bytes and should have the format described in Section 5.2.4, "Command Tail."

Any redirection of standard files must be accomplished by the parent program. Including redirection characters (<, >, and |) in a command tail does not redirect files.

ldFCB_1   Specifies a 32-bit address (segment:offset) of the first default FCB. The system copies the FCB to offset 5Ch in the child program's PSP (**pspFCB_1** field).

ldFCB_2   Specifies a 32-bit address (segment:offset) of the second default FCB. The system copies the FCB to offset 6Ch in the child program's PSP (**pspFCB_2** field).

ldCSIP   Receives a 32-bit address (segment:offset) of the entry point of the loaded program. This field is filled on return by Load Program (Interrupt 21h Function 4B01h).

ldSSSP   Receives a 32-bit address (segment:offset) of the start of the stack for the loaded program. This field is filled on return by Load Program (Interrupt 21h Function 4B01h).

Comments   If the **ldEnvironment** field contains a segment address, the parent program must fill the corresponding memory with zero-terminated ASCII strings, each having the form described in Section 5.2.3, "Environment Block." The new environment must itself be zero-terminated and must not exceed 32K. Whether the child program receives a duplicate environment or a new environment, the system allocates unique memory for the child program and copies the environment specified by the parent program to that memory. The system places the segment address of this unique memory at offset 2Ch in the child program's PSP (**pspEnvironment** field). The system automatically frees the memory when the child program terminates.

See Also   Interrupt 21h Function 4B01h Load Program

■ LOADEXEC

```
LOADEXEC STRUC
    leEnvironment    dw ?     ;environment-block segment
    leCommandTail    dd ?     ;address of command tail
    leFCB_1          dd ?     ;address of default FCB #1
    leFCB_2          dd ?     ;address of default FCB #2
LOADEXEC ENDS
```

The **LOADEXEC** structure contains addresses of the environment block, command tail, and default file control blocks (FCBs) to be used by the child program.

Fields   **leEnvironment**   Specifies whether the child program receives a copy of the parent program's environment or a new environment created by the parent program. If this field is zero, the child program receives an exact duplicate of the parent program's environment block. If the field is nonzero, the value entered must be the segment address of a block of memory containing a copy of the new environment for the child program.

leCommandTail   Specifies a 32-bit address (segment:offset) of the command tail. The system copies the command tail to offset 80h (**pspCommandTail** field) in the program segment prefix (PSP). The command tail must not exceed 128 bytes and should have the format described in Section 5.2.4, "Command Tail."

Any redirection of standard files must be accomplished by the parent program. Including redirection characters (<, >, and |) in a command tail does not redirect files.

leFCB_1   Specifies a 32-bit address (segment:offset) of the first default FCB. The system copies the FCB to offset 5Ch in the child program's PSP (**pspFCB_1** field).

leFCB_2   Specifies a 32-bit address (segment:offset) of the second default FCB. The system copies the FCB to offset 6Ch in the child program's PSP (**pspFCB_2** field).

Comments	If the **leEnvironment** field contains a segment address, the parent program must fill the corresponding memory with zero-terminated ASCII strings, each having the form described in Section 5.2.3, "Environment Block." The new environment must itself be zero-terminated and must not exceed 32K. Whether the child program receives a duplicate environment or a new environment, the system allocates unique memory for the child program and copies the environment specified by the parent program to that memory. The system places the segment address of this unique memory at offset 2Ch in the child program's PSP (**pspEnvironment** field). The system automatically frees the memory when the child program terminates.
See Also	Interrupt 21h Function 4B00h Load and Execute Program

■ LOADOVERLAY

```
LOADOVERLAY STRUC
    loStartSegment      dw ?     ;segment address of overlay's memory
    loRelocationFactor  dw ?     ;relocation factor
LOADOVERLAY ENDS
```

The **LOADOVERLAY** structure contains information used to load overlays.

Fields	**loStartSegment** Specifies the segment address of the memory allocated for the overlay. MS-DOS loads the overlay into memory, starting at this address.
	loRelocationFactor Specifies a relocation factor. For .EXE programs, this value is typically the same as the **loStartSegment** value. For .COM programs, it is zero.
See Also	Interrupt 21h Function 4B03h Load Overlay

■ PSP

```
PSP     STRUC
    pspInt20            dw ?            ;Int 20h instruction
    pspNextParagraph    dw ?            ;segment addr of next paragraph
                        db ?            ;reserved
    pspDispatcher       db 5 dup(?)     ;long call to MS-DOS
    pspTerminateVector  dd ?            ;Termination Address (Int 22h)
    pspControlCVector   dd ?            ;CTRL+C Handler (Int 23h) addr
    pspCritErrorVector  dd ?            ;Crit-Err Handler (Int 24h) addr
                        dw 11 dup(?)    ;reserved
    pspEnvironment      dw ?            ;segment address of environment
                        dw 23 dup(?)    ;reserved
    pspFCB_1            db 16 dup(?)    ;default FCB #1
    pspFCB_2            db 16 dup(?)    ;default FCB #2
                        dd ?            ;reserved
    pspCommandTail      db 128 dup(?)   ;command tail (also default DTA)
PSP     ENDS
```

The **PSP** structure contains information about the program's execution environment, such as the amount of memory the system allocates for the program, the location of the program's environment block, and the command-line arguments supplied to the program.

Fields

pspInt20   Contains a Terminate Program (Interrupt 20h) instruction. This field is provided for compatibility with earlier versions of MS-DOS.

pspNextParagraph   Specifies the segment address of the first paragraph immediately following the program. (This address does not point to free memory available for the program to use.) Programs use this field to determine quickly whether they were allocated sufficient memory to run successfully.

pspDispatcher   Contains a long call to the MS-DOS function-request handler. This field is provided for compatibility with earlier versions of MS-DOS.

pspTerminateVector   Specifies Termination Address (Interrupt 22h). MS-DOS uses this address to restore the corresponding entry in the interrupt-vector table when the process terminates.

pspControlCVector   Specifies the address of CTRL+C Handler (Interrupt 23h). MS-DOS uses this address to restore the corresponding entry in the interrupt-vector table when the process terminates.

pspCritErrorVector   Specifies the address of Critical-Error Handler (Interrupt 24h). MS-DOS uses this address to restore the corresponding entry in the interrupt-vector table when the process terminates.

pspEnvironment   Specifies the segment address of the environment block for the program.

pspFCB_1   Specifies the first 16 bytes of the first default file control block (FCB) for the program. If the FCB contains a filename, it usually matches the first argument in the command tail. This field is provided for compatibility with earlier versions of MS-DOS.

pspFCB_2   Specifies the first 16 bytes of the second default FCB for the program. If the FCB contains a filename, it usually matches the second argument in the command tail. This field is provided for compatibility with earlier versions of MS-DOS.

pspCommandTail   Specifies an ASCII string containing command-line arguments, such as filenames and switches.

Comments

The system places the PSP in the first 256 bytes of memory allocated for the program. The PSP is followed immediately by the program code and data.

The **pspCommandTail** field is also used as the default buffer pointed to by the default disk transfer address (DTA). Unless a program explicitly changes the DTA, the system uses this area as a buffer for file information returned by Find First File (Interrupt 21h Function 4Eh) and Find Next File (Interrupt 21h Function 4Fh), as well as for all FCB-type read and write operations.

See Also

Interrupt 20h Terminate Program
Interrupt 21h Function 4Eh Find First File
Interrupt 21h Function 4Fh Find Next File
Interrupt 21h Function 50h Set PSP Address
Interrupt 21h Function 51h Get PSP Address
Interrupt 22h Termination Address
Interrupt 23h CTRL+C Handler
Interrupt 24h Critical-Error Handler

Chapter

6

National Language Support

6.1 Introduction

Programs use MS-DOS national-language-support functions to adapt the keyboard, screen, and printer devices for use in different countries. This chapter describes the functions and structures used in five aspects of national language support:

- Country information
- Code pages
- Keyboard layouts
- Screen and printer fonts
- Code-page information files

6.2 Country Information

Programs use country information to prepare the characters and formats for date, time, currency, and other displayed information. Country information includes the following:

- Time, date, and currency formats
- Lowercase-to-uppercase character-conversion tables
- Collating sequence for character sorting
- Valid single-byte characters for use in filenames

All country information is stored in the COUNTRY.SYS file. Default values are set by the system if a **country** command is not included in the CONFIG.SYS file. A program can retrieve information for any nondefault countries or code pages; however, this information may not be available if the Nlsfunc program has not been loaded. If the **country** command does not specify the path to the COUNTRY.SYS file, the path must be given as an argument when Nlsfunc is started. Retrieving country information does not change the system's current country code.

6.2.1 Time, Date, and Other Formats

A program can retrieve information about the characters and formats used for such values as time, date, currency, and numbers by using either Get/Set Country Information (Interrupt 21h Function 38h) or Get Extended Country Information (Interrupt 21h Function 6501h). Get/Set Country Information copies the country information specified by the current code page to a buffer supplied by the program. Get Extended Country Information also copies country information to a buffer, but it uses the country code and code page specified by the program to determine which information to copy.

The country information corresponds to an **EXTCOUNTRYINFO** structure:

```
EXTCOUNTRYINFO      STRUC
      eciLength          dw   ?               ;size of the structure, in bytes
      eciCountryCode     dw   ?               ;country code
      eciCodePageID      dw   ?               ;code-page identifier
      eciDateFormat      dw   ?               ;date format
      eciCurrency        db   5 dup (?)       ;currency symbol (ASCIIZ)
      eciThousands       db   2 dup (?)       ;thousands separator (ASCIIZ)
      eciDecimal         db   2 dup (?)       ;decimal separator (ASCIIZ)
      eciDateSep         db   2 dup (?)       ;date separator (ASCIIZ)
      eciTimeSep         db   2 dup (?)       ;time separator (ASCIIZ)
      eciBitField        db   ?               ;currency format
      eciCurrencyPlaces  db   ?               ;places after decimal point
      eciTimeFormat      db   ?               ;12- or 24-hour format
      eciCaseMap         dd   ?               ;address of case-mapping routine
      eciDataSep         db   2 dup (?)       ;data-list separator (ASCIIZ)
      eciReserved        db   10 dup (?)      ;reserved
EXTCOUNTRYINFO      ENDS
```

Get/Set Country Information returns the same information, but without the first three fields.

For a full description of the **EXTCOUNTRYINFO** structure, see Section 6.7, "Structures."

6.2.2 Character and String Conversions

A program can convert lowercase characters to uppercase by using Convert Character (Interrupt 21h Function 6520h), Convert String (Interrupt 21h Function 6521h), or Convert ASCIIZ String (Interrupt 21h Function 6522h). Using the uppercase conversion table associated with the current country and code page, Convert Character converts the character in the DL register, and Convert String and Convert ASCIIZ String replace each character in a string with its uppercase equivalent.

Although the case-conversion functions are available to all programs, it is often faster to carry out case conversions within the program itself.

6.2.3 Conversion Tables

Programs can retrieve the conversion tables associated with a specified country and code page by using the following functions:

Get Uppercase Table (Interrupt 21h Function 6502h)
Get Filename Uppercase Table (Interrupt 21h Function 6504h)
Get Filename-Character Table (Interrupt 21h Function 6505h)
Get Collate-Sequence Table (Interrupt 21h Function 6506h)

The conversion tables contain the information a program needs to convert lowercase characters to uppercase, to sort characters or strings, and to determine which characters can be used in filenames. These functions return the 32-bit addresses (segment:offset) of the conversion tables in memory owned by MS-DOS. Programs should copy the tables to their own memory if they intend to alter them.

Programs use the uppercase table to convert lowercase text characters to uppercase; they use the filename uppercase table to convert lowercase filename characters to uppercase. Each table begins with a 16-bit value that specifies the size, in bytes, of the character-value array in the table. This value is followed by the array of uppercase-character values. Programs convert a lowercase character to its uppercase equivalent by using the value of the lowercase character as an index to the array. Since the uppercase and filename uppercase tables apply only to extended ASCII characters (that is, characters with values greater than 127), the program must subtract 128 from the lowercase character value to create the index.

Programs use the collate-sequence table to sort characters and strings. The table begins with a 16-bit value that specifies the size, in bytes, of the character-weight array in the table. This value is followed by the array of 1-byte character weights. Programs sort two characters by using the character values as indexes to the character-weight array and comparing the resulting values. The character with the lower weight appears first in a sorted list.

Programs use the filename-character table to determine which characters are permitted in filenames. The beginning of the filename-character table corresponds to a **FILECHARTABLE** structure, which has the following form:

```
FILECHARTABLE        STRUC
    fctLength        dw  ?    ;table length, in bytes, excl this field
                     db  ?
    fctFirst         db  ?    ;lowest permissible character value
    fctLast          db  ?    ;highest permissible character value
                     db  ?
    ftcExcludeFirst  db  ?    ;first in range of excluded characters
    ftcExcludeLast   db  ?    ;last in range of excluded characters
                     db  ?
    fctIllegals      db  ?    ;number of illegal characters in array
                              ;start of array of illegal characters
FILECHARTABLE        ENDS
```

For a full description of the **FILECHARTABLE** structure, see Section 6.7, "Structures."

The filename-character table is followed by an array of illegal characters. The illegal characters differ for each country, so the number of characters in a given array is specified by the **fctIllegals** field.

6.3 Code Pages

To display or print characters, MS-DOS uses code pages to translate character values into images. Each code page defines a set of 255 characters. The set includes language-specific and graphics characters in addition to the characters corresponding to keyboard keys.

At startup, MS-DOS uses the default code page, called the system code page (usually code page 437). A user can select a different code page by using the **country** command in the CONFIG.SYS file or by using the **chcp** command at the DOS prompt. A program can select a different code page by using Set Global Code Page (Interrupt 21h Function 6602h). This function is similar to the **chcp** command in that it changes the code page for the screen, keyboard, and printer, if these devices have been prepared for the new code page. Neither Set Global Code Page nor the **chcp** command can be used unless the Nlsfunc program is loaded.

A program can determine the active code page by using Get Global Code Page (Interrupt 21h Function 6601h). This function returns both the system code page and the code page set by the user or a program, if any.

For more information about code pages, see Appendix A, "Code Pages."

6.4 Keyboard Layouts

The layout of a keyboard defines the letters, numbers, and symbols represented by its keys, in addition to the character values generated by pressing the keys. Different keyboard layouts are used in different countries. Users can adapt MS-DOS for these keyboard layouts by using the Keyb program. Programs cannot adapt MS-DOS directly, but they also can use the Keyb program, by starting it as a child program.

At startup, MS-DOS installs a default keyboard layout. When a user or program changes the layout by using the Keyb program, the default layout remains available but inactive. Programs can switch between the new and default layouts by using Set KEYB.COM Country Flag (Interrupt 2Fh Function 0AD82h). (Pressing the CTRL+ALT+F1 or CTRL+ALT+F2 key combination has the same effect.) A program can determine which layout is active by using Get KEYB.COM Country Flag (Interrupt 2Fh Function 0AD83h).

Programs can set the keyboard code page by using either Set Global Code Page or Set KEYB.COM Active Code Page (Interrupt 2Fh Function 0AD81h). Set KEYB.COM Active Code Page sets only the keyboard's code page; it has no effect on other devices. The current code page determines which character codes are generated for a keyboard's keys. In general, programs should check that the code page for the keyboard matches the code page for the screen.

A program can determine whether the Keyb program is loaded by using Get KEYB.COM Version Number (Interrupt 2Fh Function 0AD80h).

For more information about the keyboard layouts supported by MS-DOS, see the *Microsoft MS-DOS User's Guide and Reference*.

6.5 Screen and Printer Fonts

Screen and printer fonts provide the bitmap or escape-sequence data required to generate character images for displaying or printing. Different code pages have different font data, so a program that changes the code page must also change the fonts for the screen and printer devices. To do this, a font corresponding to the specified code page must be available. The program can determine this by using Query Code-Page Prepare List (Interrupt 21h Function 440Ch Minor Code 6Bh) to retrieve an array of code pages for which hardware or prepared fonts exist. If a code page has a corresponding font (either hardware or prepared), the program can either select it for global system use by using Set Global Code Page or select it for only the specified device by using Select Code Page (Interrupt 21h Function 440Ch Minor Code 4Ah). A program can determine the current code page of the device by using Query Selected Code Page (Interrupt 21h Function 440Ch Minor Code 6Ah).

If a corresponding font for a code page does not exist, a program can prepare a new font by using the following procedure:

1 Use Start Code-Page Prepare (Interrupt 21h Function 440Ch Minor Code 4Ch) to begin the preparation, identifying the device and the code pages for which to prepare the new font.

2 Use Send Control Data to Character Device (Interrupt 21h Function 4403h) to copy the contents of the device's corresponding code-page information (.CPI) file to the device. For example, the program must copy the EGA.CPI file to an EGA device.

3 Use End Code-Page Prepare (Interrupt 21h Function 440Ch Minor Code 4Dh) to complete the preparation.

This procedure may fail if the DISPLAY.SYS and PRINTER.SYS drivers are not installed by using **device** commands in the CONFIG.SYS file.

Note that users can carry out a similar preparation procedure by using the **mode** command and the **cp prepare** switch.

6.6 Code-Page Information Files (.CPI)

Code-page information files, also called font files, contain the bitmap and escape-sequence data required to support multiple code pages for screen or printer devices. Included with MS-DOS are five font files, each identified by a filename extension of .CPI:

File	Supported device
EGA.CPI	Color console used with EGA and VGA display adapters
LCD.CPI	Liquid crystal display
4201.CPI	IBM Proprinters II and III Model 4201 and IBM Pro-printers II and IIIXL Model 4202
4208.CPI	IBM Proprinter X24 Model 4207 and IBM Proprinter XL24 Model 4208
5202.CPI	IBM Quietwriter III Model 5202

A font file has the following form:

```
FONTFILEHEADER   <>   ;font file header
FONTINFOHEADER   <>   ;font information header
CPENTRYHEADER    <>   ;first code-page entry header
         .
         .
         .

FONTDATAHEADER   <>   ;first font data
         .
         .
Copyright        db 150 dup(?)   ;copyright notice
```

A font file begins with a **FONTFILEHEADER** structure that identifies the file as a valid font file and specifies how many fonts it has. Currently, only one font per file is permitted. A font file always ends with a copyright notice.

Each font in a font file has a corresponding **FONTINFOHEADER** structure that specifies how many code pages the font file supports. This structure begins at the offset contained in **ffhOffset** field in the **FONTFILEHEADER** structure.

For each code page, the file contains one **CPENTRYHEADER** structure, which defines the code page and device for which the font was designed. This structure also points to the next **CPENTRYHEADER** structure if the font file supports more than one code page. The first **CPENTRYHEADER** structure immediately follows the **FONTINFOHEADER** structure.

The **cpeOffset** field in each **CPENTRYHEADER** structure points to a font-data block consisting of a **FONTDATAHEADER** structure and data for either a screen font or a printer font. The **cpeDevType** field specifies whether the font data defines a screen font or a downloadable printer font.

The **FONTDATAHEADER** structure specifies the number of fonts defined for the code page. Each screen font begins with a **SCREENFONTHEADER** structure that specifies the raster dimensions of each character in the font and the number of characters in the font. This structure is followed by the raster bitmaps for the characters. A printer font begins with a **PRINTERFONTHEADER** structure that specifies which of two formats the font data has. This structure is followed by control sequences that initialize and define the font.

For a full description of these structures, see Section 6.7, "Structures."

6.7 Structures

This section describes the structures MS-DOS uses for national language support.

■ CODEPAGE

```
CODEPAGE      STRUC
    cpLength    dw   2      ;structure size, excl this field (always 2)
    cpId        dw   ?      ;code-page identifier
CODEPAGE      ENDS
```

Fields   **cpLength**   Specifies the size of the structure, in bytes. This value must be 2.

cpId   Identifies the code page. This field can be one of the following values:

Value	Meaning
437	United States
850	Multilingual (Latin I)
852	Slavic (Latin II)
860	Portuguese
863	Canadian-French
865	Nordic

See Also   Interrupt 21h Function 440Ch Minor Code 4Ah   Select Code Page
Interrupt 21h Function 440Ch Minor Code 4Dh   End Code-Page Prepare
Interrupt 21h Function 440Ch Minor Code 6Ah   Query Selected Code Page

■ COUNTRYINFO

```
COUNTRYINFO        STRUC
    ciDateFormat      dw   ?              ;date format
    ciCurrency        db   5 dup (?)      ;currency symbol (ASCIIZ)
    ciThousands       db   2 dup (?)      ;thousands separator (ASCIIZ)
    ciDecimal         db   2 dup (?)      ;decimal separator (ASCIIZ)
    ciDateSep         db   2 dup (?)      ;date separator (ASCIIZ)
    ciTimeSep         db   2 dup (?)      ;time separator (ASCIIZ)
    ciBitField        db   ?              ;currency format
    ciCurrencyPlaces  db   ?              ;places after decimal point
    ciTimeFormat      db   ?              ;12-hour or 24-hour format
    ciCaseMap         dd   ?              ;address of case-mapping routine
    ciDataSep         db   2 dup (?)      ;data-list separator (ASCIIZ)
    ciReserved        db   10 dup (?)     ;reserved
COUNTRYINFO        ENDS
```

The **COUNTRYINFO** structure contains country-specific information that programs use to format dates, times, currency, and other information.

Fields   **ciDateFormat**   Specifies the format for the date. This field can be one of the following values:

Value	Meaning
DATE_USA (0000h)	Month/day/year
DATE_EUROPE (0001h)	Day/month/year
DATE_JAPAN (0002h)	Year/month/day

ciCurrency   Specifies a zero-terminated ASCII (ASCIIZ) string containing the currency symbol.

ciThousands   Specifies an ASCIIZ string containing the thousands separator.

ciDecimal   Specifies an ASCIIZ string containing the decimal separator.

ciDateSep   Specifies an ASCIIZ string containing the date separator.

ciTimeSep   Specifies an ASCIIZ string containing the time separator.

ciBitField   Specifies the format for currency. This field can be a combination of the following settings:

Bit	Meaning
0	0 = Currency symbol precedes amount
	1 = Currency symbol follows amount
1	0 = No space between currency symbol and amount
	1 = One space between currency symbol and amount

All other bits in **ciBitField** are undefined.

ciCurrencyPlaces   Specifies the number of digits that appear after the decimal place in currency figures.

ciTimeFormat   Specifies the format for time. This field can be one of the following values:

Value	Meaning
TIME_12HOUR (00h)	12-hour time format
TIME_24HOUR (01h)	24-hour time format

ciCaseMap   Contains the 32-bit address (segment:offset) of the case-conversion routine. The routine performs lowercase-to-uppercase mapping (country-specific) for character values in the range 80h through 0FFh and does not convert characters with values less than 80h.

ciDataSep   Specifies an ASCIIZ string containing the data-list separator.

ciReserved   Reserved; do not use.

Comments   To convert a character by using the case-conversion routine, a program copies the character value to the AL register and calls the routine, using the address in the **ciCaseMap** field. If there is a matching uppercase character, the routine returns its value in the AL register. Otherwise, the routine returns the initial value unchanged. The AL and **FLAGS** registers are the only altered registers.

See Also   Interrupt 21h Function 38h Get/Set Country Information
Interrupt 21h Function 6501h Get Extended Country Information

■ CPENTRYHEADER

```
CPENTRYHEADER     STRUC
    cpeLength       dw ?              ;size of this structure, in bytes
    cpeNext         dd ?              ;offset to next CPENTRYHEADER structure
    cpeDevType      dw ?              ;device type
    cpeDevSubtype   db 8 dup(?)       ;device name and font-file name
    cpeCodepageID   dw ?              ;code-page identifier
    cpeReserved     db 6 dup(?)       ;reserved
    cpeOffset       dd ?              ;offset to font data
CPENTRYHEADER     ENDS
```

The **CPENTRYHEADER** structure contains information about a code-page entry in a font file.

Fields

cpeLength   Specifies the size of the **CPENTRYHEADER** structure, in bytes. This field must be 28.

cpeNext   Contains the offset to the next **CPENTRYHEADER** structure, in bytes. For the last structure in the chain, this field must be zero.

cpeDevType   Specifies the type of the device for which the font is designed. This field is 1 if the device is a screen device, or 2 if the device is a printer.

cpeDevSubtype   Contains a character string that names the screen or printer type. This field also determines the name of the font file. For example, if the subtype is EGA, the font-file name is EGA.CPI. If the string contains fewer than eight characters, it is left-justified and padded with space characters (ASCII 20h).

cpeCodepageID   Identifies the code page for which the font was designed. This field can be one of the following values:

Value	Meaning
437	United States
850	Multilingual (Latin I)
852	Slavic (Latin II)
860	Portuguese
863	Canadian-French
865	Nordic

cpeReserved   Reserved; must be zero.

cpeOffset   Contains the offset, in bytes, to the font data associated with this code page.

■ CPLIST

```
CPLIST  STRUC
    cplLength     dw   ((HARDWARE_IDS+1)+(PREPARED_IDS+1))*2
                       ;structure length, in bytes, excluding this field

    cplHIds       dw   HARDWARE_IDS            ;number of hardware code pages
    cplHid        dw   HARDWARE_IDS dup(?)     ;array of hardware code pages
    cplPIds       dw   PREPARED_IDS            ;number of prepared code pages
    cplPid        dw   PREPARED_IDS dup(?)     ;array of prepared code pages
CPLIST  ENDS
```

The **CPLIST** structure contains two arrays of code-page identifiers.

Fields

cplLength   Specifies the length of the list, in bytes. This value does not include the length of the **cplLength** field.

cplHIds   Specifies the number of hardware code pages.

cplHid   Specifies an array of hardware code-page identifiers. The array contains the number of elements specified in the **cplHIds** field.

cplPIds   Specifies the number of prepared code pages.

cplPid   Specifies an array of prepared code-page identifiers. The array contains the number of elements specified in the **cplPIds** field.

See Also   Interrupt 21h Function 440Ch Minor Code 6Bh   Query Code-Page Prepare List

■ CPPREPARE

```
CPPREPARE    STRUC
    cppFlags     dw  O                    ;flags (device-specific)
    cppLength    dw  (CODEPAGE_IDS+1)*2   ;structure length, in bytes,
                                          ;excluding first two fields
    cppIds       dw  CODEPAGE_IDS         ;number of code pages in list
    cppId        dw  CODEPAGE_IDS dup(?)  ;array of code pages
CPPREPARE    ENDS
```

The **CPPREPARE** structure contains an array of code-page identifiers.

Fields

cppFlags   Specifies device-specific flags.

cppLength   Specifies the length of the structure, in bytes, excluding the **cppFlags** and **cppLength** fields.

cppIds   Specifies the number of code pages in the list.

cppId   Specifies an array of code-page identifiers. The array contains the number of elements specified in the **cppIds** field.

Comments   If 0FFFFh is given as a code-page identifier, the device driver does not change the code-page identifier at that position in its own list.

See Also   Interrupt 21h Function 440Ch Minor Code 4Ch Start Code-Page Prepare

■ EXTCOUNTRYINFO

```
EXTCOUNTRYINFO        STRUC
    eciLength            dw  ?              ;size of the structure, in bytes
    eciCountryCode       dw  ?              ;country code
    eciCodePageID        dw  ?              ;code-page identifier
    eciDateFormat        dw  ?              ;date format
    eciCurrency          db  5 dup (?)      ;currency symbol (ASCIIZ)
    eciThousands         db  2 dup (?)      ;thousands separator (ASCIIZ)
    eciDecimal           db  2 dup (?)      ;decimal separator (ASCIIZ)
    eciDateSep           db  2 dup (?)      ;date separator (ASCIIZ)
    eciTimeSep           db  2 dup (?)      ;time separator (ASCIIZ)
    eciBitField          db  ?              ;currency format
    eciCurrencyPlaces    db  ?              ;places after decimal point
    eciTimeFormat        db  ?              ;12- or 24-hour format
    eciCaseMap           dd  ?              ;address of case-mapping routine
    eciDataSep           db  2 dup (?)      ;data-list separator (ASCIIZ)
    eciReserved          db  10 dup (?)     ;reserved
EXTCOUNTRYINFO        ENDS
```

The **EXTCOUNTRYINFO** structure contains country-specific information that programs use to format dates, times, currency, and other information.

Fields   **eciLength**   Specifies the length of the structure, in bytes, not including this field.

eciCountryCode   Specifies the country code for the given information. It can be one of the following:

Value	Meaning
001	United States
002	Canadian-French
003	Latin America

Value	Meaning
031	Netherlands
032	Belgium
033	France
034	Spain
036	Hungary
038	Yugoslavia
039	Italy
041	Switzerland
042	Czechoslovakia
044	United Kingdom
045	Denmark
046	Sweden
047	Norway
048	Poland
049	Germany
055	Brazil
061	International (English)
351	Portugal
358	Finland

eciCodePageID   Identifies the code page for the information given. This field can be one of the following values:

Value	Meaning
437	United States
850	Multilingual (Latin I)
852	Slavic (Latin II)
860	Portuguese
863	Canadian-French
865	Nordic

eciDateFormat   Specifies the format for the date. This field can be one of the following values:

Value	Meaning
DATE_USA (0000h)	Month/day/year
DATE_EUROPE (0001h)	Day/month/year
DATE_JAPAN (0002h)	Year/month/day

eciCurrency   Specifies a zero-terminated ASCII (ASCIIZ) string containing the currency symbol.

eciThousands   Specifies an ASCIIZ string containing the thousands separator.

eciDecimal   Specifies an ASCIIZ string containing the decimal separator.

eciDateSep   Specifies an ASCIIZ string containing the date separator.

eciTimeSep   Specifies an ASCIIZ string containing the time separator.

eciBitField   Specifies the format for currency. This field can be a combination of the following settings:

Bit	Meaning
0	0 = Currency symbol precedes amount
	1 = Currency symbol follows amount
1	0 = No space between currency symbol and amount
	1 = One space between currency symbol and amount

All other bits in **eciBitField** are undefined.

eciCurrencyPlaces   Specifies the number of digits that appear after the decimal place in currency format.

eciTimeFormat   Specifies the format for time. This field can be one of the following values:

Value	Meaning
TIME_12HOUR (00h)	12-hour time format
TIME_24HOUR (01h)	24-hour time format

eciCaseMap   Contains the 32-bit address (segment:offset) of the case-conversion routine. The routine performs lowercase-to-uppercase mapping (country-specific) for character values in the range 80h through 0FFh and does not convert characters with values less than 80h.

eciDataSep   Specifies an ASCIIZ string containing the data-list separator.

eciReserved   Reserved; do not use.

Comments   To convert a character using the case-conversion routine, the program copies the character value to the AL register and calls the routine, using the address in the **eciCaseMap** field. If there is a matching uppercase character, the routine returns its value in the AL register. Otherwise, the routine returns the initial value unchanged. The AL register and **FLAGS** registers are the only altered registers.

See Also   Interrupt 21h Function 6501h Get Extended Country Information

■ FILECHARTABLE

```
FILECHARTABLE       STRUC
    fctLength       dw  ?     ;table length, in bytes, excl this field
                    db  ?
    fctFirst        db  ?     ;lowest permissible character value
    fctLast         db  ?     ;highest permissible character value
                    db  ?
    ftcExcludeFirst db  ?     ;first in range of excluded characters
    ftcExcludeLast  db  ?     ;last in range of excluded characters
                    db  ?
    fctIllegals     db  ?     ;number of illegal characters in array
                              ;start of array of illegal characters
FILECHARTABLE       ENDS
```

The **FILECHARTABLE** structure contains a list of characters that are and are *not* permitted in filenames.

Fields

fctLength   Specifies the length of the table, in bytes, not counting this field.

fctFirst   Specifies the lowest permissible character value.

fctLast   Specifies the highest permissible character value.

fctExcludeFirst   Specifies the first character value in a range of excluded characters.

fctExcludeLast   Specifies the last character value in a range of excluded characters.

fctIllegals   Specifies the number of illegal characters in the table. The array of illegal characters immediately follows this field.

See Also   Function 6505h Get Filename-Character Table

■ FONTDATAHEADER

```
FONTDATAHEADER  STRUC
    fdhReserved  dw ?      ;reserved
    fdhFonts     dw ?      ;number of fonts
    fdhLength    dw ?      ;size of font data, in bytes
FONTDATAHEADER  ENDS
```

The **FONTDATAHEADER** structure contains information about the number and size of the font descriptions for a code page. This structure is followed immediately by the screen or printer font descriptions.

Fields

fdhReserved   Reserved. This field must be 1.

fdhFonts   Specifies the number of fonts (font descriptions) that immediately follow this structure. These font descriptions must contain definitions for characters in the associated code page. For printer devices, no more than one font description can be given, so this field must be 1.

fdhLength   Specifies the size, in bytes, of the font descriptions that immediately follow this structure.

■ FONTFILEHEADER

```
FONTFILEHEADER  STRUC
    ffhFileTag     db 8 dup(?)  ;font-file identifier
    ffhReserved    db 8 dup(?)  ;reserved
    ffhPointers    dw ?         ;number of pointers
    ffhPointerType db ?         ;type of pointer
    ffhOffset      dd ?         ;offset to information header
FONTFILEHEADER  ENDS
```

The **FONTFILEHEADER** contains information that identifies the file as a valid font file and specifies the number of fonts defined in the file.

Fields

ffhFileTag   Identifies the font file. This field must contain the byte value 0FFh, followed by the characters F, O, N, and T (ASCII 46h, 4Fh, 4Eh, and 54h, respectively), and three space characters (ASCII 20h).

ffhReserved   Reserved; must be zero.

ffhPointers   Specifies the number of information pointers in the header. For current versions of MS-DOS, this value should be 1.

ffhPointerType   Specifies the type of information pointers in the header. For current versions of MS-DOS, this value should be 1.

ffhOffset   Specifies the offset, in bytes, from the beginning of the file to the information header.

■ FONTINFOHEADER

```
FONTINFOHEADER   STRUC
    fihCodePages    dw   ?    ;number of code-page entries
FONTINFOHEADER   ENDS
```

The **FONTINFOHEADER** structure specifies the number of code-page entries contained in the font file.

Field   **fihCodePages**   Specifies the number of code-page entries in the file.

■ PRINTERFONTHEADER

```
PRINTERFONTHEADER STRUC
    pfhSelType      dw ?     ;selection type
    pfhSeqLength    dw ?     ;sequence length, in bytes
PRINTERFONTHEADER ENDS
```

The **PRINTERFONTHEADER** structure contains information about the length and content of the control-sequence data used for the printer font. The structure is followed immediately by control-sequence data and possibly one or more bytes of downloadable font data.

Fields   **pfhSelType**   Specifies the selection type for the printer font. This field can be either of the following values:

Value	Meaning
1	The control-sequence data consists of hardware escape data followed by downloadable escape data. The hardware escape data contains the sequence of characters that selects the hardware (default) font of the printer. The first byte of the hardware escape data specifies the number of characters in the sequence. The downloadable escape data contains the sequence of control characters that selects the downloaded font currently resident in the printer. The first byte of the downloadable escape data specifies the number of characters in the sequence. The total number of bytes in the hardware and downloadable escape data must equal the number of bytes specified in the **pfhSeqLength** field.
2	The control-sequence data consists of a single escape sequence that selects the font for this code page. This font may have been downloaded.

pfhSeqLength   Specifies the length of the control-sequence data, in bytes. This value must always be less than 31.

Comments   The control-sequence data is used for initializing the printer for the code page associated with this font.

Unlike the size of a screen-font description, the size of the printer-font description cannot be determined directly. Instead, its size must be calculated from the **fdhLength** field of the **FONTDATAHEADER** structure. As a result, only one printer-font description can immediately follow a **FONTDATAHEADER** structure.

The downloadable font data consists of the escape sequence required to download the font description. This escape sequence depends on the printer. Its size is determined by subtracting the size of the **PRINTERFONTHEADER** structure from the **fdhLength** value in the corresponding **FONTDATAHEADER** structure. Since the 4208 and 5202 printers have hardware support for code pages, they do not need any font data to be downloaded. Therefore, the **fdhLength** field is nonexistent in those font files.

These existing printer files use the following selection types:

Type	Filename
1	4201.CPI
2	4208.CPI or 5202.CPI

■ SCREENFONTHEADER

```
SCREENFONTHEADER  STRUC
        sfhHeight       db  ?    ;character height
        sfhWidth        db  ?    ;character width
        sfhRelHeight    db  ?    ;must be zero
        sfhRelWidth     db  ?    ;must be zero
        sfhCharacters   dw  ?    ;number of characters defined in bitmap
SCREENFONTHEADER  ENDS
```

The **SCREENFONTHEADER** structure specifies the raster dimensions of each character in the font and the number of characters in the font. This structure is followed by a raster bitmap for each character.

Fields

sfhHeight   Specifies the number of rows, in pixels, that this character occupies on the screen.

sfhWidth   Specifies the number of columns, in pixels, that this character occupies on the screen.

sfhRelHeight   Specifies the relative height, a part of the aspect ratio. This field is currently unused and must be zero.

sfhRelWidth   Specifies the relative width, a part of the aspect ratio. This field is currently unused and must be zero.

sfhCharacters   Specifies the number of characters defined in the bitmaps immediately following this structure. Normally, the entire ASCII character set is defined, so this value is usually 256.

Comments

The bitmap data following the structure consists of one bitmap for each character in the font. Each character bitmap is a packed array of bits organized by row and column, starting at the upper left corner of the character's image. Since all current screen fonts are 8 bits wide, the number of bytes needed to encode this packed array is equal to the square area of a character in the font divided by 8.

The total length of the screen-font description is 6 bytes plus the product of the number of characters in the descriptions and the number of bytes needed to encode a character bitmap.

Chapter

7

Interrupts

7.1 Introduction

This chapter describes the interrupts that provide the primary interface between programs and the MS-DOS kernel and its supporting programs.

This chapter discusses the following:

- MS-DOS interrupts
- System interrupts
- Exceptions
- Interrupt and exception handlers
- Interrupt chains
- Multiplex interrupt handlers
- Terminate-and-stay-resident programs
- MS-DOS structures

7.2 MS-DOS Interrupts

MS-DOS reserves software interrupts 20h through 3Fh for its own use. Among the features these interrupts provide are the interfaces to the MS-DOS system functions and to MS-DOS programs that provide services to other programs.

Following are the MS-DOS interrupts:

Interrupt	Description	Comments
20h	Terminate Program	For use by .COM programs
21h	MS-DOS System Function	For use by all programs
22h	Termination Address	For storage only (Do not issue)
23h	CTRL+C Handler	Replaceable
24h	Critical-Error Handler	Replaceable
25h	Absolute Disk Read	
26h	Absolute Disk Write	
27h	Terminate and Stay Resident	For use by .COM programs
28h	MS-DOS Idle Handler	Extendable
29h	Fast Console	For use by MS-DOS character I/O
2Ah	Network/Critical Sections	For use by MS-DOS
2Eh	Reload Transient	For use by COMMAND.COM only
2Fh	Multiplex Interrupt	Extendable

Interrupt	Description	Comments
30h	MS-DOS Entry Point	For storage only (Do not issue)
31h	MS-DOS Entry Point	For storage only (Do not issue)

All other reserved interrupts—2Bh through 2Dh and 32h through 3Fh—are not currently used by MS-DOS. MS-DOS assigns a default interrupt handler to each reserved interrupt it does not use. The default handler does nothing more than return to the program that issued the interrupt.

For interrupts marked "Replaceable" or "Extendable" in the preceding table, a program can provide its own interrupt handlers to replace or enhance the existing handlers. The program should leave all other interrupts unchanged. An exception to this rule is a terminate-and-stay-resident program (TSR) that must intercept interrupts to determine when MS-DOS system functions have been called.

7.3 System Interrupts

On most computers, Interrupt 05h and Interrupts 10h through 1Fh are reserved for use by ROM BIOS routines. Although these interrupts provide an interface to low-level services for the computer, a program that uses these services cannot be guaranteed to run correctly on all MS-DOS computers.

The following are typical low-level services:

Interrupt	Service
05h	Print screen (issued when SHIFT+PRINT SCREEN is pressed)
08h	Timer tick
09h	Keyboard
0Ah	Slave interrupt controller
0Bh	COM1
0Ch	COM2
0Dh	LPT2
0Eh	Floppy disk
0Fh	LPT1
10h	Video services
11h	Peripheral equipment list
12h	Memory size
13h	Disk services

Interrupt	Service
14h	Serial-port services
15h	Miscellaneous system services
16h	Keyboard services
17h	Printer services
18h	ROM Basic
19h	Restart computer
1Ah	Time of day
1Bh	Break (issued when CTRL+BREAK is pressed)
1Ch	Timer
1Dh	Video parameters (address only)
1Eh	Diskette parameters (address only)
1Fh	Graphics fonts (address only)
70h	Real-time clock
75h	Numeric coprocessor
76h	Hard disk

In some cases, MS-DOS may replace or extend ROM BIOS routines and other device-specific interrupt handlers for the following interrupts:

Interrupt	MS-DOS handler action
00h	Displays "divide overflow" message and terminates program
01h	Returns immediately
02h*	Switches stack
03h	Returns immediately
04h	Returns immediately
08h-0Eh*	Switches stack
15h	If CTRL+ALT+DEL is detected, prepares MS-DOS before restarting computer
19h	Prepares MS-DOS before restarting computer
1Bh	Places CTRL+C character value (03h) at top of keyboard input buffer
70h*	Switches stack
72h-74h*	Switches stack
76h-77h*	Switches stack

Stack-switching interrupt handlers (marked * in the preceding list) are used in conjunction with routines that support hardware interrupts. A stack-switching handler sets up a new stack when a hardware interrupt occurs, allowing the corresponding interrupt routine to carry out operations without inadvertently overflowing the stack that was active when the interrupt occurred. The stack-switching handler restores the original stack when the interrupt routine returns. Stack-switching interrupt handlers are enabled only if the **stacks** command in the CONFIG.SYS file specifies eight or more stacks.

7.4 Exceptions

MS-DOS provides default handlers for some exceptions, such as the divide-error exception (Interrupt 00h). A computer may also provide default exception handlers as part of its ROM BIOS routines.

A program can provide its own exception-handling routines by replacing the default handlers. For example, a debugging program can install its own handlers for the single-step exception (Interrupt 01h) and the breakpoint exception (Interrupt 03h). CPU capabilities determine what types of exceptions can occur while a program is running and what information is available about them.

A program that replaces an exception handler must restore it before terminating.

7.5 Interrupt and Exception Handlers

Programs install interrupt and exception handlers to provide special responses to software interrupts, hardware interrupts, errors, or other conditions detected by the CPU. The handler determines what action to take. Most handlers carry out the action and return to the program at the point of the interruption, although some default handlers terminate the program that caused the interruption or exception.

In general, an interrupt or exception handler should do the following:

- Save the registers it uses and restore them before returning.
- Take precautions to avoid stack overflow. If a handler uses more than a few bytes of stack, it should use its own stack, restoring the original stack before returning.
- Disable interrupts only when performing critical processing such as changing stacks or updating critical data. Enable the interrupts immediately after completing the task.
- Use the **iret** instruction to return.

When the handler receives control, the SS:SP registers point to whatever stack was active when the interrupt or exception occurred. This could be a stack belonging to MS-DOS, to a program, or to other software. A handler that uses more than a few bytes of stack should switch to its own stack.

To install an interrupt or exception handler, a program must use the following procedure:

1   Retrieve the address of the current handler by using Get Interrupt Vector (Interrupt 21h Function 35h).

2   Save the address of the current handler. Before terminating, the program must restore this handler by using Set Interrupt Vector (Interrupt 21h Function 25h).

3   Install the new handler by using Set Interrupt Vector.

Programs that install interrupt or exception handlers must restore the original handlers before terminating. Since the default (MS-DOS) CTRL+C and critical-error handlers (Interrupts 23h and 24h) terminate programs without restoring interrupts, programs that install new handlers must also install custom handlers for Interrupts 23h and 24h. The custom Interrupt 23h and Interrupt 24h handlers must determine whether the program that installed the new handler is about to terminate; if it is, they must restore the original interrupt handlers before the program terminates. Note that MS-DOS automatically restores the original Interrupt 23h and Interrupt 24h handlers.

In general, if an interrupt occurs while a program is running, the corresponding interrupt handler can use any MS-DOS system function. In any other case, the handler can use only the character I/O functions (Interrupt 21h Functions 01h through 0Ch). For example, if a divide-error exception occurs in a program, the divide-error handler can display a message by using Write File or Device (Interrupt 21h Function 40h). However, if the error occurs in MS-DOS, the handler must use a character I/O function, such as Display String (Interrupt 21h Function 09h). If a critical disk error is being processed, the handler must not use *any* MS-DOS system function.

A handler can determine whether an interrupt or exception occurred in MS-DOS by examining the InDOS flag. If MS-DOS is processing a system function, this one-byte flag is nonzero. The handler can retrieve the address of the InDOS flag by using Get InDOS Flag Address (Interrupt 21h Function 34h). The handler can determine whether a critical disk error is being processed by examining the ErrorMode flag (the byte immediately before the InDOS flag). If the ErrorMode flag is nonzero, MS-DOS is processing a critical disk error.

Although a program can install interrupt handlers that service hardware interrupts, these handlers are device-specific and are not guaranteed to work with all MS-DOS computers. To support hardware interrupts, the program installs an interrupt service routine (ISR) and either programs the computer's interrupt controller to support interrupts from the specified device or uses interrupts defined by the device's ROM BIOS. In either case, the information required to carry out these steps is beyond the scope of this book.

7.6 Interrupt Chains

An interrupt chain is two or more interrupt handlers that process the same interrupt. Programs create interrupt chains either to extend the capabilities of existing interrupt handlers or to permit replacement handlers to take advantage of features in existing handlers. For example, some programs intercept Interrupt 21h to detect when certain MS-DOS system functions have been called. Such programs do not then carry out the system functions themselves; instead, they pass control to the original Interrupt 21h handler.

A program creates an interrupt chain by installing an interrupt handler and saving the address of the original handler. When the new handler processes the interrupt, it can either call or jump to the original handler if it needs help processing the interrupt. A new handler *calls* the original handler if it needs to carry out additional processing after the original handler completes its work. Otherwise, it *jumps to* the original handler.

When a new handler calls an original handler, it can modify the registers and stack before passing control to the original handler, but it must push the flags onto the stack (by using the **pushf** instruction) before making the call. In all cases, a handler should use the **iret** instruction to return from the interrupt.

A handler should assume nothing about the state of the system and should do the following:

■ Disable interrupts if it needs them disabled, and explicitly enable them otherwise. Previous handlers in the interrupt chain may or may not have enabled them.

■ Set the direction flag before executing string instructions.

■ Call the next handler in the chain immediately if the interrupt is a time-critical interrupt (for example, a timer interrupt). This ensures that handlers expecting control immediately after the interrupt get it as soon as possible.

7.7 Multiplex Interrupt Handlers

A program can provide services to other programs by installing an interrupt handler for Multiplex Interrupt (Interrupt 2Fh). Multiplex Interrupt is a common entry point for MS-DOS resident programs and device drivers that carry out requests for other programs. For example, a program can add files to the print queue (maintained by the resident program PRINT.EXE) by setting registers and issuing Multiplex Interrupt.

To provide services to other programs, a service program must add its multiplex handler to the interrupt chain and choose a multiplex identifier. This identifier is an integer that distinguishes the program's multiplex handler from all others in the interrupt chain. When other programs request service, they place the service program's multiplex identifier in the AH register. When Multiplex Interrupt is issued, each multiplex handler in the interrupt chain must check the AH register; if the register contains its identifier, the handler must process the service request.

Program identifiers must be in the range 0C0h through 0FFh. All other values are reserved for MS-DOS programs and related software. The following are a few of the reserved multiplex identifiers and their associated programs:

Multiplex identifier	Provider
01h	PRINT.EXE
06h	ASSIGN.COM
10h	SHARE.EXE
11h	Network Redirector
14h	NLSFUNC.EXE
1Ah	ANSI.SYS
43h	Extended Memory Manager (HIMEM.SYS)
48h	DOSKEY.COM
4Bh	Task Switcher
0ADh	KEYB.COM
0AEh	APPEND.EXE
0B0h	GRAFTABL.COM
0B7h	APPEND.EXE

The AL register specifies the function to carry out. Whenever a multiplex handler processes a request, it checks the contents of the AL register to determine what action to take. By convention, 00h in the AL register specifies the Installed State function. A multiplex handler processes this function by returning a nonzero value (typically 0FFh) in the AL register to indicate that it is installed.

7.8 Terminate-and-Stay-Resident Programs

When a terminate-and-stay-resident program (often called a TSR) returns control to its parent program, its code and data remain in memory to be used by other programs.

There are three types of terminate-and-stay-resident programs:

■ Service programs. These provide useful functions for other programs. For example, PRINT.EXE is a TSR that maintains the print queue and provides functions that other programs can use to examine the queue and add files to it. Service programs install an interrupt handler before terminating. Subsequent programs then use the corresponding interrupt, much as they use MS-DOS System Function (Interrupt 21h), to call the service program's functions.

- Pop-up programs. These monitor the keyboard and resume executing upon receiving particular keystrokes. To monitor the keyboard, a pop-up program intercepts an interrupt associated with the keyboard or with a key combination, such as SHIFT+PRINT SCREEN or CTRL+BREAK.

- Hardware-support programs. These operate much like low-level device drivers, controlling the operation of specific devices while providing functions that permit other programs to access the device.

A terminate-and-stay-resident program consists of at least two parts: an initialization routine and one or more interrupt handlers. The initialization routine is generally the same for all programs. The interrupt handlers depend largely on the program type, although they may carry out the same housekeeping tasks and are installed by using the same procedure.

7.8.1 Initialization Routine

The initialization routine prepares the terminate-and-stay-resident program to be used by other programs or to service interrupts generated by a device. The initialization routine must do the following:

- Make sure the TSR is not already loaded.
- Install the interrupt handler (or handlers).
- Free unneeded resources.
- Call Keep Program (Interrupt 21h Function 31h).

Unless a TSR is designed to be loaded more than once, it should safeguard against the user's starting it multiple times. The TSR can do this by using Multiplex Interrupt (Interrupt 2Fh) and a custom interrupt handler. An MS-DOS TSR, such as PRINT.EXE, uses this technique. In general, each time it starts, the TSR issues Interrupt 2Fh, supplying an identifier unique to the TSR. If the interrupt returns a reply, a copy of the TSR has already been loaded. Otherwise, the TSR must install a custom handler that replies to all subsequent calls to the TSR.

The TSR must install its interrupt handlers by using Set Interrupt Vector (Interrupt 21h Function 25h). This function copies the address of the interrupt handler to the interrupt table. If a program or device issues the corresponding interrupt, control passes to the interrupt handler. Before installing the interrupt handler, the TSR should also use Get Interrupt Vector (Interrupt 21h Function 35h) to retrieve the address of the current handler so that it can be restored if the TSR is removed from memory.

Before calling Keep Program, the initialization routine should do the following:

- Close all unneeded files, including standard devices.
- Free the environment block if it is not needed.
- Free all memory not needed to support the interrupt handler.

When it calls Keep Program, the routine should specify the smallest possible amount of program memory to retain. In particular, the code and data for the initialization routine should be at the end of the TSR, to ensure that they are freed by Keep Program.

7.8.2 Service-Program Interrupt Handler

A service program's interrupt handler receives execution control from programs that use the **int** instruction to issue an interrupt. The calling program, before issuing the interrupt, fills registers with whatever values are needed. The interrupt handler determines which function to carry out and uses the values passed to it to complete the function.

The service program may install a handler for any nonreserved interrupt. (Most interrupts from 00h through 7Fh are reserved by MS-DOS or by the computer's ROM BIOS.) Rather than use a new interrupt, however, many service programs expand the multiplex-interrupt handler they install so that it also receives and processes function requests and replies to queries about the installation state.

When the interrupt handler receives control, the stack, the current program segment prefix (PSP), and the current disk transfer address (DTA) belong to the calling program. In addition, any registers not explicitly used with the function request may contain values that the calling program expects to remain unchanged. If the interrupt handler changes any of these resources, it must save and then restore the original resource before returning.

The current program's PSP determines which open files are available to the interrupt handler. To access files other than those opened by the calling program, the interrupt handler must change the current PSP by using Set PSP Address (Interrupt 21h Function 50h). It can retrieve the current PSP by using Get PSP Address (Interrupt 21h Function 51h).

If the interrupt handler uses the buffer pointed to by the current DTA, it should change the current address to the address of its own buffer by using Set Disk Transfer Address (Interrupt 21h Function 1Ah). This change ensures that any data in the buffer pointed to by the calling program's DTA is not overwritten. The interrupt handler can retrieve the current DTA by using Get Disk Transfer Address (Interrupt 21h Function 2Fh).

7.8.3 Pop-up and Hardware-Support Interrupt Handlers

A pop-up or hardware-support program's interrupt handler receives control asynchronously—that is, whenever the user presses a key or a device generates an interrupt. To service the interrupt, the system temporarily suspends the current instruction and passes control to the interrupt handler. Since an asynchronous interrupt may occur at any time, the interrupt handler must determine the state of MS-DOS and possibly of the ROM BIOS before carrying out any operations. If a pop-up or hardware-support interrupt occurs while an MS-DOS system function or ROM BIOS routine is being carried out, the interrupt handler should ignore the interrupt and return immediately.

If the interrupt handler uses MS-DOS system functions, it must check the InDOS flag before calling a function and must check the ErrorMode flag before calling any character I/O function (Interrupt 21h Functions 01h through 0Ch).

The one-byte InDOS flag specifies whether MS-DOS is currently processing a system function. If the flag is nonzero, the interrupt handler can call only the character I/O functions; it must not call other MS-DOS system functions. A program can retrieve the address of the InDOS flag by using Get InDOS Flag Address (Interrupt 21h Function 34h).

The one-byte ErrorMode flag specifies whether MS-DOS is currently processing a critical disk error. If it is, the flag is nonzero and the interrupt handler must not call *any* MS-DOS system function, including the character I/O functions. The ErrorMode flag occupies the byte immediately before the InDOS flag, so a program can determine the ErrorMode flag address by subtracting 1 from the InDOS flag address.

The interrupt handler must check whether any ROM BIOS routine it calls directly has been interrupted, and it must not call an interrupted ROM BIOS routine that is not reentrant. Since MS-DOS provides no means to determine whether a ROM BIOS routine has been interrupted, a TSR must intercept these interrupts and record when control enters and leaves the routines. The interrupt handler can then check this record before making a call to the ROM BIOS.

The interrupt handler must not continue if another hardware interrupt is being processed. To determine whether an interrupt is active, the TSR must query the system interrupt controller.

7.9 MS-DOS Interrupt Reference

This section describes MS-DOS Interrupts 20h through 28h and Interrupt 2Fh in detail. The reference page for each interrupt provides the syntax, a statement of purpose, any parameter descriptions, and cross-references to similar or related interrupts and to related functions.

Interrupts 2Bh through 2Dh and 32h through 3Fh are not currently used by MS-DOS and are not documented here. Interrupts 29h, 2Ah, 2Eh, 30h, and 31h are also not documented.

■ Interrupt 20h Terminate Program   Superseded

```
int 20h      ;Terminate Program
```

Terminate Program (Interrupt 20h) terminates the current program and returns control to its parent program.

This interrupt has been superseded. Programs should use the Interrupt 21h function End Program (Function 4Ch).

Parameters   This function has no parameters.

Return Value   This interrupt does not return.

Comments   This interrupt is intended to be used by .COM programs. When a program issues the interrupt, the CS register must contain the segment address of the program segment prefix (PSP).

This interrupt carries out the following actions:

- Flushes the file buffers and closes files, unlocking any regions locked by the program.
- Restores Termination Address (Interrupt 22h) from offset 0Ah in the PSP (**pspTerminateVector** field).
- Restores the CTRL+C Handler (Interrupt 23h) from offset 0Eh in the PSP (**pspControlCVector** field).
- Restores the Critical-Error Handler (Interrupt 24h) from offset 12h in the PSP (**pspCritErrorVector** field).
- Frees any memory owned by the terminating program.

After completing these actions, this interrupt transfers control to the address specified by offset 0Ah in the PSP.

See Also   Interrupt 21h Function 00h Terminate Program
Interrupt 21h Function 4Ch End Program
Interrupt 22h Termination Address
Interrupt 23h CTRL+C Handler
Interrupt 24h Critical-Error Handler

■ Interrupt 21h MS-DOS System Function

MS-DOS System Function (Interrupt 21h) carries out one of the functions described in Chapter 8, "Interrupt 21h Functions."

■ Interrupt 22h Termination Address

Termination Address (Interrupt 22h) is not used as an interrupt. Instead, MS-DOS stores the termination address for the current program in the corresponding vector-table entry. This address is also specified in offset 0Ah in the current program's PSP (**pspTerminateVector** field).

Programs must not issue Interrupt 22h.

Comments

The termination address is a return address back to the program that started the current program. MS-DOS transfers control to the termination address as the last step in completing Terminate Program (Interrupt 20h), Terminate Program (Interrupt 21h Function 00h), Keep Program (Interrupt 21h Function 31h), End Program (Interrupt 21h Function 4Ch), and Terminate and Stay Resident (Interrupt 27h). These functions always restore the vector-table entry from offset 0Ah in the current PSP before transferring control, so changes to the vector-table entry are ignored.

Before transferring control to the termination address, MS-DOS restores the parent program's stack and PSP. Furthermore, if a program terminates by using Terminate Program (Interrupt 20h or Interrupt 21h Function 00h) or End Program (Interrupt 21h Function 4Ch), MS-DOS frees all resources for the program, such as allocated memory, stack, files, and standard devices. This means that changes to the termination address in the PSP or direct calls to the termination address may corrupt the operation of the system.

See Also

Interrupt 20h Terminate Program
Interrupt 21h Function 00h Terminate Program
Interrupt 21h Function 31h Keep Program
Interrupt 21h Function 4Ch End Program
Interrupt 27h Terminate and Stay Resident

■ Interrupt 23h CTRL+C Handler

CTRL+C Handler (Interrupt 23h) carries out program-specific actions in response to the CTRL+C (ASCII 03h) key combination being pressed. MS-DOS issues this interrupt if it receives the CTRL+C character while processing a system function. The handler carries out its actions then returns to the system in order to restart the system function or terminate the current program.

Programs must not issue Interrupt 23h.

Comments

MS-DOS sets the current CTRL+C handler when starting a program, copying the address of the parent program's handler to both the vector-table entry and offset 0Eh in the new program's PSP (**pspControlCVector** field). Although a program can change the vector-table entry, it must not change the address in its PSP, since MS-DOS uses this address to restore the parent program's handler.

MS-DOS does not immediately issue Interrupt 23h when the user presses the CTRL+C key combination. Instead, the system places the CTRL+C character (ASCII 03h) in the keyboard buffer; if no other characters are ahead of the control character, the system processes it while carrying out a system function. For most computers, MS-DOS also places a CTRL+C character in a buffer when the user presses the CTRL+BREAK key combination. Pressing this combination places a CTRL+C character ahead of all other characters in the keyboard buffer.

MS-DOS checks for the CTRL+C character while carrying out character I/O functions (Interrupt 21h Functions 01h through 0Ch). It also checks for the character while carrying out other system functions—but only if the CTRL+C check flag is set. If the I/O mode for the keyboard (or input device) is binary, the system disables CTRL+C character processing while a program uses Read File or Device (Interrupt 21h Function 3Fh) and the CTRL+C character is read as input.

Before issuing Interrupt 23h, MS-DOS does the following:

- Sets all registers to the values they had when the interrupted system function was initially called.
- Sets the program's stack to be the current stack. When the handler receives control, the stack has the following contents (from the top of the stack):

    The return address (CS:IP) and the flags needed for the **iret** instruction back to the system.

    The return address (CS:IP) and the flags needed for the **iret** instruction back to the program.

- Sets to zero any internal system variables, such as the ErrorMode and InDOS variables, so that the handler can call system functions or even return directly to the program without disrupting system operations.

A CTRL+C handler can call any system function.

Upon returning from Interrupt 23h, MS-DOS checks the method of return to determine what action to take. If the handler sets the carry flag and returns with the **retf** instruction, MS-DOS terminates the program by calling End Program

(Interrupt 21h Function 4Ch). If the handler returns with the **iret** instruction or with the **retf** instruction after clearing the carry flag, the system repeats the call to the system function, starting the function's action again from the beginning. In this case, the handler must preserve all registers, restoring them before returning to the system.

COMMAND.COM provides the default CTRL+C handler, which terminates the current program unless a batch file is running, in which case the handler prompts the user to continue (or not) with the next command in the file. Since prompting the user suspends execution of the current program until the user responds, programs that lock resources (especially over a network) should replace the default handler. In general, a program should make sure that other programs can access resources even while it is suspended.

See Also   Interrupt 21h Function 3Fh Read File or Device
Interrupt 21h Function 4Ch End Program

■ Interrupt 24h Critical-Error Handler

Critical-Error Handler (Interrupt 24h) carries out program-specific actions in response to critical errors during read and write operations. MS-DOS issues this interrupt if a critical error occurs while a system function is attempting to read from or write to a device or file. The handler carries out its actions then returns to the system to retry the function, terminate the function, or terminate the current program.

Programs must not issue Interrupt 24h.

Comments   MS-DOS sets the current critical-error handler when starting a program, copying the address of the parent program's handler to both the vector-table entry and offset 12h in the new program's PSP (**pspCritErrorVector** field). Although a program can change the vector-table entry, it must not change the address in its PSP, since MS-DOS uses this address to restore the parent program's handler.

Before issuing Interrupt 24h, MS-DOS does the following:

■ Sets the AX, DI, BP, and SI registers with information about the error, such as the error value, location of the error, type of device, and type of operation.

■ Sets the program's stack to be the current stack. When the handler receives control, the stack has the following contents (from the top of the stack):

The return address (CS:IP) and the flags needed for the **iret** instruction back to the system.

The contents of the program's registers at the time the system function that caused the error was called. The registers are preserved in the following order: AX, BX, CX, DX, SI, DI, BP, DS, and ES.

The return address (CS:IP) and the flags needed for the **iret** instruction back to the program.

■ Sets internal system variables, such as those for InDOS and ErrorMode. InDOS is set to zero to permit the handler to call system functions. ErrorMode is set to 1 to prevent the system from issuing Interrupt 24h again before the handler returns; MS-DOS issues only one Interrupt 24h at a time.

MS-DOS passes information about the error to the handler by using the following registers:

Register	Description
AH	Specifies information about when and where the error occurred, as well as how the critical-error handler can respond to the error. The bits in this register can have the following values:

Bit	Meaning
0	Specifies the operation that caused the error. If this bit is 0, the error occurred during a read operation. Otherwise, the error occurred during a write operation.

Register	Description

	Bit	Meaning
	1,2	Specify the location of the error, but only if the error occurred on a block device. These bits can have the following values: 00 = error in reserved sector (MS-DOS area) 01 = error in file allocation table (FAT) 10 = error in directory 11 = error in data area
	3	Specifies whether the handler can terminate the function. If this bit is 1, the handler can terminate the function. Otherwise, it must not.
	4	Specifies whether the handler can retry the function. If this bit is 1, the handler can retry the function. Otherwise, it must not.
	5	Specifies whether the handler can ignore the error. If this bit is 1, the handler can ignore the error. Otherwise, it must not.
	6	Reserved.
	7	Specifies the type of device on which the error occurred. If this bit is 0, the error occurred on a block drive. If this bit is 1, it indicates that the error occurred either on a character device or in the memory image of the FAT, and that the handler must check bit 15 in the **dhAttributes** field (offset 04h) of the **DEVICEHEADER** structure to determine the exact location. If bit 15 is set, the error occurred on a character device. Otherwise, the error occurred in the memory image of the FAT.

Register	Description
AL	Specifies the drive number (0 = A, 1 = B, 2 = C, and so on) if the error occurred on a block device. This register is not used for errors that occur on character devices.
DI	Specifies the error value. The error value, in the lower byte only, can be one of the following:

Value	Meaning
00h	Attempt to write on write-protected disk
01h	Unknown unit
02h	Drive not ready
03h	Unknown command
04h	CRC error in data

Register	Description		
	Value	**Meaning**	
	05h	Incorrect length of drive-request structure	
	06h	Seek error	
	07h	Unknown media type	
	08h	Sector not found	
	09h	Printer out of paper	
	0Ah	Write fault	
	0Bh	Read fault	
	0Ch	General failure	

The upper byte of the DI register is undefined.

BP:SI   Points to the **DEVICEHEADER** structure that contains information about the device on which the error occurred. The **DEVICE-HEADER** structure has the following form:

```
DEVICEHEADER STRUC
    dhLink          dd  ?           ;link to next driver
    dhAttributes    dw  ?           ;device attributes
    dhStrategy      dw  ?           ;strat-routine offset
    dhInterrupt     dw  ?           ;intrpt-routine offset
    dhNameOrUnits   db  '????????'  ;logical-device name
                                    ;(char device only)
                                    ;or number of units
                                    ;(block device only)

DEVICEHEADER ENDS
```

For a full description of the **DEVICEHEADER** structure, see Chapter 9, "Device Drivers."

The handler must not change the contents of the **DEVICEHEADER** structure.

The critical-error handler must determine what action to take in response to the error. For example, the default handler displays information about the error and prompts the user for input on how to proceed.

The critical-error handler can call the following Interrupt 21h functions:

Character I/O (Functions 01h through 0Ch)
Get CTRL+C Check Flag (Function 3300h)
Set CTRL+C Check Flag (Function 3301h)
Get Startup Drive (Function 3305h)
Get MS-DOS Version (Function 3306h)
Set PSP Address (Function 50h)
Get PSP Address (Functions 51h and 62h)
Get Extended Error (Function 59h)

No other system functions are permitted. Get Extended Error (Function 59h) retrieves detailed information about the error and is useful for handlers that display as much information as possible about the error.

The handler must preserve the BX, CX, DX, DS, ES, SS, and SP registers and restore the preserved values before returning to the system. The critical-error handler returns to the system by using the **iret** instruction. Before returning, it also must set the AL register to a value specifying the action the system should take. Depending on what actions are allowed (as specified by bits 3, 4, and 5 in the AH register), the AL register can contain one of the following values:

Value	Meaning
00h	Ignore the error. The system permits the system function to return to the program as if it had completed successfully.
01h	Retry the operation. The system calls the system function again. In this case, the system expects the handler to have preserved and restored registers before returning.
02h	Terminate the program. The system sets the termination type to be EXIT_CRITICAL_ERROR (02h) and carries out the same actions as End Program (Interrupt 21h Function 4Ch).
03h	Terminate the function. The system permits the system function to return to the program with an error value.

MS-DOS checks the value to ensure that it is allowed. If values 00h and 01h are not allowed, the system terminates the function. If value 03h is not allowed, the system terminates the program.

COMMAND.COM provides the default critical-error handler, which displays a message about the error and, after displaying a question such as "Abort, Retry, Fail, or Ignore?", prompts the user for a response.

See Also

Interrupt 21h Functions 01h through 12h (Character I/O Functions)
Interrupt 21h Function 3300h Get CTRL+C Check Flag
Interrupt 21h Function 3301h Set CTRL+C Check Flag
Interrupt 21h Function 3305h Get Startup Drive
Interrupt 21h Function 3306h Get MS-DOS Version
Interrupt 21h Function 50h Set PSP Address
Interrupt 21h Function 51h Get PSP Address
Interrupt 21h Function 59h Get Extended Error

■ Interrupt 25h Absolute Disk Read   **Superseded**

```
        mov     al, Drive               ;0 = A, 1 = B, 2 = C, etc.
        mov     bx, seg Buffer
        mov     ds, bx
        mov     bx, offset Buffer       ;ds:bx points to data buffer
        mov     cx, Sectors             ;number of sectors to read
        mov     dx, FirstSector         ;first logical sector to read

        int     25h                     ;Absolute Disk Read
        jc      error_handler

        popf                            ;MUST pop registers after int returns
```

Absolute Disk Read (Interrupt 25h) reads from one or more logical sectors on the specified drive and copies the data to the specified buffer.

This interrupt has been superseded. Programs should use Read Track on Logical Drive (Interrupt 21h Function 440Dh Minor Code 61h).

Parameters

Drive   Specifies the number of the drive to read (0 = A, 1 = B, 2 = C, and so on).

Buffer   Points to either a buffer that receives data or to a **DISKIO** structure, depending on the value of the *Sectors* parameter. If *Sectors* is 0FFFFh, *Buffer* must point to a **DISKIO** structure that contains the starting sector, count of sectors, and address of the buffer to receive the data. The **DISKIO** structure has the following form:

```
DISKIO  STRUC
    diStartSector   dd  ?    ;sector number to start
    diSectors       dw  ?    ;number of sectors
    diBuffer        dd  ?    ;address of buffer
DISKIO  ENDS
```

For a full description of the **DISKIO** structure, see Chapter 3, "File System."

The **DISKIO** structure is required if the size of the specified drive is greater than 32 MB.

Sectors   Specifies either the number of sectors to read or 0FFFFh, depending on the size of the specified drive. If the drive size is greater than 32 MB, *Sectors* must be 0FFFFh.

FirstSector   Specifies the number of the first logical sector to read. If *Sectors* is 0FFFFh, this number is ignored and the starting sector must be specified in the **DISKIO** structure.

Return Value

If the interrupt is successful, the carry flag is clear and the buffer contains the information read from the disk. Otherwise, the carry flag is set and the AL and AH registers contain error values. The AL register specifies device-driver errors and contains one of the following values:

Value	Meaning
01h	Unknown unit
02h	Drive not ready
04h	Data error (CRC error)
06h	Seek error

Value	Meaning
07h	Unknown media
08h	Sector not found
0Bh	Read fault
0Ch	General failure
0Fh	Invalid media change

For most computers, the AH register specifies ROM BIOS errors and may contain one of the following values:

Value	Description
01h	Bad command
02h	Address mark not found
04h	Sector not found
10h	Data error (CRC error)
20h	Controller failure
40h	Seek failure
80h	No response from drive

Comments   Upon returning, Interrupt 25h leaves the CPU flags on the stack. Programs should check the carry flag for an error before popping the flags from the stack.

Interrupt 25h does not process critical errors. If one occurs, the interrupt routine returns an error value to the program but does not issue Critical-Error Handler (Interrupt 24h).

Interrupt 25h reads logical sectors only. This means, for example, that it cannot read hidden sectors.

See Also   Interrupt 21h Function 440Dh Minor Code 61h Read Track on Logical Drive
Interrupt 24h Critical-Error Handler
Interrupt 26h Absolute Disk Write

■ Interrupt 26h Absolute Disk Write   Superseded

```
mov    al, Drive              ;0 = A, 1 = B, 2 = C, etc.
mov    bx, seg Buffer
mov    ds, bx
mov    bx, offset Buffer      ;ds:bx points to data buffer
mov    cx, Sectors            ;number of sectors to write
mov    dx, FirstSector        ;first logical sector to write

int    26h                    ;Absolute Disk Write
jc     error_handler

popf                          ;MUST pop registers after int returns
```

Absolute Disk Write (Interrupt 26h) writes data from the specified buffer to one or more logical sectors on the specified drive.

This interrupt has been superseded. Programs should use Write Track on Logical Drive (Interrupt 21h Function 440Dh Minor Code 41h).

Parameters

Drive   Specifies the number of the drive to write to (0 = A, 1 = B, 2 = C, and so on).

Buffer   Points to either a buffer that contains data to write or a **DISKIO** structure, depending on the value of the *Sectors* parameter. If *Sectors* is 0FFFFh, *Buffer* must point to a **DISKIO** structure that contains the starting sector, count of sectors, and address of the buffer containing the data. The **DISKIO** structure has the following form:

```
DISKIO  STRUC
    diStartSector    dd    ?    ;sector number to start
    diSectors        dw    ?    ;number of sectors
    diBuffer         dd    ?    ;address of buffer
DISKIO  ENDS
```

For a full description of the **DISKIO** structure, see Chapter 3, "File System."

The **DISKIO** structure is required if the size of the specified drive is greater than 32 MB.

Sectors   Specifies either the number of sectors to write or 0FFFFh, depending on the size of the specified drive. If the drive size is greater than 32 MB, *Sectors* must be 0FFFFh.

FirstSector   Specifies the number of the first logical sector to write. If *Sectors* is 0FFFFh, this number is ignored and the starting sector must be specified in the **DISKIO** structure.

Return Value

If the interrupt is successful, the carry flag is clear. Otherwise, the carry flag is set and the AL and AH registers contain error values. The AL register specifies device-driver errors and contains one of the following values:

Value	Meaning
00h	Write-protection violation
01h	Unknown unit
02h	Drive not ready
04h	Data error (CRC error)
06h	Seek error

Value	Meaning
07h	Unknown media
08h	Sector not found
0Ah	Write fault
0Ch	General failure
0Fh	Invalid media change

For most computers, the AH register specifies ROM BIOS errors and may contain one of the following values:

Value	Description
01h	Bad command
02h	Address mark not found
03h	Write-protection fault
04h	Sector not found
10h	Data error (CRC error)
20h	Controller failure
40h	Seek failure
80h	No response from drive

Comments

Upon returning, Interrupt 26h leaves the CPU flags on the stack. Programs should check the carry flag for an error before popping the flags from the stack.

Interrupt 26h does not process critical errors. If one occurs, the interrupt routine returns an error value to the program but does not issue Critical-Error Handler (Interrupt 24h).

Interrupt 26h writes logical sectors only. This means, for example, that the interrupt cannot write to hidden sectors.

See Also

Interrupt 21h Function 440Dh Minor Code 41h Write Track on Logical Drive
Interrupt 24h Critical-Error Handler
Interrupt 25h Absolute Disk Read

■ Interrupt 27h Terminate and Stay Resident   Superseded

```
mov    dx, offset Bytes      ;number of bytes to remain resident
int    27h                   ;Terminate and Stay Resident
```

Terminate and Stay Resident (Interrupt 27h) ends the current program by returning control to its parent program, but it leaves the program in memory and preserves such program resources as open files and allocated memory.

This interrupt has been superseded. Programs should use Keep Program (Interrupt 21h Function 31h).

Parameter   *Bytes*   Specifies the number of program bytes to remain in memory. This number must be in the range 0000h through 0FFFFh.

Return Value   This interrupt does not return.

Comments   This interrupt is intended to be used by .COM programs. When a program issues the interrupt, the CS register must contain the segment address of the program segment prefix (PSP).

This interrupt carries out the following actions:

■ Sets the new size of the program by converting the value of the *Bytes* parameter to a corresponding number of paragraphs and reallocating the program memory. Program memory includes only the PSP and program data and code. The reallocation does not affect the program's environment block, nor does it affect the memory allocated by the program after it was loaded.

■ Flushes the file buffers but leaves files open.

■ Restores Termination Address (Interrupt 22h) from offset 0Ah in the PSP (**pspTerminateVector** field).

■ Restores the address of CTRL+C Handler (Interrupt 23h) from offset 0Eh in the PSP (**pspControlCVector** field).

■ Restores the address of Critical-Error Handler (Interrupt 24h) from offset 12h in the PSP (**pspCritErrorVector** field).

After completing these actions, this interrupt transfers control to the address specified by offset 0Ah in the PSP.

See Also   Interrupt 21h Function 31h Keep Program
Interrupt 22h Termination Address
Interrupt 23h CTRL+C Handler
Interrupt 24h Critical-Error Handler

■ **Interrupt 28h   MS-DOS Idle Handler**   **Superseded**

MS-DOS Idle Handler (Interrupt 28h) carries out background operations, such as printing from a queue, while the system waits for user input. MS-DOS issues this interrupt while waiting for completion of character I/O functions (Interrupt 21h Functions 01h through 0Ch).

Programs that are idle (for example, programs that are polling for user input) can issue Interrupt 28h. Programs should also issue MS-DOS Idle Call (Interrupt 2Fh Function 1680h).

Comments   MS-DOS provides a minimal MS-DOS idle handler that returns immediately. System commands, such as **print**, install their own handlers to carry out background processing. Although other programs can install MS-DOS idle handlers, these programs must take great care to prevent corrupting internal stacks and registers.

MS-DOS issues Interrupt 28h only if a character I/O function has not yet completed, but does not issue the interrupt if a critical-error handler is currently running (that is, the ErrorMode internal variable is not zero). MS-DOS issues the interrupt each time it loops through a low-level read or write operation, and continues to issue the interrupt until a character is read or written.

Programs that install an MS-DOS idle handler should create a chain of handlers—that is, save the original address from the Interrupt 28h vector-table entry and call the address as part of processing.

MS-DOS makes few preparations before issuing Interrupt 28h. When control transfers to the MS-DOS idle handler, segment registers point to internal MS-DOS data segments. The SS:SP registers point to the top of the MS-DOS internal I/O stack. To prevent corrupting the system data and stack, the MS-DOS idle handler must switch to its own stack, preserve all registers, and set segment registers to point to its own data segments.

Although the MS-DOS idle handler can call system functions, it must not call character I/O functions (Interrupt 21h Functions 01h through 0Ch) without first setting the ErrorMode variable to 1. If the handler calls these functions without setting ErrorMode, the call will corrupt the internal I/O stack and MS-DOS operation.

Before returning to the system, the MS-DOS idle handler must restore the SS:SP registers to point to the I/O stack, restore all registers, and set the Error-Mode variable to zero.

See Also   Interrupt 2Fh Function 1680h MS-DOS Idle Call

■ Interrupt 2Fh Multiplex Interrupt

Multiplex Interrupt (Interrupt 2Fh) is a common entry point for terminate-and-stay-resident programs (TSRs) that provide services to other programs. Programs use this interrupt to request services from and to check the status of such MS-DOS commands as **print**, **assign**, and **append**.

A program requests service by placing a specified function number in the AX register and issuing Interrupt 2Fh. Some functions may require additional values in registers before issuing the interrupt.

Comments   Following is a list of the Interrupt 2Fh functions:

Value	Function name
0100h	Get PRINT.EXE Installed State
0101h	Add File to Queue
0102h	Remove File from Print Queue
0103h	Cancel All Files in Print Queue
0104h	Hold Print Jobs and Get Status
0105h	Release Print Jobs
0106h	Get Printer Device
0600h	Get ASSIGN.COM Installed State
1000h	Get SHARE.EXE Installed State
1100h	Get Network Installed State
1400h	Get NLSFUNC.EXE Installed State
1680h	MS-DOS Idle Call
1A00h	Get ANSI.SYS Installed State
4300h	Get HIMEM.SYS Installed State
4310h	Get HIMEM.SYS Entry-Point Address
4800h	Get DOSKEY.COM Installed State
4810h	Read Command Line
4B01h	Build Notification Chain
4B02h	Detect Switcher
4B03h	Allocate Switcher ID
4B04h	Free Switcher ID
4B05h	Identify Instance Data
0AD80h	Get KEYB.COM Version Number
0AD81h	Set KEYB.COM Active Code Page
0AD82h	Set KEYB.COM Country Flag

Value	Function name
0AD83h	Get KEYB.COM Country Flag
0B000h	Get GRAFTABL.COM Installed State
0B700h	Get APPEND.EXE Installed State
0B702h	Get APPEND.EXE Version
0B704h	Get APPEND.EXE Directory List Address
0B706h	Get APPEND.EXE Modes Flag
0B707h	Set APPEND.EXE Modes Flag
0B711h	Set True-Name Flag

These functions are available only if the corresponding MS-DOS command or program has been loaded. If the command or program is not loaded, MS-DOS carries out a default action, such as setting the carry flag and setting the AX register to 0001h (ERROR_INVALID_FUNCTION).

Programs that install their own Interrupt 2Fh handler must create a chain of handlers—that is, save the original address from the Interrupt 2Fh vector-table entry and call the address as part of their processing. Note that Interrupt 2Fh function numbers 0000h through 0BFFFh are reserved for system programs and commands. Other programs can use function numbers 0C000h through 0FFFFh.

Interrupt 2Fh Function 0100h Get PRINT.EXE Installed State

```
mov     ax, 0100h           ;Get PRINT.EXE Installed State
int     2Fh                 ;Multiplex Interrupt
```

Get PRINT.EXE Installed State (Interrupt 2Fh Function 0100h) determines
whether the resident portion of the **print** command has been loaded.

Parameters   This function has no parameters.

Return Value   The AL register contains 0FFh if **print** has been loaded or 00h if it has not.

■ Interrupt 2Fh Function 0101h Add File to Queue

```
mov     dx, seg AddPacket
mov     ds, dx
mov     dx, offset AddPacket     ;ds:dx points to level and filename

mov     ax, 0101h               ;Add File to Queue
int     2Fh                     ;Multiplex Interrupt
```

Add File to Queue (Interrupt 2Fh Function 0101h) adds a file to the print queue.

Parameter   *AddPacket*   Points to a **QUEUEPACKET** structure that contains the name of the file to add. The **QUEUEPACKET** structure has the following form:

```
QUEUEPACKET STRUC
    qpLevel     db 0    ;level, must be zero
    qpFilename  dd ?    ;segment:offset pointing to ASCIIZ path
QUEUEPACKET ENDS
```

For a full description of the **QUEUEPACKET** structure, see Section 7.11, "Structures."

Return Value   If the function is successful, the carry flag is clear. Otherwise, the carry flag is set and the AX register contains an error value, which may be one of the following:

Value	Name
0001h	ERROR_INVALID_FUNCTION
0002h	ERROR_FILE_NOT_FOUND
0003h	ERROR_PATH_NOT_FOUND
0004h	ERROR_TOO_MANY_OPEN_FILES
0005h	ERROR_ACCESS_DENIED
0008h	ERROR_QUEUE_FULL
000Ch	ERROR_INVALID_ACCESS
000Fh	ERROR_INVALID_DRIVE

See Also   Interrupt 2Fh Function 0102h Remove File from Print Queue

Interrupt 2Fh Function 0102h Remove File from Print Queue

```
        mov     dx, seg FileName
        mov     ds, dx
        mov     dx, offset FileName      ;ds:dx points to ASCIIZ filename

        mov     ax, 0102h                ;Remove File from Print Queue
        int     2Fh                      ;Multiplex Interrupt
```

Remove File from Print Queue (Interrupt 2Fh Function 0102h) removes a
specified file or files from the print queue.

Parameter   *FileName*   Points to a zero-terminated string that specifies the file or files to be
removed from the queue. The string must be a valid MS-DOS filename, but may
contain wildcards to remove multiple files from the print queue.

Return Value   If the function is successful, the carry flag is clear. Otherwise, the carry flag is
set and the AX register contains an error value, which may be 0002h
(ERROR_FILE_NOT_FOUND).

See Also   Interrupt 2Fh Function 0101h Add File to Queue

■ Interrupt 2Fh Function 0103h Cancel All Files in Print Queue

```
mov     ax, 0103h               ;Cancel All Files in Print Queue
int     2Fh                     ;Multiplex Interrupt
```

Cancel All Files in Print Queue (Interrupt 2Fh Function 0103h) stops the current print job and removes all files from the print queue.

Parameters   This function has no parameters.

Return Value   This function has no return value.

See Also   Interrupt 2Fh Function 0102h Remove File from Print Queue

■ Interrupt 2Fh Function 0104h Hold Print Jobs and Get Status

```
mov     ax, 0104h               ;Hold Print Jobs and Get Status
int     2Fh                     ;Multiplex Interrupt

mov     ErrorCount, dx          ;errors during printing
mov     [PrintQueue], si
mov     ax, ds
mov     [PrintQueue+2], ax      ;ds:si points to print queue
```

Hold Print Jobs and Get Status (Interrupt 2Fh Function 0104h) stops the current print job and returns the address of the print queue.

Parameters   This function has no parameters.

Return Value   When the function returns, the DX register contains an error count and DS:SI contains the 32-bit address (segment:offset) of the print queue.

Comments   The print queue consists of a series of 64-byte entries, each containing a zero-terminated string specifying the path of a file in the queue. The first file in the list is the one currently being printed. The last entry in the list consists of a single null character (00h).

Programs must not change the contents of the print queue. To add a file, use Add File to Queue (Interrupt 2Fh Function 0101h); to remove a file, use Remove File from Print Queue (Interrupt 2Fh Function 0102h).

The print spooler continues to hold the current print job until Release Print Jobs (Interrupt 2Fh Function 0105h) is called.

See Also   Interrupt 2Fh Function 0101h Add File to Queue
Interrupt 2Fh Function 0102h Remove File from Print Queue
Interrupt 2Fh Function 0105h Release Print Jobs

■ Interrupt 2Fh Function 0105h Release Print Jobs

```
mov     ax, 0105h                  ;Release Print Jobs
int     2Fh                        ;Multiplex Interrupt
```

Release Print Jobs (Interrupt 2Fh Function 0105h) restarts the print queue. Programs must use this function after calling Hold Print Jobs and Get Status (Interrupt 2Fh Function 0104h) to restart the current print job.

Parameters   This function has no parameters.

Return Value   This function has no return value.

See Also   Interrupt 2Fh Function 0104h Hold Print Jobs and Get Status

■ Interrupt 2Fh Function 0106h Get Printer Device

```
mov     ax, 0106h               ;Get Printer Device
int     2Fh                     ;Multiplex Interrupt
jnc     queue_empty             ;carry clear means print queue is empty

mov     [DevHeader], si
mov     [DevHeader+2], ds       ;ds:si points to print device header
```

Get Printer Device (Interrupt 2Fh Function 0106h) returns the address of the device header for the current printer.

Parameters   This function has no parameters.

Return Value   If the queue is empty, the carry flag is clear and the AX register contains zero. Otherwise, the carry flag is set, the DS:SI registers point to a **DEVICEHEADER** structure corresponding to the printer device header, and AX contains 0008h (ERROR_QUEUE_FULL).

■ Interrupt 2Fh Function 0600h Get ASSIGN.COM Installed State

```
mov      ax, 0600h    ;Get ASSIGN.COM Installed State
int      2Fh          ;Multiplex Interrupt
```

Get ASSIGN.COM Installed State (Interrupt 2Fh Function 0600h) determines whether the resident portion of the **assign** command has been loaded.

Parameters   This function has no parameters.

Return Value   The AL register contains 0FFh if **assign** has been loaded or 00h if it has not.

■ Interrupt 2Fh Function 1000h Get SHARE.EXE Installed State

```
mov     ax, 1000h    ;Get SHARE.EXE Installed State
int     2Fh          ;Multiplex Interrupt

cmp     al, 0FFh     ;0FFh means installed
```

Get SHARE.EXE Installed State (Interrupt 2Fh Function 1000h) determines whether the resident portion of the Share program has been loaded.

Parameters   This function has no parameters.

Return Value   The AL register contains 0FFh if the Share program has been loaded or 00h if it has not.

Comments   Some operating environments, such as Windows, intercept this multiplex interrupt and always return a nonzero value whether the Share program is loaded or not. To determine whether file sharing is available, a program should check for error values upon returning from carrying out a file-sharing function, such as Lock/Unlock File (Interrupt 21h Function 5Ch).

See Also   Interrupt 21h Function 5Ch Lock/Unlock File

■ Interrupt 2Fh Function 1100h Get Network Installed State

```
mov     ax, 1100h    ;Get Network Installed State
int     2Fh          ;Multiplex Interrupt
```

Get Network Installed State (Interrupt 2Fh Function 1100h) determines whether the resident portion of the network software has been installed.

Parameters   This function has no parameters.

Return Value   The AL register contains 0FFh if the network software has been installed or 00h if it has not.

■ Interrupt 2Fh Function 1400h Get NLSFUNC.EXE Installed State

```
mov     ax, 1400h    ;Get NLSFUNC.EXE Installed State
int     2Fh          ;Multiplex Interrupt

cmp     al, 0FFh     ;0FFh means installed
```

Get NLSFUNC.EXE Installed State (Interrupt 2Fh Function 1400h) determines whether the resident portion of the Nlsfunc program is loaded.

Parameters   This function has no parameters.

Return Value   The AL register contains 0FFh if the Nlsfunc program has been loaded or 00h if it has not.

■ Interrupt 2Fh Function 1680h MS-DOS Idle Call

```
mov     ax, 1680h           ;MS-DOS Idle Call
int     2Fh                 ;Multiplex Interrupt
```

MS-DOS Idle Call (Interrupt 2Fh Function 1680h) informs the system that the program is idle—for example, waiting for user input. The function permits the system to suspend the idle program temporarily and transfer control to another program.

Parameters

This function has no parameters.

Return Value

The function returns the function status in the AL register. If AL is zero, the system supports suspension of idle programs. Otherwise, the system does not support suspension.

Comments

Programs should use this interrupt when they are idle. Before using this interrupt, however, a program should use Get Interrupt Vector (Interrupt 21h Function 35h) to ensure that the interrupt-handler address for Interrupt 2Fh is not zero.

This interrupt is nonblocking, meaning the system does not suspend the program unless another program is ready to be run. In most cases, the interrupt returns immediately and the program continues running. To make sure the system can suspend the program, a program that remains idle should repeatedly call the interrupt as part of its idle loop.

See Also

Interrupt 21h Function 35h Get Interrupt Vector
Interrupt 28h MS-DOS Idle Handler

■ Interrupt 2Fh Function 1A00h Get ANSI.SYS Installed State

```
mov     ax, 1A00h           ;Get ANSI.SYS Installed State
int     2Fh                 ;Multiplex Interrupt

cmp     al, 0FFh            ;0FFh means installed
```

Get ANSI.SYS Installed State (Interrupt 2Fh Function 1A00h) determines whether the ANSI.SYS device driver has been loaded.

Parameters   This function has no parameters.

Return Value   The AL register contains 0FFh if ANSI.SYS has been loaded or 00h if it has not.

■ Interrupt 2Fh Function 4300h Get HIMEM.SYS Installed State

```
mov     ax, 4300h       ;Get HIMEM.SYS Installed State
int     2Fh             ;Multiplex Interrupt

cmp     al, 80h         ;80h means installed
```

Get HIMEM.SYS Installed State (Interrupt 2Fh Function 4300h) determines whether the extended-memory manager, HIMEM.SYS, has been loaded.

Parameters   This function has no parameters.

Return Value   The AL register contains 80h if the driver has been loaded or 00h if it has not.

Comments   The HIMEM.SYS driver provides a set of functions that programs use to independently manage extended memory. Although programs can also use these functions to manage the high memory area (HMA) and upper memory blocks (UMBs), programs should not do so if MS-DOS already manages these areas.

This function returns the installed state of any extended-memory manager as long as the manager conforms to the Lotus/Intel/Microsoft/AST eXtended Memory Specification (XMS) version 2.0.

See Also   Interrupt 2Fh Function 4310h Get HIMEM.SYS Entry-Point Address

Interrupt 2Fh Function 4310h Get HIMEM.SYS Entry-Point Address

```
mov      ax, 4310h                  ;Get HIMEM.SYS Entry-Point Address
int      2Fh                        ;Multiplex Interrupt

mov      word ptr [XMMAddr], bx
mov      word ptr [XMMAddr+2], es   ;es:bx contains entry-point address
```

Get HIMEM.SYS Entry-Point Address (Interrupt 2Fh Function 4310h) returns the 32-bit address (segment:offset) of the entry point for the extended-memory-management functions for HIMEM.SYS.

Parameters   This function has no parameters.

Return Value   The ES:BX registers contain the 32-bit address (segment:offset) of the entry point.

Comments   Before retrieving and calling this entry point, programs must use Get HIMEM.SYS Installed State (Interrupt 2Fh Function 4300h) to ensure that HIMEM.SYS has been loaded.

The extended-memory-management functions enable programs to manage extended memory, the high memory area (HMA), and upper memory blocks (UMBs). Programs also use the functions to enable and disable the A20 address line. A program calls a function by placing the function number in the AH register, filling other registers as needed, and calling the entry point. Following is a list of the extended-memory-management functions:

Number	Name
00h	Get XMS Version
01h	Allocate HMA
02h	Free HMA
03h	Global Enable A20 Line
04h	Global Disable A20 Line
05h	Local Enable A20 Line
06h	Local Disable A20 Line
07h	Query A20 Line Status
08h	Query Free Extended Memory
09h	Allocate EMB
0Ah	Free EMB
0Bh	Move EMB
0Ch	Lock EMB
0Dh	Unlock EMB
0Eh	Get Handle Information
0Fh	Resize EMB
10h	Allocate UMB
11h	Free UMB

A full description of these functions is beyond the scope of this book. For more information about them, see the Lotus/Intel/Microsoft/AST eXtended Memory Specification (XMS) version 2.0.

Programs must not use extended-memory-management functions to manage the HMA or UMBs if MS-DOS already manages these areas.

This function returns the entry-point address of any extended-memory manager as long as the manager conforms to the eXtended Memory Specification.

See Also   Interrupt 2Fh Function 4300h Get HIMEM.SYS Installed State

Interrupt 2Fh Function 4800h Get DOSKEY.COM Installed State

```
mov     ax, 4800h    ;Get DOSKEY.COM Installed State
int     2Fh          ;Multiplex Interrupt

cmp     al, 00h      ;00h means not installed
```

Get DOSKEY.COM Installed State (Interrupt 2Fh Function 4800h) determines whether the resident portion of the Doskey program has been loaded.

Parameters   This function has no parameters.

Return Value   The AL register contains a nonzero value if the Doskey program has been loaded or 00h if it has not.

See Also   Interrupt 2Fh Function 4810h Read Command Line

■ Interrupt 2Fh Function 4810h Read Command Line

```
mov     dx, seg Line
mov     ds, dx
mov     dx, offset Line ;ds:dx points to buffer to receive input

mov     ax, 4810h       ;Read Command Line
int     2Fh             ;Multiplex Interrupt
```

Read Command Line (Interrupt 2Fh Function 4810h) reads a line of up to 126 characters and copies it to the specified buffer. While the line is being read, all Doskey function keys and macros are enabled. This means, for example, that the user can select a line from the Doskey history, edit a line, or enter macros that are automatically expanded.

Parameter

Line   Points to a buffer that receives the command line. The buffer must have the following form:

Offset	Contents
00h	The maximum size of the buffer. It must be 128 bytes.
01h	A number that is one less than the number of characters read. The function copies a carriage-return character (ASCII 0Dh) to the buffer but does not include the byte in its total.
02h	The first byte of the input line.

Return Value

If the function is successful, the AX register contains zero and the input line is copied, along with the number of bytes in the line, to the buffer pointed to by the *Line* parameter.

If the user types a macro name, AX contains zero, but no text is copied to the buffer. Instead, the program must immediately call the function a second time to expand the macro and copy the macro text to the buffer.

Comments

This function adds the command line to the Doskey history. If the user types a macro name or a special parameter (such as $*), the program must call the function a second time to expand the macro or parameter. On the second call, the function automatically writes the expanded macro to the screen, overwriting the macro name. It also copies the expanded macro text to the buffer.

■ Interrupt 2Fh Function 4B01h Build Notification Chain

```
mov     bx, O
mov     es, bx                      ;es:bx is zero
mov     dx, WORD PTR [Service]
mov     cx, WORD PTR [Service+2]
                                    ;cx:dx is service-function handler addr
mov     ax, 4B01h                   ;Build Notification Chain
int     2Fh                         ;Multiplex Interrupt

mov     cx, es
or      cx, di
je      no_notifychain              ;es:bx is zero if no notification chain
```

Build Notification Chain (Interrupt 2Fh Function 4B01h) creates a linked list of notification-function handlers for global client programs and for client programs running in the current session. The task switcher calls this function to determine which client programs are to be notified about changes to the session. To receive notification, client programs must intercept Interrupt 2Fh and process Build Notification Chain when they receive the function call.

Parameter

Service   Points to the service-function handler for the task switcher. A client program can use this address to call the task switcher's service functions, such as Get Version (Service Function 0000h) and Test Memory Region (Service Function 0001h).

Return Value

If a client program is to be notified, the ES:BX registers contain the address of an **SWCALLBACKINFO** structure containing information about the client program. Otherwise, the ES:BX registers contain zero.

Comments

A client program's Interrupt 2Fh handler processes this function. If the client program does not require notifications, its handler must use the **jmp** instruction to transfer control to the previous Interrupt 2Fh handler (whose address the client program must save when it installs its own handler). If a client program requires notification, its Interrupt 2Fh handler must first pass Build Notification Chain to any other client programs that also require notification, by pushing the flags and using the **call** instruction to call the previous handler. The handler must not modify registers before calling the previous handler.

When the previous handler returns, the ES:BX registers contain either zero or the address of an **SWCALLBACKINFO** structure for another client program. In either case, before the client program can return from the interrupt, it must fill its own **SWCALLBACKINFO** structure, copy the contents of the ES:BX registers to the **scbiNext** field of its own structure, and copy the address of its **SWCALLBACKINFO** structure into the ES:BX registers.

The **SWCALLBACKINFO** structure has the following form:

```
SWCALLBACKINFO  STRUC
    scbiNext        dd   ?   ;address of next structure in chain
    scbiEntryPoint  dd   ?   ;address of notification-function handler
    scbiReserved    dd   ?   ;reserved
    scbiAPI         dd   ?   ;address of list of SWAPIINFO structures
SWCALLBACKINFO  ENDS
```

For a full description of the **SWCALLBACKINFO** and **SWAPIINFO** structures, see Section 7.11, "Structures."

A client program processes Build Notification Chain only after all previously loaded client programs have processed it. The most recently loaded client program is always first in the notification chain, followed by the next most recently loaded, and so on.

The relationship between loading order and processing order is important, since it gives a client program requesting asynchronous services from other clients a chance to cancel those requests when the task switcher notifies it of a pending switch. If the order were reversed, the client program providing the asynchronous service would have to block the switch until it completed the service.

Any client program that provides services to other programs must add itself to the notification chain.

A client program should not save the *Service* address, since the task switcher may change its current service-function-handler address at any time. To ensure that a client program always has the latest address of the service-function handler, the task switcher sends the latest address with each notification function.

Although a client program modifies the ES and BX registers, it must preserve all other registers.

See Also   Service Function 0000h Get Version
Service Function 0001h Test Memory Region

■ Interrupt 2Fh Function 4B02h Detect Switcher

```
mov      bx, 0            ;must be zero
mov      di, 0
mov      es, di           ;es:di must be zero

mov      ax,4B02h         ;Detect Switcher
int      2Fh              ;Multiplex Interrupt

mov      cx, es
or       cx, di
je       no_switcher      ;es:di is zero if no task switcher loaded

mov      WORD PTR [Service], di
mov      ax, es
mov      WORD PTR [Service+2], ax
                          ;es:di is service-function handler address
```

Detect Switcher (Interrupt 2Fh Function 4B02h) determines whether a task switcher is loaded. Client programs (such as a session manager) that need to prevent or control the interruptions caused by task switching should call this function during initialization.

Parameters   This function has no parameters.

Return Value   If a task switcher is loaded, the AX register contains 0000h and the ES:DI registers contain the address of the service-function handler for the task switcher. Otherwise, the ES:DI registers contain zero.

Comments   If a task switcher is loaded, the function returns the address of the task switcher's service-function handler. A client program can use this address to call the task switcher's service functions, such as Get Version (Service Function 0000h) and Hook Notification Chain (Service Function 0004h).

Detect Switcher returns the service-function handler address of the most recently loaded task switcher. A client program can check for other task switchers by examining the **svsPrevSwitcher** field in the **SWVERSION** structure returned by Get Version (Service Function 0000h). If this field contains a nonzero value, it points to the service-function handler for another task switcher. The client program can call this handler to retrieve and examine the other task switcher's **SWVERSION** structure, and it can continue this process until reaching the **svsPrevSwitcher** field for the first task switcher loaded, which contains zero.

The **SWVERSION** structure has the following form:

```
SWVERSION    STRUC
    svsAPIMajor     dw   ?    ;protocol supported major version
    svsAPIMinor     dw   ?    ;protocol supported minor version
    svsProductMajor dw   ?    ;task switcher's major version
    svsProductMinor dw   ?    ;task switcher's minor version
    svsSwitcherID   dw   ?    ;task-switcher identifier
    svsFlags        dw   ?    ;operation flags
    svsName         dd   ?    ;points to task-switcher name (ASCIIZ)
    svsPrevSwitcher dd   ?    ;previous task switcher's entry address
SWVERSION    ENDS
```

For a full description of the **SWVERSION** structure, see Section 7.11, "Structures."

A task switcher processing Detect Switcher can enable interrupts and call any MS-DOS system function. Although the task switcher modifies the AX, ES, and DI registers, it must preserve all other registers.

See Also

Service Function 0000h Get Version
Service Function 0004h Hook Notification Change

■ Interrupt 2Fh Function 4B03h Allocate Switcher ID

```
mov     bx, 0              ;required for future versions
les     di, Service        ;address of service-function handler

mov     ax, 4B03h          ;Allocate Switcher ID
int     2Fh                ;Multiplex Interrupt

cmp     bx, 0              ;zero means could not allocate identifier
je      error_handler

mov     [ID], bx           ;switcher identifier
```

Allocate Switcher ID (Interrupt 2Fh Function 4B03h) returns a unique switcher identifier (in the range 0001h through 000Fh). A task switcher (or controlling session manager) calls this function on initialization and then uses the switcher identifier to create session identifiers for programs that it manages. The first-loaded task switcher is responsible for processing this function.

Client programs must not call this function.

Parameter   *Service*   Points to the service-function handler for the calling task switcher. The task switcher that processes this function can use this address to call service functions, such as Get Version (Service Function 0000h).

Return Value   If Allocate Switcher ID is successful, the AX register contains 0000h and the BX register contains the new task switcher's identifier. Otherwise, the BX register contains 0000h.

Comments   A task switcher must determine whether it is the first to load by calling Detect Switcher (Interrupt 2Fh Function 4B02h). If it is the first (that is, no other task switcher is loaded), it is responsible for creating a switcher identifier for itself and for processing all subsequent calls to Allocate Switcher ID. If another task switcher is already running, the new task switcher must call Allocate Switcher ID to get a switcher identifier for itself. If Allocate Switcher ID returns zero in the BX register, the first task switcher was unable to allocate a new identifier and the calling task switcher must exit or disable itself.

A task switcher uses its switcher identifier as the high 4 bits of any session identifiers it creates to ensure that no two session identifiers are the same. The switcher identifier must be a 4-bit nonzero value.

The task switcher that processes this function must keep track of the switcher identifiers that it creates. One method is to maintain a 16-bit array, setting and freeing bits as other task switchers call Allocate Switcher ID and Free Switcher ID (Interrupt 2Fh Function 4B04h). In this method, bit 0 must be set (zero is not a valid switcher identifier). Regardless of the method used, the task switcher must disable interrupts when it examines and changes its record of allocated switcher identifiers.

A task switcher processing Allocate Switcher ID can enable interrupts (except when examining and recording allocated identifiers) and call any MS-DOS system function. Although the task switcher modifies the AX and BX registers, it must preserve all other registers.

See Also   Interrupt 2Fh Function 4B02h Detect Switcher
Interrupt 2Fh Function 4B04h Free Switcher ID
Service Function 0000h Get Version

■ Interrupt 2Fh Function 4B04h Free Switcher ID

```
mov     bx, ID              ;switcher identifier to be freed
les     di, Service         ;address of service-function handler

mov     ax, 4B04h           ;Free Switcher ID
int     2Fh                 ;Multiplex Interrupt

cmp     bx, 0
jne     error_handler       ;nonzero means invalid switcher identifier
```

Free Switcher ID (Interrupt 2Fh Function 4B04h) frees the switcher identifier associated with the task switcher having the specified service-function handler. When a task switcher terminates it calls this function.

Client programs must not call this function.

Parameters

ID   Specifies the switcher identifier to be freed. It must have been allocated by using Allocate Switcher ID (Interrupt 2Fh Function 4B03h).

Service   Points to the terminating task switcher's service-function handler. The processing task switcher can use this address to call the terminating task switcher's service functions, such as Test Memory Region (Service Function 0001h).

Return Value

If Free Switcher ID is successful, the AX and BX registers both contain 0000h. Otherwise, the BX register contains a nonzero value, indicating an invalid switcher identifier.

Comments

The task switcher processing this function can enable interrupts (except when examining and recording allocated identifiers) and call any MS-DOS system function. Although the task switcher modifies the AX and BX registers, it must preserve all other registers.

See Also

Interrupt 2Fh Function 4B03h Allocate Switcher ID
Service Function 0001h Test Memory Region

Interrupt 2Fh Function 4B05h Identify Instance Data

```
mov      bx, 0
mov      es, bx                     ;es:bx = zero
mov      dx, WORD PTR [Service]
mov      cx, WORD PTR [Service+2]   ;cx:dx = addr of serv-function handler

mov      ax, 4B05h                  ;Identify Instance Data
int      2Fh                        ;Multiplex Interrupt

mov      cx, es
or       cx, bx
je       no_instancedata            ;es:bx = zero if no inst data chain
```

Identify Instance Data (Interrupt 2Fh Function 4B05h) identifies instance data maintained by a client program. A task switcher calls this function to create a linked list of instance data blocks for all client programs running on the system. Client programs with instance data must intercept Interrupt 2Fh and process Identify Instance Data when they receive the function call.

Parameter   *Service*   Points to the service-function handler for the task switcher. A client program can use this address to call the task switcher's service functions, such as Test Memory Region (Service Function 0001h).

Return Value   If any client programs have instance data, the ES:BX registers contain the address of an **SWSTARTUPINFO** structure. Otherwise, the ES:BX registers contain zero.

Comments   A client program's Interrupt 2Fh handler processes this function. If the client program does not have instance data, its handler must use the **jmp** instruction to transfer control to the previous Interrupt 2Fh handler (whose address the client program must save when it installs its own handler). If a client has instance data, its Interrupt 2Fh handler must first pass Identify Instance Data to any other client programs by pushing the flags and using the **call** instruction to call the previous handler. The handler must not modify registers before calling the previous handler.

When the previous handler returns, the ES:BX registers contain either zero or the address of an **SWSTARTUPINFO** structure for another client program. In either case, before the client program can return from the interrupt, it must fill its own **SWSTARTUPINFO** structure, copy the ES:BX contents to the **sisNextDev** field of its own structure, and copy the address of its **SWSTART-UPINFO** structure into the ES:BX registers.

The **SWSTARTUPINFO** structure has the following form:

```
SWSTARTUPINFO STRUC
     sisVersion        dw   3     ;ignored
     sisNextDev        dd   ?     ;points to prev handler's SWSTARTUPINFO
     sisVirtDevFile    dd   0     ;ignored
     sisReferenceData  dd   ?     ;ignored
     sisInstanceData   dd   ?     ;points to SWINSTANCEITEM structures
SWSTARTUPINFO ENDS
```

For a full description of the **SWSTARTUPINFO** and **SWINSTANCEITEM** structures, see Section 7.11, "Structures."

A client program processing Identify Instance Data can enable interrupts and call any MS-DOS system function. Although the client program modifies the AX, ES, and BX registers, it must preserve all other registers.

See Also   Service Function 0001h Test Memory Region

Interrupt 2Fh Function 0AD80h Get KEYB.COM Version Number

```
mov     ax, OAD80h      ;Get KEYB.COM Version Number
int     2Fh             ;Multiplex Interrupt

mov     MajorV, bh      ;major version number
mov     MinorV, bl      ;minor version number
```

Get KEYB.COM Version Number (Interrupt 2Fh Function 0AD80h) returns the major and minor version numbers for the Keyb program.

Parameters   This function has no parameters.

Return Value   The BX register contains a nonzero version number if the Keyb program has been loaded or zero if it has not.

■ Interrupt 2Fh Function 0AD81h Set KEYB.COM Active Code Page

```
mov      bx, CodePageID    ;new code page

mov      ax, 0AD81h        ;Set KEYB.COM Active Code Page
int      2Fh               ;Multiplex Interrupt
jc       error_handler
```

Set KEYB.COM Active Code Page (Interrupt 2Fh Function 0AD81h) sets the active code page for KEYB.COM to the specified code page.

Parameter   *CodePageID*   Identifies the code page. This parameter can be one of the following values:

Value	Meaning
437	United States
850	Multilingual (Latin I)
852	Slavic (Latin II)
860	Portuguese
863	Canadian-French
865	Nordic

Return Value   If the function is successful, the carry flag is clear. Otherwise, the carry flag is set and the AX register contains 0001h if the code page is not valid.

■ Interrupt 2Fh Function 0AD82h Set KEYB.COM Country Flag

```
mov     bl, CountryFlag ;00h = domestic, 0FFh = foreign

mov     ax, 0AD82h      ;Set KEYB.COM Country Flag
int     2Fh             ;Multiplex Interrupt
```

Set KEYB.COM Country Flag (Interrupt 2Fh Function 0AD82h) sets the current value of the KEYB.COM country flag.

Parameter   *CountryFlag*   Specifies whether the keyboard being set is domestic (00h) or foreign (0FFh).

Return Value   If the function is successful, the carry flag is clear. Otherwise, the carry flag is set if the *CountryFlag* parameter is neither 00h nor 0FFh.

See Also   Interrupt 2Fh Function 0AD83h Get KEYB.COM Country Flag

■ Interrupt 2Fh Function 0AD83h Get KEYB.COM Country Flag

```
mov     ax, OAD83h          ;Get KEYB.COM Country Flag
int     2Fh                 ;Multiplex Interrupt

mov CountryFlag, bl         ;OOh = domestic, OFFh = foreign
```

Get KEYB.COM Country Flag (Interrupt 2Fh Function 0AD83h) returns the current value of the KEYB.COM country flag.

Parameters   This function has no parameters.

Return Value   The BL register contains the current country-flag value.

See Also   Interrupt 2Fh Function 0AD82h Set KEYB.COM Country Flag

■ Interrupt 2Fh Function 0B000h Get GRAFTABL.COM Installed State

```
mov     ax, 0B000h   ;Get GRAFTABL.COM Installed State
int     2Fh          ;Multiplex Interrupt
```

Get GRAFTABL.COM Installed State (Interrupt 2Fh Function 0B000h) determines whether the resident portion of the **graftabl** command has been loaded.

Parameters   This function has no parameters.

Return Value   The AL register contains 0FFh if the **graftabl** command has been loaded or 00h
if it has not.

■ Interrupt 2Fh Function 0B700h Get APPEND.EXE Installed State

```
mov     ax, OB700h      ;Get APPEND.EXE Installed State
int     2Fh             ;Multiplex Interrupt

cmp     al, OFFh        ;OFFh means installed
je      installed
```

Get APPEND.EXE Installed State (Interrupt 2Fh Function 0B700h) determines whether the resident portion of the **append** command has been loaded.

Parameters   This function has no parameters.

Return Value   The AL register contains 0FFh if the **append** command has been loaded or 00h if it has not.

Interrupt 2Fh Function 0B702h Get APPEND.EXE Version

```
mov     ax, 0B702h      ;Get APPEND.EXE Version
int     2Fh             ;Multiplex Interrupt
```

Get APPEND.EXE Version (Interrupt 2Fh Function 0B702h) returns the version flag for the **append** command.

Parameters   This function has no parameters.

Return Value   The AX register contains 0FFFFh for versions compatible with MS-DOS version 5.0.

Interrupt 2Fh Function 0B704h Get APPEND.EXE Directory List Address

```
mov     ax, 0B704h        ;Get APPEND.EXE Directory List Address
int     2Fh               ;Multiplex Interrupt

mov     [DirList], di
mov     ax, es
mov     [DirList+2], ax ;es:di points to directory list
```

Get APPEND.EXE Directory List Address (Interrupt 2Fh Function 0B704h) returns a 32-bit address (segment:offset) of a list of the currently appended directories.

Parameters   This function has no parameters.

Return Value   The ES:DI registers contain the address of the currently appended directories.

Comments   The directory list is a zero-terminated ASCII string consisting of one or more directory paths separated by semicolons.

■ Interrupt 2Fh Function 0B706h Get APPEND.EXE Modes Flag

```
mov     ax, 0B706h          ;Get APPEND.EXE Modes Flag
int     2Fh                 ;Multiplex Interrupt

mov     Modes, bx           ;APPEND.EXE operation modes
```

Get APPEND.EXE Modes Flag (Interrupt 2Fh Function 0B706h) returns the current operation modes for the **append** command.

Parameters   This function has no parameters.

Return Value   If the function is successful, the BX register contains the operation modes, which can be a combination of the following values:

Bit	Meaning
0	The **append** command is enabled.
12	The **append** command applies appended directories to file requests that already specify a drive.
13	The **append** command applies appended directories to file requests that already specify a path. This bit is set if the **/path** switch is **on**.
14	The **append** command stores the appended directories in the APPEND environment variable. This bit is set if the **/e** switch has been specified.
15	The **append** command applies appended directories to functions such as Load and Execute Program, and Find First File (Interrupt 21h Functions 4B00h and 4Eh). This bit is set if the **/x** switch is **on**.

All other bits are reserved and must be zero.

See Also   Interrupt 2Fh Function 0B707h Set APPEND.EXE Modes Flag

Interrupt 2Fh Function 0B707h Set APPEND.EXE Modes Flag

```
mov      bx, Modes          ;APPEND.EXE operation modes

mov      ax, OB707h         ;Set APPEND.EXE Modes Flag
int      2Fh                ;Multiplex Interrupt
```

Set APPEND.EXE Modes Flag (Interrupt 2Fh Function 0B707h) sets the current operation modes for the **append** command.

Parameter

Modes   Specifies the operation modes. This parameter can be a combination of the following values:

Bit	Meaning
0	The **append** command is enabled.
12	The **append** command applies appended directories to file requests that already specify a drive.
13	The **append** command applies appended directories to file requests that already specify a path. This bit is set if the **/path** switch is **on**.
14	The **append** command stores the appended directories in the APPEND environment variable. This bit is set if the **/e** switch is specified.
15	The **append** command applies appended directories to functions such as Load and Execute Program, and Find First File (Interrupt 21h Functions 4B00h and $Eh). This bit is set if the **/x** switch is **on**.

All other bits are reserved and must be zero.

Return Value   This function has no return value.

See Also   Interrupt 2Fh Function 0B706h Get APPEND.EXE Modes Flag

■ Interrupt 2Fh Function 0B711h Set True-Name Flag

```
mov     ax, 0B711h          ;Set True-Name Flag
int     2Fh                 ;Multiplex Interrupt
```

Set True-Name Flag (Interrupt 2Fh Function 0B711h) sets the current program's flag that specifies whether the **append** command converts a filename to a full path when it processes system functions such as Open File with Handle (Interrupt 21h Function 3Dh).

Parameters   This function has no parameters.

Return Value   This function has no return value.

Comments   If the true-name flag is set, **append** expands filenames that are passed to the following functions:

Open File with Handle (Interrupt 21h Function 3Dh)
Get File Attributes (Interrupt 21h Function 4300h)
Find First File (Interrupt 21h Function 4Eh)
Extended Open/Create (Interrupt 21h Function 6Ch)

For each function, the program passes an address to the zero-terminated filename and **append** copies the zero-terminated path to the same address. The program making the call must ensure that the buffer at the address is large enough to contain the full path. The **append** command resets the true-name flag after expanding a filename.

See Also   Interrupt 21h Function 3Dh Open File with Handle
Interrupt 21h Function 4300h Get File Attributes
Interrupt 21h Function 4Eh Find First File
Interrupt 21h Function 6Ch Extended Open/Create

7.10 Task-Switching Reference

This section describes the functions used for task switching:

- Notification functions
- Service functions

7.10.1 Notification Functions

This section describes the notification functions used for task switching. Client programs provide these functions, and task switchers call them to notify the client programs about task switches and the creation or deletion of sessions. The reference page for each notification function provides the syntax, a statement of purpose, descriptions of any parameters, and cross-references to similar or related functions.

■ Notification Function 0000h Init Switcher

```
les     di, Service      ;addr of task switcher's serv-function handler

mov     ax, 0000h        ;Init Switcher
call    [Notification]   ;client program's notification-function handler

cmp     ax, 0
jne     no_load          ;if nonzero, don't load
```

Init Switcher (Notification Function 0000h) notifies client programs that a new task switcher is being initialized.

Parameter

Service   Points to the service-function handler for the task switcher or controlling session manager. A client program can use this address to call the task switcher's service functions, such as Get Version (Service Function 0000h) and Hook Notification Chain (Service Function 0004h).

Return Value

The AX register contains 0000h if the task switcher can be loaded safely. Otherwise, it contains a nonzero value.

Comments

Task switchers (and controlling session managers) must call this function when they are initialized. A client program that runs in global memory and needs to take special action to coexist with a task switcher should do so when receiving this call.

The task switcher's service function handler (specified by the ES:DI registers) must support Get Version (Service Function 0000h).

Typically, a program that invokes and controls the task switcher calls Init Switcher, rather than the task switcher itself. If any client program returns a nonzero value to the Init Switcher call, the controlling program disables its task-switching option. Other task-switching programs may simply terminate if a client returns a nonzero value.

If any client program returns nonzero to Init Switcher, all client programs may receive a call to Switcher Exit (Notification Function 0007h), including the client program that returned nonzero. Client programs can ignore a Switcher Exit call that is not preceded by an Init Switcher call.

Because it is not necessarily the task switcher itself that calls this function, client programs should not assume that the service-function-handler address passed in the ES:DI registers will be the same address passed with subsequent notification functions. In particular, this address can be NULL.

The task switcher enables interrupts before calling the client program. The client program can call any MS-DOS system function. Although the client program modifies the AX register, it must preserve all other registers.

See Also

Service Function 0000h   Get Version
Service Function 0004h   Hook Notification Chain
Notification Function 0007h Switcher Exit

■ Notification Function 0001h Query Suspend

```
mov    bx, SessionID      ;current session identifier
les    di, Service        ;es:di is address of service-function handler

mov    ax, 0001h          ;Query Suspend
call   [Notification]     ;client program's notification-function handler

mov    [Result], ax       ;0 = session switch okay, 1 = do not switch
```

Query Suspend (Notification Function 0001h) notifies client programs that the task switcher is preparing to perform a session switch. A task switcher calls this function when a session switch has been requested. The client program can prevent the session switch, or it can perform any operation needed to allow the switch before returning.

Parameters   *SessionID*   Identifies the session to be suspended.

Service   Points to the service-function handler for the task switcher. A client program can use this address to call the task switcher's service functions, such as Test Memory Region (Service Function 0001h).

Return Value   The AX register contains 0000h if a session switch can be performed safely or 0001h if it cannot.

All other values are reserved.

Comments   A client program in global memory can tell from the current session identifier which session will be suspended when the switch occurs. It also can use this identifier to maintain information about the session when the session is suspended, and to restore the information when the session is resumed. The session identifier is an arbitrary value provided by the task switcher; values are not necessarily sequential and may be reused after a session is destroyed.

A client program can call Test Memory Region (Service Function 0001h) to determine whether specific code or data in memory will be affected by the session switch, and whether the switch should be allowed. For example, a network redirector can run through a chain of outstanding request descriptors and, using Test Memory Region, determine whether any of the buffers or callback addresses are located in local memory. If any are in local memory, the redirector can prevent the session switch or invoke special code to handle the case.

Before preventing a session switch because of the state of an asynchronous API, a client program should call Query API Support (Service Function 0006h) to make sure the API is not being handled by another client program.

If any client program returns a nonzero value from a call to Query Suspend, all client programs may receive a call to Session Active (Notification Function 0004h), including the client program that returned nonzero. Client programs can ignore a call to Session Active without a preceding call to Query Suspend or Suspend Session (Notification Function 0002h).

The task switcher enables interrupts before calling the client program. The client program can call any MS-DOS system function. Although the client program modifies the AX register, it must preserve all other registers.

See Also

Service Function 0001h Test Memory Region
Service Function 0006h Query API Support
Notification Function 0002h Suspend Session
Notification Function 0004h Session Active

■ Notification Function 0002h Suspend Session

```
mov     bx, SessionID      ;current session identifier
les     di, Service        ;address of service-function handler

mov     ax, 0002h          ;Suspend Session
call    [Notification]     ;client program's notification-function handler

mov     [Result], ax       ;0 = session switch okay, 1 = do not switch
```

Suspend Session (Notification Function 0002h) notifies client programs that a
session switch is about to take place, providing them a last opportunity to
prevent the session switch.

Parameters   *SessionID*   Identifies the session to be suspended.

Service   Points to the service-function handler for the task switcher. A client
program can use this address to call the task switcher's service functions, such
as Test Memory Region (Service Function 0001h).

Return Value   The AX register contains 0000h if a session switch can be performed safely or
0001h if it cannot.

All other values are reserved.

Comment   If all client programs return 0000h to Query Suspend (Notification Function
0001h), the task switcher disables interrupts and calls Suspend Session, providing clients with a final chance to prevent the session switch. Client programs
must not issue software interrupts or make any calls that might enable interrupts.

If all client programs return with 0000h in the AX register, the task switcher
replaces the current interrupt-vector table with a saved copy before enabling
interrupts. The saved copy represents the global state present when the task
switcher first started. This guarantees that interrupt handlers local to the session
being suspended will not be called in the interim between when Suspend Session
returns to the task switcher and the next call is made to Activate Session
(Notification Function 0003h). This prevents programs in local memory from
gaining control on a hardware interrupt and making a call into programs in global memory before the global programs receive the resumed session's identifier.

Client programs in global memory can receive interrupts between the Suspend
Session and Activate Session notifications but should not assume the contents of
nonglobal memory if they do. Test Memory Region (Service Function 0001h) is
used to determine whether a block of memory is local or global.

Before preventing a session switch because of the state of an asynchronous API,
a client program should call Query API Support (Service Function 0006h) to
determine that the API is not being handled by another client program.

If any client program returns a nonzero value to Suspend Session, all client
programs may receive a call to Session Active (Notification Function 0004h),
including the client program that returned nonzero. Client programs can ignore a
call to Session Active received without a preceding call to Query Suspend
(Notification Function 0001h) or Suspend Session.

The task switcher disables interrupts before calling the client program, and the client program must not enable them or call MS-DOS system functions. Although the client program modifies the AX register, it must preserve all other registers.

See Also

Service Function 0001h Test Memory Region
Service Function 0006h Query API Support
Notification Function 0001h Query Suspend
Notification Function 0003h Activate Session
Notification Function 0004h Session Active

■ Notification Function 0003h Activate Session

```
mov     bx, SessionID       ;identifier for new session
mov     cx, Flags           ;session status flags
les     di, Service         ;es:di is address of service-function handler

mov     ax, 0003h           ;Activate Session
call    [Notification]      ;client program's notification-function handler
```

Activate Session (Notification Function 0003h) notifies client programs that a session is about to become active. If the session is a previously suspended session, it has been reinstalled in memory, including its local memory and interrupt-vector table. However, interrupts are disabled and must remain disabled.

Parameters   *SessionID*   Identifies the session to be activated.

Flags   Specifies the session's status. If bit 0 is 1, the session is being activated for the first time. If bit 0 is zero, the session has been suspended and is now being resumed. All other bits are reserved and must be zero.

Service   Points to the service-function handler for the task switcher.

Return Value   The AX register contains 0000h.

Comment   If interrupts are enabled while the session memory is being swapped, global programs can receive interrupts but local programs cannot. Once the new session's interrupt-vector table has been loaded, a problem can arise if a hardware interrupt occurs just as interrupts are enabled. The task switcher disables interrupts before calling the client program, to prevent local programs from receiving the interrupt and calling global programs that cannot handle such an interrupt correctly until they receive the new session identifier.

If this is a newly created session being activated for the first time, Activate Session will be preceded by a call to Create Session (Notification Function 0005h).

The task switcher disables interrupts before calling the client program, and the client program must not enable interrupts or call MS-DOS system functions. Although the client program modifies the AX register, it must preserve all other registers.

See Also   Notification Function 0005h Create Session

■ Notification Function 0004h Session Active

```
mov     bx, SessionID     ;identifier for new session
mov     cx, Flags         ;session status flags
les     di, Service       ;es:di is address of service-function handler

mov     ax, 0004h         ;Session Active
call    [Notification]    ;client program's notification-function handler
```

Session Active (Notification Function 0004h) notifies client programs that a session has become active. If the session was previously suspended, the function notifies client programs that the session has been reinstalled in memory, including its local memory and interrupt-vector table.

Parameters

SessionID   Identifies the session that is now active.

Flags   Specifies the session's status. If bit 0 is set, the session has just been created and is now active for the first time. If bit 0 is not set, the session was previously suspended and now has resumed. All other bits are reserved and must be zero.

Service   Points to the service-function handler for the task switcher.

Return Value

The AX register contains 0000h.

Comments

If any client program fails a call to Query Suspend (Notification Function 0001h) or Suspend Session (Notification Function 0002h), all client programs may receive a Session Active notification, including the client program that denied the call to Suspend Session. Client programs can ignore a Session Active notification received without a preceding call to Query Suspend or Suspend Session.

The task switcher enables interrupts before calling the client program. The client program can call any MS-DOS system function. Although the client program modifies the AX register, it must preserve all other registers.

See Also

Notification Function 0001h Query Suspend
Notification Function 0002h Suspend Session

■ Notification Function 0005h Create Session

```
mov     bx, SessionID    ;identifier for new session
les     di, Service      ;es:di is address of service-function handler

mov     ax, 0005h        ;Create Session
call    [Notification]   ;client program's notification-function handler

cmp     ax, 1
je      no_create        ;1 = don't create session
```

Create Session (Notification Function 0005h) notifies client programs that the task switcher is about to create a new session.

Parameters

sessionID   Identifies the session to be created. This parameter consists of a 4-bit switcher identifier (in the most significant 4 bits) and a 12-bit session number (in the low-order 12 bits).

Service   Points to the service-function handler for the task switcher.

Return Value

The AX register contains 0000h if a new session can be created safely or 0001h if the client program cannot safely handle a new session.

All other values are reserved.

Comments

Before creating a new session, the task switcher calls Create Session to allow client programs to prevent the session from being created. If, for example, global client programs keep information for each session in a fixed-length data structure, they may respond to the notification by preventing the new session if the structure does not have enough room for it.

A newly created session does not have to be activated immediately; other sessions can be created, destroyed, and switched before the new session is activated.

If any client program returns 0001h to Create Session, all client programs may receive a call to Destroy Session (Notification Function 0006h), including the program that returned 0001h. Client programs can ignore a call to Destroy Session received without a preceding call to Create Session.

The task switcher enables interrupts before calling the client program. The client program can call any MS-DOS system function. Although the client program modifies the AX register, it must preserve all other registers.

See Also

Notification Function 0006h Destroy Session

■ Notification Function 0006h Destroy Session

```
mov     bx, SessionID   ;identifier for new session
les     di, Service     ;es:di is address of service-function handler

mov     ax, 0006h       ;Destroy Session
call    [Notification]  ;client program's notification-function handler
```

Destroy Session (Notification Function 0006h) notifies client programs that the task switcher is destroying a session.

Parameters   *SessionID*   Identifies the session to be destroyed.

Service   Points to the service-function handler for the task switcher.

Return Value   The AX register contains 0000h.

Comments   A task switcher calls Destroy Session whenever a session is being destroyed. Typically, this will occur when the program in the current session ends. However, any session manager that controls the task switcher can also provide a way for the user to destroy a session while the program is still running, or to destroy a session that is suspended. As a result, the session being destroyed is not necessarily the current session.

If any client program returns 0001h to Create Session (Notification Function 0005h), all client programs may receive a call to Destroy Session, including the program that returned 0001h. Client programs can ignore a call to Destroy Session received without a preceding call to Create Session.

The task switcher enables interrupts before calling the client program. The client program can call any MS-DOS system function. Although the client program modifies the AX register, it must preserve all other registers.

See Also   Notification Function 0005h Create Session

■ Notification Function 0007h Switcher Exit

```
mov      bx, Flags        ;indicates whether other task switchers present
les      di, Service      ;es:di is address of service-function handler

mov      ax, 0007h        ;Switcher Exit
call     [Notification]   ;client program's notification-function handler
```

Switcher Exit (Notification Function 0007h) notifies global client programs that the task switcher is no longer active.

Parameters   *Flags*   Specifies whether other task switchers are present in the system. If bit 0 is 1, the calling task switcher is the only switcher present. If bit 0 is zero, at least one other task switcher remains after the calling task switcher exits. All other bits are reserved and must be zero.

Service   Points to the service-function handler for the task switcher. If this address is NULL, the call-in function handler is no longer present and cannot be called.

Return Value   The AX register contains 0000h.

Comments   A task switcher calls this function. Global programs that receive this call should disable any extra processing they were running in order to coexist with the task switcher.

This function can be called by programs that control the task switcher, rather than by the task switcher itself. For this reason, the service-function-handler address specified in the ES:DI registers may differ from addresses passed with other notification functions and may be NULL.

The task switcher enables interrupts before calling the client program. The client program can call any MS-DOS system function. Although the client program modifies the AX register, it must preserve all other registers.

See Also   Notification Function 0000h Init Switcher

7.10.2 Service Functions

This section describes the service functions used for task switching. Client programs use these functions to control switching and to retrieve information about the task switcher and about the capabilities of other client programs. The reference page for each service function provides the syntax, a statement of purpose, parameter descriptions, and cross-references to similar or related functions.

■ Service Function 0000h Get Version

```
mov     ax, 0000h                       ;Get Version
call    [Service]                       ;service-function handler

jc      error_handler

mov     WORD PTR [Version], bx
mov     ax, es
mov     WORD PTR [Version+2], ax    ;es:bx points to SWVERSION struct
```

Get Version (Service Function 0000h) returns the address of an **SWVERSION** structure that identifies the current task switcher, its version number, and the protocol it supports.

Client programs and task switchers can call this function.

Parameters   This function has no parameters.

Return Value   If the function is successful, the carry flag is clear, the AX register contains 0000h, and the ES:BX registers contain the address of the **SWVERSION** structure for the current task switcher. If the task switcher does not support this function, the carry flag is set.

Comments   The **SWVERSION** structure has the following form:

```
SWVERSION    STRUC
    svsAPIMajor      dw   ?    ;protocol supported major version
    svsAPIMinor      dw   ?    ;protocol supported minor version
    svsProductMajor  dw   ?    ;task switcher's major version
    svsProductMinor  dw   ?    ;task switcher's minor version
    svsSwitcherID    dw   ?    ;task-switcher identifier
    svsFlags         dw   ?    ;operation flags
    svsName          dd   ?    ;points to task-switcher name (ASCIIZ)
    svsPrevSwitcher  dd   ?    ;previous task switcher's entry address
SWVERSION    ENDS
```

For a full description of the **SWVERSION** structure, see Section 7.11, "Structures."

A task switcher processing Get Version can enable interrupts and call any MS-DOS system function. Although the task switcher modifies the AX, ES, and DI registers, it must preserve all other registers.

See Also   Interrupt 2Fh Function 4B02h Detect Switcher

■ Service Function 0001h Test Memory Region

```
les      di, Buffer       ;points to first byte to be tested
mov      cx, Size         ;size of buffer, in bytes

mov      ax, 0001h        ;Test Memory Region
call     [Service]        ;service-function handler

jc       error_handler

mov      [Result], ax     ;0 = global, 1 = global and local, 2 = local
```

Test Memory Region (Service Function 0001h) determines whether a given block of memory is global or local in the current session. Local memory is replaced when a session switch occurs.

Client programs and task switchers can call this function. The task switcher corresponding to the specified service-function handler is responsible for processing the function.

Parameters

Buffer   Points to the first byte of memory to be tested.

Size   Specifies the buffer size, in bytes. This value must be in the range 0 through 65,535, where 0 indicates 64K (65,536). Buffers larger than 64K require more than one call to Test Memory Region to test the entire region.

Return Value

If the function is successful, the carry flag is clear and the AX register contains values specifying whether the memory is global or local. This can be one of the following values:

Value	Meaning
0000h	The buffer is in global memory.
0001h	The buffer is in both global and local memory.
0002h	The buffer is in local memory.

All other values are reserved.

If the task switcher does not support this function, the carry flag is set.

Comments

The task switcher corresponding to the specified service-function handler determines whether memory is global or local. If more than one task switcher is active, the one that creates a client program's session determines whether its memory is local or global. For this reason, a client program should test its memory region each time it receives the call Query Suspend (Notification Function 0001h) or Session Active (Notification Function 0004h), to determine whether the memory it occupies is global or local relative to the task switcher performing the session switch.

Client programs in global memory can use Test Memory Region to identify requests for asynchronous operations coming from other client programs in global memory. Client programs that service these requests do not have to take special action when a session switch occurs, because a requesting program's buffer and callback address remain accessible even after the session switch.

Since location sometimes affects operation, memory-resident programs can use Test Memory Region to determine whether they are in local or global memory. For example, a communication program in local memory should temporarily shut down before being suspended, but the same program in global memory can continue to run, since a session switch does not affect it.

A task switcher processing Test Memory Region must not enable interrupts or call any MS-DOS system function. Although the task switcher modifies the AX register, it must preserve all other registers.

See Also

Notification Function 0001h Query Suspend
Notification Function 0004h Session Active

■ Service Function 0002h Suspend Switcher

```
les     di, NewService    ;new address of service-function handler

mov     ax, 0002h         ;Suspend Switcher
call    [Service]         ;service-function handler

jc      error_handler

mov     [Result], ax      ;0 = suspended, 1 = not suspended, don't start
                          ;2 = not suspended, okay to start
```

Suspend Switcher (Service Function 0002h) notifies the current task switcher that it should suspend operations because another task switcher is being initialized.

Only a task switcher that needs to suspend the current task switcher should call this function. Client programs, especially programs in global memory, must not call it.

Parameter

NewService Points to the new task switcher's service-function handler. The current task switcher can use this address to call the new task switcher's service functions, such as Get Version (Service Function 0000h).

Return Value

If Suspend Switcher is successful, the carry flag is clear and the AX register contains a value specifying whether the task switcher has suspended operations. This value can be one of the following:

Value	Meaning
0000h	Current task switcher has suspended operations.
0001h	Current task switcher has not suspended operations. The new task switcher must not start.
0002h	Current task switcher has not suspended operations, but the new task switcher can start and run in conjunction with it.

All other values are reserved.

If the current task switcher does not support this function, the carry flag is set.

Comments

As long as they conform to the task-switching protocol, two or more active task switchers can safely coexist. Suspend Switcher helps the user avoid the confusion sometimes caused by the presence of multiple task switchers.

If the current task switcher returns 0001h, the new task switcher should not disable its session-switching capabilities unless another task switcher denies the new task switcher's call to Init Switcher (Notification Function 0000h).

After a task switcher has received a Suspend Switcher call, it should continue to respond to service functions, but it should neither respond to keyboard interrupts nor attempt to switch sessions until it receives a corresponding call to Resume Switcher (Service Function 0003h).

Suspend Switcher calls can be nested, so suspended task switchers should not become active until they have received an equal number of calls to Suspend Switcher and Resume Switcher. An exception to this rule occurs when a child program running a separate task switcher suspends its session manager's task switcher and does not reactivate it before returning control to the session manager. In this case, the session manager can safely reactivate its own task switcher.

A task switcher processing Suspend Switcher can enable interrupts and call any MS-DOS system function. Although the task switcher modifies the AX register, it must preserve all other registers.

Client programs that need to suspend session switching should return 0001h to Query Suspend (Notification Function 0001h).

A task switcher normally calls Suspend Switcher by using the service-function-handler address received from Detect Switcher (Interrupt 2Fh Function 4B02h), rather than in response to a notification function.

See Also

Interrupt 2Fh Function 4B02h Detect Switcher
Service Function 0000h Get Version
Service Function 0003h Resume Switcher
Notification Function 0000h Init Switcher
Notification Function 0001h Query Suspend

■ Service Function 0003h Resume Switcher

```
les     di, NewService   ;new address of service-function handler

mov     ax, 0003h        ;Resume Switcher
call    [Service]        ;Service-function handler

jc      error_handler
```

Resume Switcher (Function 0003h) notifies a suspended task switcher that it can resume operation.

Client programs must not call this function.

Parameter

NewService   Points to the new task switcher's service-function handler. The task switcher that is being resumed can use this address to call the new task switcher's service functions, such as Get Version (Service Function 0000h).

Return Value

If the function is successful, the carry flag is clear and the AX register contains 0000h. If the task switcher does not support this function, the carry flag is set.

Comments

A task switcher that has disabled another task switcher by using Suspend Switcher (Service Function 0002h) should call Resume Switcher to reenable it, and should use the same service-function-handler address that it used to call Suspend Switcher.

A task switcher processing Resume Switcher can enable interrupts and call any MS-DOS system function. Although the task switcher modifies the AX register, it must preserve all other registers.

See Also

Service Function 0000h Get Version
Service Function 0002h Suspend Switcher

■ Service Function 0004h Hook Notification Chain

```
les     di, CBInfo       ;es:di points to SWCALLBACKINFO structure

mov     ax, 0004h        ;Hook Notification Chain
call    [Service]        ;service-function handler

jc      error_handler    ;carry set on error
```

Hook Notification Chain (Service Function 0004h) directs the task switcher to add the specified **SWCALLBACKINFO** structure to its notification chain. Client programs that must be notified of session changes call this function during initialization.

Parameter   *CBInfo*   Points to the client program's **SWCALLBACKINFO** structure. The client program does not need to fill in the **scbiNext** field of this structure. The **SWCALLBACKINFO** structure has the following form:

```
SWCALLBACKINFO   STRUC
    scbiNext          dd   ?   ;address of next structure in chain
    scbiEntryPoint    dd   ?   ;address of notification-function handler
    scbiReserved      dd   ?   ;reserved
    scbiAPI           dd   ?   ;address of list of SWAPIINFO structures
SWCALLBACKINFO   ENDS
```

For a full description of the **SWCALLBACKINFO** and **SWAPIINFO** structures, see Section 7.11, "Structures."

Return Value   If Hook Notification Chain is successful, the carry flag is clear and the AX register contains 0000h. If the task switcher does not support this function, the carry flag is set.

Comments   Client programs can check for a task switcher by using Detect Switcher (Interrupt 2Fh Function 4B02h). If a task switcher is present, the client programs add themselves to its notification chain by calling Hook Notification Chain. A client program must fill the **SWCALLBACKINFO** structure before calling the task switcher.

Some task switchers call Build Notification Chain (Interrupt 2Fh Function 4B01h) to create a notification chain before each session switch. These task switchers can simply return from Hook Notification Chain with no other action.

Most task switchers, however, generate the notification chain only during initialization, and client programs that start later must add themselves to it. For example, a task switcher may keep a separate notification chain for each session and supply each new session it creates with a copy of its original notification chain. A client program that runs within that new session must add its notification-function handler address to the local chain by calling Hook Notification Chain.

Before terminating, a client program must unhook itself from the task switcher's notification chain by calling Unhook Notification Chain (Function 0005h).

A task switcher processing Hook Notification Chain can enable interrupts and call any MS-DOS system function. Although the task switcher modifies the AX register, it must preserve all other registers.

See Also   Interrupt 2Fh Function 4B01h Build Notification Chain
Interrupt 2Fh Function 4B02h Detect Switcher
Service Function 0005h Unhook Notification Chain

■ Service Function 0005h Unhook Notification Chain

```
les     di, CBInfo        ;es:di points to SWCALLBACKINFO structure

mov     ax, 0005h         ;Unhook Notification Chain
call    [Service]         ;service-function handler

jc      error_handler     ;carry set on error
```

Unhook Notification Chain (Service Function 0005h) directs the task switcher to remove the specified **SWCALLBACKINFO** structure from its notification chain. Client programs that are on the notification chain must call this function when they terminate.

Parameter   *CBInfo*   Points to the client program's **SWCALLBACKINFO** structure. The **SWCALLBACKINFO** structure has the following form:

```
SWCALLBACKINFO  STRUC
    scbiNext        dd  ?   ;address of next structure in chain
    scbiEntryPoint  dd  ?   ;address of notification-function handler
    scbiReserved    dd  ?   ;reserved
    scbiAPI         dd  ?   ;address of list of SWAPIINFO structures
SWCALLBACKINFO  ENDS
```

For a full description of the **SWCALLBACKINFO** and **SWAPIINFO** structures, see Section 7.11, "Structures."

Return Value   If the function is successful, the carry flag is clear and the AX register contains 0000h. If the task switcher does not support this function, the carry flag is set.

Comments   Whether a client program has used Build Notification Chain (Interrupt 2Fh Function 4B01h) or Hook Notification Chain (Service Function 0004h), it must call Unhook Notification Chain to remove itself from the notification chain of every task switcher to which it belongs.

A task switcher that rebuilds its notification chain at every session switch can return from Unhook Notification Chain with no other action.

A task switcher processing Unhook Notification Chain can enable interrupts and call any MS-DOS system function. Although the task switcher modifies the AX register, it must preserve all other registers.

See Also   Interrupt 2Fh Function 4B01h Build Notification Chain Service Function 0004h Hook Notification Chain

■ Service Function 0006h Query API Support

```
mov     bx, ApiID              ;asynchronous API identifier
mov     ax, 0006h              ;Query API Support
call    [Service]              ;service-function handler

jc      error_handler          ;carry set on error

mov     WORD PTR [ApiInfo], bx
mov     ax, es
mov     WORD PTR [ApiInfo+2], ax ;es:bx points to SWAPIINFO structure
```

Query API Support (Service Function 0006h) returns the address of the **SWAPI-INFO** structure of the client program that provides the highest level of support for the specified asynchronous API. Client programs that support asynchronous APIs call this function to determine which program should control session switching and handle the specified asynchronous API. control session switching and handle the specified asynchronous API.

Parameter   *ApiID*   Identifies an asynchronous API. This value can be one of the following:

Value	Meaning
API_NETBIOS (0001h)	NETBIOS
API_8022 (0002h)	802.2
API_TCPIP (0003h)	TCP/IP
API_LANMAN (0004h)	LAN Manager named pipes
API_IPX (0005h)	NetWare IPX

Return Value   If the function is successful, the carry flag is clear, the AX register contains 0000h, and the ES:BX registers contain the address of the **SWAPIINFO** structure of the client program that provides the highest level of support for the specified asynchronous API. If the task switcher does not support this function, the carry flag is set.

The **SWAPIINFO** structure has the following form:

```
SWAPIINFO   STRUC
    aisLength   dw 10      ;size of this structure, in bytes
    aisAPI      dw ?       ;API identifier
    aisMajor    dw ?       ;major version number
    aisMinor    dw ?       ;minor version number
    aisSupport  dw ?       ;support level
SWAPIINFO   ENDS
```

For a full description of the **SWAPIINFO** structure, see Section 7.11, "Structures."

Comments   This function allows client programs that provide support for the same asynchronous API to negotiate which program controls session switching. Each client program maintains information about the asynchronous APIs it supports and the level of support provided to each API in a list of **SWAPIINFO** structures. The program provides a pointer to the beginning of this list in its **SWCALLBACK-INFO** structure. (For a full description of the **SWCALLBACKINFO** structure, see Section 7.11, "Structures.") Since any number of client programs can provide support for the same API, the task switcher uses the **aisSupport** field in the **SWAPIINFO** structures to determine which client program provides the highest level of support and therefore receives control. In general, a client program provides the highest level of support if it allows session switching for the greatest number of special cases.

When a client program that supports an asynchronous API is processing Query Suspend (Notification Function 0001h) or Suspend Session (Notification Function 0002h), it must call Query API Support to determine whether it is the client program that should handle the API. If the function returns the address of the client program's own **SWAPIINFO** structure, the client program should prevent the session switch. If it returns the address of another client program's structure, the calling client program should not prevent the session switch, relying instead on the more capable client program to prevent the session switch if necessary.

When a task switcher processes Query API Support, interrupts are disabled if a client program calls this function while handling a notification function for which interrupts also are disabled. Otherwise, interrupts are enabled. If interrupts are disabled, the task switcher must not enable them or call MS-DOS system functions. Although the task switcher modifies the AX, ES, and BX registers, it must preserve all other registers.

See Also   Notification Function 0001h Query Suspend
Notification Function 0002h Suspend Session

7.11 Structures

This section describes the **QUEUEPACKET** structure and the structures MS-DOS task switchers use.

■ QUEUEPACKET

```
QUEUEPACKET STRUC
    qpLevel     db 0    ;level, must be zero
    qpFilename  dd ?    ;segment:offset pointing to ASCIIZ path
QUEUEPACKET ENDS
```

The **QUEUEPACKET** structure contains information used to add a file to the printing queue.

Fields   *qpLevel*   Specifies the queue level. This field must be 00h for current versions of MS-DOS.

qpFilename   Contains the 32-bit address of a zero-terminated string specifying the path of the file to add to the queue. This string must be a valid MS-DOS path and must not contain wildcards. If the specified file exists, PRINT.EXE adds the file to the queue.

See Also   Interrupt 2Fh Function 0101h Add File to Queue

■ SWAPIINFO

```
SWAPIINFO   STRUC
    aisLength   dw 10   ;size of this structure, in bytes
    aisAPI      dw ?    ;API identifier
    aisMajor    dw ?    ;major version number
    aisMinor    dw ?    ;minor version number
    aisSupport  dw ?    ;support level
SWAPIINFO   ENDS
```

The **SWAPIINFO** structure contains information about the level of support that a client program provides for a particular type of asynchronous API.

Fields   **aisLength**   Specifies the length of the structure, in bytes.

aisAPI   Identifies the asynchronous API supported by the client program. This value can be one of the following:

Value	Meaning
API_NETBIOS (0001h)	NETBIOS
API_8022 (0002h)	802.2
API_TCPIP (0003h)	TCP/IP
API_LANMAN (0004h)	LAN Manager named pipes
API_IPX (0005h)	NetWare IPX

All other values are reserved.

aisMajor   Specifies the highest major version of the API for which the client program provides the level of support specified by the **aisSupport** field. For example, if the highest version of the API supported by the client program at the specified level is 3.10, this field would be set to 0003h.

aisMinor   Specifies the highest minor version of the API for which the client program provides the specified level of support. For example, if the highest version of the API supported by the client program at the specified level is 3.10, this field would be set to 000Ah.

aisSupport   Specifies the level of support provided by the client program for the particular version of the API. The range and significance of values in this field depend upon the particular API. The following definitions are used for NETBIOS:

Value	Meaning
0001h	Minimal support. The client program prevents a session switch after an application has called a function supported in an asynchronous API, even after the request has been completed.
0002h	API-level support. The client program tracks asynchronous requests, prevents task switches when requests are outstanding, and allows task switches when all requests have been completed.
0003h	Switcher compatibility. The API provider allows switches to occur even when asynchronous requests are outstanding. However, this may be limited by such factors as buffer size, and some requests might fail.
0004h	Seamless compatibility. The API provider always allows session switches to occur.

■ SWCALLBACKINFO

```
SWCALLBACKINFO   STRUC
    scbiNext       dd   ?    ;address of next structure in chain
    scbiEntryPoint dd   ?    ;address of notification-function handler
    scbiReserved   dd   ?    ;reserved
    scbiAPI        dd   ?    ;address of list of SWAPIINFO structures
SWCALLBACKINFO   ENDS
```

The **SWCALLBACKINFO** structure contains information about the client program.

Fields

scbiNext   Specifies the 32-bit address (segment:offset) of the next structure in the notification chain.

scbiEntryPoint   Specifies the 32-bit address (segment:offset) of the client program's notification-function handler. The task switcher uses this address to call the client program's notification functions.

scbiReserved   Reserved; do not use.

scbiAPI   Specifies the 32-bit address (segment:offset) of a zero-terminated list of **SWAPIINFO** structures specifying the type of support the client program provides for various asynchronous APIs.

See Also

Interrupt 2Fh Function 4B01h Build Notification Chain
Service Function 0004h Hook Notification Chain

■ SWINSTANCEITEM

```
SWINSTANCEITEM   STRUC
    iisPtr       dd  ?          ;points to the instance data
    iisSize      dw  ?          ;size of the instance data, in bytes
SWINSTANCEITEM   ENDS
```

The **SWINSTANCEITEM** structure contains information about a block of instance data.

Fields   **iisPtr**   Specifies the 32-bit address (segment:offset) of the first byte of the block of instance data.

iisSize   Specifies the instance data's block size, in bytes.

■ SWSTARTUPINFO

```
SWSTARTUPINFO STRUC
    sisVersion           dw  3    ;ignored
    sisNextDev           dd  ?    ;points to prev handler's SWSTARTUPINFO
    sisVirtDevFile       dd  O    ;ignored
    sisReferenceData     dd  ?    ;ignored
    sisInstanceData      dd  ?    ;points to SWINSTANCEITEM structures
SWSTARTUPINFO ENDS
```

The **SWSTARTUPINFO** contains information about a client program's instance data.

Fields   **sisVersion**   Not used.

sisNextDev   Specifies the 32-bit address (segment:offset) of the next structure in the client chain.

sisVirtDevFile   Not used.

sisReferenceData   Not used.

sisInstanceData   Specifies the 32-bit address (segment:offset) of a list of **SWINSTANCEITEM** structures, each of which describes one contiguous block of instance data. The list is terminated by a 32-bit zero value.

Comments   This structure is also used with the Microsoft Windows startup Interrupt 2Fh function. However, task switchers use only the **sisNextDev** and **sisInstanceData** fields. For detailed information about the other fields in the **SWSTARTUPINFO** structure, see the *Microsoft Windows Device Driver Kit Virtual Device Adaptation Guide*.

See Also   Interrupt 2Fh Function 4B05h Identify Instance Data

■ SWVERSION

```
SWVERSION    STRUC
    svsAPIMajor     dw    ?    ;protocol supported major version
    svsAPIMinor     dw    ?    ;protocol supported minor version
    svsProductMajor dw    ?    ;task switcher's major version
    svsProductMinor dw    ?    ;task switcher's minor version
    svsSwitcherID   dw    ?    ;task-switcher identifier
    svsFlags        dw    ?    ;operation flags
    svsName         dd    ?    ;points to task-switcher name (ASCIIZ)
    svsPrevSwitcher dd    ?    ;previous task switcher's entry address
SWVERSION    ENDS
```

The **SWVERSION** structure contains information about a task switcher.

Fields

svsAPIMajor   Specifies the highest major version of the task-switching protocol that the task switcher supports. For example, if the highest version of the protocol supported is 3.10, this field would be set to 0003h. The current version is 1.0.

svsAPIMinor   Specifies the highest minor version of the task-switching protocol that the task switcher supports. For example, if the highest version of the protocol supported is 3.10, this field would be set to 000Ah. The current version is 1.0.

svsProductMajor   Specifies the major version of the task switcher, in the same format as the **svsAPIMajor** field.

svsProductMinor   Specifies the minor version of the task switcher, in the same format as **svsAPIMinor** field.

svsSwitcherID   Specifies the switcher identifier (low-order 4 bits). The task switcher uses Allocate Switcher ID (Interrupt 2Fh Function 4B03h) to generate this identifier.

svsFlags   Specifies the task-switcher flags. In this version of the task-switching protocol, only bit 0 has meaning. If bit 0 is 1, the task switcher is currently disabled; otherwise, the task switcher is enabled. All other bits are reserved and must be zero.

svsName   Specifies the 32-bit address (segment:offset) of a zero-terminated ASCII string that names the task switcher (for example, "Microsoft MS-DOS Shell Task Switcher").

svsPrevSwitcher   Specifies the 32-bit entry address (segment:offset) of the previously loaded task switcher. This entry address can be used to call the previously loaded task switcher's service-function handler.

See Also

Interrupt 2Fh Function 4B02h Detect Switcher
Interrupt 2Fh Function 4B03h Allocate Switcher ID
Service Function 0000h Get Version

Chapter

8

Interrupt 21h Functions

8.1 Introduction

This chapter describes the MS-DOS functions that a program can call to manage system operation and resources. Using these functions makes it easier to write computer-independent programs and increases the likelihood that a program will be compatible with future versions of MS-DOS.

Programs use MS-DOS services by issuing software interrupts. Interrupt 21h is the function request service; it provides access to a wide variety of MS-DOS services. Each function request uses values in various registers to receive or return function-specific information.

8.2 Function Groups

The following list shows the categories of MS-DOS functions:

- File management
- Directory management
- Drive management
- File sharing
- File control blocks (FCBs)
- Input/output control (IOCTL)
- Character input/output (I/O)
- Memory management
- Program management
- Networks
- National language support
- System management

The following sections show the functions in each category. For information about superseded functions, see Section 8.3, "Superseded Functions." For information about obsolete functions, see Section 8.4, "Obsolete Functions."

8.2.1 File-Handle Functions

Beginning with version 2.0, MS-DOS has included file-handle functions. All programs (except those that must be compatible with MS-DOS versions earlier than version 2.0) should use these functions for file management.

When a program opens or creates a file, MS-DOS assigns a unique handle to that file. The program can use the handle to access the file until the program closes the file. In some cases, a program can use a handle to read from and write to a device as if it were a file.

Following are the MS-DOS file-handle functions:

Function	Description	Version
3Ch	Create File with Handle	2.0
3Dh	Open File with Handle	2.0
3Eh	Close File with Handle	2.0
3Fh	Read File or Device	2.0
40h	Write File or Device	2.0
41h	Delete File	2.0
42h	Move File Pointer	2.0
4300h	Get File Attributes	2.0
4301h	Set File Attributes	2.0
45h	Duplicate File Handle	2.0
46h	Force Duplicate File Handle	2.0
56h	Rename File	2.0
5700h	Get File Date and Time	2.0
5701h	Set File Date and Time	2.0
5Ah	Create Temporary File	3.0
5Bh	Create New File	3.0
67h	Set Maximum Handle Count	3.3
68h	Commit File	3.3
6Ch	Extended Open/Create	4.0

8.2.2 Directory-Management Functions

Following are the MS-DOS directory-management functions:

Function	Description	Version
39h	Create Directory	2.0
3Ah	Remove Directory	2.0
3Bh	Change Current Directory	2.0
41h	Delete File	2.0
47h	Get Current Directory	2.0
4Eh	Find First File	2.0
4Fh	Find Next File	2.0
56h	Rename File	2.0

8.2.3 Drive-Management Functions

Following are the MS-DOS drive-management functions:

Function	Description	Version
0Dh	Reset Drive	1.0
0Eh	Set Default Drive	1.0
19h	Get Default Drive	1.0
1Ah	Set Disk Transfer Address	1.0
1Bh	Get Default Drive Data	2.0
1Ch	Get Drive Data	2.0
1Fh	Get Default DPB	5.0
2Fh	Get Disk Transfer Address	2.0
32h	Get DPB	5.0
3305h	Get Startup Drive	2.0
36h	Get Disk Free Space	2.0

8.2.4 File-Sharing Functions

With file sharing, multiple programs can share access to a file. File sharing operates only after the Share program has been loaded.

Following are the MS-DOS functions that are affected by file sharing:

Function	Description	Version
440Bh	Set Sharing Retry Count	3.1
5Ch	Lock/Unlock File	3.1

8.2.5 File-Control-Block (FCB) Functions

Early versions of MS-DOS used file control blocks (FCBs) for file management. Although MS-DOS still supports the FCB functions, new programs should use the file-handle functions.

This chapter includes reference information about the FCB functions for programmers who maintain older programs that may still use these functions. Following are the MS-DOS FCB functions:

Function	Description	Version
0Fh	Open File with FCB	1.0
10h	Close File with FCB	1.0
11h	Find First File with FCB	1.0

Function	Description	Version
12h	Find Next File with FCB	1.0
13h	Delete File with FCB	1.0
14h	Sequential Read	1.0
15h	Sequential Write	1.0
16h	Create File with FCB	1.0
17h	Rename File with FCB	1.0
21h	Random Read	1.0
22h	Random Write	1.0
23h	Get File Size	1.0
24h	Set Random Record Number	1.0
27h	Random Block Read	1.0
28h	Random Block Write	1.0
29h	Parse Filename	1.0

8.2.6 Input/Output Control (IOCTL) Functions

The MS-DOS input/output control (IOCTL) functions provide a consistent and expandable interface between programs and device drivers.

Following are the MS-DOS IOCTL functions. Minor codes associated with Generic IOCTL for Character Devices (Function 440Ch) and Generic IOCTL for Block Devices (Function 440Dh) are indented.

Function	Description	Version
4400h	Get Device Data	2.0
4401h	Set Device Data	2.0
4402h	Receive Control Data from Character Device	2.0
4403h	Send Control Data to Character Device	2.0
4404h	Receive Control Data from Block Device	2.0
4405h	Send Control Data to Block Device	2.0
4406h	Check Device Input Status	2.0
4407h	Check Device Output Status	2.0
4408h	Does Device Use Removable Media	3.0
4409h	Is Drive Remote	3.1
440Ah	Is File or Device Remote	3.1
440Bh	Set Sharing Retry Count	3.0

Function	Description	Version
440Ch	Generic IOCTL for Character Devices	
45h	Set Iteration Count	3.3
4Ah	Select Code Page	3.3
4Ch	Start Code-Page Prepare	3.3
4Dh	End Code-Page Prepare	3.3
5Fh	Set Display Mode	4.0
65h	Get Iteration Count	3.3
6Ah	Query Selected Code Page	3.3
6Bh	Query Code-Page Prepare List	3.3
7Fh	Get Display Mode	4.0
440Dh	Generic IOCTL for Block Devices	
40h	Set Device Parameters	3.2
41h	Write Track on Logical Drive	3.2
42h	Format Track on Logical Drive	3.2
46h	Set Media ID	4.0
60h	Get Device Parameters	3.2
61h	Read Track on Logical Drive	3.2
62h	Verify Track on Logical Drive	3.2
66h	Get Media ID	4.0
68h	Sense Media Type	5.0
440Eh	Get Logical Drive Map	3.2
440Fh	Set Logical Drive Map	3.2
4410h	Query IOCTL Handle	5.0
4411h	Query IOCTL Device	5.0

8.2.7 Character Input/Output (I/O) Functions

The standard character input/output (I/O) functions handle all input to and output from character devices, such as consoles, printers, and serial ports.

Following are the MS-DOS character I/O functions:

Function	Description	Version
01h	Read Keyboard with Echo	1.0
02h	Display Character	1.0
03h	Auxiliary Input	1.0
04h	Auxiliary Output	1.0

Function	Description	Version
05h	Print Character	1.0
06h	Direct Console I/O	1.0
07h	Direct Console Input	1.0
08h	Read Keyboard Without Echo	1.0
09h	Display String	1.0
0Ah	Buffered Keyboard Input	1.0
0Bh	Check Keyboard Status	1.0
0Ch	Flush Buffer, Read Keyboard	1.0

8.2.8 Memory-Management Functions

MS-DOS provides Interrupt 21h functions for allocating and freeing memory. The system keeps track of memory allocations by using a memory control block at the beginning of each allocated area. To avoid overwriting memory control blocks, other resident programs, or portions of the operating system or device drivers, programs should use the MS-DOS memory-management functions and use only allocated memory.

Following are the MS-DOS memory-management functions:

Function	Description	Version
48h	Allocate Memory	2.0
49h	Free Allocated Memory	2.0
4Ah	Set Memory Block Size	2.0
5800h	Get Allocation Strategy	3.0
5801h	Set Allocation Strategy	3.0
5802h	Get Upper-Memory Link	5.0
5803h	Set Upper-Memory Link	5.0

8.2.9 Program-Management Functions

MS-DOS uses several Interrupt 21h functions to load, execute, and terminate programs. Programs can use these same functions to manage other programs.

Following are the MS-DOS program-management functions:

Function	Description	Version
00h	Terminate Program	1.0
26h	Create New PSP	1.0
31h	Keep Program	2.0
34h	Get InDOS Flag Address	2.0

Function	Description	Version
4B00h	Load and Execute Program	2.0
4B01h	Load Program	2.0
4B03h	Load Overlay	2.0
4B05h	Set Execution State	5.0
4Ch	End Program	2.0
4Dh	Get Child-Program Return Value	2.0
50h	Set PSP Address	2.0
51h	Get PSP Address	2.0
59h	Get Extended Error	3.0
5D0Ah	Set Extended Error	4.0

8.2.10 Network Functions

A network consists of a server and one or more workstations. MS-DOS maintains an *assign list* to keep track of which workstation disk drives and devices have been redirected to the server.

Following are the MS-DOS network functions:

Function	Description	Version
4409h	Is Drive Remote	3.1
440Ah	Is File or Device Remote	3.1
5E00h	Get Machine Name	3.1
5E02h	Set Printer Setup	3.1
5E03h	Get Printer Setup	3.1
5F02h	Get Assign-List Entry	3.1
5F03h	Make Network Connection	3.1
5F04h	Delete Network Connection	3.1

8.2.11 National-Language-Support (NLS) Functions

Programs use the MS-DOS national-language-support (NLS) functions to retrieve and set country information, such as the time format, the currency symbol, and the screen and printer code pages.

Following are the MS-DOS NLS-related functions:

Function	Description	Version
38h	Get/Set Country Information	2.0
6501h	Get Extended Country Information	3.3

Function	Description	Version
6502h	Get Uppercase Table	3.3
6504h	Get Filename Uppercase Table	3.3
6505h	Get Filename-Character Table	3.3
6506h	Get Collate-Sequence Table	3.3
6507h	Get Double-Byte Character Set	3.3
6520h	Convert Character	3.3
6521h	Convert String	3.3
6522h	Convert ASCIIZ String	3.3
6601h	Get Global Code Page	3.3
6602h	Set Global Code Page	3.3

8.2.12 System-Management Functions

MS-DOS also provides Interrupt 21h functions for such system-management tasks as setting and examining the system time and date, the state of the Verify flag, and the state of the CTRL+C check flag. The Verify and CTRL+C check flags control how MS-DOS responds to input from programs and users.

Following are the MS-DOS system-management functions:

Function	Description	Version
25h	Set Interrupt Vector	1.0
2Ah	Get Date	1.0
2Bh	Set Date	1.0
2Ch	Get Time	1.0
2Dh	Set Time	1.0
2Eh	Set/Reset Verify Flag	1.0
30h	Get Version Number	2.0
3300h	Get CTRL+C Check Flag	2.0
3301h	Set CTRL+C Check Flag	2.0
3306h	Get MS-DOS Version	5.0
35h	Get Interrupt Vector	2.0
54h	Get Verify State	2.0

8.3 Superseded Functions

MS-DOS version 2.0 and later versions have introduced functions that supersede many of the functions introduced in earlier versions. The newer functions are more efficient and easier to use. A programmer should not use a superseded function except to maintain compatibility with versions of MS-DOS earlier than version 2.0.

The following table shows the number and name of each superseded Interrupt 21h function and of any functions that supersede it:

Old function	New function
00h Terminate Program	4Ch End Program
01h Read Keyboard with Echo	3Fh Read File or Device
02h Display Character	40h Write File or Device
03h Auxiliary Input	3Fh Read File or Device
04h Auxiliary Output	40h Write File or Device
05h Print Character	40h Write File or Device
09h Display String	40h Write File or Device
0Ah Buffered Keyboard Input	3Fh Read File or Device
0Fh Open File with FCB	3Dh Open File with Handle
10h Close File with FCB	3Eh Close File with Handle
11h Find First File with FCB	4Eh Find First File
12h Find Next File with FCB	4Fh Find Next File
13h Delete File with FCB	41h Delete File
14h Sequential Read	3Fh Read File or Device
15h Sequential Write	40h Write File or Device
16h Create File with FCB	3Ch Create File with Handle
17h Rename File with FCB	56h Rename File
1Bh Get Default Drive Data	36h Get Disk Free Space
1Ch Get Drive Data	36h Get Disk Free Space
21h Random Read	3Fh Read File or Device
22h Random Write	40h Write File or Device
23h Get File Size	42h Move File Pointer
24h Set Random Record Number	42h Move File Pointer
26h Create New PSP	4B00h Load and Execute Program

Old function	New function
27h Random Block Read	3Fh Read File or Device
	42h Move File Pointer
28h Random Block Write	40h Write File or Device
	42h Move File Pointer

Some programmers may work on older software that still uses superseded functions. For the convenience of these programmers, this chapter includes reference pages for the superseded functions. New programs should not use superseded functions, because Microsoft may remove support for these functions at any time.

8.4 Obsolete Functions

This chapter does not include reference pages for Interrupt 21h functions that are obsolete—that is, not supported by MS-DOS version 5.0. Following are the numbers of the six obsolete functions: 18h, 1Dh, 1Eh, 20h, 61h, and 63h.

8.5 Interrupt 21h Function Reference

The remainder of this chapter describes the MS-DOS Interrupt 21h functions in detail. The reference page for each function provides the syntax, a statement of purpose, any parameter descriptions, and cross-references to any similar or related functions.

All the MS-DOS Interrupt 21h functions share a common interface. To use an Interrupt 21h function, a program should carry out the following actions:

- Load control information into each appropriate register, as shown in the syntax section for the function.
- Load the function number into the AH or AX register.
- Issue Interrupt 21h.

When MS-DOS returns control to a program, that program should examine any appropriate registers for error and return information, as shown in the syntax section for the function.

The reference pages that follow present the MS-DOS Interrupt 21h functions in numeric order.

■ Function 00h Terminate Program   Superseded

```
mov    ah, 00h    ;Terminate Program
int    21h
```

Terminate Program (Function 00h) terminates the current program and returns control to its parent program.

This function has been superseded by End Program (Function 4Ch).

Parameters   This function has no parameters.

Return Value   This function does not return.

Comments   This function is intended to be used by .COM programs. When a program calls this function, the CS register must contain the segment address of the program segment prefix (PSP).

This function carries out the following actions:

- Flushes the file buffers and closes files, unlocking any regions locked by the program.
- Restores Termination Address (Interrupt 22h) from offset 0Ah in the PSP (**pspTerminateVector** field).
- Restores the address of CTRL+C Handler (Interrupt 23h) from offset 0Eh in the PSP (**pspControlCVector** field).
- Restores the address of Critical-Error Handler (Interrupt 24h) from offset 12h in the PSP (**pspCritErrorVector** field).
- Frees any memory owned by the terminating process.

After completing these actions, this function transfers control to the address specified by offset 0Ah in the PSP.

See Also   Interrupt 20h Terminate Program
Interrupt 22h Termination Address
Interrupt 23h CTRL+C Handler
Interrupt 24h Critical-Error Handler
Function 4Ch End Program

■ Function 01h Read Keyboard with Echo   Superseded

```
mov    ah, 01h        ;Read Keyboard with Echo
int    21h

mov    InputChar, al  ;character from standard input
```

Read Keyboard with Echo (Function 01h) reads a character from the standard input device and writes it to the standard output device. If no character is ready, MS-DOS waits until one is available.

This function has been superseded by Read File or Device (Function 3Fh).

Parameters   This function has no parameters.

Return Value   The AL register contains the input character.

Comments   Upon reading a carriage-return character (0Dh), this function sends the standard output device a carriage return but not a linefeed (that is, it sets the cursor to the beginning of the current line).

If the character read from the keyboard is an extended key code (for example, if the user presses one of the function keys), Read Keyboard with Echo returns 00h and the program must call the function again to get the second byte of the extended key code.

See Also   Function 3Fh Read File or Device

■ Function 02h Display Character   **Superseded**

```
mov      dl, OutputChar   ;character to display

mov      ah, 02h          ;Display Character
int      21h
```

Display Character (Function 02h) displays a character on the standard output device.

This function has been superseded by Write File or Device (Function 40h).

Parameter   *OutputChar*   Specifies the ASCII value of the character to be displayed.

Return Value   This function has no return value.

Comment   When the standard output device is the screen, displaying a backspace character (ASCII 08h) moves the cursor back one position but does not erase characters.

See Also   Function 40h Write File or Device

■ Function 03h Auxiliary Input   Superseded

```
mov     ah, 03h         ;Auxiliary Input
int     21h

mov     InputChar, al   ;character from auxiliary input
```

Auxiliary Input (Function 03h) reads a character from the standard auxiliary device. If no character is available, MS-DOS waits.

This function has been superseded by Read File or Device (Function 3Fh).

Parameters   This function has no parameters.

Return Value   The AL register contains the ASCII value of the input character.

Comment   As this function receives characters from the standard auxiliary device, it does not save them in a buffer. Therefore, if the device is sending data faster than the program can process it, characters may be lost.

See Also   Function 04h Auxiliary Output
                    Function 3Fh Read File or Device

■ Function 04h Auxiliary Output   Superseded

```
mov     dl, OutputChar      ;character to output
mov     ah, 04h             ;Auxiliary Output
int     21h
```

Auxiliary Output (Function 04h) sends a character to the auxiliary output device. This function has been superseded by Write File or Device (Function 40h).

Parameter   *OutputChar*   Specifies the ASCII value of the character to be displayed.

Return Value   This function has no return value.

Comment   If the output device is busy, this function waits until the device is ready.

See Also   Function 03h Auxiliary Input
                   Function 40h Write File or Device

■ Function 05h Print Character   Superseded

```
mov     dl, OutputChar      ;character to print
mov     ah, 05h             ;Print Character
int     21h
```

Print Character (Function 05h) sends a character to the standard printer device. This function has been superseded by Write File or Device (Function 40h).

Parameter   *OutputChar*   Specifies the ASCII value of the character to be printed.

Return Value   This function has no return value.

Comment   If the printer device is busy, this function waits until the device is ready.

See Also   Function 40h Write File or Device

■ Function 06h Direct Console I/O

```
mov     dl, IOSwitch      ;0FFh = read, 00h through 0FEh = write

mov     ah, 06h           ;Direct Console I/O
int     21h
```

Direct Console I/O (Function 06h) reads a character from standard input or writes a character to standard output. If no character is available, MS-DOS does not wait. When this function reads a character from standard input; it does not send the character to standard output.

Parameter

IOSwitch   Specifies whether the function is to read from standard input or write to standard output. This parameter can be any value in the range 00h through 0FFh. The values result in the following actions:

Value	Action
0FFh	Reads a character from standard input; returns immediately if no character is ready.
00–0FEh	Writes the character to standard output.

Return Value

If output is requested, this function has no return value.

If input is requested and a character is ready, the AL register contains the character and the zero flag is cleared. If no character is ready, the AL register is undefined and the zero flag is set.

Comments

This function is typically used by programs that must be able to read and write any character or control code.

If the character read from the keyboard is an extended key code (for example, if the user presses one of the function keys), Direct Console I/O returns 00h and the program must call the function again to get the second byte of the extended key code.

This function does *not* check for CTRL+C.

See Also

Function 02h Display Character
Function 04h Auxiliary Output
Function 05h Print Character
Function 07h Direct Console Input
Function 08h Read Keyboard Without Echo
Function 09h Display String
Function 0Ah Buffered Keyboard Input
Function 0Bh Check Keyboard Status
Function 0Ch Flush Buffer, Read Keyboard
Function 3Fh Read File or Device
Function 40h Write File or Device

■ Function 07h Direct Console Input

```
mov      ah, 07h          ;Direct Console Input
int      21h

mov      InputChar, al    ;character from standard input
```

Direct Console Input (Function 07h) reads a character from standard input. If no character is available, MS-DOS waits until one is available. This function does not send the character to standard output.

Parameters   This function has no parameters.

Return Value   The AL register contains the ASCII value of the input character.

Comments   If the character read from standard input is an extended key code (for example, if the user presses one of the function keys), Direct Console Input returns 00h and the program must call the function again to get the second byte of the extended key code.

This function does *not* check for CTRL+C.

See Also   Function 06h Direct Console I/O
Function 08h Read Keyboard Without Echo
Function 0Ah Buffered Keyboard Input
Function 0Bh Check Keyboard Status
Function 0Ch Flush Buffer, Read Keyboard
Function 3Fh Read File or Device

▪ Function 08h Read Keyboard Without Echo

```
mov     ah, 08h         ;Read Keyboard Without Echo
int     21h

mov     InputChar, al   ;character from standard input
```

Read Keyboard Without Echo (Function 08h) reads a character from standard input.

This function does not send the character to an output device.

Parameters   This function has no parameters.

Return Value   The AL register contains the ASCII value of the input character.

Comment   If the character read from the keyboard is an extended key code (for example, if the user presses one of the function keys), Read Keyboard Without Echo returns 00h and the program must call the function again to get the second byte of the extended key code.

See Also   Function 06h Direct Console I/O
                    Function 07h Direct Console Input
                    Function 0Ah Buffered Keyboard Input
                    Function 0Bh Check Keyboard Status
                    Function 0Ch Flush Buffer, Read Keyboard
                    Function 3Fh Read File or Device

■ Function 09h Display String   Superseded

```
mov     dx, seg String
mov     ds, dx
mov     dx, offset String        ;ds:dx points to string to display

mov     ah, 09h                  ;Display String
int     21h
```

Display String (Function 09h) sends a string to standard output. The string must end with a dollar sign (ASCII 24h). MS-DOS displays characters up to but not including the dollar sign.

This function has been superseded by Write File or Device (Function 40h).

Parameter   *String*   Points to the buffer containing the string to be displayed.

Return Value   This function has no return value.

Comment   This function cannot send a string containing a dollar sign (ASCII 24h) to standard output. The string may contain any other characters.

See Also   Function 40h Write File or Device

■ Function 0Ah Buffered Keyboard Input   Superseded

```
mov     dx, seg Buffer
mov     ds, dx
mov     dx, offset Buffer        ;ds:dx points to buffer for input
mov     al, MaxLength
mov     byte ptr Buffer[0], al   ;maximum amount of input

mov     ah, 0Ah                  ;Buffered Keyboard Input
int     21h
```

Buffered Keyboard Input (Function 0Ah) reads a string from standard input and echoes it to standard output until a program-defined number of characters is reached or until the user presses the ENTER key.

This function has been superseded by Read File or Device (Function 3Fh).

Parameters   *Buffer*   Points to the buffer where the string will be returned. The buffer must have the following form:

Offset	Contents
00h	Specifies the maximum number of characters, including the carriage return, to be copied to the buffer. This value, set by the program, must not exceed 255 (0FFh).
01h	Receives the actual number of characters copied to the buffer, not counting the carriage return. The function sets this value.

Bytes from offset 02h up to the end of the buffer receive the typed characters. The entire buffer must be at least two bytes longer than the size specified at offset 00h.

MaxLength   Specifies the maximum length of the input string.

Return Value   The string area of the buffer (starting at the third byte in the buffer) contains the input string, and the second byte of the buffer contains the number of characters read (not counting the carriage return).

Comment   Characters are read from standard input and placed in the buffer, beginning at the third byte, until a carriage-return character (ASCII 0Dh) is read. When the number of characters in the buffer reaches one fewer than the maximum, additional characters read are ignored and a beep character (ASCII 07h) is sent to standard output until a carriage-return character is read.

See Also   Function 3Fh Read File or Device

Function 0Bh Check Keyboard Status

```
mov     ah, OBh     ;Check Keyboard Status
int     21h

cmp     al, O       ;zero means not ready
je      not_ready
```

Check Keyboard Status (Function 0Bh) determines whether a character is available from standard input.

Parameters

This function has no parameters.

Return Value

If a character is available, the AL register contains 0FFh. Otherwise, the AL register contains 00h.

Comment

This function does not indicate how many characters are available, only that there is at least one.

See Also

Function 01h Read Keyboard with Echo
Function 06h Direct Console I/O
Function 07h Direct Console Input
Function 08h Read Keyboard Without Echo
Function 0Ah Buffered Keyboard Input
Function 3Fh Read File or Device

■ Function 0Ch Flush Buffer, Read Keyboard

```
mov     al, FunctionNumber    ;input function (01h, 06h, 07h, or 08h)

mov     ah, 0Ch               ;Flush Buffer, Read Keyboard
int     21h

mov     InputChar, al         ;character from standard input
```

Flush Buffer, Read Keyboard (Function 0Ch) empties the standard input buffer. Further processing depends on the value in AL when the function is called.

Parameter   *FunctionNumber*   Specifies the number of a read-keyboard function that is to be executed after the standard input buffer is flushed. The following functions can be specified:

Value	Function name
01h	Read Keyboard with Echo
06h	Direct Console I/O
07h	Direct Console Input
08h	Read Keyboard Without Echo

The value 0Ah is reserved and must not be used.

Return Value   If a function number is specified, the AL register contains the return value for that function. If no function number is specified (that is, *FunctionNumber* is not 01h, 06h, 07h, or 08h), the AL register contains 00h and the standard input buffer is empty.

Comments   This function clears all keyboard input received before a program requests new input, so that the program does not receive a character that was entered before the request.

If Flush Buffer, Read Keyboard is used to call Direct Console I/O (Function 06h), the DL register must contain 0FFh (Flush Buffer, Read Keyboard cannot be used to call Direct Console I/O and write a character).

See Also   Function 01h Read Keyboard with Echo
Function 06h Direct Console I/O
Function 07h Direct Console Input
Function 08h Read Keyboard Without Echo
Function 3Fh Read File or Device

■ Function 0Dh Reset Drive

```
mov     ah, 0Dh        ;Reset Drive
int     21h
```

Reset Drive (Function 0Dh) flushes all file buffers. Any write operations that are buffered by MS-DOS are performed, and all waiting data is written to the appropriate drive.

Parameters   This function has no parameters.

Return Value   This function has no return value.

Comments   Reset Drive is normally used by CTRL+C interrupt handlers.

This function does not update directory entries; programs must close changed files to update their directory entries.

See Also   Function 10h Close File with FCB
                      Function 3Eh Close File with Handle

■ Function 0Eh Set Default Drive

```
mov     dl, DriveNumber      ;drive (0 = A, 1 = B, 2 = C, etc.)

mov     ah, 0Eh              ;Set Default Drive
int     21h

mov     LogicalDrives, al    ;number of logical drives
```

Set Default Drive (Function 0Eh) sets the specified drive to be the default drive and returns a count of the logical drives in the system.

Parameter

DriveNumber Specifies the number of the drive to be made the default drive (0 = A, 1 = B, 2 = C, and so on).

Return Value

The AL register contains the number of logical drives in the system. This number includes floppy disk drives, RAM disks, and logical drives on any hard disks in the system.

Comment

The number of logical drives in the system is not necessarily the same as the number of physical drives. In addition, the number of logical drives returned may not map directly to drive letters. For example, if the function returns 5, drives A, B, C, D, and E are not necessarily valid drive letters.

See Also

Function 19h Get Default Drive
Function 3Bh Change Current Directory

■ Function 0Fh Open File with FCB   Superseded

```
        mov     dx, seg FileFCB
        mov     ds, dx
        mov     dx, offset FileFCB   ;ds:dx points to FCB

        mov     ah, OFh              ;Open File with FCB
        int     21h

        cmp     al, O                ;zero means success
        jne     error_handler
```

Open File with FCB (Function 0Fh) opens a file identified by the file control block (FCB).

This function has been superseded by Open File with Handle (Function 3Dh).

Parameter   *FileFCB*   Points to an **FCB** structure that identifies the file to open. The **fcbDriveId**, **fcbFileName**, and **fcbExtent** fields must specify the filename and drive; all other fields must be set to zero. The **FCB** structure has the following form:

```
FCB     STRUC
        fcbDriveID      db   ?             ;drive no. (O=default, 1=A, etc.)
        fcbFileName     db   '????????'    ;filename
        fcbExtent       db   '???'         ;file extension
        fcbCurBlockNo   dw   ?             ;current block number
        fcbRecSize      dw   ?             ;record size
        fcbFileSize     db   4 dup (?)     ;size of file, in bytes
        fcbFileDate     dw   ?             ;date file last modified
        fcbFileTime     dw   ?             ;time file last modified
        fcbReserved     db   8 dup (?)     ;reserved
        fcbCurRecNo     db   ?             ;current record number
        fcbRandomRecNo  db   4 dup (?)     ;random record number
FCB     ENDS
```

For a full description of the **FCB** structure, see Chapter 3, "File System."

Return Value   If the file is found, the AL register contains 00h and the remaining fields in the **FCB** structure are filled in. Otherwise, the AL register contains 0FFh.

Comments   This function does not support paths, so it is possible to open only files in the current directory.

If the calling program specifies zero for the drive number, MS-DOS searches for the file on the default drive. If the system finds the file, it fills in the **fcbDriveId** field with the correct drive.

When a file is opened, MS-DOS sets the current block number in the FCB to zero (the file pointer is at the beginning of the file).

MS-DOS initially sets the record size to 128 bytes. If some other record size is to be used, the size must be set after the call to Open File with FCB but before any other disk operation.

See Also   Function 10h Close File with FCB
Function 3Dh Open File with Handle

■ Function 10h Close File with FCB   Superseded

```
        mov     dx, seg FileFCB
        mov     ds, dx
        mov     dx, offset FileFCB    ;ds:dx points to FCB

        mov     ah, 10h               ;Close File with FCB
        int     21h

        cmp     al, 0                 ;zero means success
        jne     error_handler
```

Close File with FCB (Function 10h) closes the open file identified by the file control block (FCB).

This function has been superseded by Close File with Handle (Function 3Eh).

Parameter   *FileFCB*   Points to an **FCB** structure that identifies the file to close. The structure must have been previously opened by using Open File with FCB (Function 0Fh) or Create File with FCB (Function 16h). The **FCB** structure has the following form:

```
FCB       STRUC
     fcbDriveID      db    ?               ;drive no. (0=default, 1=A, etc.)
     fcbFileName     db    '????????'      ;filename
     fcbExtent       db    '???'           ;file extension
     fcbCurBlockNo   dw    ?               ;current block number
     fcbRecSize      dw    ?               ;record size
     fcbFileSize     db    4 dup (?)       ;size of file, in bytes
     fcbFileDate     dw    ?               ;date file last modified
     fcbFileTime     dw    ?               ;time file last modified
     fcbReserved     db    8 dup (?)       ;reserved
     fcbCurRecNo     db    ?               ;current record number
     fcbRandomRecNo  db    4 dup (?)       ;random record number
FCB       ENDS
```

For a full description of the **FCB** structure, see Chapter 3, "File System."

Return Value   If the file is found, the AL register contains 00h and the remaining fields in the **FCB** structure are filled in. Otherwise, the AL register contains 0FFh.

Comments   Close File with FCB searches the current directory for the file named in the **FCB** structure. If it finds a directory entry for the file, it completes any buffered write operations (buffered information is written to the disk, and the buffers are freed). MS-DOS then updates the directory entry, if necessary, to match the **FCB** structure and closes the file. Further requests to read from or write to the file will fail.

After a program changes a file, it must call this function to update the directory entry. Programs should close any **FCB** structure (even one for a file that has not been changed) when they no longer need access to the file.

This function does not support paths, so it is possible to close only files in the current directory.

See Also   Function 0Fh Open File with FCB
Function 3Eh Close File with Handle

■ Function 11h Find First File with FCB   Superseded

```
mov     dx, seg FileFCB
mov     ds, dx
mov     dx, offset FileFCB    ;ds:dx points to FCB

mov     ah, 11h               ;Find First File with FCB
int     21h

cmp     al, O                 ;zero means success
jne     error_handler
```

Find First File with FCB (Function 11h) searches the current directory for the first file matching the filename specified by the file control block (FCB).

This function has been superseded by Find First File (Function 4Eh).

Parameter   *FileFCB*   Points to an **FCB** structure or **EXTENDEDFCB** structure that identifies the file or files to search for.

If an **FCB** structure is given, the fields **fcbDriveID**, **fcbFileName**, and **fcbExtent** must specify the filename(s). The filename can include wildcards. All other fields should be zero. The **FCB** structure has the following form:

```
FCB        STRUC
    fcbDriveID      db   ?              ;drive no. (O=default, 1=A, etc.)
    fcbFileName     db   '????????'     ;filename
    fcbExtent       db   '???'          ;file extension
    fcbCurBlockNo   dw   ?              ;current block number
    fcbRecSize      dw   ?              ;record size
    fcbFileSize     db   4 dup (?)      ;size of file, in bytes
    fcbFileDate     dw   ?              ;date file last modified
    fcbFileTime     dw   ?              ;time file last modified
    fcbReserved     db   8 dup (?)      ;reserved
    fcbCurRecNo     db   ?              ;current record number
    fcbRandomRecNo  db   4 dup (?)      ;random record number
FCB        ENDS
```

For a full description of the **FCB** structure, see Chapter 3, "File System."

If an **EXTENDEDFCB** structure is given, the fields **extDriveID**, **extFileName**, and **extExtent** must specify the filename(s). The filename can include wildcards. The **extAttribute** field must specify the attributes of the file to search for. All other fields should be zero. The **EXTENDEDFCB** structure has the following form:

```
EXTENDEDFCB    STRUC
    extSignature    db   Offh           ;extended FCB signature
    extReserved     db   5 dup(O)       ;reserved bytes
    extAttribute    db   ?              ;attribute byte
                                        ;file control block (FCB)
    extDriveID      db   ?              ;drive no. (O=default, 1=A, etc.)
    extFileName     db   '????????'     ;filename
    extExtent       db   '???'          ;file extension
    extCurBlockNo   dw   ?              ;current block number
    extRecSize      dw   ?              ;record size
    extFileSize     db   4 dup (?)      ;size of file, in bytes
    extFileDate     dw   ?              ;date file last modified
    extFileTime     dw   ?              ;time file last modified
    extReserved     db   8 dup (?)      ;reserved bytes
    extCurRecNo     db   ?              ;current record number
    extRandomRecNo  db   4 dup (?)      ;random record number
EXTENDEDFCB    ENDS
```

For a full description of the **EXTENDEDFCB** structure, see Chapter 3, "File System."

Return Value

If a file matching the name in the **FCB** structure or **EXTENDEDFCB** structure is found, the AL register contains 00h and the buffer at the current disk transfer address (DTA) receives a **DIRENTRY** structure defining the file. Otherwise, the AL register contains 0FFh.

Comments

If a program uses Find Next File with FCB (Function 12h) to continue searching for matching filenames, it must not alter or open the original **FCB** structure.

If the function is successful and an **FCB** structure was given, the function copies the drive number used in the search (1 = A, 2 = B, and so on) to the first byte at the DTA. It copies a **DIRENTRY** structure that defines the file starting at the second byte at the DTA.

If the function is successful and an **EXTENDEDFCB** was given, the function copies an **EXTHEADER** structure that starts at the first byte at the DTA and then copies a **DIRENTRY** structure that defines the file immediately after the **EXTHEADER** structure.

The **DIRENTRY** structure has the following form:

```
DIRENTRY      STRUC
    deName          db  '????????'      ;name
    deExtension     db  '???'           ;extension
    deAttributes    db  ?               ;attributes
    deReserved      db  10 dup (?)      ;reserved
    deTime          dw  ?               ;time
    deDate          dw  ?               ;date
    deStartCluster  dw  ?               ;starting cluster
    deFileSize      dd  ?               ;file size
DIRENTRY      ENDS
```

For a full description of the **DIRENTRY** structure, see Chapter 3, "File System."

The **EXTHEADER** structure has the following form:

```
EXTHEADER STRUC
    ehSignature     db  0ffh            ;extended signature
    ehReserved      db  5 dup (0)       ;reserved
    ehSearchAttrs   db  ?               ;attribute byte
EXTHEADER ENDS
```

For a full description of the **EXTHEADER** structure, see Chapter 3, "File System."

See Also

Function 4Eh Find First File

Function 12h Find Next File with FCB   Superseded

```
mov     dx, seg FileFCB
mov     ds, dx
mov     dx, offset FileFCB    ;ds:dx points to FCB

mov     ah, 12h               ;Find Next File with FCB
int     21h

cmp     al, 0                 ;zero means success
jne     error_handler
```

Find Next File with FCB (Function 12h) searches the current directory for additional files matching the filename specified by the file control block (FCB).

A program must initiate a file search with Find First File with FCB (Function 11h) before it can use Find Next File with FCB.

This function has been superseded by Find Next File (Function 4Fh).

Parameter   *FileFCB*   Points to an **FCB** or **EXTENDEDFCB** structure that identifies the file or files to search for. The structure must have been previously filled by using Find First File with FCB (Function 11h). The **FCB** structure has the following form:

```
FCB        STRUC
    fcbDriveID     db ?              ;drive no. (0=default, 1=A, etc.)
    fcbFileName    db '????????'     ;filename
    fcbExtent      db '???'          ;file extension
    fcbCurBlockNo  dw ?              ;current block number
    fcbRecSize     dw ?              ;record size
    fcbFileSize    db 4 dup (?)      ;size of file, in bytes
    fcbFileDate    dw ?              ;date file last modified
    fcbFileTime    dw ?              ;time file last modified
    fcbReserved    db 8 dup (?)      ;reserved
    fcbCurRecNo    db ?              ;current record number
    fcbRandomRecNo db 4 dup (?)      ;random record number
FCB        ENDS
```

For a full description of the **FCB** structure, see Chapter 3, "File System."

The **EXTENDEDFCB** structure has the following form:

```
EXTENDEDFCB     STRUC
    extSignature   db 0ffh           ;extended FCB signature
    extReserved    db 5 dup(0)       ;reserved bytes
    extAttribute   db ?              ;attribute byte
                                     ;file control block (FCB)
    extDriveID     db ?              ;drive no. (0=default, 1=A, etc.)
    extFileName    db '????????'     ;filename
    extExtent      db '???'          ;file extension
    extCurBlockNo  dw ?              ;current block number
    extRecSize     dw ?              ;record size
    extFileSize    db 4 dup (?)      ;size of file, in bytes
    extFileDate    dw ?              ;date file last modified
    extFileTime    dw ?              ;time file last modified
    extReserved    db 8 dup (?)      ;reserved bytes
    extCurRecNo    db ?              ;current record number
    extRandomRecNo db 4 dup (?)      ;random record number
EXTENDEDFCB     ENDS
```

For a full description of the **EXTENDEDFCB** structure, see Chapter 3, "File System."

Return Value

If a file matching the name in the **FCB** structure or **EXTENDEDFCB** structure is found, the AL register contains 00h and the buffer at the current disk transfer address (DTA) receives a **DIRENTRY** structure defining the file. Otherwise, the AL register contains 0FFh.

Comments

If the function is successful and an **FCB** structure was given, the function copies the drive number used in the search (1 = A, 2 = B, and so on) to the first byte at the DTA. It copies a **DIRENTRY** structure that defines the file starting at the second byte at the DTA.

If the function is successful and an **EXTENDEDFCB** was given, the function copies an **EXTHEADER** structure that starts at the first byte at the DTA and then copies a **DIRENTRY** structure that defines the file immediately after the **EXTHEADER** structure.

The **DIRENTRY** structure has the following form:

```
DIRENTRY        STRUC
    deName          db  '????????'      ;name
    deExtension     db  '???'           ;extension
    deAttributes    db  ?               ;attributes
    deReserved      db  10 dup(?)       ;reserved
    deTime          dw  ?               ;time
    deDate          dw  ?               ;date
    deStartCluster  dw  ?               ;starting cluster
    deFileSize      dd  ?               ;file size
DIRENTRY        ENDS
```

For a full description of the **DIRENTRY** structure, see Chapter 3, "File System."

The **EXTHEADER** structure has the following form:

```
EXTHEADER STRUC
    ehSignature     db  0ffh            ;extended signature
    ehReserved      db  5 dup(0)        ;reserved
    ehSearchAttrs   db  ?               ;attribute byte
EXTHEADER ENDS
```

For a full description of the **EXTHEADER** structure, see Chapter 3, "File System."

See Also

Function 4Fh Find Next File

■ Function 13h Delete File with FCB   Superseded

```
mov     dx, seg FileFCB
mov     ds, dx
mov     dx, offset FileFCB   ;ds:dx points to FCB

mov     ah, 13h              ;Delete File with FCB
int     21h

cmp     al, 0                ;zero means success
jne     error_handler
```

Delete File with FCB (Function 13h) deletes the file or files identified by the file control block (FCB).

This function has been superseded by Delete File (Function 41h).

Parameter   *FileFCB*   Points to an **FCB** structure that identifies the file or files to delete. The **fcbDriveId**, **fcbFileName**, and **fcbExtent** fields must specify the filename and drive. The filename can include wildcards. All other fields must be zero. The **FCB** structure has the following form:

```
FCB     STRUC
        fcbDriveID      db   ?                  ;drive no. (0=default, 1=A, etc.)
        fcbFileName     db   '????????'         ;filename
        fcbExtent       db   '???'              ;file extension
        fcbCurBlockNo   dw   ?                  ;current block number
        fcbRecSize      dw   ?                  ;record size
        fcbFileSize     db   4 dup (?)          ;size of file, in bytes
        fcbFileDate     dw   ?                  ;date file last modified
        fcbFileTime     dw   ?                  ;time file last modified
        fcbReserved     db   8 dup (?)          ;reserved
        fcbCurRecNo     db   ?                  ;current record number
        fcbRandomRecNo  db   4 dup (?)          ;random record number
FCB     ENDS
```

For a full description of the **FCB** structure, see Chapter 3, "File System."

Return Value   If a file matching the name in the **FCB** structure is found and deleted, the AL register contains 00h. Otherwise (if a matching file cannot be found), the AL register contains 0FFh.

Comments   Programs should not delete open files.

If the filename in the **FCB** structure contains wildcards, all matching files are deleted.

This function can be used to delete files on a network drive but only if the network has granted delete (or similar) access to the given file or drive.

See Also   Function 41h Delete File

■ Function 14h Sequential Read   Superseded

```
mov     dx, seg FileFCB
mov     ds, dx
mov     dx, offset FileFCB    ;ds:dx points to FCB

mov     ah, 14h               ;Sequential Read
int     21h

cmp     al, 0                 ;zero means success
jne     error_handler
```

Sequential Read (Function 14h) reads a record from the file identified by the file control block (FCB). Data read from the file is written to the memory at the current disk transfer address (DTA).

This function has been superseded by Read File or Device (Function 3Fh).

Parameter   *FileFCB*   Points to an **FCB** structure that identifies an open file. The structure must have been previously filled by using Open File with FCB (Function 0Fh) or Create File with FCB (Function 16h). The **fcbCurBlockNo** and **fcbCurRecNo** fields in the **FCB** structure must specify the record to read. The **FCB** structure has the following form:

```
FCB     STRUC
    fcbDriveID      db  ?                ;drive no. (0=default, 1=A, etc.)
    fcbFileName     db  '????????'       ;filename
    fcbExtent       db  '???'            ;file extension
    fcbCurBlockNo   dw  ?                ;current block number
    fcbRecSize      dw  ?                ;record size
    fcbFileSize     db  4 dup (?)        ;size of file, in bytes
    fcbFileDate     dw  ?                ;date file last modified
    fcbFileTime     dw  ?                ;time file last modified
    fcbReserved     db  8 dup (?)        ;reserved
    fcbCurRecNo     db  ?                ;current record number
    fcbRandomRecNo db  4 dup (?)         ;random record number
FCB     ENDS
```

For a full description of the **FCB** structure, see Chapter 3, "File System."

Return Value   If the function is successful, the AL register contains 00h, and the memory at the DTA contains the record read from the file. Otherwise, the AL register contains an error value, which may be one of the following values:

Value	Meaning
01h	End of file encountered, no data in record
02h	Segment boundary overlapped by DTA, read canceled
03h	End of file encountered, partial record at DTA (rest of record filled with zeros)

Comments   MS-DOS increments the **fcbCurBlockNo** and **fcbCurRecNo** fields in the **FCB** structure after a successful read operation.

This function can be used to read files on a network drive but only if the network has granted read (or similar) access to the given file or drive.

See Also   Function 0Fh Open File with FCB
Function 15h Sequential Write
Function 16h Create File with FCB
Function 3Fh Read File or Device

■ Function 15h Sequential Write   Superseded

```
mov     dx, seg FileFCB
mov     ds, dx
mov     dx, offset FileFCB   ;ds:dx points to FCB

mov     ah, 15h              ;Sequential Write
int     21h

cmp     al, 0                ;zero means success
jne     error_handler
```

Sequential Write (Function 15h) writes the data at the current disk transfer address (DTA) to a record in the file identified by the file control block (FCB).

This function has been superseded by Write File or Device (Function 40h).

Parameter   *FileFCB*   Points to an **FCB** structure that identifies an open file. The structure must have been previously filled by using Open File with FCB (Function 0Fh) or Create File with FCB (Function 16h). The **fcbCurBlockNo** and **fcbCurRecNo** fields in the **FCB** structure specify the record to write. The **FCB** structure has the following form:

```
FCB     STRUC
        fcbDriveID      db   ?            ;drive no. (0=default, 1=A, etc.)
        fcbFileName     db   '????????'   ;filename
        fcbExtent       db   '???'        ;file extension
        fcbCurBlockNo   dw   ?            ;current block number
        fcbRecSize      dw   ?            ;record size
        fcbFileSize     db   4 dup (?)    ;size of file, in bytes
        fcbFileDate     dw   ?            ;date file last modified
        fcbFileTime     dw   ?            ;time file last modified
        fcbReserved     db   8 dup (?)    ;reserved
        fcbCurRecNo     db   ?            ;current record number
        fcbRandomRecNo  db   4 dup (?)    ;random record number
FCB     ENDS
```

For a full description of the **FCB** structure, see Chapter 3, "File System."

Return Value   If the function is successful, the AL register contains 00h. Otherwise, the AL register contains 01h if the disk is full or 02h if the DTA overlapped a segment boundary. In either case, the write operation is canceled.

Comments   MS-DOS increments the **fcbCurBlockNo** and **fcbCurRecNo** fields in the **FCB** structure after a successful write operation.

This function can be used to write files on a network drive but only if the network has granted write (or similar) access to the given file or drive.

See Also   Function 0Fh Open File with FCB
Function 14h Sequential Read
Function 16h Create File with FCB
Function 40h Write File or Device

■ Function 16h Create File with FCB   Superseded

```
mov     dx, seg FileFCB
mov     ds, dx
mov     dx, offset FileFCB    ;ds:dx points to FCB

mov     ah, 16h               ;Create File with FCB
int     21h

cmp     al, 0                 ;zero means success
jne     error_handler
```

Create File with FCB (16h) creates a new file having the filename specified by the file control block (FCB). If a file with the specified name already exists, MS-DOS opens it and truncates it to zero length.

This function has been superseded by Create File with Handle (Function 3Ch).

Parameter

FileFCB   Points to an **FCB** structure that identifies the file to create. The **fcbDriveId**, **fcbFileName**, and **fcbExtent** fields must specify the filename and drive. All other fields must be zero. The **FCB** structure has the following form:

```
FCB     STRUC
        fcbDriveID    db  ?               ;drive no. (0=default, 1=A, etc.)
        fcbFileName   db  '????????'      ;filename
        fcbExtent     db  '???'           ;file extension
        fcbCurBlockNo dw  ?               ;current block number
        fcbRecSize    dw  ?               ;record size
        fcbFileSize   db  4 dup (?)       ;size of file, in bytes
        fcbFileDate   dw  ?               ;date file last modified
        fcbFileTime   dw  ?               ;time file last modified
        fcbReserved   db  8 dup (?)       ;reserved
        fcbCurRecNo   db  ?               ;current record number
        fcbRandomRecNo db 4 dup (?)       ;random record number
FCB     ENDS
```

For a full description of the **FCB** structure, see Chapter 3, "File System."

Return Value

If the function is successful, the AL register contains 00h. Otherwise, the AL register contains 0FFh.

Comments

This function can be used to create files on a network drive but only if the network has granted create (or similar) access to the given drive.

The **EXTENDEDFCB** structure can be used in place of the **FCB** structure to assign attributes to the file when creating it. In this case, the **EXTENDEDFCB** structure is used for all subsequent read, write, and close operations.

See Also

Function 3Ch Create File with Handle

■ Function 17h Rename File with FCB   Superseded

```
        mov     dx, seg FilesFCB
        mov     ds, dx
        mov     dx, offset FilesFCB     ;ds:dx points to RENAMEFCB structure

        mov     ah, 17h                 ;Rename File with FCB
        int     21h

        cmp     al, O                   ;zero means success
        jne     error_handler
```

Rename File with FCB (Function 17h) changes the name of an existing file.

This function has been superseded by Rename File (Function 56h).

Parameter   *FilesFCB*   Points to a **RENAMEFCB** structure that contains the old and new names for the file. The **RENAMEFCB** structure has the following form:

```
RENAMEFCB    STRUC
    renDriveID      db ?                ;drive no. (O=default, 1=A, etc.)
    renOldName      db '????????'       ;old filename
    renOldExtent    db '???'            ;old file extension
    renReserved1    db 5 dup (?)        ;reserved
    renNewName      db '????????'       ;new filename
    renNewExtent    db '???'            ;new extension
    renReserved2    db 9 dup (?)        ;reserved
RENAMEFCB    ENDS
```

For a full description of the **RENAMEFCB** structure, see Chapter 3, "File System."

Return Value   If the function is successful, the AL register contains 00h. Otherwise, the AL register contains 0FFh.

Comments   If the filename in the **RENAMEFCB** structure contains wildcards, all matching files are renamed.

If the new name matches the name of an existing file, the function returns 0FFh without renaming the file.

See Also   Function 56h Rename File

■ Function 19h Get Default Drive

```
mov     ah, 19h             ;Get Default Drive
int     21h

mov     DriveNumber, al     ;drive (0 = A, 1 = B, etc.)
```

Get Default Drive (Function 19h) returns the number of the default drive.

Parameters   This function has no parameters.

Return Value   The AL register contains the drive number (0 = A, 1 = B, and so on).

See Also   Function 0Eh Set Default Drive

■ Function 1Ah Set Disk Transfer Address

```
mov     dx, seg DTA
mov     ds, dx
mov     dx, offset DTA   ;ds:dx is new disk transfer address

mov     ah, 1Ah          ;Set Disk Transfer Address
int     21h
```

Set Disk Transfer Address (Function 1Ah) sets the address of the buffer that MS-DOS uses for file I/O (with file control blocks, or FCBs) and disk searches (with and without FCBs).

Parameter   *DTA*   Points to the buffer MS-DOS is to use for file operations.

Return Value   This function has no return value.

Comments   When a program starts, the default disk transfer address (DTA) is offset 0080h in the program segment prefix (PSP). If a program sets the DTA, the new buffer must be large enough to accommodate the file record size (for example, if the file record size is 128 bytes, the buffer must be at least 128 bytes). In addition, the buffer must not overlap a segment boundary. The default DTA should not be used for read or write operations with record sizes that exceed 128 bytes.

Programs can retrieve the current DTA with Get Disk Transfer Address (Function 2Fh).

See Also   Function 11h Find First File with FCB
Function 12h Find Next File with FCB
Function 14h Sequential Read
Function 15h Sequential Write
Function 21h Random Read
Function 22h Random Write
Function 27h Random Block Read
Function 28h Random Block Write
Function 2Fh Get Disk Transfer Address
Function 4Eh Find First File
Function 4Fh Find Next File

■ Function 1Bh Get Default Drive Data   Superseded

```
mov     ah, 1Bh                 ;Get Default Drive Data
int     21h

cmp     al, OFFh                ;OFFh means error
je      error_handler

mov     SecPerCluster, al       ;sectors per cluster
mov     BytesPerSector, cx      ;bytes per sector
mov     NumClusters, dx         ;number of clusters
mov     al, byte ptr [bx]       ;ds:bx points to media descriptor
mov     MediaDesc, al
```

Get Default Drive Data (1Bh) retrieves information about the disk in the default drive.

This function has been superseded by Get Disk Free Space (Function 36h).

Parameters   This function has no parameters.

Return Values   If the function is successful, the AL, CX, DX, and DS:BX registers contain the following information:

Register	Contents
AL	Number of sectors in a cluster.
CX	Number of bytes in a sector.
DX	Number of clusters on the disk.
DS:BX	Points to the media descriptor.

Otherwise, the AL register contains 0FFh.

Comments   If Get Default Drive Data fails, the default drive was invalid or a disk error occurred. A program must check the return values from this function to determine whether it has valid disk information.

Following are the most commonly used media descriptors and their corresponding media:

Value	Type of medium
0F0h	3.5-inch, 2 sides, 18 sectors/track (1.44 MB); 3.5-inch, 2 sides, 36 sectors/track (2.88 MB); 5.25-inch, 2 sides, 15 sectors/track (1.2 MB). This value is also used to describe other media types.
0F8h	Hard disk, any capacity.
0F9h	3.5-inch, 2 sides, 9 sectors/track, 80 tracks/side (720K); 5.25-inch, 2 sides, 15 sectors/track, 40 tracks/side (1.2 MB).
0FAh	5.25-inch, 1 side, 8 sectors/track, (320K).
0FBh	3.5-inch, 2 sides, 8 sectors/track (640K).
0FCh	5.25-inch, 1 side, 9 sectors/track, 40 tracks/side (180K).
0FDh	5.25-inch, 2 sides, 9 sectors/track, 40 tracks/side (360K). This value is also used for 8-inch disks.
0FEh	5.25-inch, 1 side, 8 sectors/track, 40 tracks/side (160K). This value is also used for 8-inch disks.
0FFh	5.25-inch, 2 sides, 8 sectors/track, 40 tracks/side (320K).

Get Default Drive Data modifies the DS register. A program should save the contents of the register before calling this function and restore the contents of the register after retrieving the media descriptor.

See Also   Function 1Ch Get Drive Data
Function 36h Get Disk Free Space

■ Function 1Ch Get Drive Data   Superseded

```
mov     dl, DriveNum          ;drive (0 = default, 1 = A, 2 = B, etc.)

mov     ah, 1Ch               ;Get Drive Data
int     21h

cmp     al, 0FFh              ;0FFh means error
jz      error_handler

mov     SecPerCluster, al     ;sectors per cluster
mov     BytesPerSector, cx    ;bytes per sector
mov     NumClusters, dx       ;number of clusters
mov     al, byte ptr [bx]     ;ds:bx points to media descriptor
mov     MediaDesc, al
```

Get Drive Data (Function 1Ch) retrieves information about the disk in the specified drive.

This function has been superseded by Get Disk Free Space (Function 36h).

Parameter   *DriveNum*   Specifies the number of the drive for which to return information (0 = default, 1 = A, 2 = B, and so on).

Return Values   If the function is successful, the AL, CX, DX, and DS:BX registers contain the following information:

Register	Contents
AL	Number of sectors in a cluster.
CX	Number of bytes in a sector.
DX	Number of clusters on the disk.
DS:BX	Points to the media descriptor.

Otherwise, the AL register contains 0FFh.

Comments   If Get Drive Data fails, the default drive was invalid or a disk error occurred. A program must check the return values from this function to determine whether it has valid disk information.

Following are the most commonly used media descriptors and their corresponding media:

Value	Type of medium
0F0h	3.5-inch, 2 sides, 18 sectors/track (1.44 MB); 3.5-inch, 2 sides, 36 sectors/track (2.88 MB); 5.25-inch, 2 sides, 15 sectors/track (1.2 MB). This value is also used to describe other media types.
0F8h	Hard disk, any capacity.
0F9h	3.5-inch, 2 sides, 9 sectors/track, 80 tracks/side (720K); 5.25-inch, 2 sides, 15 sectors/track, 40 tracks/side (1.2 MB).
0FAh	5.25-inch, 1 side, 8 sectors/track, (320K).
0FBh	3.5-inch, 2 sides, 8 sectors/track (640K).
0FCh	5.25-inch, 1 side, 9 sectors/track, 40 tracks/side (180K).
0FDh	5.25-inch, 2 sides, 9 sectors/track, 40 tracks/side (360K). This value is also used for 8-inch disks.

Value	Type of medium
0FEh	5.25-inch, 1 side, 8 sectors/track, 40 tracks/side (160K). This value is also used for 8-inch disks.
0FFh	5.25-inch, 2 sides, 8 sectors/track, 40 tracks/side (320K).

Get Drive Data modifies the DS register. A program should save the contents of the register before calling this function and restore the contents of the register after retrieving the media descriptor.

See Also

Function 1Bh Get Default Drive Data
Function 36h Get Disk Free Space

■ Function 1Fh Get Default DPB

```
mov     ah, 1Fh                             ;Get Default DPB
int     21h

cmp     al, OFFh                            ;OFFh means error
jz      error_handler

mov     word ptr [defaultDPB], bx
mov     word ptr [defaultDPB+2], ds         ;ds:bx points to default DPB
```

Get Default DPB (Function 1Fh) retrieves drive parameters for the default drive.

Parameters   This function has no parameters.

Return Value   If the function is successful, the AL register contains zero and the DS:BX registers point to a **DPB** structure that contains the drive parameters. The DS register contains the segment address, and the BX register contains the offset. Otherwise, if the default drive was invalid or a disk error occurred, the AL register contains 0FFh.

Comments   If Get Default DPB is successful, the DS:BX registers point to a **DPB** structure, which has the following form:

```
DPB     STRUC
        dpbDrive        db  ?       ;drive number (O = A, 1 = B, etc.)
        dpbUnit         db  ?       ;unit number for driver
        dpbSectorSize   dw  ?       ;sector size, in bytes
        dpbClusterMask  db  ?       ;sectors per cluster - 1
        dpbClusterShift db  ?       ;sectors per cluster, as power of 2
        dpbFirstFAT     dw  ?       ;first sector containing FAT
        dpbFATCount     db  ?       ;number of FATs
        dpbRootEntries  dw  ?       ;number of root-directory entries
        dpbFirstSector  dw  ?       ;first sector of first cluster
        dpbMaxCluster   dw  ?       ;number of clusters on drive + 1
        dpbFATSize      dw  ?       ;number of sectors occupied by FAT
        dpbDirSector    dw  ?       ;first sector containing directory
        dpbDriverAddr   dd  ?       ;address of device driver
        dpbMedia        db  ?       ;media descriptor
        dpbFirstAccess  db  ?       ;indicates access to drive
        dpbNextDPB      dd  ?       ;address of next drive parameter block
        dpbNextFree     dw  ?       ;last allocated cluster
        dpbFreeCnt      dw  ?       ;number of free clusters
DPB     ENDS
```

For more information about the **DPB** structure, see Chapter 3, "File System."

See Also   Function 32h Get DPB

■ Function 21h Random Read   **Superseded**

```
mov     dx, seg FileFCB
mov     ds, dx
mov     dx, offset FileFCB   ;ds:dx points to FCB

mov     ah, 21h              ;Random Read
int     21h

cmp     al, 0                ;zero means success
jne     error_handler
```

Random Read (Function 21h) reads a record from the file identified by the file control block (FCB). Data read from the file is written to the memory at the current disk transfer address (DTA).

This function has been superseded by Read File or Device (Function 3Fh).

Parameter

FileFCB   Points to an **FCB** structure that identifies an open file. The structure must have been previously filled by using Open File with FCB (Function 0Fh) or Create File with FCB (Function 16h). Also, the **fcbRandomRecNo** field must specify the record to read. The **FCB** structure has the following form:

```
FCB     STRUC
    fcbDriveID      db  ?               ;drive no. (0=default, 1=A, etc.)
    fcbFileName     db  '????????'      ;filename
    fcbExtent       db  '???'           ;file extension
    fcbCurBlockNo   dw  ?               ;current block number
    fcbRecSize      dw  ?               ;record size
    fcbFileSize     db  4 dup (?)       ;size of file, in bytes
    fcbFileDate     dw  ?               ;date file last modified
    fcbFileTime     dw  ?               ;time file last modified
    fcbReserved     db  8 dup (?)       ;reserved
    fcbCurRecNo     db  ?               ;current record number
    fcbRandomRecNo  db  4 dup (?)       ;random record number
FCB     ENDS
```

For a full description of the **FCB** structure, see Chapter 3, "File System."

Return Value

If the function is successful, the AL register contains 00h and the memory at the DTA contains the record read from the file. Otherwise, the AL register contains an error value, which may be one of the following:

Value	Meaning
01h	End of file encountered, no data in record
02h	Segment boundary overlapped by DTA, read canceled
03h	End of file encountered, partial record at DTA (rest of record filled with zeros)

Comments

MS-DOS updates the **fcbCurBlockNo** and **fcbCurRecNo** fields in the **FCB** structure to agree with the **fcbRandomRecNo** field before attempting to read the record from the disk. No record numbers are incremented; successive calls to the function repeatedly read the same record.

This function can be used to read files on a network drive but only if the network has granted read (or similar) access to the given file or drive.

See Also

Function 0Fh Open File with FCB
Function 14h Sequential Read
Function 16h Create File with FCB
Function 22h Random Write
Function 3Fh Read File or Device

■ Function 22h   Random Write   Superseded

```
mov     dx, seg FileFCB
mov     ds, dx
mov     dx, offset FileFCB   ;ds:dx points to FCB

mov     ah, 22h              ;Random Write
int     21h

cmp     al, O                ;zero means success
jne     error_handler
```

Random Write (Function 22h) writes data at the current disk transfer address (DTA) to a record in the file identified by the file control block (FCB).

This function has been superseded by Write File or Device (Function 40h).

Parameter   *FileFCB*   Points to an **FCB** structure that identifies an open file. The structure must have been previously filled by using Open File with FCB (Function 0Fh) or Create File with FCB (Function 16h). Also, the **fcbRandomRecNo** field must specify the record to write. The **FCB** structure has the following form:

```
FCB       STRUC
    fcbDriveID      db   ?              ;drive no. (O=default, 1=A, etc.)
    fcbFileName     db   '????????'     ;filename
    fcbExtent       db   '???'          ;file extension
    fcbCurBlockNo   dw   ?              ;current block number
    fcbRecSize      dw   ?              ;record size
    fcbFileSize     db   4 dup (?)      ;size of file, in bytes
    fcbFileDate     dw   ?              ;date file last modified
    fcbFileTime     dw   ?              ;time file last modified
    fcbReserved     db   8 dup (?)      ;reserved
    fcbCurRecNo     db   ?              ;current record number
    fcbRandomRecNo  db   4 dup (?)      ;random record number
FCB       ENDS
```

For a full description of the **FCB** structure, see Chapter 3, "File System."

Return Value   If the function is successful, the AL register contains 00h. Otherwise, the AL register contains 01h if the disk is full or 02h if the DTA overlapped a segment boundary. In either case, the write operation is canceled.

Comments   MS-DOS updates the **fcbCurBlockNo** and **fcbCurRecNo** fields in the **FCB** structure to agree with the **fcbRandomRecNo** field before attempting to write the record to the disk. No record numbers are incremented; successive calls to this function write to the same record in the file.

This function can be used to write files on a network drive but only if the network has granted write (or similar) access to the given file or drive.

See Also   Function 0Fh   Open File with FCB
Function 15h   Sequential Write
Function 16h   Create File with FCB
Function 21h   Random Read
Function 40h   Write File or Device

■ Function 23h Get File Size   Superseded

```
mov     dx, seg FileFCB
mov     ds, dx
mov     dx, offset FileFCB   ;ds:dx points to FCB

mov     ah, 23h              ;Get File Size
int     21h

cmp     al, 0                ;zero means success
jne     error_handler
```

Get File Size (Function 23h) returns the number of records in a file specified by a file control block (FCB).

This function has been superseded by Move File Pointer (Function 42h).

Parameter   *FileFCB*   Points to an **FCB** structure that identifies the file to examine. The **fcbDriveID**, **fcbFileName**, and **fcbExtent** fields must contain the filename information. Also, the **fcbRecSize** field must contain the size of a single file record. Other fields should contain zero. The **FCB** structure has the following form:

```
FCB     STRUC
        fcbDriveID      db  ?              ;drive no. (0=default, 1=A, etc.)
        fcbFileName     db  '????????'     ;filename
        fcbExtent       db  '???'          ;file extension
        fcbCurBlockNo   dw  ?              ;current block number
        fcbRecSize      dw  ?              ;record size
        fcbFileSize     db  4 dup (?)      ;size of file, in bytes
        fcbFileDate     dw  ?              ;date file last modified
        fcbFileTime     dw  ?              ;time file last modified
        fcbReserved     db  8 dup (?)      ;reserved
        fcbCurRecNo     db  ?              ;current record number
        fcbRandomRecNo  db  4 dup (?)      ;random record number
FCB     ENDS
```

For a full description of the **FCB** structure, see Chapter 3, "File System."

Return Value   If the function is successful, the AL register contains 00h and the **fcbRandomRecNo** field contains the number of records in the file. Otherwise, the AL register contains 0FFh.

Comment   MS-DOS returns the size of the file in records by dividing the size in bytes by the size of a single record (as specified by the **fcbRecSize** field). If the **fcbRecSize** field in the **FCB** structure is set to 1 byte, MS-DOS returns the size of the file in bytes.

See Also   Function 42h Move File Pointer

■ Function 24h Set Random Record Number   Superseded

```
mov     dx, seg FileFCB
mov     ds, dx
mov     dx, offset FileFCB  ;ds:dx points to FCB

mov     ah, 24h             ;Set Random Record Number
int     21h
```

Set Random Record Number (Function 24h) sets the random record field in a file control block (FCB) to match the file position indicated by the current block and current record fields.

This function has been superseded by Move File Pointer (Function 42h).

Parameter   *FileFCB*   Points to an **FCB** structure that identifies an open file. The structure must have been previously filled by using Open File with FCB (Function 0Fh) or Create File with FCB (Function 16h). Also, the **fcbRandomRecNo** field must contain zero before this function is called. The **FCB** structure has the following form:

```
FCB     STRUC
    fcbDriveID      db    ?               ;drive no. (0=default, 1=A, etc.)
    fcbFileName     db    '????????'      ;filename
    fcbExtent       db    '???'           ;file extension
    fcbCurBlockNo   dw    ?               ;current block number
    fcbRecSize      dw    ?               ;record size
    fcbFileSize     db    4 dup (?)       ;size of file, in bytes
    fcbFileDate     dw    ?               ;date file last modified
    fcbFileTime     dw    ?               ;time file last modified
    fcbReserved     db    8 dup (?)       ;reserved
    fcbCurRecNo     db    ?               ;current record number
    fcbRandomRecNo  db    4 dup (?)       ;random record number
FCB     ENDS
```

For a full description of the **FCB** structure, see Chapter 3, "File System."

Return Value   This function has no return value.

See Also

Function 0Fh Open File with FCB
Function 16h Create File with FCB
Function 21h Random Read
Function 22h Random Write
Function 42h Move File Pointer

■ Function 25h Set Interrupt Vector

```
mov     dx, seg InterruptHandler
mov     ds, dx
mov     dx, offset InterruptHandler      ;ds:dx points to new handler
mov     al, InterruptNumber              ;interrupt vector

mov     ah, 25h                          ;Set Interrupt Vector
int     21h
```

Set Interrupt Vector (Function 25h) replaces the vector-table entry with the address of the specified interrupt handler.

Parameters   *InterruptHandler*   Specifies the address of the new interrupt handler.

InterruptNumber   Specifies the number of the interrupt (00h–0FFh) that is to cause the specified handler to be called.

Return Value   This function has no return value.

Comments   Programs should *never* set an interrupt vector directly in memory. Programs should use this function to replace an interrupt vector.

When a program installs a new interrupt handler, it should use Get Interrupt Vector (Function 35h) to retrieve the address of the original interrupt handler and restore this original address before terminating.

See Also   Function 35h Get Interrupt Vector

■ Function 26h Create New PSP   Superseded

```
mov     dx, SegmentPSP        ;segment address to receive PSP

mov     ah, 26h               ;Create New PSP
int     21h
```

Create New PSP (Function 26h) creates a new program segment prefix (PSP), copying it to the beginning of the segment specified by the *SegmentPSP* parameter.

This function has been superseded by Load and Execute Program (Function 4B00h).

Parameter   *SegmentPSP*   Specifies the address of a segment to receive the new PSP.

Return Value   This function has no return value.

Comment   This function is intended to be called only by .COM programs. When a program calls this function, the CS register must contain the segment address of the PSP.

See Also   Function 4B00h Load and Execute Program

■ Function 27h Random Block Read   Superseded

```
mov    cx, cRecords          ;number of records to read
mov    dx, seg FileFCB
mov    ds, dx
mov    dx, offset FileFCB    ;ds:dx points to FCB

mov    ah, 27h               ;Random Block Read
int    21h

cmp    al, 0                 ;zero means success
jne    error_handler
```

Random Block Read (Function 27h) reads one or more records from the file identified by the file control block (FCB). Data read from the file is written to the memory at the current disk transfer address (DTA).

This function has been superseded by Read File or Device (Function 3Fh) and Move File Pointer (Function 42h).

Parameters   *cRecords*   Specifies the number of records to read.

FileFCB   Points to an **FCB** structure that identifies an open file. The structure must have been previously filled by using Open File with FCB (Function 0Fh) or Create File with FCB (Function 16h). Also, the **fcbRandomRecNo** field must specify the first record to read. The **FCB** structure has the following form:

```
FCB      STRUC
    fcbDriveID      db   ?              ;drive no. (0=default, 1=A, etc.)
    fcbFileName     db   '????????'     ;filename
    fcbExtent       db   '???'          ;file extension
    fcbCurBlockNo   dw   ?              ;current block number
    fcbRecSize      dw   ?              ;record size
    fcbFileSize     db   4 dup (?)      ;size of file, in bytes
    fcbFileDate     dw   ?              ;date file last modified
    fcbFileTime     dw   ?              ;time file last modified
    fcbReserved     db   8 dup (?)      ;reserved
    fcbCurRecNo     db   ?              ;current record number
    fcbRandomRecNo  db   4 dup (?)      ;random record number
FCB      ENDS
```

For a full description of the **FCB** structure, see Chapter 3, "File System."

Return Value   If the function is successful, the AL register contains 00h, the memory at the DTA contains the records read from the file, and the CX register contains a count of the number of records read. Otherwise, the AL register contains an error value, which may be one of the following:

Value	Meaning
01h	End of file encountered, no data in record
02h	Segment boundary overlapped by DTA, read canceled
03h	End of file encountered, partial record at DTA (rest of record filled with zeros)

Comments   A program using this function must ensure that the buffer at the DTA is large enough to hold all the data read from the file.

MS-DOS updates the **fcbCurBlockNo** and **fcbCurRecNo** fields in the **FCB** structure to agree with the **fcbRandomRecNo** field before attempting to read the record from the disk. The block and record fields are incremented after a successful read operation; successive calls to this function read sequential groups of records from the file until MS-DOS reaches the end of the file.

This function can be used to read files on a network drive but only if the network has granted read (or similar) access to the given file or drive.

See Also

Function 0Fh Open File with FCB
Function 16h Create File with FCB
Function 21h Random Read
Function 28h Random Block Write
Function 3Fh Read File or Device
Function 42h Move File Pointer

■ Function 28h Random Block Write   Superseded

```
mov     cx, cRecords            ;number of records to write
mov     dx, seg FileFCB
mov     ds, dx
mov     dx, offset FileFCB      ;ds:dx points to FCB

mov     ah, 28h                 ;Random Block Write
int     21h

cmp     al, 0                   ;zero means success
jne     error_handler
```

Random Block Write (Function 28h) writes the data at the current disk transfer address (DTA) to one or more records in the file identified by the file control block (FCB).

This function has been superseded by Write File or Device (Function 40h) and Move File Pointer (Function 42h).

Parameters

cRecords   Specifies the number of records to write.

FileFCB   Points to an **FCB** structure that identifies an open file. The structure must have been previously filled by using Open File with FCB (Function 0Fh) or Create File with FCB (Function 16h). Also, the **fcbRandomRecNo** field must specify the first record to write. The **FCB** structure has the following form:

```
FCB     STRUC
    fcbDriveID      db  ?               ;drive no. (0=default, 1=A, etc.)
    fcbFileName     db  '????????'      ;filename
    fcbExtent       db  '???'           ;file extension
    fcbCurBlockNo   dw  ?               ;current block number
    fcbRecSize      dw  ?               ;record size
    fcbFileSize     db  4 dup (?)       ;size of file, in bytes
    fcbFileDate     dw  ?               ;date file last modified
    fcbFileTime     dw  ?               ;time file last modified
    fcbReserved     db  8 dup (?)       ;reserved
    fcbCurRecNo     db  ?               ;current record number
    fcbRandomRecNo  db  4 dup (?)       ;random record number
FCB     ENDS
```

For a full description of the **FCB** structure, see Chapter 3, "File System."

Return Value

If the function is successful, the AL register contains 00h. Otherwise, the AL register contains 01h if the disk is full or 02h if the DTA overlapped a segment boundary. In either case, the write operation is canceled.

If the function returns 00h or 01h, the CX register contains the number of records actually written.

Comments

MS-DOS updates the **fcbCurBlockNo** and **fcbCurRecNo** fields in the **FCB** structure to agree with the **fcbRandomRecNo** field before attempting to write the records to the disk. The block and record fields are incremented after a successful write operation; successive calls to this function write sequential groups of records to the file.

This function can be used to write files on a network drive but only if the network has granted write (or similar) access to the given file or drive.

See Also   Function 0Fh Open File with FCB
                     Function 16h Create File with FCB
                     Function 22h Random Write
                     Function 27h Random Block Read
                     Function 40h Write File or Device
                     Function 42h Move File Pointer

■ Function 29h Parse Filename

```
mov     si, seg ParseInput
mov     ds, si
mov     si, offset ParseInput    ;ds:si points to name(s) to parse
mov     di, seg FileFCB
mov     es, di
mov     di, offset FileFCB       ;es:di points to FCB
mov     al, ParseControl         ;controls parsing

mov     ah, 29h                  ;Parse Filename
int     21h
```

Parse Filename (Function 29h) converts a filename string that has the form *drive:filename.extension* into a string of the form required for a file control block (FCB).

This function is useful only when file control blocks are used.

Parameters   *ParseInput*   Points to a zero-terminated ASCII string specifying the filename or filenames to parse. Each filename must be in the form *drive:filename.extension* and may contain wildcards. If more than one filename is given, the names must be separated with at least one space character (ASCII 20h). Separator characters used for the MS-DOS command line are also valid.

FileFCB   Points to an **FCB** structure that receives the parsed filename. The **FCB** structure has the following form:

```
FCB     STRUC
    fcbDriveID      db  ?              ;drive no. (0=default, 1=A, etc.)
    fcbFileName     db  '????????'     ;filename
    fcbExtent       db  '???'          ;file extension
    fcbCurBlockNo   dw  ?              ;current block number
    fcbRecSize      dw  ?              ;record size .
    fcbFileSize     db  4 dup (?)      ;size of file, in bytes
    fcbFileDate     dw  ?              ;date file last modified
    fcbFileTime     dw  ?              ;time file last modified
    fcbReserved     db  8 dup (?)      ;reserved
    fcbCurRecNo     db  ?              ;current record number
    fcbRandomRecNo  db  4 dup (?)      ;random record number
FCB     ENDS
```

For a full description of the **FCB** structure, see Chapter 3, "File System."

ParseControl   Controls how MS-DOS parses the *ParseInput* parameter. This parameter has the following form:

Bit	Meaning
0	0 = Stops parsing if a file separator is encountered.
	1 = Ignores leading separators.
1	0 = Sets the drive number in the **FCB** structure to 00h (default drive) if the string does not contain a drive number.
	1 = Leaves the drive number in the **FCB** structure unchanged if the string does not contain a drive number.
2	0 = Sets the filename in the **FCB** structure to eight space characters (ASCII 20h) if the string does not contain a filename.
	1 = Leaves the filename in the **FCB** structure unchanged if the string does not contain a filename.

Bit	Meaning
3	0 = Sets the extension in the **FCB** structure to three space characters (ASCII 20h) if the string does not contain an extension.
	1 = Leaves the extension in the **FCB** structure unchanged if the string does not contain an extension.

Bits 4 through 7 are reserved and must be zero.

Return Values

If the function is successful, the AL, DS:SI, and ES:DI registers contain the following information:

Register	Description
AL	Contains 01h if at least one wildcard is in the filename or extension. Otherwise, it contains 00h.
DS:SI	Points to the first character after the parsed string.
ES:DI	Points to the first byte of the **FCB** structure.

If the drive letter is invalid, the AL register contains 0FFh. If the string does not contain a valid filename, the memory at ES:DI+1 contains a space character (ASCII 20h).

Comments

Parse Filename fills the **fcbDriveId**, **fcbFileName**, and **fcbExtent** fields of the specified **FCB** structure unless the *ParseControl* parameter specifies otherwise. To fill these fields, the function strips any leading white-space characters (spaces and tabs) from the string pointed to by *ParseInput*, then uses the remaining characters to create the drive number, filename, and filename extension. If bit 0 in *ParseControl* is set, the function also strips exactly one filename separator if one appears before the first non–white-space character. The following are valid filename separators:

: . ; , = +

Once Parse Filename begins to convert a filename, it continues to read characters from the string until it encounters a white-space character, a filename separator, a control character (ASCII 01h through 1Fh), or one of the following characters:

/ " [ ] < > |

If the filename in the string has fewer than eight characters, the function fills the remaining bytes in the **fcbFileName** field with space characters (ASCII 20h). If the filename extension has fewer than three characters, the function fills the remaining bytes in the **fcbExtent** field with space characters.

Function 2Ah Get Date

```
mov      ah, 2Ah            ;Get Date
int      21h

mov      WeekDay, al        ;day of week (0 = Sunday, 1 = Monday, etc.)
mov      Year, cx           ;year (1980 through 2099)
mov      Month, dh          ;month (1 = Jan, 2 = Feb, etc.)
mov      MonthDay, dl       ;day of month (1 through 31)
```

Get Date (Function 2Ah) returns the current MS-DOS system date (the date maintained by the clock device).

Parameters   This function has no parameters.

Return Values   The AL, CX, and DX registers contain the following information:

Register	Contents
AL	A number representing the day of the week (0 = Sunday, 1 = Monday, and so on)
CX	A year number (1980 through 2099)
DH	A number representing the month (1 = January, 2 = February, and so on)
DL	The day of the month (1 through 31)

See Also

Function 2Bh Set Date
Function 2Ch Get Time
Function 2Dh Set Time

■ Function 2Bh Set Date

```
mov     cx, Year            ;year (1980 through 2099)
mov     dh, Month           ;month (1 = Jan, 2 = Feb, etc.)
mov     dl, MonthDay        ;day of month (1 through 31)

mov     ah, 2Bh             ;Set Date
int     21h

cmp     al, O               ;zero means success
jne     error_handler
```

Set Date (Function 2Bh) sets the MS-DOS system date (the date maintained by the clock device).

Parameters   *Year*   Specifies a year number in the range 1980 through 2099.

Month   Specifies a number representing the month (1 = January, 2 = February, and so on).

MonthDay   Specifies a day of the month (1 through 31).

Return Value   If the function is successful, the AL register contains 00h. Otherwise, the AL register contains 0FFh.

See Also   Function 2Ah Get Date
Function 2Ch Get Time
Function 2Dh Set Time

■ Function 2Ch Get Time

```
mov     ah, 2Ch              ;Get Time
int     21h

mov     Hour, ch             ;hour (0 through 23)
mov     Minutes, cl          ;minutes (0 through 59)
mov     Seconds, dh          ;seconds (0 through 59)
mov     Hundredths, dl       ;hundredths of a second (0 through 99)
```

Get Time (Function 2Ch) returns the MS-DOS system time (the time maintained by the clock device).

Parameters   This function has no parameters.

Return Values   The CX and DX registers contain the following information:

Register	Contents
CH	Hour in 24-hour format (13 = 1 P.M., 14 = 2 P.M., and so on)
CL	Minutes (0 through 59)
DH	Seconds (0 through 59)
DL	Hundredths of a second (0 through 99)

See Also   Function 2Ah Get Date
Function 2Bh Set Date
Function 2Dh Set Time

Function 2Dh Set Time

```
mov     ch, Hour          ;hour (0 through 23)
mov     cl, Minutes       ;minutes (0 through 59)
mov     dh, Seconds       ;seconds (0 through 59)
mov     dl, Hundredths    ;hundredths of a second (0 through 99)

mov     ah, 2Dh           ;Set Time
int     21h

cmp     al, 0             ;zero means success
jne     error_handler
```

Set Time (Function 2Dh) sets the MS-DOS system time (the time maintained by the clock device).

Parameters

Hour   Specifies the hour to set in 24-hour format (13 = 1 P.M., 14 = 2 P.M., and so on).

Minutes   Specifies the minutes to set (0 through 59).

Seconds   Specifies the seconds to set (0 through 59).

Hundredths   Specifies the hundredths of a second to set (0 through 99).

Return Value

If the function is successful, the AL register contains 00h. Otherwise, the AL register contains 0FFh.

Comment

If the hardware does not resolve hundredths of seconds, the value of the *Hundredths* parameter is ignored.

See Also

Function 2Ah Get Date
Function 2Bh Set Date
Function 2Ch Get Time

■ Function 2Eh Set/Reset Verify Flag

```
mov     al, VerifyFlag      ;0 = reset, 1 = set

mov     ah, 2Eh             ;Set/Reset Verify Flag
int     21h
```

Set/Reset Verify Flag (Function 2Eh) turns the write verify flag on or off, thus determining whether MS-DOS verifies write operations.

Parameter

VerifyFlag   Specifies whether MS-DOS is to attempt to verify that data has been transferred correctly after write operations. If this parameter is 0, MS-DOS does not verify write operations; if this parameter is 1, MS-DOS verifies write operations.

Return Value

This function has no return value.

Comment

The system checks this flag every time it performs a write operation. The write verify flag is typically off, because disk errors are rare and verification slows writing. The write verify flag can be turned on during critical write operations.

See Also

Function 54h Get Verify State

■ Function 2Fh Get Disk Transfer Address

```
mov     ah, 2Fh                          ;Get Disk Transfer Address
int     21h

mov     word ptr [CurrentDTA], bx    ;es:bx is current DTA
mov     word ptr [CurrentDTA+2], es
```

Get Disk Transfer Address (Function 2Fh) returns the segment and offset of the current disk transfer address (DTA).

Parameters   This function has no parameters.

Return Value   The ES:BX registers contain the DTA. The ES register contains the segment address, and the BX register contains the offset.

Comments   There is no way to determine the size of the buffer at the DTA.

If Set Disk Transfer Address (Function 1Ah) has not been used to set the DTA, MS-DOS sets a program's default DTA to be offset 0080h in the program segment prefix (PSP). The default DTA cannot be used with a record size larger than 128 bytes.

See Also   Function 1Ah Set Disk Transfer Address

■ Function 30h Get Version Number

```
mov     al, VerOrOEMFlag    ;01h = version flag, 00h = OEM number

mov     ah, 30h             ;Get Version Number
int     21h

mov     MajorV, al          ;major version number (05h for version 5.0)
mov     MinorV, ah          ;minor version number (00h for version 5.0)
mov     VerOrOEM, bh        ;version flag or OEM number
mov     byte ptr [UserNum+2], bl    ;bl:cx is 24-bit user serial number
mov     word ptr [UserNum], cx
```

Get Version Number (Function 30h) returns the MS-DOS version number set by the **setver** command for the program. The function also returns either the MS-DOS version flag or the original-equipment-manufacturer (OEM) number.

Parameter   *VerOrOEMFlag*   Specifies whether the function returns the version flag or the OEM number in the BH register. It can be one of the following values:

Value	Number
00h	The OEM number
01h	The version flag

Return Values   The AX, BX, and CX registers contain the following information:

Register	Contents
AL	The major version number for the program—for example, 03h for version 3.31, 05h for version 5.0.
AH	The minor version number for the program—for example, 1Fh for version 3.31, 00h for version 5.0.
BH	Either the OEM number or the version flag. In the latter case, if the version flag is set to DOSINROM (08h), MS-DOS runs in ROM; otherwise, MS-DOS runs in RAM. All other bits are reserved and set to zero.
BL:CX	The 24-bit user serial number. The user serial number is OEM-dependent. If not used, the number is set to zero.

Comments   This function returns the MS-DOS version number set by the **setver** command. This version number can differ from the MS-DOS version number returned by Get MS-DOS Version (Function 3306h).

For more information about the **setver** command, see the *Microsoft MS-DOS User's Guide and Reference*.

See Also   Function 3306h Get MS-DOS Version

■ Function 31h Keep Program

```
mov     dx, MemSize       ;number of paragraphs to keep
mov     al, ReturnCode    ;code returned by terminating program

mov     ah, 31h           ;Keep Program
int     21h
```

Keep Program (Function 31h) ends the current program by returning control to its parent program but leaves (keeps) the program in memory and preserves the program's resources, such as open files and allocated memory.

Parameters   *MemSize*   Specifies the number of paragraphs of program code and data to keep in memory. If this parameter is less than 6, the function sets it to 6 before reallocating program memory.

ReturnCode   Specifies the code that is returned to the parent program. If the program terminates normally, *ReturnCode* should be 00h.

Return Value   This function does not return.

Comments   This function carries out the following actions:

■ Reallocates program memory to the amount specified by *MemSize*. Program memory includes only the program segment prefix (PSP) and program data and code. The reallocation does not affect the program's environment block, nor does it affect the memory allocated by the program after it was loaded.

■ Flushes the file buffers but leaves files open. Any locked regions in the open files remain locked.

■ Restores Termination Address (Interrupt 22h) from offset 0Ah in the PSP (**pspTerminateVector** field).

■ Restores the address of CTRL+C Handler (Interrupt 23h) from offset 0Eh in the PSP (**pspControlCVector** field).

■ Restores the address of Critical-Error Handler (Interrupt 24h) from offset 12h in the PSP (**pspCritErrorVector** field).

After completing these actions, this function transfers execution control to the address specified by offset 0Ah in the PSP.

See Also   Function 4B00h Load and Execute Program
Function 4Ch End Program
Function 4Dh Get Child-Program Return Value
Interrupt 22h Termination Address
Interrupt 23h CTRL+C Handler
Interrupt 24h Critical-Error Handler

■ Function 32h Get DPB

```
        mov     dl, DriveNum              ;drive (0 = default, 1 = A, etc.)

        mov     ah, 32h                   ;Get DPB
        int     21h

        cmp     al, 0FFh                  ;0FFh means error
        jz      error_handler

        mov     word ptr [defaultDPB], bx
        mov     word ptr [defaultDPB+2], ds  ;ds:bx points to default DPB
```

Get DPB (Function 32h) retrieves drive parameters for the specified drive.

Parameter   *DriveNum*   Specifies the number of the drive for which to return information (0 = default, 1 = A, 2 = B, and so on).

Return Value   If the function is successful, the AL register contains zero and the DS:BX registers point to a **DPB** structure that contains the drive parameters. The DS register contains the segment address, and the BX register contains the offset. Otherwise, if the specified drive was invalid or a disk error occurred, the AL register contains 0FFh.

Comments   If Get DPB is successful, the DS:BX registers point to a **DPB** structure, which has the following form:

```
DPB     STRUC
    dpbDrive        db  ?   ;drive number (0 = A, 1 = B, etc.)
    dpbUnit         db  ?   ;unit number for driver
    dpbSectorSize   dw  ?   ;sector size, in bytes
    dpbClusterMask  db  ?   ;sectors per cluster - 1
    dpbClusterShift db  ?   ;sectors per cluster, as power of 2
    dpbFirstFAT     dw  ?   ;first sector containing FAT
    dpbFATCount     db  ?   ;number of FATs
    dpbRootEntries  dw  ?   ;number of root-directory entries
    dpbFirstSector  dw  ?   ;first sector of first cluster
    dpbMaxCluster   dw  ?   ;number of clusters on drive + 1
    dpbFATSize      dw  ?   ;number of sectors occupied by FAT
    dpbDirSector    dw  ?   ;first sector containing directory
    dpbDriverAddr   dd  ?   ;address of device driver
    dpbMedia        db  ?   ;media descriptor
    dpbFirstAccess  db  ?   ;indicates access to drive
    dpbNextDPB      dd  ?   ;address of next drive parameter block
    dpbNextFree     dw  ?   ;last allocated cluster
    dpbFreeCnt      dw  ?   ;number of free clusters
DPB     ENDS
```

For more information about the **DPB** structure, see Chapter 3, "File System."

See Also   Function 1Fh Get Default DPB

Function 3300h Get CTRL+C Check Flag

```
mov     ax, 3300h           ;Get CTRL+C Check Flag
int     21h

mov     BreakFlag, dl       ;0 = off, 1 = on
```

Get CTRL+C Check Flag (Function 3300h) returns the status of the MS-DOS CTRL+C check flag.

Parameters   This function has no parameters.

Return Value   The DL register contains 00h if checking is disabled, or the DL register contains 01h if checking is enabled.

Comment   If the CTRL+C check flag is off, MS-DOS checks for CTRL+C only while processing character I/O functions 01h through 0Ch. If the check flag is on, MS-DOS checks for CTRL+C while processing other system functions.

See Also   Function 3301h Set CTRL+C Check Flag

■ Function 3301h Set CTRL+C Check Flag

```
mov      dl, BreakFlag    ;00h = off, 01h = on

mov      ax, 3301h        ;Set CTRL+C Check Flag
int      21h
```

Set CTRL+C Check Flag (Function 3301h) turns the CTRL+C check flag on or off.

Parameter   *BreakFlag*   Specifies whether to turn CTRL+C testing on or off. If this parameter is 00h, CTRL+C testing is turned off; if this parameter is 01h, CTRL+C testing is turned on.

Return Value   This function has no return value.

Comments   If the CTRL+C check flag is off, MS-DOS checks for CTRL+C only while processing character I/O functions 01h through 0Ch. If the check flag is on, MS-DOS checks for CTRL+C while processing other I/O functions, such as disk operations.

The CTRL+C flag affects all programs. If a program changes the state of this flag, the state change remains in effect even after the program terminates. An efficient program should save the state of the flag before changing it and restore the state before terminating.

See Also   Function 3300h Get CTRL+C Check Flag

■ Function 3305h Get Startup Drive

```
mov     ax, 3305h           ;Get Startup Drive
int     21h

mov     StartupDrive, dl    ;drive (1 = A, 2 = B, etc.)
```

Get Startup Drive (Function 3305h) returns a number representing the drive that was used to load MS-DOS.

Parameters   This function has no parameters.

Return Value   The DL register contains the number of the startup drive (1 = A, 2 = B, 3 = C, and so on).

▪ Function 3306h   Get MS-DOS Version

```
mov     ax, 3306h           ;Get MS-DOS Version
int     21h

mov     MajorV, bl          ;major version number (05h for version 5.0)
mov     MinorV, bh          ;minor version number (00h for version 5.0)
mov     RevisionNum, dl     ;revision number in bits 0 through 2
mov     VersionFlags, dh    ;version flags
```

Get MS-DOS Version (Function 3306h) returns the MS-DOS version number, the MS-DOS revision number, and version flags specifying whether MS-DOS is in the high memory area (HMA) or in read-only memory (ROM).

Parameters   This function has no parameters.

Return Values   The BX and DX registers contain the following information:

Register	Contents
BL	The major version number—for example, 05h for version 5.0.
BH	The minor version number—for example, 00h for version 5.0.
DL	In the low three bits, the revision number. All other bits are reserved and set to zero.
DH	The MS-DOS version flags. The contents may be a combination of the following values:

Value	Meaning
DOSINROM (08h)	If set, MS-DOS runs in ROM; otherwise, MS-DOS runs in RAM.
DOSINHMA (10h)	If set, MS-DOS is in the high memory area; otherwise, MS-DOS is in conventional memory.

All other bits are reserved and set to zero.

Comments   This function returns the actual MS-DOS version number rather than the version number set by the **setver** command for the program.

See Also   Function 30h Get Version Number

■ Function 34h Get InDOS Flag Address

```
mov     ah, 34h                        ;Get InDOS Flag Address
int     21h

mov     InDOS, byte ptr es:[bx]        ;es:bx points to InDOS flag
```

Get InDOS Flag Address (Function 34h) returns the address of the MS-DOS InDOS flag. The InDOS flag shows the current state of Interrupt 21h processing.

Parameters   This function has no parameters.

Return Value   The ES:BX registers contain the InDOS flag address. The ES register contains the segment address of the InDOS flag, and the BX register contains the offset.

Comment   While MS-DOS is processing an Interrupt 21h function, the value of the InDOS flag is nonzero.

■ Function 35h Get Interrupt Vector

```
mov     al, InterruptNumber      ;interrupt vector number
mov     ah, 35h                  ;Get Interrupt Vector
int     21h
mov     word ptr [Handler], bx   ;es:bx points to interrupt handler
mov     word ptr [Handler+2], es
```

Get Interrupt Vector (Function 35h) returns the address of the routine that handles the specified interrupt.

Parameter   *InterruptNumber*   Specifies the interrupt number that causes the interrupt routine to be called.

Return Value   If the function is successful, the ES:BX registers point to the routine that handles the specified interrupt. The ES register contains the segment address of the interrupt-handling routine, and the BX register contains the offset.

See Also   Function 25h Set Interrupt Vector

■ Function 36h Get Disk Free Space

```
mov     dl, Drive                   ;drive (0 = default, 1 = A, 2 = B, etc.)

mov     ah, 36h                     ;Get Disk Free Space
int     21h

cmp     ax, OFFFFh                  ;OFFFFh means drive not valid
je      error_handler

mov     SectorsPerCluster, ax       ;sectors per cluster
mov     AvailClusters, bx           ;number of available clusters
mov     BytesPerSector, cx          ;bytes per sector
mov     TotalClusters, dx           ;total number of clusters on disk
```

Get Disk Free Space (Function 36h) returns the number of clusters available on
the disk in the specified drive and the information necessary to calculate the
number of bytes available on the disk.

Parameter

Drive   The number of the drive to return information for (0 = default value,
1 = A, 2 = B, and so on).

Return Values

If the function is successful, the AX, BX, CX, and DX registers contain the following information:

Register	Contents
AX	The number of sectors in a cluster
BX	The number of clusters available on the disk
CX	The number of bytes in a sector
DX	The total number of clusters on the disk

Otherwise, the AX register contains 0FFFFh.

Comments

The number of free bytes on the disk can be calculated by multiplying the available clusters by the sectors per cluster by the bytes per sector (BX*AX*CX).

MS-DOS reports sectors allocated in the file allocation table (FAT) but not
belonging to a file (lost clusters) as used clusters, just as if they were allocated
to a file.

See Also

Function 1Bh Get Default Drive Data
Function 1Ch Get Drive Data

■ Function 38h Get/Set Country Information

```
lds     dx, InfoAddress ;ds:dx points to buffer to get country info
                        ;or
                        ;dx is OFFFFh to set country code

cmp     CountryCode, OFEh
ja      code2

mov     al, byte ptr CountryCode     ;country code if less than 254
jmp     continue

code2:
mov     bx, CountryCode              ;country code if greater than 254
mov     al, OFFh

continue:
mov     ah, 38h                      ;Get/Set Country Information
int     21h

jc      error_handler                ;carry set means error
```

Get/Set Country Information (Function 38h) either returns country information or sets the country code, depending on the contents of the DX register.

If the DX register contains any value other than 0FFFFh, this function returns a **COUNTRYINFO** structure containing country information that MS-DOS uses to control the keyboard and screen.

If the DX register contains 0FFFFh, this function sets the country code that MS-DOS uses to determine country information for the keyboard and screen.

Parameters

InfoAddress   Specifies whether this function gets country information or sets the country code. If the parameter points to a **COUNTRYINFO** structure, the function copies country information to the structure. If the low 16 bits of the parameter is 0FFFFh, the function sets the country code.

The **COUNTRYINFO** structure has the following form:

```
COUNTRYINFO        STRUC
    ciDateFormat        dw   ?              ;date format
    ciCurrency          db   5 dup (?)      ;currency symbol (ASCIIZ)
    ciThousands         db   2 dup (?)      ;thousands separator (ASCIIZ)
    ciDecimal           db   2 dup (?)      ;decimal separator (ASCIIZ)
    ciDateSep           db   2 dup (?)      ;date separator (ASCIIZ)
    ciTimeSep           db   2 dup (?)      ;time separator (ASCIIZ)
    ciBitField          db   ?              ;currency format
    ciCurrencyPlaces    db   ?              ;places after decimal point
    ciTimeFormat        db   ?              ;12-hour or 24-hour format
    ciCaseMap           dd   ?              ;address of case-mapping routine
    ciDataSep           db   2 dup (?)      ;data-list separator (ASCIIZ)
    ciReserved          db   10 dup (?)     ;reserved
COUNTRYINFO        ENDS
```

For a full description of the **COUNTRYINFO** structure, see Chapter 6, "National Language Support."

CountryCode   Specifies the country code. This parameter can be one of the following values:

Value	Meaning
001	United States
002	Canadian-French
003	Latin America

Value	Meaning
031	Netherlands
032	Belgium
033	France
034	Spain
036	Hungary
038	Yugoslavia
039	Italy
041	Switzerland
042	Czechoslovakia
044	United Kingdom
045	Denmark
046	Sweden
047	Norway
048	Poland
049	Germany
055	Brazil
061	International English
351	Portugal
358	Finland

Each country code is listed as a three-digit decimal number, the same as that used for that country's international telephone prefix.

To get country information for the current country, *CountryCode* must be zero.

Return Value

If the function is successful, the carry flag is clear. Otherwise, the carry flag is set and the AX register contains an error value, which may be one of the following values:

Value	Name
0001h	ERROR_INVALID_FUNCTION
0002h	ERROR_FILE_NOT_FOUND

Comments

When the country code is less than 254, the AL register contains the code. Otherwise, the BX register contains the country code and the AL register contains the value 0FFh.

If the DX register contains any value other than 0FFFFh, the function returns the country code in both the AL and BX registers. In this case, the AL register contains the low 8 bits of the country code.

See Also

Function 6501h Get Extended Country Information
Function 6601h Get Global Code Page
Function 6602h Set Global Code Page

■ Function 39h Create Directory

```
mov     dx, seg Dir
mov     ds, dx
mov     dx, offset Dir        ;ds:dx points to name of new directory

mov     ah, 39h               ;Create Directory
int     21h

jc      error_handler         ;carry set means error
```

Create Directory (Function 39h) creates a new directory by using the specified path.

Parameter

Dir   Points to a zero-terminated ASCII string that specifies the directory to create. This string must be a valid MS-DOS directory name and cannot contain wildcards.

Return Value

If the function is successful, the carry flag is clear. Otherwise, the carry flag is set and the AX register contains an error value, which may be one of the following values:

Value	Name
0002h	ERROR_FILE_NOT_FOUND
0003h	ERROR_PATH_NOT_FOUND
0005h	ERROR_ACCESS_DENIED

Comment

This function returns 0005h (ERROR_ACCESS_DENIED) if a file or directory with the specified name already exists in the specified path.

See Also

Function 3Ah Remove Directory
Function 3Bh Change Current Directory
Function 47h Get Current Directory

■ Function 3Ah Remove Directory

```
mov     dx, seg Dir
mov     ds, dx
mov     dx, offset Dir   ;ds:dx points to name of directory to remove

mov     ah, 3Ah          ;Remove Directory
int     21h

jc      error_handler    ;carry set means error
```

Remove Directory (Function 3Ah) removes (deletes) a specified directory.

Parameter

Dir   Points to a zero-terminated ASCII string that specifies the directory to remove. This string must be a valid MS-DOS directory name and cannot contain wildcards.

Return Value

If the function is successful, the carry flag is clear. Otherwise, the carry flag is set and the AX register contains an error value, which may be one of the following values:

Value	Name
0003h	ERROR_PATH_NOT_FOUND
0005h	ERROR_ACCESS_DENIED
0010h	ERROR_CURRENT_DIRECTORY

Comment

This function returns 0005h (ERROR_ACCESS_DENIED) if the directory to be deleted is not empty or the directory to be deleted is the root directory.

See Also

Function 39h Create Directory
Function 3Bh Change Current Directory
Function 47h Get Current Directory

■ Function 3Bh Change Current Directory

```
        mov     dx, seg Dir
        mov     ds, dx
        mov     dx, offset Dir    ;ds:dx points to name of new directory

        mov     ah, 3Bh           ;Change Current Directory
        int     21h

        jc      error_handler     ;carry set means error
```

Change Current Directory (Function 3Bh) changes the current directory to a
specified path.

Parameter   *Dir*   Points to a zero-terminated ASCII string that specifies the new current
directory. This string must be a valid MS-DOS directory name and cannot con-
tain wildcards.

Comment   If a drive other than the default drive is specified as part of the new directory
path, this function changes the current directory on that drive but does not
change the default drive. Set Default Drive (Function 0Eh) can be used to
change the default drive.

Return Value   If the function is successful, the carry flag is clear. Otherwise, the carry flag
is set and the AX register contains an error value, which may be 0003h
(ERROR_PATH_NOT_FOUND).

See Also   Function 0Eh Set Default Drive
Function 47h Get Current Directory

■ Function 3Ch Create File with Handle

```
mov     dx, seg FileName
mov     ds, dx
mov     dx, offset FileName    ;ds:dx points to name of file or device
mov     cx, Attributes         ;file attributes

mov     ah, 3Ch                ;Create File with Handle
int     21h

jc      error_handler          ;carry set means error
mov     Handle, ax             ;handle of file or device
```

Create File with Handle (Function 3Ch) creates a file and assigns it the first available handle. If the specified file already exists, MS-DOS opens it and truncates it to zero length.

Parameters

FileName   Points to a zero-terminated ASCII string that specifies the file to create. This string must be a valid MS-DOS filename and cannot contain wildcards.

Attributes   Specifies the attributes to assign to the new file. Any combination of the following values is valid:

Value	Meaning
ATTR_NORMAL (0000h)	File can be read from or written to.
ATTR_READONLY (0001h)	File can read from but not written to.
ATTR_HIDDEN (0002h)	File is hidden and does not appear in a directory listing.
ATTR_SYSTEM (0004h)	File is a system file.
ATTR_VOLUME (0008h)	*FileName* is used as the volume label for the current medium.
ATTR_ARCHIVE (0020h)	File is marked for archiving.

Return Value

If the function is successful, the carry flag is clear and the AX register contains the new file handle. Otherwise, the carry flag is set and the AX register contains an error value, which may be one of the following values:

Value	Name
0003h	ERROR_PATH_NOT_FOUND
0004h	ERROR_TOO_MANY_OPEN_FILES
0005h	ERROR_ACCESS_DENIED

Comments

This function returns 0005h (ERROR_ACCESS_DENIED) if a read-only file with the specified name already exists in the specified path or if the file to be created is in the root directory and the root directory is full.

When MS-DOS creates a file, it opens the file with read-and-write access and compatibility sharing mode and sets the file pointer to zero. If the attribute ATTR_READONLY is specified, it takes affect only after the new file is closed.

Create File with Handle creates a volume label for the medium in the specified drive only if the ATTR_VOLUME attribute is given and the current medium does not have an existing volume label.

If the specified file is on a network drive, this function creates the file only if the network has granted create (or similar) access to the drive or directory.

See Also

Function 4300h Get File Attributes
Function 4301h Set File Attributes
Function 5Ah Create Temporary File
Function 5Bh Create New File
Function 6Ch Extended Open/Create

■ Function 3Dh Open File with Handle

```
mov     dx, seg FileName
mov     ds, dx
mov     dx, offset FileName     ;ds:dx points to name of file or device
mov     al, FileAccess          ;modes with which to open file

mov     ah, 3Dh                 ;Open File with Handle
int     21h

jc      error_handler           ;carry set means error
mov     Handle, ax              ;handle of file or device
```

Open File with Handle (Function 3Dh) opens any file, including hidden and system files, for input or output.

Parameters   *FileName*   Points to a zero-terminated ASCII string that specifies the file to open. This string must be a valid MS-DOS filename and cannot contain wildcards.

FileAccess   Specifies the modes with which to open the file. *FileAccess* can be a combination of values from the following table. The access value is required; the sharing and inheritance values are optional.

Value	Meaning
OPEN_ACCESS_READONLY (0000h)	Open the file for read-only access.
OPEN_ACCESS_WRITEONLY (0001h)	Open the file for write-only access.
OPEN_ACCESS_READWRITE (0002h)	Open the file for read-and-write access.
OPEN_SHARE_COMPATIBILITY (0000h)	Permit other programs any access to the file. On a given computer, any program can open the file any number of times with this mode. This is the default sharing value.
OPEN_SHARE_DENYREADWRITE (0010h)	Do not permit any other program to open the file.
OPEN_SHARE_DENYWRITE (0020h)	Do not permit any other program to open the file for write access.
OPEN_SHARE_DENYREAD (0030h)	Do not permit any other program to open the file for read access.
OPEN_SHARE_DENYNONE (0040h)	Permit other programs read or write access, but no program may open the file for compatibility access.
OPEN_FLAGS_NOINHERIT (0080h)	A child program created with Load and Execute Program (Function 4B00h) does not inherit the file handle. If this mode is not set, child programs inherit the file handle.

Return Value   If the function is successful, the carry flag is clear and the AX register contains the file handle. Otherwise, the carry flag is set and the AX register contains an error value, which may be one of the following values:

Value	Name
0002h	ERROR_FILE_NOT_FOUND
0003h	ERROR_PATH_NOT_FOUND
0004h	ERROR_TOO_MANY_OPEN_FILES
0005h	ERROR_ACCESS_DENIED
000Ch	ERROR_INVALID_ACCESS

Comments   When the file is opened, the file pointer is set to zero (the first byte in the file).

This function returns the error value 0005h (ERROR_ACCESS_DENIED) if a program attempts to open a directory or volume identifier or to open a read-only file for write access.

If the Share program is not loaded, MS-DOS ignores the following modes: OPEN_SHARE_DENYREADWRITE, OPEN_SHARE_DENYWRITE, OPEN_SHARE_DENYREAD, and OPEN_SHARE_DENYNONE. If this function fails because of a file-sharing error, a subsequent call to Get Extended Error (Function 59h) returns the error value that specifies a sharing violation.

If the specified file is on a network drive, Open File with Handle opens the file only if the network has granted read access, write access, or read-and-write access to the drive or directory.

See Also   Function 3Eh Close File with Handle
Function 3Fh Read File or Device
Function 40h Write File or Device
Function 42h Move File Pointer
Function 59h Get Extended Error
Function 6Ch Extended Open/Create
Interrupt 2Fh Function 1000h Get SHARE.EXE Installed State

■ Function 3Eh Close File with Handle

```
mov     bx, Handle          ;handle of file or device
mov     ah, 3Eh             ;Close File with Handle
int     21h
jc      error_handler       ;carry set means error
```

Close File with Handle (Function 3Eh) closes a file opened or created with a
file-handle function.

Parameter   *Handle*   Identifies the file to close.

Return Value   If the function is successful, the carry flag is clear. Otherwise, the carry flag
is set and the AX register contains an error value, which may be 0006h
(ERROR_INVALID_HANDLE).

Comments   When MS-DOS processes this function, any internal buffer for the file is flushed
(any pending write operations are completed), any locked regions of the file are
unlocked, and the directory is updated to reflect any changes in the file size,
date, or time.

Although closing a file invalidates the corresponding handle, MS-DOS may reuse
the handle to identify a file that is subsequently opened or created. Programs can
use Is File or Device Remote (Function 440Ah) to determine whether a given
handle is valid.

See Also   Function 3Ch Create File with Handle
Function 3Dh Open File with Handle
Function 440Ah Is File or Device Remote
Function 5Ah Create Temporary File
Function 5Bh Create New File
Function 6Ch Extended Open/Create

■ Function 3Fh Read File or Device

```
mov      bx, Handle              ;handle of file or device
mov      cx, MaxBytes            ;maximum number of bytes to read
mov      dx, seg Buffer
mov      ds, dx
mov      dx, offset Buffer       ;ds:dx points to buffer to receive data

mov      ah, 3Fh                 ;Read File or Device
int      21h

jc       error_handler           ;carry set means error
mov      ActualBytes, ax         ;number of bytes read
```

Read File or Device (Function 3Fh) reads up to the specified number of bytes of data from a file or device into a buffer. MS-DOS may read fewer than the specified number of bytes if it reaches the end of the file.

Parameters   *Handle*   Identifies the file or device to be read from.

MaxBytes   Specifies the maximum number of bytes to read.

Buffer   Points to the buffer that is to receive data from the file or device. The buffer must be at least as large as *MaxBytes*.

Return Value   If the function is successful, the carry flag is clear, *Buffer* contains the data read from the file or device, and the AX register contains the number of bytes read from the file or device. Otherwise, the carry flag is set and the AX register contains an error value, which may be one of the following values:

Value	Name
0005h	ERROR_ACCESS_DENIED
0006h	ERROR_INVALID_HANDLE

Comments   *Handle* can be a handle for a standard device or a handle created by using such a function as Open File with Handle (Function 3Dh).

When MS-DOS reads from a file, it reads data starting at the current location of the file pointer. When this function returns, the file pointer is positioned at the byte immediately following the last byte read from the file.

This function can also be used to read from the standard input device (typically the keyboard). If MS-DOS is reading from standard input, this function returns if it reads a carriage-return character (ASCII 0Dh), even if it has not yet read the number of bytes specified in *MaxBytes*.

If this function returns zero for the number of bytes read, the file pointer is at the end of the file. If the number of bytes read is fewer than the number requested, MS-DOS reached the end of the file during the read operation.

See Also   Function 3Ch Create File with Handle
Function 3Dh Open File with Handle
Function 40h Write File or Device
Function 42h Move File Pointer
Function 5Ah Create Temporary File
Function 5Bh Create New File
Function 6Ch Extended Open/Create

■ Function 40h Write File or Device

```
mov      bx, Handle           ;handle of file or device
mov      cx, MaxBytes         ;maximum number of bytes to write
mov      dx, seg Buffer
mov      ds, dx
mov      dx, offset Buffer    ;ds:dx points to buffer containing data

mov      ah, 40h              ;Write File or Device
int      21h

jc       error_handler        ;carry set means error
mov      ActualBytes, ax      ;number of bytes written
```

Write File or Device (Function 40h) writes up to the specified number of bytes of data from a buffer to a file or device.

Parameters *Handle*   Identifies the file or device that is to receive the data.

MaxBytes   Specifies the maximum number of bytes to write.

Buffer   Points to a buffer that contains the data to write.

Return Value If the function is successful, the carry flag is clear and the AX register contains the number of bytes written to the file or device. Otherwise, the carry flag is set and the AX register contains an error value, which may be one of the following values:

Value	Name
0005h	ERROR_ACCESS_DENIED
0006h	ERROR_INVALID_HANDLE

Comments *Handle* can be a handle for a standard device or a handle created by using such a function as Open File with Handle (Function 3Dh).

When MS-DOS writes to a file, it writes data starting at the current location of the file pointer. When this function returns, the file pointer is positioned at the byte immediately after the last byte written to the file.

Writing 0 bytes to the file truncates the file at the current position of the file pointer.

If the number of bytes written is fewer than the number requested, the destination file or disk is full. Note that the carry flag is *not* set in this situation.

See Also Function 3Ch Create File with Handle
Function 3Dh Open File with Handle
Function 3Fh Read File or Device
Function 42h Move File Pointer
Function 5Ah Create Temporary File
Function 5Bh Create New File
Function 6Ch Extended Open/Create

■ Function 41h Delete File

```
mov     dx, seg FileName
mov     ds, dx
mov     dx, offset FileName  ;ds:dx points to filename

mov     ah, 41h              ;Delete File
int     21h

jc      error_handler        ;carry set means error
```

Delete File (Function 41h) deletes a specified file.

Parameter

FileName   Points to a zero-terminated ASCII string that specifies the file to delete. This string must be a valid MS-DOS filename and cannot contain wildcards.

Return Value

If the function is successful, the carry flag is clear. Otherwise, the carry flag is set and the AX register contains an error value, which may be one of the following values:

Value	Name
0002h	ERROR_FILE_NOT_FOUND
0003h	ERROR_PATH_NOT_FOUND
0005h	ERROR_ACCESS_DENIED

Comments

This function cannot be used to remove a directory, a volume label, or a read-only file. A program can use Set File Attributes (Function 4301h) to change the attributes of a read-only file so that the file can be deleted.

If the specified file is on a network drive, the function deletes the file only if network grants delete access to the drive or directory.

See Also

Function 3Ah Remove Directory
Function 4300h Get File Attributes
Function 4301h Set File Attributes

■ Function 42h Move File Pointer

```
mov     bx, Handle              ;file handle
mov     cx, HiOffset            ;most-significant 16 bits of offset
mov     dx, LoOffset            ;least-significant 16 bits of offset

mov     al, MoveMethod          ;move method code
or      ah, 42h                 ;Move File Pointer
int     21h

jc      error_handler           ;carry set means error

mov     HiPosition, dx          ;high 16 bits of absolute position
mov     LoPosition, ax          ;low 16 bits of absolute position
```

Move File Pointer (Function 42h) moves the file pointer to the specified position in the file. The file pointer is maintained by the system; it points to the next byte to be read from a file or to the next position in the file to receive a byte.

Parameters

Handle   Identifies an open file.

HiOffset   Specifies the most-significant 16 bits of a 32-bit offset. The offset specifies the number of bytes to move the file pointer. This value may be positive or negative.

LoOffset   Specifies the least-significant 16 bits of the 32-bit offset.

MoveMethod   Specifies where the move will start. This parameter must be one of the following values:

Value	Meaning
00h	Start move at the beginning of the file.
01h	Start move at the current location.
02h	Start move at the end of the file.

Return Value

If the function is successful, the carry flag is clear and the DX and AX registers contain the new position of the file pointer. The DX register contains the most-significant 16 bits of the 32-bit offset, and the AX register contains the least-significant 16 bits. Otherwise, the carry flag is set and the AX register contains an error value, which may be one of the following values:

Value	Name
0001h	ERROR_INVALID_FUNCTION
0006h	ERROR_INVALID_HANDLE

Comments

This function returns 0001h (ERROR_INVALID_FUNCTION) if a method other than 00h, 01h, or 02h is specified for *MoveMethod*.

With method 00h, the 32-bit value in the CX and DX registers is always interpreted as a positive value. It is not possible to move the file pointer to a position before the start of the file with method 00h. With methods 01h and 02h, however, the 32-bit offset is interpreted as a signed value; it is possible to move the file pointer either forward or backward.

A program should never attempt to move the file pointer to a position before the start of the file. Although this action does not generate an error during the move, it does generate an error on a subsequent read or write operation. A program can move the file pointer beyond the end of the file. On a subsequent write operation, MS-DOS writes data to the given position in the file, filling the gap between the previous end of the file and the given position with undefined data. This is a common way to reserve file space without writing to the file.

See Also   Function 3Fh Read File or Device
Function 40h Write File or Device

■ Function 4300h Get File Attributes

```
mov     dx, seg FileName
mov     ds, dx
mov     dx, offset FileName ;ds:dx points to filename or directory name

mov     ax, 4300h           ;Get File Attributes
int     21h

jc      error_handler       ;carry set means error
mov     Attributes, cx      ;attributes are returned in cx
```

Get File Attributes (Function 4300h) retrieves the attributes for a specified file or directory.

Parameter *FileName* Points to a zero-terminated ASCII string that specifies the file or directory to retrieve attributes for. This string must be a valid MS-DOS filename or directory name and cannot contain wildcards.

Return Value If the function is successful, the carry flag is clear and the CX register contains the attributes for the file or directory. Otherwise, the carry flag is set and the AX register contains an error value, which may be one of the following values:

Value	Name
0001h	ERROR_INVALID_FUNCTION
0002h	ERROR_FILE_NOT_FOUND
0003h	ERROR_PATH_NOT_FOUND
0005h	ERROR_ACCESS_DENIED

Comment The file attributes returned in the CX register may be a combination of the following values:

Value	Meaning
ATTR_NORMAL (0000h)	File can be read from or written to.
ATTR_READONLY (0001h)	File can read from but not written to.
ATTR_HIDDEN (0002h)	File or directory is hidden and does not appear in a directory listing.
ATTR_SYSTEM (0004h)	File or directory is a system file.
ATTR_ARCHIVE (0020h)	File has been archived.
ATTR_VOLUME (0008h)	Filename is the current volume label for the media.
ATTR_DIRECTORY (0010h)	Filename identifies a directory, not a file.

See Also Function 4301h Set File Attributes

■ Function 4301h Set File Attributes

```
mov     cx, Attributes      ;attributes to set
mov     dx, seg FileName
mov     ds, dx
mov     dx, offset FileName ;ds:dx points to filename or directory name

mov     ax, 4301h           ;Set File Attributes
int     21h

jc      error_handler       ;carry set means error
```

Set File Attributes (Function 4301h) sets the attributes for a specified file or directory.

Parameters   *Attributes*   Specifies the new attributes for the file or directory. This parameter can be a combination of the following values:

Value	Meaning
ATTR_NORMAL (0000h)	File can be read from or written to.
ATTR_READONLY (0001h)	File can read from but not written to.
ATTR_HIDDEN (0002h)	File is hidden and does not appear in a directory listing.
ATTR_SYSTEM (0004h)	File is a system file.
ATTR_ARCHIVE (0020h)	File has been archived.

FileName   Points to a zero-terminated ASCII string that specifies the file or directory to set attributes for. This string must be a valid MS-DOS filename or directory name and cannot contain wildcards.

Return Value   If the function is successful, the carry flag is clear. Otherwise, the carry flag is set and the AX register contains an error value, which may be one of the following values:

Value	Name
0001h	ERROR_INVALID_FUNCTION
0002h	ERROR_FILE_NOT_FOUND
0003h	ERROR_PATH_NOT_FOUND
0005h	ERROR_ACCESS_DENIED

Comments   Only ATTR_HIDDEN and ATTR_SYSTEM are meaningful for directories.

See Also   Function 4300h Get File Attributes

■ Function 4400h Get Device Data

```
mov     bx, Handle        ;handle of file or device

mov     ax, 4400h         ;Get Device Data
int     21h
jc      error_handler     ;carry set means error

mov     DevStatus, dx     ;device-status value
```

Get Device Data (Function 4400h) returns information about the handle, such as whether it identifies a file or a device.

Parameter   *Handle*   Identifies the file or device to return information about.

Return Value   If the function is successful, the carry flag is clear and the DX register contains the device-status value. Otherwise, the carry flag is set and the AX register contains an error value, which may be one of the following:

Value	Name
0001h	ERROR_INVALID_FUNCTION
0005h	ERROR_ACCESS_DENIED
0006h	ERROR_INVALID_HANDLE

Comments   Bit 7 in the DX register specifies whether the handle identifies a file or a device. If bit 7 is 0, the handle identifies a file, and the other bits in the DX register have the following meaning:

Bits	Meaning
0–5	Drive number (0 = A, 1 = B, etc.)
6	1 = file has not been written to

All other bits are zero. Bits 0–5 may specify an invalid drive number if the file is a network file that is not associated with a redirected drive.

If bit 7 is 1, the handle identifies a device, and the other bits in the DX register have the following meaning:

Bit	Meaning
0	1 = Console input device
1	1 = Console output device
2	1 = Null device
3	1 = Clock device
4	1 = Special device
5	1 = Binary mode, 0 = ASCII mode
6	0 = End of file returned if device is read

Bits 8 through 15 are identical to the high 8 bits of the **dhAttribute** field in the **DEVICEHEADER** structure for the device.

See Also   Function 4401h Set Device Data

■ Function 4401h Set Device Data

```
mov      bx, Handle          ;handle of file or device
mov      dx, DevStatus       ;device-status value

mov      ax, 4401h           ;Set Device Data
int      21h
jc       error_handler       ;carry set means error
```

Set Device Data (Function 4401h) tells MS-DOS how to use the device refer-
enced by the specified handle. This function cannot change how MS-DOS uses
a file.

Parameters
Handle   Identifies the device to set information for.

DevStatus   Specifies the device-status value. Bit 7 must be 1, to indicate that
the specified handle refers to a device, and other bits can be set as follows:

Bits	Meaning
0	1 = Console input device
1	1 = Console output device
2	1 = Null device
3	1 = Clock device
4	1 = Special device
5	1 = Binary mode, 0 = ASCII mode
6	0 = End of file returned if device is read

All other bits must be set to zero.

Return Value
If the function is successful, the carry flag is clear. Otherwise, the carry flag
is set and the AX register contains an error value, which may be one of the following:

Value	Name
0001h	ERROR_INVALID_FUNCTION
0005h	ERROR_ACCESS_DENIED
0006h	ERROR_INVALID_HANDLE
000Dh	ERROR_INVALID_DATA

See Also
Function 4400h Get Device Data

Function 4402h Receive Control Data from Character Device

```
mov     bx, Handle          ;handle of device
mov     cx, MaxBytes        ;maximum amount of data to receive
mov     dx, seg Buffer
mov     ds, dx
mov     dx, offset Buffer   ;ds:dx points to buffer to receive data

mov     ax, 4402h           ;Receive Control Data from Character Device
int     21h
jc      error_handler       ;carry set means error
mov     ActualBytes, ax     ;number of bytes received
```

Receive Control Data from Character Device (Function 4402h) reads control information of any length and format from a character-device driver. The format of the information is device-specific and does not follow any standard.

Parameters   *Handle*   Identifies the device to receive information from.

MaxBytes   Specifies the maximum number of bytes to read.

Buffer   Points to the buffer to receive the data read from the device. The buffer must be at least as large as *MaxBytes*.

Return Value   If the function is successful, the carry flag is clear, the buffer is filled in with the requested information, and the AX register contains the number of bytes received. Otherwise, the carry flag is set and the AX register contains an error value, which may be one of the following:

Value	Name
0001h	ERROR_INVALID_FUNCTION
0005h	ERROR_ACCESS_DENIED
0006h	ERROR_INVALID_HANDLE
000Dh	ERROR_INVALID_DATA

Comment   Character-device drivers are not required to support this function or Send Control Data to Character Device (Function 4403h). A program should use Get Device Data (Function 4400h) and examine bit 14 in the device-status value to ensure that the device driver can process control data.

See Also   Function 4400h Get Device Data
Function 4403h Send Control Data to Character Device
Function 4404h Receive Control Data from Block Device
Function 4405h Send Control Data to Block Device

■ Function 4403h Send Control Data to Character Device

```
mov      bx, Handle             ;handle of device
mov      cx, MaxBytes           ;maximum number of bytes to send
mov      dx, seg Buffer
mov      ds, dx
mov      dx, offset Buffer      ;ds:dx points to buffer with data to send

mov      ax, 4403h              ;Send Control Data to Character Device
int      21h
jc       error_handler          ;carry set means error
mov      ActualBytes, ax        ;number of bytes sent
```

Send Control Data to Character Device (Function 4403h) writes control information of any length and format to a character-device driver. The format of the
information is device-specific and does not follow any standard.

Parameters   *Handle*   Identifies the device to send information to.

MaxBytes   Specifies the number of bytes to write.

Buffer   Points to the buffer that contains the data to write to the device.

Return Value   If the function is successful, the carry flag is clear and the AX register contains
the number of bytes sent. Otherwise, the carry flag is set and the AX register
contains an error value, which may be one of the following:

Value	Name
0001h	ERROR_INVALID_FUNCTION
0005h	ERROR_ACCESS_DENIED
0006h	ERROR_INVALID_HANDLE
000Dh	ERROR_INVALID_DATA

Comment   Character-device drivers are not required to support this function or Receive
Control Data from Character Device (Function 4402h). A program should use
Get Device Data (Function 4400h) and examine bit 14 in the device-status value
to ensure that the device driver can process control data.

See Also   Function 4400h Get Device Data
Function 4402h Receive Control Data from Character Device
Function 4404h Receive Control Data from Block Device
Function 4405h Send Control Data to Block Device

Function 4404h Receive Control Data from Block Device

```
mov     bl, Drive           ;0 = default, 1 = A, 2 = B, etc.
mov     cx, MaxBytes        ;maximum number of bytes to receive
mov     dx, seg Buffer
mov     ds, dx
mov     dx, offset Buffer   ;ds:dx points to buffer to receive data

mov     ax, 4404h           ;Receive Control Data from Block Device
int     21h
jc      error_handler       ;carry set means error
mov     ActualBytes, ax     ;number of bytes received
```

Receive Control Data from Block Device (Function 4404h) reads control information of any length and format from a block-device driver. The format of the information is device-specific and does not follow any standard.

Parameters

Drive Specifies the drive for which information is requested (0 = default drive, 1 = drive A, 2 = drive B, etc.).

MaxBytes Specifies the maximum number of bytes to read.

Buffer Points to the buffer to receive the data read from the device. The buffer must be at least as large as *MaxBytes*.

Return Value

If the function is successful, the carry flag is clear, the buffer is filled in with the requested information, and the AX register contains the number of bytes received. Otherwise, the carry flag is set and the AX register contains an error value, which may be one of the following:

Value	Name
0001h	ERROR_INVALID_FUNCTION
0005h	ERROR_ACCESS_DENIED
0006h	ERROR_INVALID_HANDLE
000Dh	ERROR_INVALID_DATA

See Also

Function 4402h Receive Control Data from Character Device
Function 4403h Send Control Data to Character Device
Function 4405h Send Control Data to Block Device

■ Function 4405h Send Control Data to Block Device

```
mov     bl, Drive               ;0 = default, 1 = A, 2 = B, etc.
mov     cx, MaxBytes            ;maximum number of bytes to send
mov     dx, seg Buffer
mov     ds, dx
mov     dx, offset Buffer       ;ds:dx points to buffer containing data

mov     ax, 4405h               ;Send Control Data to Block Device
int     21h
jc      error_handler           ;carry set means error
mov     ActualBytes, ax         ;number of bytes sent
```

Send Control Data to Block Device (Function 4405h) writes control information of any length and format to a block-device driver. The format of the information is device-specific and does not follow any standard.

Parameters   *Drive*   Specifies the drive to send information to (0 = default drive, 1 = A, 2 = B, etc.).

MaxBytes   Specifies the number of bytes to write.

Buffer   Points to the buffer that contains the data to write to the device.

Return Value   If the function is successful, the carry flag is clear and the AX register contains the number of bytes sent. Otherwise, the carry flag is set and the AX register contains an error value, which may be one of the following:

Value	Name
0001h	ERROR_INVALID_FUNCTION
0005h	ERROR_ACCESS_DENIED
0006h	ERROR_INVALID_HANDLE
000Dh	ERROR_INVALID_DATA

See Also   Function 4402h Receive Control Data from Character Device
Function 4403h Send Control Data to Character Device
Function 4404h Receive Control Data from Block Device

■ Function 4406h Check Device Input Status

```
mov     bx, Handle          ;handle of file or device

mov     ax, 4406h           ;Check Device Input Status
int     21h
jc      error_handler       ;carry set means error

cmp     al, OFFh            ;OFFh means file or device is ready
jne     not_ready
```

Check Device Input Status (Function 4406h) determines whether a file or device is ready for input.

Parameter   *Handle*   Identifies the file or device to check.

Return Value   If the function is successful, the carry flag is clear and the AL register contains the input-status value. Otherwise, the carry flag is set and the AX register contains an error value, which may be one of the following:

Value	Name
0001h	ERROR_INVALID_FUNCTION
0005h	ERROR_ACCESS_DENIED
0006h	ERROR_INVALID_HANDLE

Comment   The meaning of the input-status value depends on whether the handle specifies a file or a device, as shown in the following table:

Status	Device	File
00h	Not ready	File pointer at end of file
0FFh	Ready .	·Ready

See Also   Function 4407h Check Device Output Status

■ Function 4407h Check Device Output Status

```
mov      bx, Handle        ;handle of file or device

mov      ax, 4407h         ;Check Device Output Status
int      21h
jc       error_handler     ;carry set means error

cmp      al, 0FFh          ;0FFh means file or device is ready
jne      not_ready
```

Check Device Output Status (Function 4407h) determines whether a file or device is ready for output.

Parameter *Handle* Identifies the file or device to check.

Return Value If the function is successful, the carry flag is clear and the AL register contains the output-status value. Otherwise, the carry flag is set and the AX register contains an error value, which may be one of the following:

Value	Name
0001h	ERROR_INVALID_FUNCTION
0005h	ERROR_ACCESS_DENIED
0006h	ERROR_INVALID_HANDLE

Comment The meaning of the output-status value depends on whether the handle specifies a file or a device, as shown in the following table:

Status	Device	File
00h	Not ready	Ready
0FFh	Ready	Ready

For an output file, Check Device Output Status always returns Ready, even if the disk is full or there is no disk in the drive.

See Also Function 4406h Check Device Input Status

■ Function 4408h Does Device Use Removable Media

```
mov     bl, Drive           ;0 = default, 1 = A, 2 = B, etc.

mov     ax, 4408h           ;Does Device Use Removable Media
int     21h
jc      error_handler       ;carry set means error

cmp     ax, 0               ;zero means removable media
jne     not_removable
```

Does Device Use Removable Media (Function 4408h) determines whether the specified device contains a removable storage medium, such as a floppy disk.

Parameter   *Drive*   Specifies the drive to check (0 = default drive, 1 = A, 2 = B, etc.).

Return Value   If the function is successful, the carry flag is clear and the AX register indicates whether the storage medium in the specified drive is removable (register contains 0000h) or not (register contains 0001h).

Otherwise, the carry flag is set and the AX register contains an error value, which may be one of the following:

Value	Name
0001h	ERROR_INVALID_FUNCTION
000Fh	ERROR_INVALID_DRIVE

Comments   This function returns 0001h (ERROR_INVALID_FUNCTION) for a network drive or for a device driver that does not support the function request. In these cases, the calling program should assume that the storage medium is not removable.

Function 4409h Is Drive Remote

```
mov     bl, Drive          ;0 = default, 1 = A, 2 = B, etc.

mov     ax, 4409h          ;Is Drive Remote
int     21h
jc      error_handler      ;carry set means error

test    dx, 1000h          ;bit 12 set means drive is remote
jnz     remote_device
```

Is Drive Remote (Function 4409h) determines whether the specified drive is local (attached to the computer running the program) or remote (on a network server).

Parameter   *Drive*   Specifies the drive to check (0 = default drive, 1 = A, 2 = B, etc.).

Return Value   If the function is successful, the carry flag is clear and the DX register contains the device-attribute value. Otherwise, the carry flag is set and the AX register contains an error value, which may be one of the following:

Value	Name
0001h	ERROR_INVALID_FUNCTION
000Fh	ERROR_INVALID_DRIVE

Comments   Bit 12 in the DX register specifies whether the drive is local or remote. If bit 12 is 1, the drive is remote and the other bits in the DX register are zero.

If bit 12 is zero, the drive is not a network drive, and the bits in the DX register have the following meaning:

Bit	Description
1	1 = Drive uses 32-bit sector addressing.
6	1 = Drive accepts Generic IOCTL for Block Devices, Get Logical Drive Map, and Set Logical Drive Map (Functions 440Dh, 440Eh, and 440Fh).
7	1 = Drive accepts Query IOCTL Device (Function 4411h).
9	1 = Drive is local but shared by other computers in the network.
11	1 = Drive accepts Does Device Use Removable Media (Function 4408h).
13	1 = Drive requires media descriptor in FAT.
14	1 = Drive accepts Receive Control Data from Block Device and Send Control Data to Block Device (Functions 4404h and 4405h).
15	1 = Substitution drive (for example, set by the **subst** command).

All other bits are zero.

■ Function 440Ah Is File or Device Remote

```
mov      bx, Handle          ;handle of file or device

mov      ax, 440Ah           ;Is File or Device Remote
int      21h
jc       error_handler       ;carry set means error

test     dx, 8000h           ;bit 15 set means device is remote
jnz      remote_device
```

Is File or Device Remote (Function 440Ah) determines whether the specified handle refers to a file or device that is local (on the computer running the program) or remote (on a network server).

Parameter   *Handle*   Specifies the file or device to check.

Return Value   If the function is successful, the carry flag is clear and the DX register contains the device-attribute value. Otherwise, the carry flag is set and the AX register contains an error value, which may be one of the following:

Value	Name
0001h	ERROR_INVALID_FUNCTION
0006h	ERROR_INVALID_HANDLE

Comments   Bit 15 of the device-attribute value indicates whether the file or device is local (bit is clear) or remote (bit is set).

Other bits in the DX register contain additional information about the file or device. In particular, bit 7 in the DX register specifies whether the handle identifies a file or a device. If bit 7 is 0, the handle identifies a file and the other bits in the DX register have the following meaning:

Bit	Meaning
0–5	Drive number (0 = A, 1 = B, 2 = C, etc.)
6	1 = File has not been written to
12	1 = No inherit
14	1 = Date/time not set at close
15	1 = Remote file, 0 = local file

All other bits are zero.

If bit 7 is 1, the handle identifies a device and the other bits in the DX register have the following meaning:

Bit	Meaning
0	1 = Console input device
1	1 = Console output device
2	1 = Null device
3	1 = Clock device
4	1 = Special device
5	1 = Binary mode, 0 = ASCII mode
6	0 = End of file returned if device is read

Bit	Meaning
11	1 = Network spooler
12	1 = No inherit
13	1 = Named pipe
15	1 = Remote device, 0 = local device

All other bits are zero.

■ Function 440Bh Set Sharing Retry Count

```
mov     cx, cPause       ;number of times through pause loop
mov     dx, cRetries     ;number of times to retry file operation

mov     ax, 440Bh        ;Set Sharing Retry Count
int     21h
jc      error_handler    ;carry set means error
```

Set Sharing Retry Count (Function 440Bh) sets the number of times MS-DOS retries a disk operation after a failure caused by a file-sharing operation. When the number of retries is reached without success, MS-DOS returns an error value to the program that requested the disk operation.

Parameters

cPause   Specifies the number of times MS-DOS is to go through a pause loop, thereby controlling the amount of time between retries.

cRetries   Specifies the number of times MS-DOS retries the file operation before returning an error value.

Return Value

If the function is successful, the carry flag is clear. Otherwise, the carry flag is set and the AX register contains an error value, which may be 0001h (ERROR_INVALID_FUNCTION).

Comments

Set Sharing Retry Count returns 0001h (ERROR_INVALID_FUNCTION) if file sharing is not active (SHARE.EXE has not been loaded).

The pause time depends on the computer's clock speed. The default sharing retry count is 3; the default number of times between retries is 1. If a program changes the retry count or pause value, it should restore the default values before terminating.

See Also

Function 5Ch   Lock/Unlock File
Interrupt 2Fh Function 1000h Get SHARE.EXE Installed State

■ Function 440Ch Minor Code 45h Set Iteration Count

```
mov     bx, Handle              ;handle of device
mov     ch, Category            ;device category

mov     cl, 45h                 ;Set Iteration Count

mov     dx, seg ItCount
mov     ds, dx
mov     dx, offset ItCount      ;points to buffer for iteration count

mov     ax, 440Ch               ;IOCTL for Character Device
int     21h

jc      error_handler           ;carry set means error
```

Set Iteration Count (Function 440Ch Minor Code 45h) sets the number of times the device driver is to try to send output to a device before assuming that the device is busy.

Parameters   *Handle*   Identifies the device to set the iteration count for.

Category   Specifies the type of device. This parameter must be one of the following values:

Value	Device
01h	Serial device
03h	Console (screen)
05h	Parallel printer

ItCount   Points to a buffer that contains a 16-bit iteration count. The device driver tries to send output to the device until it reaches this number of retries without success.

Return Value   If the function is successful, the carry flag is clear. Otherwise, the carry flag is set and the AX register contains an error value, which may be one of the following:

Value	Name
0001h	ERROR_INVALID_FUNCTION
0006h	ERROR_INVALID_HANDLE

This function may also return a device-dependent error value as specified by the device driver.

See Also   Function 440Ch Minor Code 65h Get Iteration Count

Function 440Ch Minor Code 4Ah Select Code Page

```
mov     bx, Handle                  ;handle of device
mov     ch, Category                ;device category

mov     cl, 4Ah                     ;Select Code Page

mov     dx, seg CodePageID
mov     ds, dx
mov     dx, offset CodePageID       ;ds:dx points to CODEPAGE structure

mov     ax, 440Ch                   ;IOCTL for Character Device
int     21h

jc      error_handler               ;carry set means error
```

Select Code Page (Function 440Ch Minor Code 4Ah) selects the code page used by the specified device. The code page must be in the list of prepared code pages for the device.

Parameters

Handle   Identifies the device to set the code page for.

Category   Specifies the type of device. This parameter must be one of the following values:

Value	Device
01h	Serial device
03h	Console (screen)
05h	Parallel printer

CodePageID   Points to a **CODEPAGE** structure that contains the identifier of the code page to be selected. The **CODEPAGE** structure has the following form:

```
CODEPAGE    STRUC
    cpLength    dw    2    ;struct size, excluding this field (always 2)
    cpId        dw    ?    ;code-page identifier
CODEPAGE    ENDS
```

For a full description of the **CODEPAGE** structure, see Chapter 6, "National Language Support."

Return Value

If the function is successful, the carry flag is clear. Otherwise, the carry flag is set.

See Also

Function 440Ch Minor Code 4Ch Start Code-Page Prepare
Function 440Ch Minor Code 4Dh End Code-Page Prepare
Function 440Ch Minor Code 6Ah Query Selected Code Page
Function 440Ch Minor Code 6Bh Query Code-Page Prepare List

■ Function 440Ch Minor Code 4Ch Start Code-Page Prepare

```
mov     bx, Handle              ;handle of device
mov     ch, Category            ;device category

mov     cl, 4Ch                 ;Start Code-Page Prepare

mov     dx, seg PrepareIDs
mov     ds, dx
mov     dx, offset PrepareIDs   ;ds:dx points to CPPREPARE structure

mov     ax, 440Ch               ;IOCTL for Character Device
int     21h

jc      error_handler           ;carry set means error
```

Start Code-Page Prepare (Function 440Ch Minor Code 4Ch) instructs a device driver to begin to prepare a new code-page list.

Parameters

Handle   Identifies the device to set code pages for.

Category   Specifies the type of device. This parameter must be one of the following values:

Value	Device
01h	Serial device
03h	Console (screen)
05h	Parallel printer

PrepareIDs   Points to a **CPPREPARE** structure that contains information for the new code-page list. The **CPPREPARE** structure has the following form:

```
CPPREPARE   STRUC
    cppFlags    dw O                    ;flags (device-specific)
    cppLength   dw (CODEPAGE_IDS+1)*2   ;structure length, in bytes,
                                        ;excluding first two fields
    cppIds      dw CODEPAGE_IDS         ;number of code pages in list
    cppId       dw CODEPAGE_IDS dup(?)  ;array of code pages
CPPREPARE   ENDS
```

For a full description of the **CPPREPARE** structure, see Chapter 6, "National Language Support."

Return Value

If the function is successful, the carry flag is clear. Otherwise, the carry flag is set.

Comments

After calling Start Code-Page Prepare, a program must write data defining the code-page fonts to the device driver by using Send Control Data to Character Device (Function 4403h). The code-page data is device-specific. The program must end the code-page preparation by using End Code-Page Prepare (Function 440Ch Minor Code 4Dh).

A program can instruct the device driver to set up the device with the most recently prepared code page by calling Start Code-Page Prepare with all code-page numbers set to 0FFFFh. This operation must be followed immediately with a call to End Code-Page Prepare (Function 440Ch Minor Code 4Dh).

See Also

Function 4403h Send Control Data to Character Device
Function 440Ch Minor Code 4Ah Select Code Page
Function 440Ch Minor Code 4Dh End Code-Page Prepare
Function 440Ch Minor Code 6Ah Query Selected Code Page
Function 440Ch Minor Code 6Bh Query Code-Page Prepare List

■ Function 440Ch Minor Code 4Dh End Code-Page Prepare

```
mov     bx, Handle              ;handle of device
mov     ch, Category            ;device category

mov     cl, 4Dh                 ;End Code-Page Prepare

mov     ax, 440Ch               ;IOCTL for Character Device
int     21h

jc      error_handler           ;carry set means error
```

End Code-Page Prepare (Function 440Ch Minor Code 4Dh) tells a device driver that code-page preparation is complete.

Parameters   *Handle*   Identifies the device the code pages are set for.

Category   Specifies the type of device. This parameter must be one of the following values:

Value	Device
01h	Serial device
03h	Console (screen)
05h	Parallel printer

Return Value   If the function is successful, the carry flag is clear. Otherwise, the carry flag is set.

Comment   End Code-Page Prepare completes code-page preparation started by using Start Code-Page Prepare (Function 440Ch Minor Code 4Ch).

See Also   Function 440Ch Minor Code 4Ah Select Code Page
Function 440Ch Minor Code 4Ch Start Code-Page Prepare
Function 440Ch Minor Code 6Ah Query Selected Code Page
Function 440Ch Minor Code 6Bh Query Code-Page Prepare List

■ Function 440Ch Minor Code 5Fh Set Display Mode

```
mov      bx, Handle           ;handle of device
mov      ch, 03h              ;screen device category

mov      cl, 5Fh              ;Set Display Mode

mov      dx, seg Mode
mov      ds, dx
mov      dx, offset Mode      ;points to buffer for display mode

mov      ax, 440Ch            ;IOCTL for Character Device
int      21h

jc       error_handler       ;carry set means error
```

Set Display Mode (Function 440Ch Minor Code 5Fh) sets the display mode for the screen device.

Parameters

Handle   Identifies the device to set the display mode for.

Mode   Points to a **DISPLAYMODE** structure that specifies the mode to set. The **dmInfoLevel** field must be 0 and the **dmDataLength** field must be 14. The structure has the following form:

```
DISPLAYMODE     STRUC
    dmInfoLevel     db 0     ;information level (must be zero)
    dmReserved1     db ?     ;reserved
    dmDataLength    dw ?     ;length of remaining data, in bytes
    dmFlags         dw ?     ;control flags
    dmMode          db ?     ;display mode
    dmReserved2     db ?     ;reserved
    dmColors        dw ?     ;number of colors
    dmWidth         dw ?     ;screen width, in pixels
    dmLength        dw ?     ;screen length, in pixels
    dmColumns       dw ?     ;columns
    dmRows          dw ?     ;rows
DISPLAYMODE     ENDS
```

For more information about the **DISPLAYMODE** structure, see Chapter 4, "Character Input and Output."

Return Value

If the function is successful, the carry flag is clear. Otherwise, the carry flag is set and the AX register contains an error value, which may be one of the following:

Value	Name
0001h	ERROR_INVALID_FUNCTION
0005h	ERROR_ACCESS_DENIED
0006h	ERROR_INVALID_HANDLE

Comments

The function returns 0001h (ERROR_INVALID_FUNCTION) if the ANSI.SYS driver has not been loaded.

See Also

Interrupt 2Fh Function 1A00h Get ANSI.SYS Installed State

Function 440Ch Minor Code 65h Get Iteration Count

```
mov     bx, Handle              ;handle of device
mov     ch, Category            ;device category

mov     cl, 65h                 ;Get Iteration Count

mov     dx, seg ItCount
mov     ds, dx
mov     dx, offset ItCount      ;points to buffer for iteration count

mov     ax, 440Ch               ;IOCTL for Character Device
int     21h

jc      error_handler           ;carry set means error
```

Get Iteration Count (Function 440Ch Minor Code 65h) returns the number of times the device driver is to try to send output to a device before assuming that the device is busy.

Parameters   *Handle*   Identifies the device to get the iteration count for.

Category   Specifies the type of device. This parameter must be one of the following values:

Value	Device
01h	Serial device
03h	Console (screen)
05h	Parallel printer

ItCount   Points to a 16-bit buffer to receive the iteration count. The device driver tries to send output to the device until it reaches this number of retries unsuccessfully.

Return Value   If the function is successful, the carry flag is clear. Otherwise, the carry flag is set and the AX register contains an error value, which may be one of the following:

Value	Name
0001h	ERROR_INVALID_FUNCTION
0006h	ERROR_INVALID_HANDLE

This function may also return a device-dependent error value as specified by the device driver.

See Also   Function 440Ch Minor Code 45h Set Iteration Count

■ Function 440Ch Minor Code 6Ah Query Selected Code Page

```
mov     bx, Handle                  ;handle of device
mov     ch, Category                ;device category

mov     cl, 6Ah                     ;Query Code Page

mov     dx, seg CodePageID
mov     ds, dx
mov     dx, offset CodePageID       ;ds:dx points to CODEPAGE structure

mov     ax, 440Ch                   ;IOCTL for Character Device
int     21h

jc      error_handler               ;carry set means error
```

Query Selected Code Page (Function 440Ch Minor Code 6Ah) returns the currently selected code page for the specified device.

Parameters   *Handle*   Identifies the device to return the selected code page for.

Category   Specifies the type of device. This parameter must be one of the following values:

Value	Device
01h	Serial device
03h	Console (screen)
05h	Parallel printer

CodePageID   Points to a **CODEPAGE** structure that receives the identifier for the selected code page. The **CODEPAGE** structure has the following form:

```
CODEPAGE    STRUC
   cpLength    dw  2    ;struct size, excluding this field (always 2)
   cpId        dw  ?    ;code-page identifier
CODEPAGE    ENDS
```

For a full description of the **CODEPAGE** structure, see Chapter 6, "National Language Support."

Return Value   If the function is successful, the carry flag is clear. Otherwise, the carry flag is set.

See Also   Function 440Ch Minor Code 4Ah Select Code Page
Function 440Ch Minor Code 4Ch Start Code-Page Prepare
Function 440Ch Minor Code 4Dh End Code-Page Prepare
Function 440Ch Minor Code 6Bh Query Code-Page Prepare List

■ Function 440Ch Minor Code 6Bh Query Code-Page Prepare List

```
mov     bx, Handle              ;handle of device
mov     ch, Category            ;device category

mov     cl, 6Bh                 ;Query Code-Page Prepare List

mov     dx, seg ListIDs
mov     ds, dx
mov     dx, offset ListIDs      ;ds:dx points to CPLIST structure

mov     ax, 440Ch               ;IOCTL for Character Device
int     21h

jc      error_handler           ;carry set means error
```

Query Code Page Prepare List (Function 440Ch Minor Code 6Bh) returns the list of currently prepared code pages for the specified device.

Parameters

Handle   Identifies the device to return the code-page list for.

Category   Specifies the type of device. This parameter must be one of the following values:

Value	Device
01h	Serial device
03h	Console (screen)
05h	Parallel printer

ListIDs   Points to a **CPLIST** structure that receives the list of prepared code pages. The **CPLIST** structure has the following form:

```
CPLIST  STRUC
    cplLength    dw    ((HARDWARE_IDS+1)+(PREPARED_IDS+1))*2
                                    ;structure length, in bytes,
                                    ;excluding this field
    cplHIds      dw    HARDWARE_IDS          ;number of hardware code pages
    cplHid       dw    HARDWARE_IDS dup(?)   ;array of hardware code pages
    cplPIds      dw    PREPARED_IDS          ;number of prepared code pages
    cplPid       dw    PREPARED_IDS dup(?)   ;array of prepared code pages
CPLIST  ENDS
```

For a full description of the **CPLIST** structure, see Chapter 6, "National Language Support."

Return Value

If the function is successful, the carry flag is clear. Otherwise, the carry flag is set.

Comment

The device driver may return up to 12 hardware code-page identifiers and 12 prepared code-page identifiers.

See Also

Function 440Ch Minor Code 4Ah Select Code Page
Function 440Ch Minor Code 4Ch Start Code-Page Prepare
Function 440Ch Minor Code 4Dh End Code-Page Prepare
Function 440Ch Minor Code 6Ah Query Selected Code Page

■ Function 440Ch Minor Code 7Fh Get Display Mode

```
        mov     bx, Handle              ;handle of device
        mov     ch, 03h                 ;screen device category

        mov     cl, 7Fh                 ;Get Display Mode

        mov     dx, seg Mode
        mov     ds, dx
        mov     dx, offset Mode         ;points to buffer for display mode

        mov     ax, 440Ch               ;IOCTL for Character Device
        int     21h

        jc      error_handler           ;carry set means error
```

Get Display Mode (Function 440Ch Minor Code 7Fh) retrieves the display mode for the screen device.

Parameters

Handle   Identifies the device to get the display mode for.

Mode   Points to a **DISPLAYMODE** structure that receives the display-mode information. Before the function is called, the **dmInfoLevel** field must be 0 and the **dmDataLength** field must be 14. The **DISPLAYMODE** structure has the following form:

```
DISPLAYMODE     STRUC
    dmInfoLevel     db 0        ;information level (must be zero)
    dmReserved1     db ?        ;reserved
    dmDataLength    dw ?        ;length of remaining data, in bytes
    dmFlags         dw ?        ;control flags
    dmMode          db ?        ;display mode
    dmReserved2     db ?        ;reserved
    dmColors        dw ?        ;number of colors
    dmWidth         dw ?        ;screen width, in pixels
    dmLength        dw ?        ;screen length, in pixels
    dmColumns       dw ?        ;columns
    dmRows          dw ?        ;rows
DISPLAYMODE     ENDS
```

For more information about the **DISPLAYMODE** structure, see Chapter 4, "Character Input and Output."

Return Value

If the function is successful, the carry flag is clear. Otherwise, the carry flag is set and the AX register contains an error value, which may be one of the following:

Value	Name
0001h	ERROR_INVALID_FUNCTION
0005h	ERROR_ACCESS_DENIED
0006h	ERROR_INVALID_HANDLE

Comments

The function returns 0001h (ERROR_INVALID_FUNCTION) if the ANSI.SYS driver has not been loaded.

See Also

Function 440Ch Minor Code 5Fh Set Display Mode
Interrupt 2Fh Function 1A00h Get ANSI.SYS Installed State

■ Function 440Dh Minor Code 40h Set Device Parameters

```
mov     bx, Drive              ;0 = default, 1 = A, 2 = B, etc.
mov     ch, 08h                ;device category (must be 08h)

mov     cl, 40h                ;Set Device Parameters

mov     dx, seg DriveDP
mov     ds, dx
mov     dx, offset DriveDP     ;ds:dx points to DEVICEPARAMS structure

mov     ax, 440Dh              ;IOCTL for Block Device
int     21h

jc      error_handler          ;carry set means error
```

Set Device Parameters (Function 440Dh Minor Code 40h) sets the device parameters for the specified block device.

Parameters

Drive   Specifies the drive that parameters are being set for (0 = default drive, 1 = A, 2 = B, etc.).

DriveDP   Points to a **DEVICEPARAMS** structure that contains the parameters for the specified block device. The **DEVICEPARAMS** structure has the following form:

```
DEVICEPARAMS    STRUC
    dpSpecFunc      db  ?    ;special functions
    dpDevType       db  ?    ;device type
    dpDevAttr       dw  ?    ;device attributes
    dpCylinders     dw  ?    ;number of cylinders
    dpMediaType     db  ?    ;media type
                             ;Start of BIOS parameter block (BPB)
    dpBytesPerSec   dw  ?    ;bytes per sector
    dpSecPerClust   db  ?    ;sectors per cluster
    dpResSectors    dw  ?    ;number of reserved sectors
    dpFATs          db  ?    ;number of file allocation tables
    dpRootDirEnts   dw  ?    ;number of root-directory entries
    dpSectors       dw  ?    ;total number of sectors
    dpMedia         db  ?    ;media descriptor
    dpFATsecs       dw  ?    ;number of sectors per FAT
    dpSecPerTrack   dw  ?    ;sectors per track
    dpHeads         dw  ?    ;number of heads
    dpHiddenSecs    dd  ?    ;number of hidden sectors
    dpHugeSectors   dd  ?    ;number of sectors if dpSectors = 0
                             ;End of BIOS parameter block (BPB)
DEVICEPARAMS    ENDS
```

For a full description of the **DEVICEPARAMS** structure, see Chapter 3, "File System."

Return Value

If the function is successful, the carry flag is clear. Otherwise, the carry flag is set and the AX register contains an error value, which may be one of the following:

Value	Name
0001h	ERROR_INVALID_FUNCTION
0002h	ERROR_FILE_NOT_FOUND
0005h	ERROR_ACCESS_DENIED

Comment

Set Device Parameters returns 0002h (ERROR_FILE_NOT_FOUND) if the specified drive number is invalid.

See Also

Function 440Dh Minor Code 60h Get Device Parameters

Function 440Dh Minor Code 41h Write Track on Logical Drive

```
        mov     bx, Drive               ;0 = default, 1 = A, 2 = B, etc.
        mov     ch, 08h                 ;device category (must be 08h)

        mov     cl, 41h                 ;Write Track on Logical Drive

        mov     dx, seg WriteBlock
        mov     ds, dx
        mov     dx, offset WriteBlock   ;ds:dx points to RWBLOCK structure

        mov     ax, 440Dh               ;IOCTL for Block Device
        int     21h

        jc      error_handler           ;carry set means error
```

Write Track on Logical Drive (Function 440Dh Minor Code 41h) writes data from a buffer to a track on the specified device.

Parameters

Drive   Specifies the drive information is to be written to (0 = default drive, 1 = A, 2 = B, etc.).

WriteBlock   Points to an **RWBLOCK** structure that contains information that specifies the sectors to be written to. The **rwBuffer** field must contain the address of the buffer that contains the data to write to the disk. The **RWBLOCK** structure has the following form:

```
RWBLOCK STRUC
    rwSpecFunc      db  0   ;special functions (must be zero)
    rwHead          dw  ?   ;head to read/write
    rwCylinder      dw  ?   ;cylinder to read/write
    rwFirstSector   dw  ?   ;first sector to read/write
    rwSectors       dw  ?   ;number of sectors to read/write
    rwBuffer        dd  ?   ;address of buffer for read/write data
RWBLOCK ENDS
```

For a full description of the **RWBLOCK** structure, see Chapter 3, "File System."

Return Value

If the function is successful, the carry flag is clear. Otherwise, the carry flag is set and the AX register contains an error value, which may be one of the following:

Value	Name
0001h	ERROR_INVALID_FUNCTION
0002h	ERROR_FILE_NOT_FOUND
0005h	ERROR_ACCESS_DENIED

Comment

Write Track on Logical Drive returns 0002h (ERROR_FILE_NOT_FOUND) if the specified drive number is invalid.

See Also

Function 440Dh Minor Code 61h Read Track on Logical Drive

■ Function 440Dh Minor Code 42h Format Track on Logical Drive

```
mov      bx, Drive                    ;0 = default, 1 = A, 2 = B, etc.
mov      ch, 08h                      ;device category (must be 08h)

mov      cl, 42h                      ;Format Track on Logical Drive

mov      dx, seg FormatBlock
mov      ds, dx
mov      dx, offset FormatBlock       ;ds:dx points to FVBLOCK structure

mov      ax, 440Dh                    ;IOCTL for Block Device
int      21h

jc       error_handler               ;carry set means error
```

Format Track on Logical Drive (Function 440Dh Minor Code 42h) formats and verifies a track on the specified device.

Parameters

Drive   Specifies the drive on which the track is to be formatted and verified (0 = default drive, 1 = A, 2 = B, etc.).

FormatBlock   Points to an **FVBLOCK** structure that specifies the head and cylinder to format. The **FVBLOCK** structure has the following form:

```
FVBLOCK STRUC
    fvSpecFunc     db   0    ;special functions (must be zero)
    fvHead         dw   ?    ;head to format/verify
    fvCylinder     dw   ?    ;cylinder to format/verify
FVBLOCK ENDS
```

For a full description of the **FVBLOCK** structure, see Chapter 3, "File System."

Return Value

If the function is successful, the carry flag is clear. Otherwise, the carry flag is set and the AX register contains an error value, which may be one of the following:

Value	Name
0001h	ERROR_INVALID_FUNCTION
0002h	ERROR_FILE_NOT_FOUND
0005h	ERROR_ACCESS_DENIED

Comment

Format Track on Logical Drive returns 0002h (ERROR_FILE_NOT_FOUND) if the specified drive number is invalid.

See Also

Function 440Dh Minor Code 62h Verify Track on Logical Drive

Function 440Dh Minor Code 46h Set Media ID

```
mov     bx, Drive           ;0 = default, 1 = A, 2 = B, etc.
mov     ch, 08h             ;device category (must be 08h)

mov     cl, 46h             ;Set Media ID

mov     dx, seg MediaID
mov     ds, dx
mov     dx, offset MediaID  ;ds:dx points to MID structure

mov     ax, 440Dh           ;IOCTL for Block  Device
int     21h

jc      error_handler       ;carry set means error
```

Set Media ID (Function 440Dh Minor Code 46h) sets the volume label, serial number, and file system for the specified drive.

Parameters

Drive   Specifies the drive for which identification is to be set (0 = default drive, 1 = A, 2 = B, etc.).

MediaID   Points to a **MID** structure that contains information that uniquely identifies a disk or other storage medium. The **MID** structure has the following form:

```
MID STRUC
    midInfoLevel    dw  0           ;information level
    midSerialNum    dd  ?           ;serial number
    midVolLabel     db  11 dup (?)  ;ASCII volume label
    midFileSysType  db  8 dup (?)   ;file system type
MID ENDS
```

For a full description of the **MID** structure, see Chapter 3, "File System."

Return Value

If the function is successful, the carry flag is clear. Otherwise, the carry flag is set and the AX register contains an error value, which may be one of the following:

Value	Name
0001h	ERROR_INVALID_FUNCTION
0002h	ERROR_FILE_NOT_FOUND
0005h	ERROR_ACCESS_DENIED

Comments

Set Media ID returns 0002h (ERROR_FILE_NOT_FOUND) if the specified drive number is invalid.

See Also

Function 440Dh Minor Code 66h Get Media ID

■ Function 440Dh Minor Code 60h Get Device Parameters

```
mov     bx, Drive           ;O = default, 1 = A, 2 = B, etc.
mov     ch, 08h             ;device category (must be 08h)

mov     cl, 60h             ;Get Device Parameters

mov     dx, seg DriveDP
mov     ds, dx
mov     dx, offset DriveDP  ;ds:dx points to DEVICEPARAMS structure

mov     ax, 440Dh           ;IOCTL for Block Device
int     21h

jc      error_handler       ;carry set means error
```

Get Device Parameters (Function 440Dh Minor Code 60h) returns the device parameters for the specified block device.

Parameters

Drive   Specifies the drive for which parameters are requested (0 = default drive, 1 = A, 2 = B, etc.).

DriveDP   Points to a **DEVICEPARAMS** structure that receives information on the device's storage capacity and characteristics. The **DEVICEPARAMS** structure has the following form:

```
DEVICEPARAMS    STRUC
    dpSpecFunc      db  ?   ;special functions
    dpDevType       db  ?   ;device type
    dpDevAttr       dw  ?   ;device attributes
    dpCylinders     dw  ?   ;number of cylinders
    dpMediaType     db  ?   ;media type
                            ;Start of BIOS parameter block (BPB)
    dpBytesPerSec   dw  ?   ;bytes per sector
    dpSecPerClust   db  ?   ;sectors per cluster
    dpResSectors    dw  ?   ;number of reserved sectors
    dpFATs          db  ?   ;number of file allocation tables
    dpRootDirEnts   dw  ?   ;number of root-directory entries
    dpSectors       dw  ?   ;total number of sectors
    dpMedia         db  ?   ;media descriptor
    dpFATsecs       dw  ?   ;number of sectors per FAT
    dpSecPerTrack   dw  ?   ;sectors per track
    dpHeads         dw  ?   ;number of heads
    dpHiddenSecs    dd  ?   ;number of hidden sectors
    dpHugeSectors   dd  ?   ;number of sectors if dpSectors = O
                            ;End of BIOS parameter block (BPB)
DEVICEPARAMS    ENDS
```

The **dpSpecFunc** field determines whether the function retrieves current or default information. If the field is set to 1, the function retrieves information about the current medium in the drive; if the field is set to 0, the function retrieves information about the default medium for the drive.

For a full description of the **DEVICEPARAMS** structure, see Chapter 3, "File System."

Return Value

If the function is successful, the carry flag is clear. Otherwise, the carry flag is set and the AX register contains an error value, which may be one of the following:

Value	Name
0001h	ERROR_INVALID_FUNCTION
0002h	ERROR_FILE_NOT_FOUND
0005h	ERROR_ACCESS_DENIED

Comment   Get Device Parameters returns 0002h (ERROR_FILE_NOT_FOUND) if the
                  specified drive number is invalid.

See Also   Function 440Dh Minor Code 40h Set Device Parameters

■ Function 440Dh Minor Code 61h Read Track on Logical Drive

```
mov     bx, Drive               ;0 = default, 1 = A, 2 = B, etc.
mov     ch, 08h                 ;device category (must be 08h)

mov     cl, 61h                 ;Read Track on Logical Drive

mov     dx, seg ReadBlock
mov     ds, dx
mov     dx, offset ReadBlock    ;ds:dx points to RWBLOCK structure

mov     ax, 440Dh               ;IOCTL for Block Device
int     21h

jc      error_handler           ;carry set means error
```

Read Track on Logical Drive (Function 440Dh Minor Code 61h) reads data from a track on the specified device and places the data in memory.

Parameters

Drive   Specifies the drive to be read from (0 = default drive, 1 = A, 2 = B, etc.).

ReadBlock   Points to an **RWBLOCK** structure that contains information that specifies the sectors to be read from. The **RWBLOCK** structure has the following form:

```
RWBLOCK STRUC
    rwSpecFunc      db  0   ;special functions (must be zero)
    rwHead          dw  ?   ;head to read/write
    rwCylinder      dw  ?   ;cylinder to read/write
    rwFirstSector   dw  ?   ;first sector to read/write
    rwSectors       dw  ?   ;number of sectors to read/write
    rwBuffer        dd  ?   ;address of buffer for read/write data
RWBLOCK ENDS
```

For a full description of the **RWBLOCK** structure, see Chapter 3, "File System."

Return Value

If the function is successful, the carry flag is clear. Otherwise, the carry flag is set and the AX register contains an error value, which may be one of the following:

Value	Name
0001h	ERROR_INVALID_FUNCTION
0002h	ERROR_FILE_NOT_FOUND
0005h	ERROR_ACCESS_DENIED

Comment

Read Track on Logical Drive returns 0002h (ERROR_FILE_NOT_FOUND) if the specified drive number is invalid.

See Also

Function 440Dh Minor Code 41h Write Track on Logical Drive

■ Function 440Dh Minor Code 62h Verify Track on Logical Drive

```
mov     bx, Drive               ;O = default, 1 = A, 2 = B, etc.
mov     ch, O8h                 ;device category (must be O8h)

mov     cl, 62h                 ;Verify Track on Logical Drive

mov     dx, seg VerifyBlock
mov     ds, dx
mov     dx, offset VerifyBlock  ;ds:dx points to FVBLOCK structure

mov     ax, 44ODh               ;IOCTL for Block Device
int     21h

jc      error_handler           ;carry set means error
```

Verify Track on Logical Drive (Function 440Dh Minor Code 62h) verifies a track on the specified device.

Parameters   *Drive*   Specifies the drive on which the track is to be verified (0 = default drive, 1 = A, 2 = B, etc.).

VerifyBlock   Points to an **FVBLOCK** structure that specifies the head and cylinder to verify. The **FVBLOCK** structure has the following form:

```
FVBLOCK STRUC
    fvSpecFunc      db  O   ;special functions (must be zero)
    fvHead          dw  ?   ;head to format/verify
    fvCylinder      dw  ?   ;cylinder to format/verify
FVBLOCK ENDS
```

For a full description of the **FVBLOCK** structure, see Chapter 3, "File System."

Return Value   If the function is successful, the carry flag is clear. Otherwise, the carry flag is set and the AX register contains an error value, which may be one of the following:

Value	Name
0001h	ERROR_INVALID_FUNCTION
0002h	ERROR_FILE_NOT_FOUND
0005h	ERROR_ACCESS_DENIED

Comment   Verify Track on Logical Drive returns 0002h (ERROR_FILE_NOT_FOUND) if the specified drive number is invalid.

See Also   Function 440Dh Minor Code 42h Format Track on Logical Drive

■ Function 440Dh Minor Code 66h Get Media ID

```
mov     bx, Drive              ;0 = default, 1 = A, 2 = B, etc.
mov     ch, 08h                ;device category (must be 08h)

mov     cl, 66h                ;Get Media ID

mov     dx, seg MediaID
mov     ds, dx
mov     dx, offset MediaID     ;ds:dx points to MID structure

mov     ax, 440Dh              ;IOCTL for Block Device
int     21h

jc      error_handler          ;carry set means error
```

Get Media ID (Function 440Dh Minor Code 66h) returns the volume label, serial number and file system for the specified drive.

Parameters   *Drive*   Specifies the drive for which information is to be returned (0 = default drive, 1 = A, 2 = B, etc.).

MediaID   Points to a **MID** structure that receives information that uniquely identifies a disk or other storage medium. The **MID** structure has the following form:

```
MID STRUC
    midInfoLevel    dw  0            ;information level
    midSerialNum    dd  ?            ;serial number
    midVolLabel     db  11 dup (?)   ;ASCII volume label
    midFileSysType  db  8 dup (?)    ;file system type
MID ENDS
```

For a full description of the **MID** structure, see Chapter 3, "File System."

Return Value   If the function is successful, the carry flag is clear, and the parameter block is filled in with information about the disk. Otherwise, the carry flag is set and the AX register contains an error value, which may be one of the following:

Value	Name
0001h	ERROR_INVALID_FUNCTION
0002h	ERROR_FILE_NOT_FOUND
0005h	ERROR_ACCESS_DENIED

Comments   Get Media ID returns 0002h (ERROR_FILE_NOT_FOUND) if the specified drive number is invalid.

See Also   Function 440Dh Minor Code 46h Set Media ID

■ Function 440Dh Minor Code 68h Sense Media Type

```
mov    bx, Drive            ;O = default, 1 = A, 2 = B, etc.
mov    ch, 08h              ;device category (must be 08h)

mov    cl, 68h              ;Sense Media Type

mov    dx, seg Media
mov    ds, dx
mov    dx, offset Media     ;ds:dx points to buffer for media type

mov    ax, 440Dh            ;IOCTL for Block Device
int    21h

jc     error_handler        ;carry set means error
```

Sense Media Type (Function 440Dh Minor Code 68h) returns the media type for the specified block device.

Parameters   *Drive*   Specifies the drive for which parameters are requested (0 = default drive, 1 = A, 2 = B, etc.).

Media   Points to a 2-byte buffer that receives information on the media type for the given drive. The buffer has the following form:

Offset	Description
00h	Receives a value specifying whether the media type is the default value. This byte is set to 01h for the default media type and to 00h for any other media type.
01h	Receives a value specifying the media type. This byte is set to 02h for 720K disks, 07h for 1.44-MB disks, and 09h for 2.88-MB disks.

Return Value   If the function is successful, the carry flag is clear. Otherwise, the carry flag is set and the AX register contains an error value, which may be one of the following:

Value	Name
0001h	ERROR_INVALID_FUNCTION
0005h	ERROR_ACCESS_DENIED

This function may also return a device-dependent error value as specified by the device driver.

Comment   Sense Media Type returns 0005h (ERROR_ACCESS_DENIED) if the media type for the specified drive cannot be determined or the given drive is not ready. Programs can use Get Extended Error (Function 59h) to retrieve additional information about the error.

■ Function 440Eh Get Logical Drive Map

```
mov     bl, Drive        ;0 = default, 1 = A, 2 = B, etc.

mov     ax, 440Eh        ;Get Logical Drive Map
int     21h

jc      error_handler    ;carry set means error
```

Get Logical Drive Map (Function 440Eh) determines whether a physical drive has more than one logical drive number and returns the active drive number if it does.

Parameter

Drive Specifies the drive number to check (0 = default drive, 1 = A, 2 = B, etc.). The function checks the physical drive that corresponds to this logical drive number.

Return Value

If the function is successful, the carry flag is clear and the AL register contains the active drive number for the corresponding physical drive. If the physical drive has only one drive number, the AL register contains 00h.

If the function is not successful, the carry flag is set and the AX register contains an error value, which may be one of the following:

Value	Name
0001h	ERROR_INVALID_FUNCTION
0005h	ERROR_ACCESS_DENIED
000Fh	ERROR_INVALID_DRIVE

Comments

If a program attempts to access the drive by using an inactive drive number, MS-DOS prompts the user with the message "Insert diskette for drive *x*: and press any key when ready."

See Also

Function 440Fh Set Logical Drive Map

■ Function 440Fh Set Logical Drive Map

```
mov      bl, Drive        ;0 = default, 1 = A, 2 = B, etc.

mov      ax, 440Fh        ;Set Logical Drive Map
int      21h

jc       error_handler    ;carry set means error
```

Set Logical Drive Map (Function 440Fh) sets the active drive number for a physical drive that has more than one logical drive number.

Parameter   *Drive*   Specifies the drive number to set (0 = default drive, 1 = A, 2 = B, etc.).

Return Value   If the function is successful, the carry flag is clear, and the AL register contains the active drive number for the corresponding physical drive. If the physical drive has only one drive number, the AL register contains 00h.

If the function is not successful, the carry flag is set and the AX register contains an error value, which may be one of the following:

Value	Meaning
0001h	ERROR_INVALID_FUNCTION
0005h	ERROR_ACCESS_DENIED
000Fh	ERROR_INVALID_DRIVE

Comments   Programs that set the active drive prevent MS-DOS from prompting the user with the message "Insert diskette for drive *x*: and press any key when ready."

See Also   Function 440Eh Get Logical Drive Map

■ Function 4410h Query IOCTL Handle

```
mov     bx, Handle        ;Device handle

mov     ch, Category      ;Category to check
mov     cl, Function      ;Function to check

mov     ax, 4410h         ;Query IOCTL Handle 4410h
int     21h
jnc     supported         ;carry clear means IOCTL supported
```

Query IOCTL Handle (Function 4410h) determines whether the specified IOCTL function is supported by the given device driver.

Parameters

Handle   Identifies the device to check.

Category   Specifies an IOCTL category code. It can be one of the following:

Value	Meaning
01h	Serial device
03h	Console (screen)
05h	Parallel printer

Function   Specifies a Function 440Ch minor code. It can be one of the following:

Value	Meaning
45h	Set Iteration Count
65h	Get Iteration Count

Return Value

If IOCTL is supported, the carry flag is clear. Otherwise, the carry flag is set and AX contains an error value, which may be one of the following:

Value	Name
0001h	ERROR_INVALID_FUNCTION
0005h	ERROR_ACCESS_DENIED

Comments

Query IOCTL Handle returns 0001h (ERROR_INVALID_FUNCTION) if the device driver has no support for IOCTL functions. The function returns 0005h (ERROR_ACCESS_DENIED) if the device driver supports IOCTL functions but does not support the specified IOCTL.

See Also

Function 3Dh Open File with Handle
Function 3Ch Create File with Handle
Function 4411h Query IOCTL Device

■ Function 4411h Query IOCTL Device

```
mov     bl, Drive        ;0 = default, 1 = A, 2 = B, etc.

mov     ch, 8            ;IOCTL category to check. Must be 8
mov     cl, Function     ;IOCTL function to check

mov     ax, 4411h        ;Query IOCTL Device 4411h
int     21h
jnc     supported        ;carry clear means IOCTL supported
```

Query IOCTL Device (Function 4411h) determines whether the specified IOCTL function is supported for the given drive.

Parameters   *Drive*   Specifies the drive (0 = default drive, 1 = A, 2 = B, etc.).

Function   Specifies a Function 4401 minor code. It can be one of the following:

Value	Meaning
40h	Set Device Parameters
41h	Write Track on Logical Drive
42h	Format Track on Logical Drive
46h	Set Media ID
60h	Get Device Parameters
61h	Read Track on Logical Drive
62h	Verify Track on Logical Drive
66h	Get Media ID
68h	Sense Media Type

Return Value   If IOCTL is supported, the carry flag is clear. Otherwise, the carry flag is set and AX contains an error value, which may be one of the following:

Value	Name
0001h	ERROR_INVALID_FUNCTION
0005h	ERROR_ACCESS_DENIED
000Fh	ERROR_INVALID_DRIVE

Comments   Query IOCTL Device returns 0001h (ERROR_INVALID_FUNCTION) if the device driver has no support for IOCTL functions. The function returns 0005h (ERROR_ACCESS_DENIED) if the device driver supports IOCTL functions but does not support the specified IOCTL.

See Also   Function 4410h Query IOCTL Handle

■ Function 45h Duplicate File Handle

```
mov      bx, OldHandle          ;handle to duplicate

mov      ah, 45h                ;Duplicate File Handle
int      21h

jc       error_handler          ;carry set means error
mov      NewHandle, ax          ;refers to same file as OldHandle
```

Duplicate File Handle (Function 45h) creates a new file handle that can be used to read from or write to the same file or device that is associated with the original handle.

Parameter *OldHandle*   Identifies the handle to be duplicated.

Return Value If the function is successful, the carry flag is clear and the AX register contains the new handle. Otherwise, the carry flag is set and the AX register contains an error value, which may be one of the following:

Value	Name
0004h	ERROR_TOO_MANY_OPEN_FILES
0006h	ERROR_INVALID_HANDLE

Comments If this function is used to duplicate the handle of an open file, the file pointer for the new handle is set to the same position as the pointer for the old handle. Using either handle to read from or write to the file changes the file pointer for both handles.

Duplicate File Handle can also be used to keep a file open while its directory entry is changed. If a program creates a duplicate handle and then closes the original handle, the file's directory entry is updated, but the duplicate handle can still be used to read from or write to the file.

See Also Function 46h Force Duplicate File Handle

■ Function 46h Force Duplicate File Handle

```
mov     bx, OpenHandle        ;handle of file or device
mov     cx, DuplicateHandle   ;new handle for same file or device

mov     ah, 46h               ;Force Duplicate File Handle
int     21h

jc      error_handler         ;carry set means error
```

Force Duplicate File Handle (Function 46h) forces the specified duplicate handle to identify the same open file or device identified by the *OpenHandle* parameter.

Parameters   *OpenHandle*   Identifies an open file or device.

DuplicateHandle   Specifies an integer value for the new handle. This integer must not exceed the current limit as specified by Set Maximum Handle Count (Function 67h).

Return Value   If the function is successful, the carry flag is clear. Otherwise, the carry flag is set and the AX register contains an error value, which may be one of the following:

Value	Name
0004h	ERROR_TOO_MANY_OPEN_FILES
0006h	ERROR_INVALID_HANDLE

Comments   After a program uses this function, both handles can be used to read from or write to the file or device specified by *OpenHandle*. Moving the file pointer with either handle moves the file pointer for the other handle.

If *DuplicateHandle* identifies an open file, MS-DOS closes that file.

See Also   Function 45h Duplicate File Handle
Function 67h Set Maximum Handle Count

■ Function 47h Get Current Directory

```
        mov     si, seg CurDir
        mov     ds, si
        mov     si, offset CurDir   ;ds:si points to buf to receive current dir
        mov     dl, Drive           ;0 = default, 1 = A, 2 = B, etc.

        mov     ah, 47h             ;Get Current Directory
        int     21h

        jc      error_handler       ;carry set means error
```

Get Current Directory (Function 47h) returns the path of the current directory on the specified drive.

Parameters   *CurDir*   Points to a buffer where the current path on the specified drive is to be placed. The buffer should be at least 64 bytes, large enough to contain the largest possible path for the current directory.

Drive   Specifies the drive number (0 = default drive, 1 = A, 2 = B, etc.).

Return Value   If the function is successful, the carry flag is clear and the *CurDir* buffer is filled in with the current default path on the specified drive. Otherwise, the carry flag is set and the AX register contains an error value, which may be 000Fh (ERROR_INVALID_DRIVE).

Comment   This function copies to the specified buffer a zero-terminated ASCII string that identifies the current directory. The string consists of one or more directory names separated by backslashes (\). The path string does not include the drive letter and does not start with a leading backslash.

See Also   Function 3Bh Change Current Directory

■ Function 48h Allocate Memory

```
mov      bx, MemSize        ;amount of memory requested, in paragraphs

mov      ah, 48h            ;Allocate Memory
int      21h

jc       error_handler      ;carry set means error
mov      SegmentMem, ax     ;segment address of allocated memory
```

Allocate Memory (Function 48h) allocates the requested amount of memory and returns the segment address of the allocated memory block.

Parameter

MemSize   Specifies the amount of memory to be allocated, in paragraphs (16 bytes).

Return Value

If the function is successful, the carry flag is clear and the AX register contains the segment address of the first byte (offset 0) of the allocated memory block. Otherwise, the carry flag is set and the AX register contains an error value, which may be one of the following:

Value	Name
0007h	ERROR_ARENA_TRASHED
0008h	ERROR_NOT_ENOUGH_MEMORY

Comments

If Allocate Memory returns 0008h (ERROR_NOT_ENOUGH_MEMORY), the BX register contains the number of paragraphs in the largest available memory block.

The contents of the allocated memory are not defined.

MS-DOS allocates all available memory to a .COM program; most .EXE programs request all available memory when they load. If a program is to subsequently use the Allocate Memory function to dynamically allocate memory, it should use Set Memory Block Size (Function 4Ah) to free as much memory as possible.

The default memory-management strategy is to allocate the first available block that contains the requested number of bytes. A program can use Set Allocation Strategy (Function 5801h) to change the way MS-DOS chooses memory blocks for allocation.

See Also

Function 49h Free Allocated Memory
Function 4Ah Set Memory Block Size
Function 5800h Get Allocation Strategy
Function 5801h Set Allocation Strategy

■ Function 49h Free Allocated Memory

```
mov     ax, SegmentMem   ;segment address of memory to free
mov     es, ax

mov     ah, 49h          ;Free Allocated Memory
int     21h

jc      error_handler    ;carry set means error
```

Free Allocated Memory (Function 49h) frees a block of memory previously allocated by Allocate Memory (Function 48h).

Parameter
SegmentMem   Specifies the segment address of the memory block to be freed. This address must have been returned from a call to the Allocate Memory function.

Return Value
If the function is successful, the carry flag is clear. Otherwise, the carry flag is set and the AX register contains an error value, which may be one of the following:

Value	Name
0007h	ERROR_ARENA_TRASHED
0009h	ERROR_INVALID_BLOCK

Comment
MS-DOS returns 0009h (ERROR_INVALID_BLOCK) if a program tries to free memory that was not allocated by Allocate Memory.

See Also
Function 48h Allocate Memory

■ Function 4Ah Set Memory Block Size

```
mov     bx, MemSize      ;amount of memory, in paragraphs
mov     ax, SegmentMem   ;segment address of memory to resize
mov     es, ax

mov     ah, 4Ah          ;Set Memory Block Size
int     21h

jc      error_handler    ;carry set means error
```

Set Memory Block Size (Function 4Ah) can be used to change the size of a
memory segment previously allocated by Allocate Memory (Function 48h) or to
change the amount of memory originally allocated to a program by MS-DOS.

Parameters

MemSize   Specifies the new size of the memory block, in paragraphs. The new
size may be smaller or larger than the current size of the block.

SegmentMem   Specifies the segment address of the memory block to resize. If
the memory block was allocated by Allocate Memory, this parameter must be
the segment address returned by that function.

Return Value

If the function is successful, the carry flag is clear. Otherwise, the carry flag
is set and the AX register contains an error value, which may be one of the
following:

Value	Name
0007h	ERROR_ARENA_TRASHED
0008h	ERROR_NOT_ENOUGH_MEMORY
0009h	ERROR_INVALID_BLOCK

Comments

If this function returns 0008h (ERROR_NOT_ENOUGH_MEMORY), the BX
register contains the number of paragraphs in the largest available memory
block.

This function returns 0009h (ERROR_INVALID_BLOCK) if a program tries to
change the size of a memory block that was not allocated by Allocate Memory
or by MS-DOS when the program was started.

If this function is used to decrease the size of a memory block, the memory
above the new limit is no longer owned by the program and should not be used.
If this function is used to increase the size of a memory block, the contents of
the new memory are not defined.

See Also

Function 48h Allocate Memory
Function 49h Free Allocated Memory

■ Function 4B00h Load and Execute Program

```
mov     dx, seg ProgName
mov     ds, dx
mov     dx, offset ProgName    ;ds:dx points to program name

mov     bx, seg ProgArgs
mov     es, bx
mov     bx, offset ProgArgs    ;es:bx points to LOADEXEC structure

mov     ax, 4B00h              ;Load and Execute Program
int     21h

jc      error_handler          ;carry set means error
```

Load and Execute Program (Function 4B00h) loads a program into memory, creates a new program segment prefix (PSP), and transfers control to the new program.

Parameters   *ProgName*   Points to a zero-terminated ASCII string that specifies the program to load. The program name must be a valid MS-DOS filename, and the file must be a valid .COM or .EXE program.

ProgArgs   Points to a **LOADEXEC** structure that contains information the child program uses. The **LOADEXEC** structure has the following form:

```
LOADEXEC STRUC
    leEnvironment    dw ?    ;environment-block segment
    leCommandTail    dd ?    ;address of command tail
    leFCB_1          dd ?    ;address of default FCB #1
    leFCB_2          dd ?    ;address of default FCB #2
LOADEXEC ENDS
```

For a full description of the **LOADEXEC** structure, see Chapter 5, "Program Management."

Return Value   If the function is successful, the carry flag is clear. Otherwise, the carry flag is set and the AX register contains an error value, which may be one of the following:

Value	Name
0001h	ERROR_INVALID_FUNCTION
0002h	ERROR_FILE_NOT_FOUND
0003h	ERROR_PATH_NOT_FOUND
0004h	ERROR_TOO_MANY_OPEN_FILES
0005h	ERROR_ACCESS_DENIED
0008h	ERROR_NOT_ENOUGH_MEMORY
000Ah	ERROR_BAD_ENVIRONMENT
000Bh	ERROR_BAD_FORMAT

Comment   There must be enough free memory for MS-DOS to load the program file. All open files of the parent program, except files that were opened in no-inheritance mode, are available to the newly loaded program.

See Also

Function 31h Keep Program
Function 4B01h Load Program
Function 4B03h Load Overlay
Function 4B05h Set Execution State
Function 4Ch End Program
Function 4Dh Get Child-Program Return Value

■ Function 4B01h Load Program

```
mov     dx, seg ProgName
mov     ds, dx
mov     dx, offset ProgName    ;ds:dx points to program name

mov     bx, seg LoadArgs
mov     es, bx
mov     bx, offset LoadArgs    ;es:bx points to LOAD structure

mov     ax, 4B01h              ;Load Program
int     21h

jc      error_handler         ;carry set means error
```

Load Program (Function 4B01h) loads a program into memory and creates a new program segment prefix (PSP) but does not transfer control to the new program.

Parameters

ProgName   Points to a zero-terminated ASCII string specifying the program to load. The program name must be a valid MS-DOS filename, and the file must be a valid .COM or .EXE program.

LoadArgs   Points to a **LOAD** structure that contains information the child program uses. The **LOAD** structure has the following form:

```
LOAD STRUC
    ldEnvironment   dw ?    ;environment-block segment
    ldCommandTail   dd ?    ;address of command tail
    ldFCB_1         dd ?    ;address of default FCB #1
    ldFCB_2         dd ?    ;address of default FCB #2
    ldCSIP          dd ?    ;starting code address
    ldSSSP          dd ?    ;starting stack address
LOAD ENDS
```

For a full description of the **LOAD** structure, see Chapter 5, "Program Management."

Return Value

If the function is successful, the carry flag is clear. Otherwise, the carry flag is set and the AX register contains an error value, which may be one of the following:

Value	Name
0001h	ERROR_INVALID_FUNCTION
0002h	ERROR_FILE_NOT_FOUND
0003h	ERROR_PATH_NOT_FOUND
0004h	ERROR_TOO_MANY_OPEN_FILES
0005h	ERROR_ACCESS_DENIED
0008h	ERROR_NOT_ENOUGH_MEMORY
000Ah	ERROR_BAD_ENVIRONMENT
000Bh	ERROR_BAD_FORMAT

Comment

There must be enough free memory for MS-DOS to load the program file.

See Also

Function 4B00h Load and Execute Program
Function 4B03h Load Overlay
Function 4B05h Set Execution State

■ Function 4B03h Load Overlay

```
mov     dx, seg ProgName
mov     ds, dx
mov     dx, offset ProgName      ;ds:dx points to program name

mov     bx, seg OvlArgs
mov     es, bx
mov     bx, offset OvlArgs       ;es:bx points to LOADOVERLAY structure

mov     ax, 4B03h                ;Load Overlay
int     21h

jc      error_handler            ;carry set means error
```

Load Overlay (Function 4B03h) loads a program as an overlay. MS-DOS loads the overlay into memory already allocated by the program.

Parameters   *ProgName*   Points to a zero-terminated ASCII string specifying the program to load. The program name must be a valid MS-DOS filename.

OvlArgs   Points to a **LOADOVERLAY** structure that contains information used to load overlays. The **LOADOVERLAY** structure has the following form:

```
LOADOVERLAY STRUC
    loStartSegment          dw ?     ;segment address of overlay's memory
    loRelocationFactor      dw ?     ;relocation factor
LOADOVERLAY ENDS
```

For a full description of the **LOADOVERLAY** structure, see Chapter 5, "Program Management."

Return Value   If the function is successful, the carry flag is clear. Otherwise, the carry flag is set and the AX register contains an error value, which may be one of the following:

Value	Name
0001h	ERROR_INVALID_FUNCTION
0002h	ERROR_FILE_NOT_FOUND
0003h	ERROR_PATH_NOT_FOUND
0004h	ERROR_TOO_MANY_OPEN_FILES
0005h	ERROR_ACCESS_DENIED
0008h	ERROR_NOT_ENOUGH_MEMORY
000Ah	ERROR_BAD_ENVIRONMENT

See Also   Function 4B00h Load and Execute Program
Function 4B01h Load Program

■ Function 4B05h Set Execution State

```
mov     dx, seg ExecState
mov     ds, dx
mov     dx, offset ExecState      ;ds:dx points to EXECSTATE structure

mov     ax, 4B05h                 ;Set Execution State
int     21h
jc      error_handler
```

Set Execution State (Function 4B05h) prepares a new program for execution. This preparation includes setting the version number for the program as specified by the **setver** command.

Parameter

ExecState   Points to an **EXECSTATE** structure that contains the execution state. The **EXECSTATE** structure has the following form:

```
EXECSTATE    STRUC
    esReserved  dw ?     ;reserved
    esFlags     dw ?     ;type flags
    esProgName  dd ?     ;points to ASCIIZ string of program name
    esPSP       dw ?     ;PSP segment of the new program
    esStartAddr dd ?     ;starting cs:ip of the new program
    esProgSize  dd ?     ;program size, including PSP
EXECSTATE    ENDS
```

For a full description of the **EXECSTATE** structure, see Chapter 5, "Program Management."

Return Value

This function has no return value.

Comments

This function is required for programs that intercept Load and Execution Program (Function 4B00h).

After the function returns, the calling program must transfer execution control to the new program as soon as possible. In particular, before starting the new program, the calling program must not call MS-DOS system functions, ROM BIOS functions, or system interrupts.

When MS-DOS is installed in the high-memory area (HMA), this function turns off the A20 line, making the HMA inaccessible. If the new program must have access to the HMA, the program must turn on the A20 line. Note that MS-DOS automatically turns on the A20 line (and usually leaves it on) when carrying out other system functions.

See Also

Function 4B00h Load and Execute Program
Function 4B01h Load Program

■ Function 4Ch End Program

```
mov     al, ReturnValue   ;program-defined return value

mov     ah, 4Ch           ;End Program
int     21h
```

End Program (Function 4Ch) terminates the current program and returns control to its parent program.

Parameter

ReturnValue   Specifies a return value. If the terminated program was started by Load and Execute Program (Function 4B00h), the parent program can use Get Child-Program Return Value (Function 4Dh) to retrieve this value.

Return Value

This function does not return.

Comment

This function performs the following actions:

■ Flushes the file buffers and closes files, unlocking any regions locked by the program.

■ Restores Termination Address (Interrupt 22h) from offset 0Ah in the PSP (**pspTerminateVector** field).

■ Restores the address of CTRL+C Handler (Interrupt 23h) from offset 0Eh in the PSP (**pspControlCVector** field).

■ Restores the address of Critical-Error Handler (Interrupt 24h) from offset 12h in the PSP (**pspCritErrorVector** field).

■ Frees any memory owned by the terminating program.

After completing these actions, this function transfers control to the address specified by offset 0Ah in the PSP.

See Also

Function 00h Terminate Program
Function 31h Keep Program
Function 4Dh Get Child-Program Return Value
Function 5Ch Lock/Unlock File
Interrupt 22h Termination Address
Interrupt 23h CTRL+C Handler
Interrupt 24h Critical-Error Handler

■ Function 4Dh Get Child-Program Return Value

```
mov     ah, 4Dh            ;Get Child-Program Return Value
int     21h

mov     ReturnValue, al ;return value from last child program
mov     Method, ah         ;termination method for child program
```

Get Child-Program Return Value (Function 4Dh) retrieves the return value specified by the last child program. The child program must have specified a return value by using either End Program (Function 4Ch) or Keep Program (Function 31h).

Parameters

This function has no parameters.

Return Value

The AX register contains the child-program return value; the AL register contains the return value specified by the child program; and the AH register contains a number that specifies the child-program termination method, which may be one of the following:

Value	Meaning
00h	Normal termination
01h	Terminated by CTRL+C
02h	Critical device error
03h	Terminated by the Keep Program function

Comments

The return value for the program is available only once. Subsequent calls to this function in relation to the same child program give meaningless results.

If there is no child-program return value to retrieve, this function does not return an error, and the information in the AX register is meaningless.

See Also

Function 31h Keep Program
Function 4Ch End Program

■ Function 4Eh Find First File

```
mov     cx, Attributes       ;attributes to search for
mov     dx, seg FileName
mov     ds, dx
mov     dx, offset FileName  ;ds:dx points to file or directory name(s)

mov     ah, 4Eh              ;Find First File
int     21h

jc      error_handler        ;carry set means error
```

Find First File (Function 4Eh) searches a directory for the first file or directory whose name and attributes match the specified name and attributes.

Parameters   *Attributes*   Specifies the attributes to search for. This parameter can be a combination of the following attributes:

Value	Meaning
ATTR_NORMAL (0000h)	File can be read from or written to.
ATTR_READONLY (0001h)	File can be read from, but not written to.
ATTR_HIDDEN (0002h)	File or directory is hidden and does not appear in a directory listing.
ATTR_SYSTEM (0004h)	File or directory is a system file or directory.
ATTR_VOLUMEID (0008h)	Filename is the volume label of media in specified drive.
ATTR_DIRECTORY (0010h)	Filename identifies a directory, not a file.

FileName   Points to a zero-terminated ASCII string that specifies the file or directory to search for. The name must be a valid MS-DOS filename or directory name and can include wildcards.

Return Value   If the function is successful, the carry flag is clear and the file information is copied as a **FILEINFO** structure to the current disk transfer address (DTA). Otherwise, the carry flag is set and the AX register contains an error value, which may be one of the following:

Value	Name
0002h	ERROR_FILE_NOT_FOUND
0003h	ERROR_PATH_NOT_FOUND
0012h	ERROR_NO_MORE_FILES

Comments   If the DTA has not been explicitly set by Set Disk Transfer Address (Function 1Ah), MS-DOS uses the default DTA, offset 80h, in the program segment prefix (PSP).

If a program specifies any combination of ATTR_SYSTEM, ATTR_HIDDEN, and ATTR_DIRECTORY, this function returns normal files in addition to the specified files. The program must examine the attribute contained in the DTA to determine the type of file found.

The **FILEINFO** structure that contains the file information has the following form:

```
FILEINFO        STRUC
    fiReserved      db   21 dup (?)   ;reserved
    fiAttribute     db   ?            ;attributes of file found
    fiFileTime      dw   ?            ;time of last write
    fiFileDate      dw   ?            ;date of last write
    fiSize          dd   ?            ;file size
    fiFileName      db   13 dup (?)   ;filename and extension
FILEINFO        ENDS
```

For a full description of the **FILEINFO** structure, see Chapter 3, "File System."

See Also   Function 1Ah Set Disk Transfer Address
Function 4Fh Find Next File

■ Function 4Fh Find Next File

```
mov     ah, 4Fh         ;Find Next File
int     21h

jc      error_handler   ;carry set means error
```

Find Next File (Function 4Fh) searches for the next directory entry that matches the name and attributes specified in a previous call to Find First File (Function 4Eh). The current disk transfer address (DTA) must contain the information filled in by the Find First File function.

Parameters   This function has no parameters.

Return Value   If the function is successful, the carry flag is clear and the file information is copied as a **FILEINFO** structure to the current DTA. Otherwise, the carry flag is set and the AX register contains an error value, which may be one of the following:

Value	Name
0002h	ERROR_FILE_NOT_FOUND
0003h	ERROR_PATH_NOT_FOUND
0012h	ERROR_NO_MORE_FILES

Comments   If a program specifies any combination of ATTR_SYSTEM, ATTR_HIDDEN, and ATTR_DIRECTORY, this function returns normal files in addition to the specified files. The program must examine the attribute contained in the DTA to determine the type of file found.

The **FILEINFO** structure that contains the file information has the following form:

```
FILEINFO    STRUC
    fiReserved      db  21 dup (?)   ;reserved
    fiAttribute     db  ?            ;attributes of file found
    fiFileTime      dw  ?            ;time of last write
    fiFileDate      dw  ?            ;date of last write
    fiSize          dd  ?            ;file size
    fiFileName      db  13 dup (?)   ;filename and extension
FILEINFO    ENDS
```

For a full description of the **FILEINFO** structure, see Chapter 3, "File System."

See Also   Function 4Eh Find First File

■ Function 50h Set PSP Address

```
mov     bx, SegmentPSP    ;segment address of new PSP

mov     ah, 50h           ;Set PSP Address
int     21h
```

Set PSP Address (Function 50h) sets the segment address of the program segment prefix (PSP) for the current program.

Parameter   *SegmentPSP*   Specifies the segment address of the PSP for the current program.

Return Value   This function has no return value.

See Also   Function 51h Get PSP Address

■ Function 51h Get PSP Address

```
mov      ah, 51h          ;Get PSP Address
int      21h

mov      SegmentPSP, bx   ;segment address of current PSP
```

Get PSP Address (Function 51h) returns the segment address of the program segment prefix (PSP) for the current program.

Parameters   This function has no parameters.

Return Value   The BX register contains the segment address of the PSP for the current program.

Comments   Functions 62h and 51h are identical. Programs can use either function number to get the segment address of the current PSP.

See Also   Function 50h Set PSP Address

■ Function 54h Get Verify State

```
mov     ah, 54h         ;Get Verify State
int     21h

mov     VerifyFlag, al ;00h = off, 01h = on
```

Get Verify State (Function 54h) returns the state of the MS-DOS verify flag.

Parameters   This function has no parameters.

Return Value   The AL register contains the state of the MS-DOS verify flag. If this value is 00h, MS-DOS does not verify write operations. If the value is 01h, MS-DOS does verify write operations.

Comment   The write-verify flag is normally off. A program can change this state by using Reset/Set Verify Flag (Function 2Eh); a user can change the state by using the **verify** command.

See Also   Function 2Eh Reset/Set Verify Flag

■ Function 56h Rename File

```
mov     dx, seg OldName
mov     ds, dx
mov     dx, offset OldName    ;ds:dx points to old file or directory name

mov     di, seg NewName
mov     es, di
mov     di, offset NewName    ;es:di points to new file or directory name

mov     ah, 56h               ;Rename File
int     21h

jc      error_handler         ;carry set means error
```

Rename File (Function 56h) renames or moves a file or directory by changing its directory entry.

Parameters   *OldName*   Points to a zero-terminated ASCII string that specifies the file or directory to rename or move. The name must be a valid MS-DOS filename or directory name and cannot include wildcards.

NewName   Points to a zero-terminated ASCII string that specifies the new name for the file or directory. The name must be a valid MS-DOS filename or directory name and cannot include wildcards.

Return Value   If the function is successful, the carry flag is clear. Otherwise, the carry flag is set and the AX register contains an error value, which may be one of the following:

Value	Name
0002h	ERROR_FILE_NOT_FOUND
0003h	ERROR_PATH_NOT_FOUND
0005h	ERROR_ACCESS_DENIED
0011h	ERROR_NOT_SAME_DEVICE

Comments   Open files or directories must be closed before they are moved or renamed with this function.

A program can use this function to move a file or directory by specifying different paths for the *OldName* and *NewName* parameters and keeping the filename or directory name the same. This function cannot be used to move files or directories from one disk drive to another; however, both the old and new names must specify the same drive either explicitly or by default.

If the specified file is on a network drive, the function renames the file only if network grants create and delete access to the drive or directory.

See Also   Function 17h Rename File with FCB

■ Function 5700h Get File Date and Time

```
mov     bx, Handle          ;handle of file

mov     ax, 5700h           ;Get Date and Time
int     21h

jc      error_handler       ;carry set means error
mov     FileTime, cx        ;time file was last modified
mov     FileDate, dx        ;date file was last modified
```

Get File Date and Time (Function 5700h) retrieves the time and date a file was last modified (the last time its directory entry was updated).

Parameter   *Handle*   Identifies the file to retrieve the date and time for.

Return Value   If the function is successful, the carry flag is clear, the CX register contains the time the file was last modified, and the DX register contains the date the file was last modified. Otherwise, the carry flag is set and the AX register contains an error value, which may be 0006h (ERROR_INVALID_HANDLE).

Comments   The file time returned in CX is a 16-bit value with the following format:

Bits	Contents
0–4	Second divided by 2
5–10	Minute (0–59)
11–15	Hour (0–23 on a 24-hour clock)

The file date returned in DX is a 16-bit value with the following format:

Bits	Contents
0–4	Day of the month (1–31)
5–8	Month (1 = January, 2 = February, etc.)
9–15	Year offset from 1980 (add 1980 to get actual year)

See Also   Function 5701h Set File Date and Time

■ Function 5701h Set File Date and Time

```
mov     bx, Handle      ;handle of file
mov     cx, FileTime    ;new file time
mov     dx, FileDate    ;new file date

mov     ax, 5701h       ;Set Date and Time
int     21h

jc      error_handler   ;carry set means error
```

Set File Date and Time (Function 5701h) sets the time and date for a file, replacing the time and date set for the file when it was last modified.

Parameters

Handle   Identifies the file to set the date and time for.

FileTime   Specifies the new time for the file. The file time is a 16-bit value with the following format:

Bits	Contents
0–4	Second divided by 2
5–10	Minute (0–59)
11–15	Hour (0–23 on a 24-hour clock)

FileDate   Specifies the new date for the file. The file date is a 16-bit value with the following format:

Bits	Contents
0–4	Day of the month (1–31)
5–8	Month (1 = January, 2 = February, etc.)
9–15	Year offset from 1980 (add 1980 to get actual year)

Return Value

If the function is successful, the carry flag is clear. Otherwise, the carry flag is set and the AX register contains an error value, which may be 0006h (ERROR_INVALID_HANDLE).

See Also

Function 5700h Get File Date and Time

■ Function 5800h Get Allocation Strategy

```
mov     ax, 5800h        ;Get Allocation Strategy
int     21h

mov     Strategy, ax     ;allocation strategy
```

Get Allocation Strategy (Function 5800h) returns the method MS-DOS uses to allocate memory.

Parameters This function has no parameters.

Return Value The carry flag is clear and the AX register contains the allocation-strategy value.

Comment The allocation-strategy value can be one of the following:

Value	Meaning
FIRST_FIT_LOW (0000h)	Search conventional memory for the available block having the lowest address. This is the default strategy.
BEST_FIT_LOW (0001h)	Search conventional memory for the available block that most closely matches the requested size.
LAST_FIT_LOW (0002h)	Search conventional memory for the available block at the highest address.
FIRST_FIT_HIGH (0080h)	Search the upper-memory area for the available block at the lowest address. If no block is found, the search continues in conventional memory.
BEST_FIT_HIGH (0081h)	Search the upper-memory area for the available block that most closely matches the requested size. If no block is found, the search continues in conventional memory.
LAST_FIT_HIGH (0082h)	Search the upper-memory area for the available block at the highest address. If no block is found, the search continues in conventional memory.
FIRST_FIT_HIGHONLY (0040h)	Search the upper-memory area for the available block at the lowest address.
BEST_FIT_HIGHONLY (0041h)	Search the upper-memory area for the available block that most closely matches the requested size.
LAST_FIT_HIGHONLY (0042h)	Search the upper-memory area for the available block at the highest address.

For more information about upper-memory blocks and memory allocation, see Chapter 5, "Program Management."

See Also Function 48h Allocate Memory
Function 5801h Set Allocation Strategy
Function 5802h Get Upper-Memory Link
Function 5803h Set Upper-Memory Link

■ Function 5801h Set Allocation Strategy

```
mov     bx, Strategy      ;allocation strategy

mov     ax, 5801h         ;Set Allocation Strategy
int     21h

jc      error_handler     ;carry set means error
```

Set Allocation Strategy (5801h) sets the method MS-DOS uses to allocate memory.

Parameter

Strategy   Specifies the allocation strategy. This parameter can be one of the following values:

Value	Meaning
FIRST_FIT_LOW (0000h)	Search conventional memory for the available block having the lowest address. This is the default strategy.
BEST_FIT_LOW (0001h)	Search conventional memory for the available block that most closely matches the requested size.
LAST_FIT_LOW (0002h)	Search conventional memory for the available block at the highest address.
FIRST_FIT_HIGH (0080h)	Search the upper-memory area for the available block at the lowest address. If no block is found, the search continues in conventional memory.
BEST_FIT_HIGH (0081h)	Search the upper-memory area for the available block that most closely matches the requested size. If no block is found, the search continues in conventional memory.
LAST_FIT_HIGH (0082h)	Search the upper-memory area for the available block at the highest address. If no block is found, the search continues in conventional memory.
FIRST_FIT_HIGHONLY (0040h)	Search the upper-memory area for the available block at the lowest address.
BEST_FIT_HIGHONLY (0041h)	Search the upper-memory area for the available block that most closely matches the requested size.
LAST_FIT_HIGHONLY (0042h)	Search the upper-memory area for the available block at the highest address.

Return Value

If the function is successful, the carry flag is clear. Otherwise, the carry flag is set and the AX register contains an error value, which may be 0001h (ERROR_INVALID_FUNCTION).

Comment

This function returns 0001h (ERROR_INVALID_FUNCTION) if *Strategy* is not one of the specified values.

If the current allocation strategy specifies the upper-memory area but the upper-memory area is not linked, MS-DOS searches conventional memory instead.

For more information about upper-memory blocks and memory allocation, see Chapter 5, "Program Management."

See Also

Function 48h Allocate Memory
Function 5800h Get Allocation Strategy
Function 5802h Get Upper-Memory Link
Function 5803h Set Upper-Memory Link

■ Function 5802h Get Upper-Memory Link

```
mov     ax, 5802h               ;Get Upper-Memory Link
int     21h

mov     LinkFlag, al            ;1 = linked, 0 = not linked
```

Get Upper-Memory Link (Function 5802h) specifies whether programs can allocate memory from the upper memory area.

Parameters   This function has no parameters.

Return Value   The carry flag is clear and the AL register contains 01h if the upper memory area is linked; otherwise, AL contains 00h.

Comments   For more information about upper memory blocks and memory allocation, see Chapter 5, "Program Management."

See Also   Function 48h Allocate Memory
Function 5803H Set Upper-Memory Link

■ Function 5803h Set Upper-Memory Link

```
mov     bx, LinkFlag        ;1= link, O = unlink

mov     ax, 5803h           ;Set Upper-Memory Link
int     21h

jc      error_handler       ;carry clear means error
```

Set Upper-Memory Link (Function 5803h) links or unlinks the upper memory area. When this area is linked, a program can allocate memory from it.

Parameters

LinkFlag   Specifies whether to link or unlink the upper memory area. If this parameter is 01h, the function links the area; if the parameter is 00h, the function unlinks the area.

Return Value

If the function is successful, the carry flag is clear. Otherwise, the carry flag is set and the AX register contains an error value, which may be one of the following:

Value	Name
0001h	ERROR_INVALID_FUNCTION.
0007h	ERROR_ARENA_TRASHED

Comments

The function returns 0001h (ERROR_INVALID_FUNCTION) if MS-DOS has been loaded without the command **dos=umb** having been specified in the CONFIG.SYS file.

For more information about upper memory blocks and memory allocation, see Chapter 5, "Program Management."

See Also

Function 48h Allocate Memory
Function 5802H Get Upper-Memory Link

■ Function 59h Get Extended Error

```
mov     ah, 59h    ;Get Extended Error
int     21h

cmp     ax, 0      ;zero means no error
jz      no_error

mov     ExtError, ax      ;extended-error value
mov     ErrClass, bh      ;error class
mov     ErrAction, bl     ;suggested action
mov     ErrLocation, ch   ;location of error
```

Get Extended Error (Function 59h) returns extended-error information, including the location where an error occurred and a suggested action, for the most recent MS-DOS Interrupt 21h function call.

Parameters   This function has no parameters.

Return Value   The carry flag is clear and the AX, BX, and CH registers contain the extended-error information. The AX register contains an extended-error value, the BH register contains the error class, the BL register contains the suggested action value, and the CH register contains the error-location value.

Comments   When MS-DOS processes this function, it alters all registers except SS:SP and CS:IP. A program should preserve the contents of any registers that will be needed after the function call.

For the table that contains the error values, see Appendix C, "Error Values."

The error class may be one of the following:

Value	Meaning
ERRCLASS_OUTRES (01h)	Out of resource, such as storage.
ERRCLASS_TEMPSIT (02h)	Not an error, but a temporary situation that is expected to end, such as a locked region in a file.
ERRCLASS_AUTH (03h)	Authorization problem.
ERRCLASS_INTRN (04h)	Internal error in system.
ERRCLASS_HRDFAIL (05h)	Hardware failure.
ERRCLASS_SYSFAIL (06h)	System software failure not the fault of the active program (caused by missing or incorrect configuration files, for example).
ERRCLASS_APPERR (07h)	Application error.
ERRCLASS_NOTFND (08h)	File or item not found.
ERRCLASS_BADFMT (09h)	File or item with an invalid format or type.
ERRCLASS_LOCKED (0Ah)	Interlocked file or item.
ERRCLASS_MEDIA (0Bh)	Wrong disk in drive, bad spot on disk, or other storage-medium problem.
ERRCLASS_ALREADY (0Ch)	Existing file or item.
ERRCLASS_UNK (0Dh)	Unknown.

The suggested action may be one of the following:

Value	Meaning
ERRACT_RETRY (01h)	Retry immediately.
ERRACT_DLYRET (02h)	Delay and retry.
ERRACT_USER (03h)	Bad user input—get new values.
ERRACT_ABORT (04h)	Terminate in an orderly manner.
ERRACT_PANIC (05h)	Terminate immediately.
ERRACT_IGNORE (06h)	Ignore the error.
ERRACT_INTRET (07h)	Prompt the user to remove the cause of the error (to change disks, for example) and then retry.

The error location may be one of the following:

Value	Location
ERRLOC_UNK (01h)	Unknown
ERRLOC_DISK (02h)	Random-access device, such as a disk drive
ERRLOC_NET (03h)	Network
ERRLOC_SERDEV (04h)	Serial device
ERRLOC_MEM (05h)	Memory

See Also   Function 5D0Ah Set Extended Error

Function 5Ah Create Temporary File

```
mov     cx, Attributes       ;file attributes
mov     dx, seg TempPath
mov     ds, dx
mov     dx, offset TempPath  ;ds:dx points to directory path

mov     ah, 5Ah              ;Create Temporary File
int     21h

jc      error_handler        ;carry set means error

mov     Handle, ax           ;handle of temporary file
```

Create Temporary File (Function 5Ah) creates a file with a unique name and returns both a handle for the file and the new filename.

Parameters

Attributes   Specifies the attributes to assign to the new file. This parameter can be some combination of the following attributes:

Value	Meaning
ATTR_NORMAL (0000h)	File can be read from or written to.
ATTR_READONLY (0001h)	File can be read from but not written to.
ATTR_HIDDEN (0002h)	File does not appear in a directory listing.
ATTR_SYSTEM (0004h)	File is a system file.
ATTR_ARCHIVE (0020h)	File is marked for archiving.

TempPath   Points to a zero-terminated ASCII string that specifies the path for the temporary file. *TempPath* must end with a backslash character (\) and a zero byte. The program must reserve the 13 bytes immediately following the terminating zero to hold the temporary filename.

Return Value

If the function is successful, the carry flag is clear, the AX register contains a handle for the temporary file, and the 13-byte buffer following *TempPath* is filled in with the name of the temporary file. Otherwise, the carry flag is set and the AX register contains an error value, which may be one of the following:

Value	Name
0003h	ERROR_PATH_NOT_FOUND
0004h	ERROR_TOO_MANY_OPEN_FILES
0005h	ERROR_ACCESS_DENIED

Comments

When MS-DOS creates a file, it opens the file with read-and-write access and compatibility sharing mode and sets the file pointer to zero. If the attribute ATTR_READONLY is specified, it takes effect only after the new file is closed.

If the specified file is on a network drive, the function creates the file only if network grants create access to the drive or directory.

MS-DOS does not delete temporary files; programs using temporary files should delete them when they are no longer in use.

See Also

Function 3Ch Create File with Handle
Function 5Bh Create New File

■ Function 5Bh Create New File

```
mov     dx, seg FileName
mov     ds, dx
mov     dx, offset FileName     ;ds:dx points to new filename

mov     cx, Attributes          ;file attributes

mov     ah, 5Bh                 ;Create New File
int     21h

jc      error_handler           ;carry set means error
mov     Handle, ax              ;handle of file
```

Create New File (Function 5Bh) creates a file and assigns it the first available handle. If the specified file already exists, this function fails.

Parameters

FileName   Points to a zero-terminated ASCII string that specifies the new filename. The name must be a valid MS-DOS filename and cannot contain wildcards.

Attributes   Specifies the attributes to assign to the new file. This parameter can be some combination of the following attributes:

Value	Meaning
ATTR_NORMAL (0000h)	File can be read from or written to.
ATTR_READONLY (0001h)	File can be read from but not written to.
ATTR_HIDDEN (0002h)	File does not appear in a directory listing.
ATTR_SYSTEM (0004h)	File is a system file.
ATTR_ARCHIVE (0020h)	File is marked for archiving.

Return Value

If the function is successful, the carry flag is clear and the AX register contains the new file handle. Otherwise, the carry flag is set and the AX register contains an error value, which may be one of the following:

Value	Name
0003h	ERROR_PATH_NOT_FOUND
0004h	ERROR_TOO_MANY_OPEN_FILES
0005h	ERROR_ACCESS_DENIED
0050h	ERROR_FILE_EXISTS

Comments

Create New File returns 0050h (ERROR_FILE_EXISTS) if a file with the specified name already exists.

When MS-DOS creates a file, it opens the file with read-and-write access and compatibility sharing mode and sets the file pointer to zero. If the attribute ATTR_READONLY is specified, it takes effect only after the new file is closed.

If the specified file is on a network drive, the function creates the file only if network grants create access to the drive or directory.

See Also

Function 3Ch Create File with Handle
Function 4300h Get File Attributes
Function 4301h Set File Attributes
Function 5Ah Create Temporary File

■ Function 5Ch Lock/Unlock File

```
mov     bx, Handle       ;handle of file to lock or unlock

mov     cx, hiOffset     ;high 16 bits of 32-bit offset
mov     dx, loOffset     ;low 16 bits of 32-bit offset

mov     si, hiLength     ;high 16 bits of 32-bit region length
mov     di, loLength     ;low 16 bits of 32-bit region length

mov     al, LockFlag     ;00h = lock, 01h = unlock
mov     ah, 5Ch          ;Lock/Unlock File
int     21h

jc      error_handler    ;carry set means error
```

Lock/Unlock File (Function 5Ch) denies or allows access to the specified region in a file.

Parameters

Handle   Identifies the file to lock or unlock.

hiOffset:loOffset   Specifies the 32-bit offset (in bytes) from the start of the file to the beginning of the region to lock or unlock.

hiLength:loLength   Specifies the 32-bit length (in bytes) of the region to lock or unlock.

LockFlag   Specifies whether to lock or unlock the specified file region (00h to lock the region, 01h to unlock the region).

Return Value

If the function is successful, the carry flag is clear. Otherwise, the carry flag is set, and the AX register contains an error value, which may be one of the following:

Value	Name
0001h	ERROR_INVALID_FUNCTION
0006h	ERROR_INVALID_HANDLE
0021h	ERROR_LOCK_VIOLATION
0024h	ERROR_SHARING_BUFFER_EXCEEDED

Comments

File sharing must be loaded (by running the Share program) before this function can be used on a local computer.

This function returns 0021h (ERROR_LOCK_VIOLATION) if all or part of the specified region is already locked or if the specified region is not identical to a region previously locked by the same procedure.

If another program attempts to write to or read from a locked region, MS-DOS retries the operation one or more times; if all retries fail, MS-DOS issues Critical-Error Handler (Interrupt 24h) for the requesting program. A program can set the number of retries by using Set Sharing Retry Count (Function 440Bh).

The locked region can be anywhere in the file. For example, locking beyond the end of the file is not an error. Duplicate File Handle (Function 45h) and Force Duplicate File Handle (Function 46h) duplicate access to any locked regions. Passing an open file to a child program by using Load and Execute Program (Function 4B00h) does not duplicate access to locked regions.

Programs should not depend on being denied access to a locked region. To determine the status of a region (locked or unlocked), a program can attempt to lock the region and then examine the error value.

See Also

Function 440Bh Set Sharing Retry Count
Function 45h Duplicate File Handle
Function 46h Force Duplicate File Handle
Function 4B00h Load and Execute Program
Interrupt 24h Critical-Error Handler
Interrupt 2Fh Function 1000h Get SHARE.EXE Installed State

■ Function 5D0Ah Set Extended Error

```
mov     si, seg ErrInfo
mov     ds, si
mov     si, offset ErrInfo        ;ds:si points to ERROR structure

mov     ax, 5D0Ah                 ;Set Extended Error
int     21h
```

Set Extended Error (Function 5D0Ah) sets the error class, location, suggested action, and other information that will be returned by the next call to Get Extended Error (Function 59h).

Parameter   *ErrInfo*   Points to an **ERROR** structure that contains error information as well as the contents of the registers when an error occurred. The **ERROR** structure has the following form:

```
ERROR   STRUC
    errAX        dw   ?    ;ax register
    errBX        dw   ?    ;bx register
    errCX        dw   ?    ;cx register
    errDX        dw   ?    ;dx register
    errSI        dw   ?    ;si register
    errDI        dw   ?    ;di register
    errDS        dw   ?    ;ds register
    errES        dw   ?    ;es register
    errReserved  dw   ?    ;reserved 16 bits
    errUID       dw   ?    ;user (computer) ID (0 = local computer)
    errPID       dw   ?    ;program ID (0 = local program)
ERROR   ENDS
```

For a full description of the **ERROR** structure, see Chapter 3, "File System."

Return Value   This function has no return value.

See Also   Function 59h Get Extended Error

■ Function 5E00h Get Machine Name

```
mov     dx, seg NetworkName
mov     ds, dx
mov     dx, offset NetworkName ;ds:dx points to buffer for network name

mov     ax, 5E00h       ;Get Machine Name
int     21h

jc      error_handler   ;carry set means error

cmp     ch, 0           ;zero means name not valid
jz      error_handler
mov     NetNum, cl      ;NETBIOS number
```

Get Machine Name (Function 5E00h) returns the network name of the local computer (machine).

Parameter

NetworkName   Points to a 16-byte buffer to receive the zero-terminated ASCII (ASCIIZ) network name. For information about network drives, see Chapter 3, "File System."

Return Value

If the function is successful, the carry flag is clear, the 16-byte buffer is filled in with the network name, and the CX register contains the NETBIOS number of the local computer. Otherwise, the carry flag is set and the AX register contains an error value, which may be 0001h (ERROR_INVALID_FUNCTION).

Comments

This function returns 0001h (ERROR_INVALID_FUNCTION) if the network is not running. If the network was never installed, the function returns zero in the CH register.

The local computer's identification number is returned in the following format:

Register	Description
CH	Specifies whether the network name is valid (CH contains a value other than zero) or not valid (CH contains zero).
CL	Specifies the NETBIOS number assigned to the local computer.

See Also

Function 5F03h Make Network Connection
Interrupt 2Fh Function 1100h Get Network Installed State

■ Function 5E02h Set Printer Setup

```
mov      bx, ListIndex      ;assign-list index
mov      cx, SetupSize      ;length of setup string

mov      dx, seg SetupString
mov      ds, dx
mov      dx, offset SetupString  ;ds:dx points to printer setup string

mov      ax, 5E02h          ;Set Printer Setup
int      21h

jc       error_handler      ;carry set means error
```

Set Printer Setup (Function 5E02h) defines a string of control characters that MS-DOS adds to the beginning of each file sent to a network printer.

Parameters *ListIndex*   Specifies the assign-list index for a network printer.

SetupSize   Specifies the length of the string that will be sent to a network printer. The setup string cannot be longer than 64 characters.

SetupString   Points to a buffer that contains the string to be sent to a network printer.

Return Value If the function is successful, the carry flag is clear. Otherwise, the carry flag is set and the AX register contains an error value, which may be 0001h (ERROR_INVALID_FUNCTION).

Comment This function returns 0001h (ERROR_INVALID_FUNCTION) if the network is not running.

See Also Function 5E03h Get Printer Setup
Function 5F02h Get Assign-List Entry

■ Function 5E03h Get Printer Setup

```
mov     bx, ListIndex     ;assign-list index

mov     di, seg SetupString
mov     es, di
mov     di, offset SetupString  ;es:di points to buf for setup string

mov     ax, 5E03h         ;Get Printer Setup
int     21h

jc      error_handler     ;carry set means error
mov     SetupSize, cx     ;length of setup string
```

Get Printer Setup (Function 5E02h) retrieves the string of control characters added to the beginning of each file sent to a network printer.

Parameters   *ListIndex*   Specifies the assign-list index for a network printer.

SetupString   Points to a 64-byte buffer that receives the current string for the specified network printer.

Return Value   If the function is successful, the carry flag is clear, the buffer pointed to by the ES:DI registers is filled in with the string currently used for printer setup, and the CX register contains the length of the printer setup string. Otherwise, the carry flag is set and the AX register contains an error value, which may be 0001h (ERROR_INVALID_FUNCTION).

Comment   This function returns 0001h (ERROR_INVALID_FUNCTION) if the network is not running.

See Also   Function 5E02h Set Printer Setup
Function 5F02h Get Assign-List Entry

■ Function 5F02h Get Assign-List Entry

```
mov     bx, ListIndex    ;assign-list index

mov     si, seg LocalBuffer
mov     ds, si
mov     si, offset LocalBuffer   ;ds:si points to buf for local name

mov     di, seg NetBuffer
mov     es, di
mov     di, offset NetBuffer     ;es:di points to buf for network name

mov     ax, 5F02h        ;Get Assign-List Entry
int     21h

jc      error_handler    ;carry set means error
```

Get Assign-List Entry (Function 5F02h) retrieves the local and network names of a device, such as a network printer. MS-DOS uses the assign-list index—which a program sets by using Make Assign-List Entry (Function 5F03h)—to search a list of network connections.

Parameters
ListIndex   Specifies the assign-list index for a network device.

LocalBuffer   Points to a 16-byte buffer that is to receive the local name of the device.

NetBuffer   Points to a 128-byte buffer that is to receive the network name of the device.

Return Value
If the function is successful, the carry flag is clear, the name buffers are filled in, the CX register contains the user value stored by Make Network Connection (Function 5F03h), and the BX register contains the device-status value. Otherwise, the carry flag is set and the AX register contains an error value, which may be one of the following:

Value	Name
0001h	ERROR_INVALID_FUNCTION
0012h	ERROR_NO_MORE_FILES

Comments
The network must be running and file sharing must be active for this function to operate successfully.

This function returns 0001h (ERROR_INVALID_FUNCTION) if the network is not running. The function returns 0002h (ERROR_NO_MORE_FILES) if the index specified in *ListIndex* is greater than the number of entries in the assign list.

The device-status value has the following format:

Register	Description
BH	Specifies whether the device is available (BH contains 01h) or temporarily unavailable (BH contains 00h).
BL	Specifies the type of device (03h = printer, 04h = drive).

MS-DOS maintains one assign-list entry for each of the currently connected network devices. As a program connects and disconnects network devices, MS-DOS adds and deletes entries from the list. Each entry receives an assign-list index. The assign-list indexes are zero-based and consecutive—the first network device to be connected receives index 0, the second receives index 1, and so on. When a program disconnects a network device, MS-DOS reindexes the entries so that the indexes remain consecutive. For example, if the first network device is disconnected, the second device receives index 0, the third receives index 1, and so on. To determine the current index for a device, a program typically retrieves assign-list entries for each index, starting with 0, until it matches either the user value returned in the CX register or the network name pointed to by the ES:DI registers.

See Also   Function 5F03h Make Network Connection
Function 5F04h Delete Network Connection

Function 5F03h Make Network Connection

```
mov     bl, DevCode                 ;device code
mov     cx, UserVal                 ;user value

mov     si, seg LocalBuffer
mov     ds, si
mov     si, offset LocalBuffer      ;ds:si points to buf for local name

mov     di, seg NetBuffer
mov     es, di
mov     di, offset NetBuffer        ;es:di points to buf for network name

mov     ax, 5F03h                   ;Make Network Connection
int     21h

jc      error_handler               ;carry set means error
```

Make Network Connection (Function 5F03h) creates a connection to a network device or drive, or redirects a local device or drive if a local name is specified.

Parameters   *DevCode*   Specifies the local-device code (03h = printer, 04h = disk drive).

UserVal   Specifies a user value to be saved and returned to a program that calls Get Assign-List Entry (Function 5F02h).

LocalBuffer   Points to a zero-terminated ASCII string that specifies the local device to redirect.

If the *DevCode* parameter is 03h, the local device is a printer and the device the *LocalBuffer* parameter points to must be PRN, LPT1, LPT2, or LPT3.

If *DevCode* is 04h, the local device is a disk drive and *LocalBuffer* must specify either a drive letter followed by a colon or a null string (a string whose first character is zero). If *LocalBuffer* specifies a drive letter, MS-DOS redirects the drive to the network device. If *LocalBuffer* is a null string, MS-DOS attempts to provide access to the network device without redirecting a local disk drive.

NetBuffer   Points to two consecutive zero-terminated ASCII strings specifying the network name and the password for the network drive or device. If the network device has no password, the second string must be a null string. For information about network drives, see Chapter 3, "File System."

Return Value   If the function is successful, the carry flag is clear. Otherwise, the carry flag is set and the AX register contains an error value, which may be one of the following:

Value	Name
0001h	ERROR_INVALID_FUNCTION
0003h	ERROR_PATH_NOT_FOUND
0005h	ERROR_ACCESS_DENIED
0008h	ERROR_NOT_ENOUGH_MEMORY
000Fh	ERROR_INVALID_DRIVE
0012h	ERROR_NO_MORE_FILES
0057h	ERROR_INVALID_PARAMETER

Comments

This function returns 0001h (ERROR_INVALID_FUNCTION) if the network is not running.

If the function returns 0005h (ERROR_ACCESS_DENIED), it may mean either that the password is not valid or that the specified device or drive could not be found on the server.

See Also

Function 5F02h Get Assign-List Entry
Function 5F04h Delete Network Connection
Interrupt 2Fh Function 1100h Get Network Installed State

■ Function 5F04h Delete Network Connection

```
mov     si, seg LocalBuffer
mov     ds, si
mov     si, offset LocalBuffer    ;ds:si points to local name

mov     ax, 5F04h                 ;Delete Network Connection
int     21h

jc      error_handler             ;carry set means error
```

Delete Network Connection (Function 5F04h) deletes the connection to the network device and restores the redirected local device or drive.

Parameter

LocalBuffer   Points to a zero-terminated ASCII string that specifies the network connection to delete. *LocalBuffer* can specify one of the following:

- The letter of a redirected drive, followed by a colon. MS-DOS cancels the redirection and restores the drive to its physical meaning.
- The name of a redirected printer (PRN, LPT1, LPT2, LPT3, or their machine-specific equivalents). MS-DOS cancels the redirection and restores the printer name to its physical meaning.
- A string starting with two backslashes (\\). MS-DOS terminates the connection between the local computer and the network directory.

Return Value

If the function is successful, the carry flag is clear. Otherwise, the carry flag is set and the AX register contains an error value, which may be one of the following:

Value	Name
0001h	ERROR_INVALID_FUNCTION
000Fh	ERROR_INVALID_DRIVE

Comment

This function returns 0001h (ERROR_INVALID_FUNCTION) if the network is not running.

See Also

Function 5F03h Make Network Connection
Interrupt 2Fh Function 1100h Get Network Installed State

Function 6501h Get Extended Country Information

```
mov     bx, CodePageID          ;code page to return info for
mov     cx, InfoSize            ;size of buffer for country info
mov     dx, CountryCode         ;country code to return info for
mov     di, seg Information
mov     es, dx
mov     di, offset Information  ;es:di points to EXTCOUNTRYINFO struct

mov     ax, 6501h               ;Get Extended Country Information
int     21h

jc      error_handler           ;carry set means error
```

Get Extended Country Information (Function 6501h) returns the country information that MS-DOS uses to control the keyboard and screen.

Parameters *CodePageID* Identifies the code page to return the country information for. This parameter can be one of the following values:

Value	Meaning
437	United States
850	Multilingual (Latin I)
852	Slavic (Latin II)
860	Portuguese
863	Canadian-French
865	Nordic

If this parameter is 0FFFFh, MS-DOS returns information about the current code page for the keyboard/screen.

InfoSize Specifies the size of the buffer for the country information. The buffer must be at least 5 bytes long.

CountryCode Specifies the country code to return information for. This parameter can be one of the following values:

Value	Meaning
001	United States
002	Canadian-French
003	Latin America
031	Netherlands
032	Belgium
033	France
034	Spain
036	Hungary
038	Yugoslavia
039	Italy
041	Switzerland
042	Czechoslovakia
044	United Kingdom
045	Denmark

Value	Meaning
046	Sweden
047	Norway
048	Poland
049	Germany
055	Brazil
061	International English
351	Portugal
358	Finland

If this parameter is 0FFFFh, MS-DOS returns information about the current country.

Information Points to a buffer that receives country information. The buffer consists of a single byte followed by an **EXTCOUNTRYINFO** structure. The **EXTCOUNTRYINFO** structure has the following form:

```
EXTCOUNTRYINFO      STRUC
    eciLength          dw    ?              ;size of the structure, in bytes
    eciCountryCode     dw    ?              ;country code
    eciCodePageID      dw    ?              ;code-page identifier
    eciDateFormat      dw    ?              ;date format
    eciCurrency        db    5 dup (?)      ;currency symbol (ASCIIZ)
    eciThousands       db    2 dup (?)      ;thousands separator (ASCIIZ)
    eciDecimal         db    2 dup (?)      ;decimal separator (ASCIIZ)
    eciDateSep         db    2 dup (?)      ;date separator (ASCIIZ)
    eciTimeSep         db    2 dup (?)      ;time separator (ASCIIZ)
    eciBitField        db    ?              ;currency format
    eciCurrencyPlaces  db    ?              ;places after decimal point
    eciTimeFormat      db    ?              ;12- or 24-hour format
    eciCaseMap         dd    ?              ;address of case-mapping routine
    eciDataSep         db    2 dup (?)      ;data-list separator (ASCIIZ)
    eciReserved        db    10 dup (?)     ;reserved
EXTCOUNTRYINFO      ENDS
```

For a full description of the **EXTCOUNTRYINFO** structure, see Chapter 6, "National Language Support."

Return Value If the function is successful, the carry flag is clear and the country information is copied to the **EXTCOUNTRYINFO** structure. Otherwise, the carry flag is set and the AX register contains an error value, which may be one of the following:

Value	Name
0001h	ERROR_INVALID_FUNCTION
0002h	ERROR_FILE_NOT_FOUND

Comments This function returns 0001h (ERROR_INVALID_FUNCTION) if the value specified in *InfoSize* is less than 5. If the *InfoSize* value is greater than 5 but less than the size of the country information, the information is truncated and no error is returned.

This function returns 0002h (ERROR_FILE_NOT_FOUND) if MS-DOS cannot retrieve country information for the specified code page and country code.

See Also Function 38h Get/Set Country Information
Function 6601h Get Global Code Page
Function 6602h Set Global Code Page

■ Function 6502h Get Uppercase Table

```
mov     bx, CodePageID          ;code page to return table for
mov     cx, 5                   ;size of buffer (must be at least 5)
mov     dx, CountryCode         ;country code to return table for
                                ;    (0FFFFh = default country)
mov     di, seg Table
mov     es, dx
mov     di, offset Table        ;es:di points to buffer for ptr to table

mov     ax, 6502h               ;Get Uppercase Table
int     21h

jc      error_handler           ;carry set means error
```

Get Uppercase Table (Function 6502h) returns the address of the uppercase table for the specified code page and country code. The uppercase table maps the extended ASCII characters (characters with ASCII values greater than 128) to their uppercase equivalents.

Parameters

CodePageID   Identifies the code page to return the uppercase table for. This parameter can be one of the following values:

Value	Meaning
437	United States
850	Multilingual (Latin I)
852	Slavic (Latin II)
860	Portuguese
863	Canadian-French
865	Nordic

If this parameter is 0FFFFh, MS-DOS returns information about the current code page for the console/screen.

CountryCode   Specifies the country code to return the uppercase table for. This parameter can be one of the following values:

Value	Meaning
001	United States
002	Canadian-French
003	Latin America
031	Netherlands
032	Belgium
033	France
034	Spain
036	Hungary
038	Yugoslavia
039	Italy
041	Switzerland
042	Czechoslovakia
044	United Kingdom
045	Denmark

Value	Meaning
046	Sweden
047	Norway
048	Poland
049	Germany
055	Brazil
061	International English
351	Portugal
358	Finland

If this parameter is 0FFFFh, MS-DOS returns the table for the current country.

Table   Points to a buffer in which MS-DOS places the 8-bit identifier (02h) of the uppercase table and the 32-bit address (segment:offset) of the table. The buffer must be at least 5 bytes long.

Return Value   If the function is successful, the carry flag is clear and the 32-bit address of the uppercase table is copied to the buffer pointed to by the *Table* parameter. Otherwise, the carry flag is set and the AX register contains an error value, which may be one of the following:

Value	Name
0001h	ERROR_INVALID_FUNCTION
0002h	ERROR_FILE_NOT_FOUND

Comments   This function returns 0001h (ERROR_INVALID_FUNCTION) if the buffer size specified by the CX register is less than 5.

This function returns 0002h (ERROR_FILE_NOT_FOUND) if MS-DOS cannot retrieve country information for the specified code page and country code.

The uppercase table starts with a 16-bit value that specifies the length of the table; the remainder of the table specifies the uppercase equivalents of the ASCII characters from 80h to 0FFh.

See Also   Function 38h Get/Set Country Information
Function 6501h Get Extended Country Information
Function 6504h Get Filename Uppercase Table
Function 6601h Get Global Code Page
Function 6602h Set Global Code Page

■ Function 6504h Get Filename Uppercase Table

```
mov     bx, CodePageID       ;code page to return table for
mov     cx, 5                ;size of buffer (must be at least 5)
mov     dx, CountryCode      ;country code to return table for
mov     di, seg Table
mov     es, dx
mov     di, offset Table     ;es:di points to buffer for ptr to table

mov     ax, 6504h            ;Get Filename Uppercase Table
int     21h

jc      error_handler        ;carry set means error
```

Get Filename Uppercase Table (Function 6504h) returns the address of the file-name uppercase table for the specified country code and code page. The table maps extended ASCII characters in filenames (characters with ASCII values greater than 128) to their uppercase equivalents.

Parameters   *CodePageID*   Identifies the code page to return the table for. This parameter can be one of the following values:

Value	Meaning
437	United States
850	Multilingual (Latin I)
852	Slavic (Latin II)
860	Portuguese
863	Canadian-French
865	Nordic

If this parameter is 0FFFFh, MS-DOS returns a table for the current code page.

CountryCode   Specifies the country code to return the table for. This parameter can be one of the following values:

Value	Meaning
001	United States
002	Canadian-French
003	Latin America
031	Netherlands
032	Belgium
033	France
034	Spain
036	Hungary
038	Yugoslavia
039	Italy
041	Switzerland
042	Czechoslovakia
044	United Kingdom
045	Denmark
046	Sweden

Value	Meaning
047	Norway
048	Poland
049	Germany
055	Brazil
061	International English
351	Portugal
358	Finland

If this parameter is 0FFFFh, MS-DOS returns the table for the current country.

Table   Points to a buffer in which MS-DOS places the 8-bit identifier (04h) of the filename uppercase table and the 32-bit address (segment:offset) of the table. The buffer must be at least 5 bytes long.

Return Value

If the function is successful, the carry flag is clear and the 32-bit address of the filename uppercase table is copied to the buffer pointed to by the *Table* parameter. Otherwise, the carry flag is set and the AX register contains an error value, which may be one of the following:

Value	Name
0001h	ERROR_INVALID_FUNCTION
0002h	ERROR_FILE_NOT_FOUND

Comments

This function returns 0001h (ERROR_INVALID_FUNCTION) if the buffer size specified by the CX register is less than 5.

This function returns 0002h (ERROR_FILE_NOT_FOUND) if MS-DOS cannot retrieve country information for the specified code page and country code.

The filename uppercase table starts with a 16-bit value that specifies the length of the table; the remainder of the table specifies the uppercase equivalents of the ASCII characters from 80h to 0FFh.

See Also

Function 38h Get/Set Country Information
Function 6501h Get Extended Country Information
Function 6502h Get Uppercase Table
Function 6601h Get Global Code Page
Function 6602h Set Global Code Page

■ Function 6505h Get Filename-Character Table

```
mov    bx, CodePageID      ;code page to return sequence for
mov    cx, 5               ;size of buffer (must be at least 5)
mov    dx, CountryCode     ;country code to return sequence for
mov    di, seg Table
mov    es, si
mov    di, offset Table    ;es:di points to buffer for ptr to sequence

mov    ax, 6505h           ;Get Filename-Character Table
int    21h

jc     error_handler       ;carry set means error
```

Get Filename-Character Table (Function 6506h) returns the address of the filename-character table for the specified code page and country code. The table specifies which characters must not be used in filenames.

Parameters *CodePageID* Identifies the code page to return the filename-character table for. This parameter can be one of the following values:

Value	Meaning
437	United States
850	Multilingual (Latin I)
852	Slavic (Latin II)
860	Portuguese
863	Canadian-French
865	Nordic

If this parameter is 0FFFFh, MS-DOS returns information for the current code page.

CountryCode Specifies the country code to return the filename-character table for. This parameter can be one of the following values:

Value	Meaning
001	United States
002	Canadian-French
003	Latin America
031	Netherlands
032	Belgium
033	France
034	Spain
036	Hungary
038	Yugoslavia
039	Italy
041	Switzerland
042	Czechoslovakia
044	United Kingdom
045	Denmark

Value	Meaning
046	Sweden
047	Norway
048	Poland
049	Germany
055	Brazil
061	International English
351	Portugal
358	Finland

If this parameter is 0FFFFh, MS-DOS returns the table for the current country.

Table   Points to a buffer in which MS-DOS places the 8-bit identifier (05h) of the filename-character table and the 32-bit address (segment:offset) of the table. The buffer must be at least 5 bytes long.

Return Value   If the function is successful, the carry flag is clear and the 32-bit address of the filename-character table is copied to the buffer pointed to by the *Table* parameter. Otherwise, the carry flag is set and the AX register contains an error value, which may be one of the following:

Value	Name
0001h	ERROR_INVALID_FUNCTION
0002h	ERROR_FILE_NOT_FOUND

Comments   This function returns 0001h (ERROR_INVALID_FUNCTION) if the buffer size specified in the CX register is less than 5.

This function returns 0002h (ERROR_FILE_NOT_FOUND) if MS-DOS cannot retrieve country information for the specified code page and country code.

The filename-character table starts with a 16-bit value that specifies the length of the table.

See Also   Function 38h Get/Set Country Information
Function 6501h Get Extended Country Information
Function 6601h Get Global Code Page
Function 6602h Set Global Code Page

■ Function 6506h Get Collate-Sequence Table

```
mov     bx, CodePageID     ;code page to return sequence for
mov     cx, 5              ;size of buffer (must be at least 5)
mov     dx, CountryCode    ;country code to return sequence for
mov     di, seg Table
mov     es, di
mov     di, offset Table ;es:di points to buffer for ptr to sequence

mov     ax, 6506h          ;Get Collate Table
int     21h

jc      error_handler      ;carry set means error
```

Get Collate-Sequence Table (Function 6506h) returns the address of the collate-sequence table for the specified code page and country code. The table is a character array of 256 elements; each element specifies the sorting weight of the corresponding character. (The sorting weight is the value used to determine whether a character appears before or after another character in a sorted list.) Sorting weights and character values are not necessarily the same—for example, in a given character set, the sorting weights for the letters A and B might be 1 and 2, even though their character values are 65 and 66.

Parameters   *CodePageID*   Identifies the code page to return the collate-sequence table for. This parameter can be one of the following values:

Value	Meaning
437	United States
850	Multilingual (Latin I)
852	Slavic (Latin II)
860	Portuguese
863	Canadian-French
865	Nordic

If this parameter is 0FFFFh, MS-DOS returns information for the current code page.

CountryCode   Specifies the country code to return the collate-sequence table for. This parameter can be one of the following values:

Value	Meaning
001	United States
002	Canadian-French
003	Latin America
031	Netherlands
032	Belgium
033	France
034	Spain
036	Hungary
038	Yugoslavia

Value	Meaning
039	Italy
041	Switzerland
042	Czechoslovakia
044	United Kingdom
045	Denmark
046	Sweden
047	Norway
048	Poland
049	Germany
055	Brazil
061	International English
351	Portugal
358	Finland

If this parameter is 0FFFFh, MS-DOS returns the table for the current country.

Table   Points to a buffer in which MS-DOS places the 8-bit identifier (06h) of the collate-sequence table and the 32-bit address (segment:offset) of the table. The buffer must be at least 5 bytes long.

Return Value   If the function is successful, the carry flag is clear and the 32-bit address to the collate-sequence table is copied to the buffer pointed to by the *Table* parameter. Otherwise, the carry flag is set and the AX register contains an error value, which may be one of the following:

Value	Name
0001h	ERROR_INVALID_FUNCTION
0002h	ERROR_FILE_NOT_FOUND

Comments   This function returns 0001h (ERROR_INVALID_FUNCTION) if the buffer size specified in the CX register is less than 5.

This function returns 0002h (ERROR_FILE_NOT_FOUND) if MS-DOS cannot retrieve country information for the specified code page and country code.

The collate-sequence table starts with a 16-bit value that specifies the length of the table; the remainder of the table specifies the sorting weight for each character.

See Also   Function 38h Get/Set Country Information
Function 6501h Get Extended Country Information
Function 6601h Get Global Code Page
Function 6602h Set Global Code Page

■ Function 6507h Get Double-Byte Character Set

```
        mov     bx, CodePageID      ;code page to return DBCS for
        mov     cx, 5               ;size of buffer (must be at least 5)
        mov     dx, CountryCode     ;country code to return DBCS for
        mov     di, seg DBCS
        mov     es, di
        mov     di, offset DBCS     ;es:di points to buffer for pointer to DBCS

        mov     ax, 6507h           ;Get Double-Byte Character Set
        int     21h

        jc      error_handler       ;carry set means error
```

Get Double-Byte Character Set (Function 6507h) returns the address of a buffer containing values that specify the valid ranges for lead bytes in the given double-byte character set (DBCS).

Parameters   *CodePageID*   Identifies the code page to return the DBCS values for. This parameter can be one of the following values:

Value	Meaning
437	United States
850	Multilingual (Latin I)
852	Slavic (Latin II)
860	Portuguese
863	Canadian-French
865	Nordic

If this parameter is 0FFFFh, MS-DOS returns information for the current code page.

CountryCode   Specifies the country code to return the DBCS values for. This parameter can be one of the following values:

Value	Meaning
001	United States
002	Canadian-French
003	Latin America
031	Netherlands
032	Belgium
033	France
034	Spain
036	Hungary
038	Yugoslavia
039	Italy
041	Switzerland
042	Czechoslovakia
044	United Kingdom

Value	Meaning
045	Denmark
046	Sweden
047	Norway
048	Poland
049	Germany
055	Brazil
061	International English
351	Portugal
358	Finland

If this value is 0FFFFh, MS-DOS returns information for the current country.

DBCS   Points to a buffer in which MS-DOS places the 8-bit identifier (07h) of the DBCS values and the 32-bit address (segment:offset) of the table. The buffer must be at least 5 bytes long.

Return Value

If the function is successful, the carry flag is clear and the 32-bit address to the DBCS values is copied to the buffer pointed to by the *DBCS* parameter. Otherwise, the carry flag is set and the AX register contains an error value, which may be one of the following:

Value	Name
0001h	ERROR_INVALID_FUNCTION
0002h	ERROR_FILE_NOT_FOUND

Comments

This function returns 0001h (ERROR_INVALID_FUNCTION) if the buffer size specified in the CX register is less than 5.

This function returns 0002h (ERROR_FILE_NOT_FOUND) if MS-DOS cannot retrieve information for the specified code page and country code.

The DBCS values starts with a 16-bit value that specifies the length of the table. The remainder of the table consists of pairs of bytes with each pair specifying the low and high character values for a valid range of lead byte values.

See Also

Function 38h Get/Set Country Information
Function 6501h Get Extended Country Information
Function 6601h Get Global Code Page
Function 6602h Set Global Code Page

■ Function 6520h Convert Character

```
mov     dl, Character        ;character to convert

mov     ax, 6520h            ;Convert Character
int     21h

jc      error_handler        ;carry set means error
```

Convert Character (Function 6520h) converts the specified character to an uppercase character using the current uppercase table.

Parameter   *Character*   Specifies the character to convert.

Return Value   The function copies the corresponding uppercase character (if any) to the DL register.

See Also   Function 6521h Convert String
                   Function 6522h Convert ASCIIZ String

■ Function 6521h Convert String

```
mov     cx, StringLength      ;length of string in bytes
mov     dx, seg String
mov     ds, dx
mov     dx, offset String     ;ds:dx points to string to convert

mov     ax, 6521h             ;Convert String
int     21h

jc      error_handler         ;carry set means error
```

Convert String (Function 6521h) converts each character in the specified string to an uppercase character using the current uppercase table.

Parameters

StringLength   Specifies the length of the string in bytes.

String   Points to the string to convert.

Return Value

The function replaces the original characters in the string with the corresponding uppercase characters (if any).

See Also

Function 6520h Convert Character
Function 6522h Convert ASCIIZ String

■ Function 6522h Convert ASCIIZ String

```
mov     dx, seg String
mov     ds, dx
mov     dx, offset String     ;ds:dx points to string to convert

mov     ax, 6522h             ;Convert ASCIIZ String
int     21h

jc      error_handler         ;carry set means error
```

Convert ASCIIZ String (Function 6522h) converts each character in the specified string to an uppercase character using the current uppercase table.

Parameter   *String*   Points to a zero-terminated string.

Return Value   The function replaces the original characters in the string with the corresponding uppercase characters (if any).

See Also   Function 6520h Convert Character
Function 6521h Convert String

▪ Function 6601h Get Global Code Page

```
mov     ax, 6601h            ;Get Global Code Page
int     21h

jc      error_handler        ;carry set means error

mov     UserCodePageID, bx   ;user code page
mov     SysCodePageID, dx    ;system code page
```

Get Global Code Page (Function 6601h) identifies the code page currently used by all programs.

Parameters   This function has no parameters.

Return Value   If the function is successful, the carry flag is clear, the BX register contains the active code page (the code page set by the user), and the DX register contains the number of the system code page (the code page specified at startup). Otherwise, the carry flag is set and the AX register contains an error value, which may be 0002h (ERROR_FILE_NOT_FOUND).

Comment   The code-page identifier can be one of the following:

Value	Meaning
437	United States
850	Multilingual (Latin I)
852	Slavic (Latin II)
860	Portuguese
863	Canadian-French
865	Nordic

See Also   Function 6602h Set Global Code Page

■ Function 6602h Set Global Code Page

```
mov      bx, CodePageID       ;code page to set

mov      ax, 6602h            ;Set Global Code Page
int      21h

jc       error_handler        ;carry set means error
```

Set Global Code Page (Function 6602h) sets the code page used by all programs.

Parameter   *CodePageID*   Identifies the code page to set. This parameter can be set to one of the following values:

Value	Meaning
437	United States
850	Multilingual (Latin I)
852	Slavic (Latin II)
860	Portuguese
863	Canadian-French
865	Nordic

Return Value   If the function is successful, the carry flag is clear. Otherwise, the carry flag is set and the AX register contains an error value, which may be 0002h (ERROR_FILE_NOT_FOUND).

Comments   Before a code page can be selected for use on a device, the device must be prepared for code-page switching. The selected code page must be compatible with the country code specified in CONFIG.SYS. MS-DOS returns 0002h (ERROR_FILE_NOT_FOUND) if it cannot read the COUNTRY.SYS file or another specified country-information file.

See Also   Function 6601h Get Global Code Page

■ Function 67h Set Maximum Handle Count

```
mov     bx, Handles     ;new maximum handle count

mov     ah, 67h         ;Set Maximum Handle Count
int     21h

jc      error_handler
```

Set Maximum Handle Count (Function 67h) sets the maximum number of handles a program can use at any one time.

Parameter   *Handles*   Identifies the new maximum number of handles.

Return Value   If the function is successful, the carry flag is clear. Otherwise, the carry flag is set and the AX register contains an error value.

Comments   This function sets the maximum number of handles for the program but does not change the number of handles available in the system. The total number of system handles is set by the **files** command in the CONFIG.SYS file.

The maximum handle count specified in the *Handles* parameter is a property of the given program and is not inherited by child programs. This count must be in the range 20 to 65,535. If a number less than 20 is specified, the function uses 20 by default.

If Set Maximum Handle Count is used to reduce the number of "allowed" handles, the new limit does not take effect until any handles above the new limit are closed.

See Also   Function 46h Force Duplicate File Handle

■ Function 68h Commit File

```
mov     bx, Handle      ;handle of file to commit

mov     ah, 68h         ;Commit File
int     21h

jc      error_handler   ;carry set means error
```

Commit File (Function 68h) flushes all stored data for a file without closing the file; this ensures that the contents of the file are current.

Parameter   *Handle*   Identifies the file to commit.

Return Value   If the function is successful, the carry flag is clear. Otherwise, the carry flag is set and the AX register contains an error value.

Comment   This function provides a more efficient way to update file contents than closing a file and immediately reopening it. However, if a program opens or creates a file by specifying the flag OPEN_FLAGS_COMMIT (4000h) with Extended Open/Create (Function 6Ch), the system updates the file each time the file is written to.

See Also   Function 0Dh Reset Drive
                   Function 6Ch Extended Open/Create

■ Function 6Ch Extended Open/Create

```
mov     bx, OpenMode      ;access and sharing values
mov     cx, Attributes    ;file attributes
mov     dx, Action        ;action to take if file exists/does not exist

mov     si, seg FileName
mov     ds, si
mov     si, offset FileName     ;ds:si points to filename

mov     ah, 6Ch           ;Extended Open/Create
int     21h

jc      error_handler     ;carry set means error
```

Extended Open/Create (Function 6Ch) combines Create File with Handle
(Function 3Ch), Open File with Handle (Function 3Dh), and Commit File
(Function 68h).

Parameters   *OpenMode*   Specifies the modes with which to open the file. This parameter
consists of one access value, one sharing value, and, optionally, other values,
which can be given in any combination.

Value	Meaning
OPEN_ACCESS_READONLY (0000h)	Open the file for read-only access.
OPEN_ACCESS_WRITEONLY (0001h)	Open the file for write-only access.
OPEN_ACCESS_READWRITE (0002h)	Open the file for read-and-write access.
OPEN_SHARE_COMPATIBILITY (0000h)	Permit other programs any access to the file. On a given computer, any program can open the file any number of times with this value. This is the default value.
OPEN_SHARE_DENYREADWRITE (0010h)	Do not permit any other program to open the file.
OPEN_SHARE_DENYWRITE (0020h)	Do not permit any other program to open the file for write access.
OPEN_SHARE_DENYREAD (0030h)	Do not permit any other program to open the file for read access.
OPEN_SHARE_DENYNONE (0040h)	Permit other programs read or write access, but no program may open the file for compatibility access.

Value	Meaning
OPEN_FLAGS_NOINHERIT (0080h)	A child program created with Load and Execute Program (Function 4B00h) does not inherit the file handle. If this mode is not set, child programs inherit the file handle.
OPEN_FLAGS_NOCRIT_ERR (2000h)	Critical-Error Handler (Interrupt 24h) will not be called if a critical error occurs while MS-DOS is opening this file. Instead, MS-DOS returns an error value to the program.
OPEN_FLAGS_COMMIT (4000h)	MS-DOS commits the file (updates the file contents on disk) after each write operation.

Attributes Specifies the attributes to assign to the file if the specified file is created. This parameter can be a combination of the following values:

Value	Meaning
ATTR_NORMAL (0000h)	File can be read from or written to.
ATTR_READONLY (0001h)	File can be read from, but not written to.
ATTR_HIDDEN (0002h)	File does not appear in a directory listing.
ATTR_SYSTEM (0004h)	File is a system file.
ATTR_ARCHIVE (0020h)	File is marked for archiving.

If the file is opened instead of created, this parameter is ignored.

Action Specifies the action to take if the file exists or if it does not exist. This parameter can be a combination of the following values:

Value	Meaning
FILE_CREATE (0001h)	Create a new file. Fail if the file already exists.
FILE_OPEN (0010h)	Open the file. Fail if the file does not exist.
FILE_TRUNCATE (0020h)	Open the file and set the file pointer to zero (replace the existing file).

FileName Points to a zero-terminated ASCII string that specifies the file to open or create. The name must be a valid MS-DOS filename.

Return Value   If the function is successful, the carry flag is clear. Otherwise, the carry flag is set and the AX register contains an error value, which may be one of the following:

Value	Name
0003h	ERROR_PATH_NOT_FOUND
0004h	ERROR_TOO_MANY_OPEN_FILES
0005h	ERROR_ACCESS_DENIED

Comment   If the specified file is on a network drive, the function creates the file only if network grants create access to the drive or directory. Similarly, the function opens the file only if the network grants read, write, or both read and write access to the drive or directory.

See Also   Function 3Ch Create File with Handle
Function 3Dh Open File with Handle
Function 68h Commit File
Interrupt 24h Critical-Error Handler

Chapter

9

Device Drivers

9.1 Introduction

Device drivers are special programs, loaded when the system starts, that give MS-DOS a device-independent hardware interface that it uses to carry out input and output operations with system hardware devices. This chapter describes device-driver formats, functions, and operations.

As part of its BIOS, MS-DOS provides resident device drivers that support required devices: keyboard, screen, serial port, parallel port, real-time clock, and disk drive. Computer manufacturers create resident drivers and incorporate them in MS-DOS for their computers.

Installable device drivers support printers, plotters, and pointing devices that are not part of the original computer's equipment but are installed by the user. Manufacturers who develop add-on devices for MS-DOS computers create installable device drivers to support them. Users install the drivers by using **device** or **devicehigh** commands in the CONFIG.SYS file.

Installable device drivers can also be used to extend or replace existing resident device drivers. The device driver ANSI.SYS provided with MS-DOS, for example, extends the resident device driver for the screen, enabling programs to use ANSI escape sequences to move the cursor and control the color and format of characters on the screen.

Although the focus of this chapter is on installable device drivers, the discussion also applies to resident device drivers.

9.2 Character and Block Devices

MS-DOS recognizes two types of device: character and block. A character device performs input and output a single character at a time. Examples are the keyboard, screen, serial port, and parallel port. A block device performs input and output in structured pieces called blocks. Block devices include all disk drives and other mass-storage devices on the computer.

A device driver supports either a character device or a block device, but never both. The type of device a driver supports determines both the functions the driver implements and the information the driver supplies in its device-driver header and to MS-DOS when the driver is initialized.

9.3 Device-Driver Format

Every device driver, whether it supports a character device or a block device, consists of a device-driver header, a strategy routine, and an interrupt routine. These elements provide the information and code needed to carry out requests from MS-DOS for device input and output.

Installable device drivers are contained in either binary image files, containing absolute load images, or .EXE-format files. (Binary image files that contain device drivers are often given the filename extension .SYS to distinguish the files from other binary image files, such as .COM program files). Although most device-driver files contain a single device driver, some contain more than one, in which case the file must contain one header for each driver.

9.3.1 Device-Driver Header

The device-driver header, which must be at the beginning of the device driver, identifies the device driver, specifies the driver's strategy and interrupt routines, and defines the attributes of the device the driver supports. The form of the device-driver header corresponds to a **DEVICEHEADER** structure:

```
DEVICEHEADER STRUC
    dhLink          dd ?            ;link to next driver
    dhAttributes    dw ?            ;device attributes
    dhStrategy      dw ?            ;strategy-routine offset
    dhInterrupt     dw ?            ;interrupt-routine offset
    dhNameOrUnits   db '????????'   ;logical-device name (char dev only)
                                    ;number of units (block dev only)
DEVICEHEADER ENDS
```

The **dhLink** field must be 0FFFFh if there are no other device-driver headers in the file. Otherwise, the low 16 bits must contain the offset (from the beginning of the load image) to the next device-driver header, and the high 16 bits must contain zero. When loading the driver, MS-DOS sets this field to point to the next driver in the driver chain.

The **dhAttributes** field specifies the device type and provides additional information that MS-DOS uses when creating requests. The bits in this field must be set as follows:

Bit	Meaning
0	**For a character-device driver.** Specifies that the device is the standard input device. This bit must be set to 1 if the driver replaces the resident device driver that supports the standard input device.
1	**For a character-device driver.** Specifies that the device is the standard output device. This bit must be set to 1 if the driver replaces the resident device driver that supports the standard output device.
	For a block-device driver. Specifies whether the driver can process 32-bit sector addresses. This bit must be set to 1 if the driver supports 32-bit sector addressing. MS-DOS checks this bit to determine whether it should use the **rwrHugeSector** field at the end of the **READWRITEREQUEST** structure used with Read, Write, and Write with Verify (Device-Driver Functions 04h, 08h, and 09h).
	This bit must be zero if the device supports only 16-bit sector addressing.
2	**For a character-device driver.** Specifies that the device is the NUL device. The resident NUL device driver cannot be replaced. This bit must be zero for all other device drivers.
3	**For a character-device driver.** Specifies that the device is the clock device. This bit must be set to 1 if the driver replaces the resident device driver that supports the clock device.

Bit	Meaning
4	**For a character-device driver.** Specifies that the driver supports fast character output. If this bit is set, MS-DOS issues Interrupt 29h (with the character value in the AL register) when a program writes to the device—for example, when using Direct Console I/O (Interrupt 21h Function 06h). During its initialization, the device driver must install a handler (for Interrupt 29h) that carries out the fast output.
6	Specifies whether the device supports logical-drive mapping or generic IOCTL functions, or both. This bit must be set to 1 if the device driver implements Get Logical Drive and Set Logical Drive (Device-Driver Functions 17h and 18h) or Generic IOCTL (Device-Driver Function 13h).
7	Specifies whether the device supports IOCTL queries. This bit must be set to 1 if the device driver implements IOCTL Query (Device-Driver Function 19h).
11	Specifies whether the driver supports Open Device, Close Device, and Removable Media (Device-Driver Functions 0Dh, 0Eh, and 0Fh). This bit must be set to 1 if the driver implements these functions. Only block-device drivers support Removable Media.
13	**For a character-device driver.** Specifies whether the driver supports Output Until Busy (Device-Driver Function 10h). This bit must be set to 1 if the driver implements this function.
	For a block-device driver. Specifies whether the driver requires MS-DOS to supply the first sector of the first file allocation table (FAT) when it calls Build BPB (Device-Driver Function 02h). Drivers that have no other means of determining the current medium type use the media descriptor in the first byte of the FAT. This bit must be set to 1 if the driver requires the FAT.
14	Specifies whether the driver supports IOCTL Read and IOCTL Write (Device-Driver Functions 03h and 0Ch). This bit must be set to 1 if the driver implements these functions.
15	Specifies whether the driver supports a character device or a block device. This bit must be set to 1 if the driver supports a character device.

Any bits in the **dhAttributes** field that are not used for a given device type must be zero.

The **dhStrategy** and **dhInterrupt** fields contain the offsets to the entry points of the strategy and interrupt routines. Since these fields are 16-bit values, the entry points must be in the same segment as the device-driver file header. For a device driver in a binary image file, the offsets are in bytes from the beginning of the file; for a driver in an .EXE-format file, the offsets are in bytes from the beginning of the file's load image.

The **dhNameOrUnits** field is an 8-byte field that contains either a logical-device name or a 1-byte value specifying the number of units supported. A character-device driver must supply a logical-device name of no more than eight characters. If it has fewer than eight characters, the name must be left-aligned and any remaining bytes in the field must be filled with space characters (ASCII 20h). The device name must not contain a colon (:). A block-device driver does not supply a name; instead, it can supply the number of units it supports. This is optional, however, since MS-DOS fills in this field with the value the driver returns by using Init (Device-Driver Function 00h).

For a full description of the **DEVICEHEADER** structure, see Section 9.9, "Structures."

9.3.2 Strategy and Interrupt Routines

Each driver has two routines: a strategy routine and an interrupt routine. Both routines are called by MS-DOS, but only the interrupt routine carries out any work.

MS-DOS first makes a far call to the device driver's strategy routine, passing (in the ES:BX registers) the 32-bit address (segment:offset) of a request packet. The strategy routine saves this address and returns immediately by using a far return. MS-DOS then calls the interrupt routine. At this point, the device driver carries out the requested function, accessing the hardware either directly or by using ROM BIOS calls. When processing is complete, the interrupt routine must set the status value in the request packet and return to MS-DOS by using a far return. The request is completed when the interrupt routine returns.

The interrupt routine, despite its name, is never started as a result of an interrupt. Instead, the routine always receives control from an explicit call made by MS-DOS. When called, the interrupt routine must examine the function field in the request packet to determine what action to take. Since a device driver must never have more than one pending request at any given time, the interrupt routine must, for each request, either carry out an action or indicate to MS-DOS that the device is busy or in error.

The strategy and interrupt routines must preserve any registers they use, including flags. The routines can save registers on the stack (restoring them before returning), although there is limited space on the stack when these routines are called (usually about 40 to 50 bytes). If the driver requires more room, it should set up its own stack. The direction flag and interrupt-enable bits are especially critical and must be preserved in all cases.

9.4 Block-Device Drivers

A block-device driver handles input and output for a mass-storage device, such as a disk drive. The driver must implement the following device-driver functions:

Function	Name	Comments
00h	Init	
01h	Media Check	

Function	Name	Comments
02h	Build BPB	
03h	IOCTL Read	Required only if bit 14 is set in the **dhAttributes** field of the **DEVICE-HEADER** structure
04h	Read	
08h	Write	
09h	Write with Verify	
0Ch	IOCTL Write	Required only if bit 14 in **dhAttributes** is set
0Dh	Open Device	Required only if bit 11 in **dhAttributes** is set
0Eh	Close Device	Required only if bit 11 in **dhAttributes** is set
0Fh	Removable Media	Required only if bit 11 in **dhAttributes** is set
13h	Generic IOCTL	Required only if bit 6 in **dhAttributes** is set
17h	Get Logical Device	Required only if bit 6 in **dhAttributes** is set
18h	Set Logical Device	Required only if bit 6 in **dhAttributes** is set
19h	IOCTL Query	Required only if bit 7 in **dhAttributes** is set

Every block-device driver controls one or more devices. A device can be a physical drive, such as a floppy disk drive, or a logical drive, such as a partition on a hard disk. In either case, MS-DOS assigns a unique drive number that programs use to access the device. The driver is responsible for determining and reporting how many devices it supports when it returns from a call to Init (Device-Driver Function 00h).

MS-DOS allows no more than 26 drives for the entire system. If a device driver reports a number that would push the system total beyond 26, MS-DOS terminates the driver. To ensure that a driver does not exceed this limit, MS-DOS passes the next available drive number to the driver during initialization. As long as the sum of this number and the driver's number of units is less than 26, the driver's initialization will succeed.

It is not possible to replace the resident block-device driver with an installable device driver. Installable block-device drivers can be used only for devices not directly supported by resident drivers. Note that MS-DOS always initializes resident block-device drivers before installable drivers and always assigns drive numbers in the same order as it initialized the drivers.

9.5 Character-Device Drivers

An installable character-device driver handles input and output for a device such as a keyboard, screen, or serial port. A character-device driver must implement the following device-driver functions:

Function	Name	Comments
00h	Init	
03h	IOCTL Read	Required only if bit 14 is set in the **dhAttributes** field of the **DEVICE-HEADER** structure
04h	Read	
05h	Nondestructive Read	
06h	Input Status	
07h	Input Flush	
08h	Write	
09h	Write with Verify	
0Ah	Output Status	
0Bh	Output Flush	
0Ch	IOCTL Write	Required only if bit 14 in **dhAttributes** is set
0Dh	Open Device	Required only if bit 11 in **dhAttributes** is set
0Eh	Close Device	Required only if bit 11 in **dhAttributes** is set
10h	Output Until Busy	Required only if bit 13 in **dhAttributes** is set
13h	Generic IOCTL	Required only if bit 6 in **dhAttributes** is set
19h	IOCTL Query	Required only if bit 7 in **dhAttributes** is set

Every character-device driver must have a logical-device name that identifies the driver and is used by programs to open the device. Logical-device names do not need to be unique, but using the same name in two or more drivers prevents MS-DOS from accessing all but the last driver to be initialized. This is because MS-DOS, when opening a device, searches the driver chain from the beginning until it finds a driver that has a matching logical-device name. Since the last driver initialized is always closest to the beginning, MS-DOS stops its search there. Note that resident device drivers can be replaced by giving an installable driver the same logical-device name as the resident driver.

9.6 Request Packets and Function Requests

MS-DOS generates function requests when programs call MS-DOS system functions that require input from or output to a given device. Each function request consists of a request packet that MS-DOS passes to the device driver. A request packet contains information the driver uses to identify and carry out the request. The size and format of a packet depend on the function to be carried out, but all request packets have two parts: a request header (which has the same format for all requests), and request-specific fields. The form of the request header corresponds to a **REQUESTHEADER** structure:

```
REQUESTHEADER     STRUC
    rhLength      db ?              ;length of record, in bytes
    rhUnit        db ?              ;unit number (block device only)
    rhFunction    db ?              ;function number
    rhStatus      dw ?              ;status
    rhReserved    db 8 dup(?)       ;reserved
REQUESTHEADER     ENDS
```

For a full description of the **REQUESTHEADER** structure, see Section 9.9, "Structures."

MS-DOS writes the request packet in a reserved area of memory, setting the **rhFunction** field (offset 02h) to specify the action to be performed by the device driver and setting the **rhUnit** field (offset 01h), if the driver supports a block device, to identify the drive the request is for. The **rhLength** field (offset 00h) contains the length, in bytes, of the complete request packet. This is important for requests that have additional request-specific fields.

MS-DOS first calls the device driver's strategy routine, passing (in the ES:BX registers) the 32-bit address (segment:offset) of the request packet. The strategy routine saves this address and immediately returns to the system. MS-DOS then calls the interrupt routine, which retrieves the address of the request packet and reads the **rhFunction** field to determine what action to take. If the device driver supports a block device, the interrupt routine also reads the **rhUnit** field to determine which drive to access. This field specifies a zero-based unit number. (For example, if the driver controls four devices, a request to access the first one specifies number 0.) Note that the drive number and the unit number are not the same. Although programs use drive numbers to access a driver's devices, MS-DOS converts these numbers to zero-based unit numbers before calling the driver with a function request.

Depending on the function, the interrupt routine may read from or write to additional fields. The request packet for Write (Device-Driver Function 08h), for example, includes a transfer address (offset 0Dh), a sector count (offset 12h), and a starting sector (offset 14h). The interrupt routine must translate the starting sector into a physical sector (consisting of track, head, and sector numbers) and then write the specified number of sectors from the transfer address to the designated sectors on the specified drive.

When the interrupt routine completes its actions, it must report the status of the request to MS-DOS by setting one or more bits in the **rhStatus** field (offset 03h) in the request packet. If the function is successful, the routine sets the done bit

(bit 8). If an error occurred, the routine sets the done bit and the error bit (bit 15) and copies an error value to bits 0 through 7 of the **rhStatus** field. (For a list of these error values, see the **REQUESTHEADER** structure in Section 9.9, "Structures.") Finally, the routine returns to MS-DOS.

9.7 Device-Driver Initialization

MS-DOS loads and initializes installable device drivers in the order their corresponding **device** or **devicehigh** commands appear in the CONFIG.SYS file. When loading a driver, MS-DOS does not create a program segment prefix (PSP) or an environment block. Instead, it allocates enough memory to load the contents of the driver file and copies the contents from disk, placing the device-driver header at the beginning of the allocated memory. MS-DOS then calls the strategy routine and the interrupt routine with a request packet for Init (Device-Driver Function 00h). The form of this request packet corresponds to an **INITREQUEST** structure:

```
INITREQUEST STRUC
    irLength        db ?            ;length of record, in bytes
    irUnit          db ?            ;not used
    irFunction      db 00h          ;function number
    irStatus        dw ?            ;status
    irReserved      db 8 dup(?)     ;reserved
    irUnits         db ?            ;OUTPUT: number of units
    irEndAddress    dd ?            ;INPUT:  end available driver memory
                                    ;OUTPUT: end resident code
    irParamAddress  dd ?            ;INPUT:  addr CONFIG.SYS device= line
                                    ;OUTPUT: addr BPB pointer array
    irDriveNumber   db ?            ;INPUT:  first drive number
    irMessageFlag   dw ?            ;OUTPUT: error-message flag
INITREQUEST ENDS
```

For a full description of the **INITREQUEST** structure, see Init (Device-Driver Function 00h).

When processing the Init function, the interrupt routine should carry out any initialization required, such as processing arguments specified on the **device** or **devicehigh** command line. Note that only a few MS-DOS system functions are available during initialization (Interrupt 21h Functions 01h through 0Ch, 25h, 30h, and 35h). In general, the interrupt routine can display messages at the standard output device, but it cannot open files or allocate additional memory.

Initially, the **irEndAddress** value in the request packet contains the segment address of the next memory block after the driver, regardless of whether the device driver is loaded using the **device** or **devicehigh** command. The driver can use the memory up to this address. If the **devicehigh** command is used to load a driver into the upper memory area, the driver's code-segment and data-segment addresses may be greater than A000h, and the address space immediately following the driver may contain ROM or memory-mapped devices and not necessarily RAM.

To complete the initialization, the interrupt routine must copy the address of the end of the driver to the **irEndAddress** field in the request packet. Block-device drivers must also copy the number of units they support and the address of an array of BIOS parameter blocks (BPBs) to corresponding fields in the request packet. Finally, the interrupt routine must set the done bit (bit 8) in the **irStatus** field and return.

If a driver cannot be initialized, it must set both the error bit (bit 15) and the done bit (bit 8) in the **irStatus** field. It must also set the **irUnits** field to zero and set **irEndAddress** the driver's starting address. MS-DOS then discards the driver and frees its memory for use by the next driver.

MS-DOS initializes a driver only once. This means the interrupt routine should free the memory containing its initialization code and data. The driver cannot free memory directly, but MS-DOS frees it for the driver when the driver specifies its ending address in the request packet. MS-DOS uses this ending addess to reallocate the memory block containing the driver. If the initialization code and data are at the end of the driver and the driver sets the **irEndAddress** field properly, MS-DOS frees their memory when reallocating the block.

An installable device driver that has the same logical-device name as an existing character-device driver effectively replaces the existing driver. The old driver remains in memory, however, and its strategy and interrupt routines can be called by the new driver to access the given device. This is one way a new driver can extend the capabilities of an existing driver.

The new driver can retrieve the addresses of the old driver's strategy and interrupt routines by searching the driver chain for device-driver headers that have matching logical-device names. (The new driver is at the top of the driver chain, and the **dhLink** field in its device-driver header contains the address of the next driver in the chain. For the last driver in the chain, the **dhLink** field contains 0FFFFh.) The old driver's address can be retrieved only after the new driver has completed its initialization.

9.8 Device-Driver Function Reference

The following pages describe the MS-DOS device-driver functions, in numeric order. Each description includes the function's syntax and return values. Fields are designated as INPUT where information is filled in by MS-DOS before it calls the device driver and as OUTPUT where information must be supplied by the driver.

Init (Device-Driver Function 00h)

```
INITREQUEST STRUC
    irLength          db ?              ;length of record, in bytes
    irUnit            db ?              ;not used
    irFunction        db 00h            ;function number
    irStatus          dw ?              ;status
    irReserved        db 8 dup(?)       ;reserved
    irUnits           db ?              ;OUTPUT: number of units
    irEndAddress      dd ?              ;INPUT:  end available driver memory
                                        ;OUTPUT: end resident code
    irParamAddress    dd ?              ;INPUT:  addr CONFIG.SYS device= line
                                        ;OUTPUT: addr BPB pointer array
    irDriveNumber     db ?              ;INPUT:  first drive number
    irMessageFlag     dw ?              ;OUTPUT: error-message flag
INITREQUEST ENDS
```

Init (Device-Driver Function 00h) directs the driver to initialize the device driver and corresponding device. This function is called only once, when the driver is loaded.

This function is required for both block- and character-device drivers.

Fields

irLength   Specifies the length, in bytes, of the **INITREQUEST** structure.

irUnit   Not used.

irFunction   Specifies the Init function: 00h.

irStatus   Specifies the status of the completed function. If the function is successful, the driver must set the done bit (bit 8). Otherwise, the driver must set both the error and done bits (bits 15 and 8) and copy an error value to the low-order byte.

irReserved   Reserved; do not use.

irUnits   Specifies the number of units supported by the driver. MS-DOS uses this number to assign sequential drive numbers to the units. The driver must set this field.

Character-device drivers should set this field to zero.

irEndAddress   Contains the 32-bit address (segment:offset) of the end of memory available to the device driver and receives the 32-bit address of the end of the initialized driver. The following table describes input and output:

Input/output	Description
Input	Points to the first byte of memory that immediately follows the device driver and which must not be used by the driver. During initialization, the driver may use any memory between its starting address and this address. The driver can also reserve some or all of this memory for use after initialization. (This field is not used for input in MS-DOS versions earlier than version 5.0. The driver should check the MS-DOS version number before using the value in this field.)
Output	Points to the first byte of memory that immediately follows the initialized driver. The driver must set this field to an address that is not greater than the end of available memory. If the driver fails to initialize, it should set this field to its starting address. This directs MS-DOS to remove the driver and free all memory associated with it.

irParamAddress   Contains a 32-bit address (segment:offset) of the initialization parameters and receives a 32-bit address of an array of pointers to **BPB** structures. The following table describes input and output:

Input/output	Description
Input	Points to the initialization parameters for the driver as copied from the CONFIG.SYS file. The parameters consist of the filename for the driver and any command-line switches—that is, all text on the corresponding **device** or **devicehigh** command line up to the terminating carriage-return character (ASCII 0Dh) or linefeed character (ASCII 0Ah) but not including the **device** or **devicehigh** command and equal sign.
Output	Points to an array of pointers to **BPB** structures. These structures specify the BIOS parameters for each unit supported by the drive. (Each pointer is a 16-bit offset relative to the start of the driver.)

The **BPB** structure has the following form:

```
BPB       STRUC
    bpbBytesPerSec   dw   ?
    bpbSecPerClust   db   ?
    bpbResSectors    dw   ?
    bpbFATs          db   ?
    bpbRootDirEnts   dw   ?
    bpbSectors       dw   ?
    bpbMedia         db   ?
    bpbFATsecs       dw   ?
    bpbSecPerTrack   dw   ?
    bpbHeads         dw   ?
    bpbHiddenSecs    dd   ?
    bpbHugeSectors   dd   ?
BPB       ENDS
```

For a full description of the **BPB** structure, see Section 9.9, "Structures." If all units are the same, all pointers in the array can be the same.

Character device drivers must set the **irParamAddress** field to zero.

irDriveNumber   Contains the zero-based drive number for the driver's first unit as assigned by MS-DOS. MS-DOS supplies this number so that the driver can determine whether MS-DOS will accept all its supported units. MS-DOS allows no more than 26 units in the system.

irMessageFlag   Specifies whether MS-DOS displays an error message on initialization failure. To direct MS-DOS to display the message, the driver must set this field to 1. The message is displayed only if the driver also sets the **irStatus** field to indicate failure.

Comments

The Init function is called only once; its code and data need not be retained after it has initialized its device. A device driver can release the Init function's code and data by placing the function at the end of the driver and returning the function's starting address in the **irEndAddress** field.

If the Init function uses Interrupt 21h system functions, it may use only the functions in the following table:

Function number	Description
01h-0Ch	Character I/O
25h	Set Interrupt Vector
30h	Get Version Number
35h	Get Interrupt Vector

See Also   Interrupt 21h Functions 01h-0Ch Character Input and Output
Interrupt 21h Function 25h Set Interrupt Vector
Interrupt 21h Function 30h Get Version Number
Interrupt 21h Function 35h Get Interrupt Vector

■ Media Check (Device-Driver Function 01h)

```
MEDIAREQUEST      STRUC
    mrLength      db  ?              ;length of record, in bytes
    mrUnit        db  ?              ;unit number
    mrFunction    db  01h            ;function number
    mrStatus      dw  ?              ;status
    mrReserved    db  8 dup(?)       ;reserved
    mrMediaID     db  ?              ;INPUT:   current media descriptor
    mrReturn      db  ?              ;OUTPUT: return value
    mrVolumeID    dd  ?              ;OUTPUT: previous volume identifier
MEDIAREQUEST      ENDS
```

Media Check (Device-Driver Function 01h) determines whether the medium in the specified drive has changed.

This function is required by block-device drivers only.

Fields

mrLength   Specifies the length, in bytes, of the **MEDIAREQUEST** structure.

mrUnit   Specifies the unit for which the medium is to be checked.

mrFunction   Specifies the Media Check function: 01h.

mrStatus   Specifies the status of the completed function. If the function is successful, the driver must set the done bit (bit 8). Otherwise, the driver must set both the error and done bits (bits 15 and 8) and copy an error value to the low-order byte.

mrReserved   Reserved; do not use.

mrMediaID   Specifies the media descriptor for the medium MS-DOS assumes is in the drive. Following are the most commonly used media descriptors and their corresponding media:

Value	Type of medium
0F0h	3.5-inch, 2 sides, 18 sectors/track (1.44 MB); 3.5-inch, 2 sides, 36 sectors/track (2.88 MB); 5.25-inch, 2 sides, 15 sectors/track (1.2 MB). This value is also used to describe other media types.
0F8h	Hard disk, any capacity.
0F9h	3.5-inch, 2 sides, 9 sectors/track, 80 tracks/side (720K); 5.25-inch, 2 sides, 15 sectors/track, 40 tracks/side (1.2 MB).
0FAh	5.25-inch, 1 side, 8 sectors/track, (320K).
0FBh	3.5-inch, 2 sides, 8 sectors/track (640K).
0FCh	5.25-inch, 1 side, 9 sectors/track, 40 tracks/side (180K).
0FDh	5.25-inch, 2 sides, 9 sectors/track, 40 tracks/side (360K). This value is also used for 8-inch disks.
0FEh	5.25-inch, 1 side, 8 sectors/track, 40 tracks/side (160K). This value is also used for 8-inch disks.
0FFh	5.25-inch, 2 sides, 8 sectors/track, 40 tracks/side (320K).

mrReturn   Receives a return value identifying whether the medium has changed. The driver must set the field to one of the following values:

Value	Meaning
0FFh	Medium has been changed.
00h	Driver cannot determine whether medium has been changed.
01h	Medium is unchanged.

mrVolumeID   Receives the 32-bit address (segment:offset) of a zero-terminated ASCII string specifying the volume identifier of the previous disk in the drive. The driver must set this field to the address of the volume identifier. If the disk does not have a volume identifier, the driver must set the field to the address of the string "NO NAME".

Comments   If the medium in the drive has not changed, MS-DOS proceeds with the disk operation.

If the medium in the drive has changed, MS-DOS invalidates all buffers associated with the drive, including any buffers containing data waiting to be written (this data is lost). MS-DOS then calls Build BPB (Device-Driver Function 02h) to request a **BPB** structure for the new disk and reads the disk's file allocation table (FAT) and directory.

If the driver cannot determine whether the disk has changed, MS-DOS checks its internal disk buffers. If data is waiting to be written to the disk, the system assumes that the disk has not changed and attempts to write the data to the disk. If the disk buffers are empty, MS-DOS assumes the disk has changed and updates the disk information as if the driver had returned 0FFh.

See Also   Device-Driver Function 02h Build BPB

■ Build BPB (Device-Driver Function 02h)

```
BUILDBPBREQUEST STRUC
    bbrLength       db  ?              ;length of record, in bytes
    bbrUnit         db  ?              ;unit number
    bbrFunction     db  02h            ;function number
    bbrStatus       dw  ?              ;status
    bbrReserved     db  8 dup(?)       ;reserved
    bbrMediaID      db  ?              ;INPUT:  media descriptor
    bbrFATSector    dd  ?              ;INPUT:  buffer with first FAT sector
    bbrBPBAddress   dd  ?              ;OUTPUT: BPB address
BUILDBPBREQUEST ENDS
```

Build BPB (Device-Driver Function 02h) returns a **BPB** structure for the medium in the specified drive. MS-DOS calls this function whenever Media Check (Device-Driver Function 01h) specifies that the medium has changed or that it might have been changed and no disk-write operations are pending.

This function is required for block-device drivers.

Fields   **bbrLength**   Specifies the length, in bytes, of the **BUILDBPBREQUEST** structure.

bbrUnit   Specifies the unit for which to return the **BPB** structure.

bbrFunction   Specifies the Build BPB function: 02h.

bbrStatus   Specifies the status of the completed function. If the function is successful, the driver must set the done bit (bit 8). Otherwise, the driver must set both the error and done bits (bits 15 and 8) and copy an error value to the low-order byte.

bbrReserved   Reserved; do not use.

bbrMediaID   Specifies the media descriptor for the medium that MS-DOS assumes is in the drive. Following are the most commonly used media descriptors and their corresponding media:

Value	Type of medium
0F0h	3.5-inch, 2 sides, 18 sectors/track (1.44 MB); 3.5-inch, 2 sides, 36 sectors/track (2.88 MB); 5.25-inch, 2 sides, 15 sectors/track (1.2 MB). This value is also used to describe other media types.
0F8h	Hard disk, any capacity.
0F9h	3.5-inch, 2 sides, 9 sectors/track, 80 tracks/side (720K); 5.25-inch, 2 sides, 15 sectors/track, 40 tracks/side (1.2 MB).
0FAh	5.25-inch, 1 side, 8 sectors/track, (320K).
0FBh	3.5-inch, 2 sides, 8 sectors/track (640K).
0FCh	5.25-inch, 1 side, 9 sectors/track, 40 tracks/side (180K).
0FDh	5.25-inch, 2 sides, 9 sectors/track, 40 tracks/side (360K). This value is also used for 8-inch disks.
0FEh	5.25-inch, 1 side, 8 sectors/track, 40 tracks/side (160K). This value is also used for 8-inch disks.
0FFh	5.25-inch, 2 sides, 8 sectors/track, 40 tracks/side (320K).

For more information about media descriptors, see Chapter 3, "File System."

bbrFATSector   Contains the 32-bit address (segment:offset) of a buffer. The contents of the buffer depend on bit 13 in the **dhAttributes** field in the driver's **DEVICEHEADER** structure. If bit 13 is zero, the buffer contains the first sector of the first FAT on the disk; the driver uses the first byte in this buffer to determine the disk's media descriptor. In this case, the driver must not alter this buffer. If bit 13 is set, the contents of the buffer are meaningless and the driver may use the buffer as scratch space.

bbrBPBAddress   Receives the 32-bit address (segment:offset) of the **BPB** structure for the medium in the drive. The **BPB** structure has the following form:

```
BPB     STRUC
    bpbBytesPerSec   dw   ?   ;bytes per sector
    bpbSecPerClust   db   ?   ;sectors per cluster
    bpbResSectors    dw   ?   ;number of reserved sectors
    bpbFATs          db   ?   ;number of file allocation tables
    bpbRootDirEnts   dw   ?   ;number of root-directory entries
    bpbSectors       dw   ?   ;total number of sectors
    bpbMedia         db   ?   ;media descriptor
    bpbFATsecs       dw   ?   ;number of sectors per FAT
    bpbSecPerTrack   dw   ?   ;sectors per track
    bpbHeads         dw   ?   ;number of heads
    bpbHiddenSecs    dd   ?   ;number of hidden sectors
    bpbHugeSectors   dd   ?   ;number of sectors if bpbSectors = 0
BPB     ENDS
```

For a full description of the **DEVICEHEADER** and **BPB** structures, see Section 9.9, "Structures."

Comments

If the driver supports removable media, Build BPB should read the volume label from the disk and save it.

See Also

Device-Driver Function 01h Media Check
Interrupt 21h Function 440Dh Minor Code 40h Set Device Parameters
Interrupt 21h Function 440Dh Minor Code 60h Get Device Parameters

■ IOCTL Read (Device-Driver Function 03h)

```
IOCTLRWREQUEST  STRUC
     irwrLength      db  ?          ;length of record, in bytes
     irwrUnit        db  ?          ;unit number
     irwrFunction    db  03h        ;function number
     irwrStatus      dw  ?          ;status
     irwrReserved    db  8 dup(?)   ;reserved
     irwrData        db  ?          ;not used
     irwrBuffer      dd  ?          ;INPUT:   buffer address
     irwrBytes       dw  ?          ;INPUT:   number of bytes requested
                                    ;OUTPUT:  number of bytes read
IOCTLRWREQUEST  ENDS
```

IOCTL Read (Device-Driver Function 03h) transfers data from a device driver into the specified buffer.

This function can be used for both block- and character-device drivers.

Fields   **irwrLength**   Specifies the length, in bytes, of the **IOCTLRWREQUEST** structure.

irwrUnit   Specifies the device driver from which data is to be read. This field is used for block-device drivers only.

irwrFunction   Specifies the IOCTL Read function: 03h.

irwrStatus   Specifies the status of the completed function. If the function is successful, the driver must set the done bit (bit 8). Otherwise, the driver must set both the error and done bits (bits 15 and 8) and copy an error value to the low-order byte.

irwrReserved   Reserved; do not use.

irwrData   Not used.

irwrBuffer   Contains the 32-bit address (segment:offset) of the buffer that receives data read from the device.

irwrBytes   Contains the number of bytes to read and receives the number of bytes read. The following table describes input and output:

Input/output	Description
Input	Specifies the number of bytes to read. This number must not exceed the size, in bytes, of the specified buffer.
Output	Specifies the number of bytes read. This number cannot exceed the requested number of bytes.

Comments   MS-DOS calls this function only if bit 14 is set in the **dhAttributes** field of the **DEVICEHEADER** structure for the driver. For a full description of the **DEVICEHEADER** structure, see Section 9.9, "Structures."

The format of the returned data is device-specific and does not follow any standard.

See Also   Device-Driver Function 0Ch IOCTL Write
Interrupt 21h Function 4402h Receive Control Data from Character Device
Interrupt 21h Function 4404h Receive Control Data from Block Device

■ Read (Device-Driver Function 04h)

```
READWRITEREQUEST       STRUC
     rwrLength         db  ?           ;length of record, in bytes
     rwrUnit           db  ?           ;unit number
     rwrFunction       db  04h         ;function number
     rwrStatus         dw  ?           ;status
     rwrReserved       db  8 dup(?)    ;reserved
     rwrMediaID        db  ?           ;INPUT:   media descriptor
     rwrBuffer         dd  ?           ;INPUT:   buffer address
     rwrBytesSec       dw  ?           ;INPUT:   number bytes/sectors to read
                                       ;OUTPUT: number bytes/sectors read
     rwrStartSec       dw  ?           ;INPUT:   starting-sector number
     rwrVolumeID       dd  ?           ;OUTPUT: volume identifier
     rwrHugeStartSec   dd  ?           ;INPUT:   32-bit starting-sector number
READWRITEREQUEST       ENDS
```

Read (Device-Driver Function 04h) transfers data from a device into the specified buffer.

This function is required for both block- and character-device drivers.

Fields

rwrLength   Specifies the length, in bytes, of the **READWRITEREQUEST** structure.

rwrUnit   Specifies the device from which data is to be read. This field is used for block-device drivers only.

rwrFunction   Specifies the Read function: 04h.

rwrStatus   Specifies the status of the completed function. If the function is successful, the driver must set the done bit (bit 8). Otherwise, the driver must set both the error and done bits (bits 15 and 8) and copy an error value to the low-order byte.

rwrReserved   Reserved; do not use.

rwrMediaID   Specifies the media descriptor for the medium that MS-DOS assumes is in the drive. This field can be any one of the media-descriptor values specified in Media Check (Device-Driver Function 01h). This field is used for block-device drivers only.

rwrBuffer   Contains the 32-bit address (segment:offset) of the buffer that receives the data read from the device.

rwrBytesSec   Contains the number of bytes or sectors to read and receives the number of bytes or sectors read. The following table describes input and output:

Input/output	Description
Input	Specifies the number of bytes to read from a character device, or the number of sectors to read from a block device.
Output	Specifies the number of bytes read from a character device, or the number of sectors read from the block device. The driver must set this field; if there is an error, the driver should return the number of bytes or sectors read before the error occurred.

rwrStartSec   Specifies the first logical sector to read. If the first sector is larger than 65,535 bytes, this field contains 0FFFFh and the **rwrHugeStartSec** field specifies the first sector. This field is used for block-device drivers only.

rwrVolumeID   Contains the 32-bit address (segment:offset) of a zero-terminated ASCII string specifying the volume identifier for the disk most recently accessed. If the driver returns error value 0Fh (invalid disk change), MS-DOS uses the volume identifier to prompt the user to insert the appropriate disk. This field is used for block-device drivers only.

rwrHugeStartSec   Specifies the first logical sector to read. This field is used only if the **rwrStartSec** field contains 0FFFFh. This field is used for block-device drivers only.

Comments

The driver must translate the logical-sector number supplied in the **rwrStartSec** or **rwrHugeStartSec** field to the appropriate head, track, and sector numbers.

The **rwrHugeStartSec** field is used only if bit 1 is set in the **dhAttributes** field in the block-device driver's **DEVICEHEADER** structure. For a full description of the **DEVICEHEADER** structure, see Section 9.9, "Structures."

See Also

Device-Driver Function 01h Media Check
Device-Driver Function 08h Write
Device-Driver Function 09h Write with Verify
Interrupt 21h Function 3Fh Read File or Device

■ Nondestructive Read (Device-Driver Function 05h)

```
NDREADREQUEST    STRUC
    nrrLength    db ?              ;length of record, in bytes
    nrrUnit      db ?              ;not used
    nrrFunction  db 05h            ;function number
    nrrStatus    dw ?              ;status
    nrrReserved  db 8 dup(?)       ;reserved
    nrrChar      db ?              ;OUTPUT: character read from device
NDREADREQUEST    ENDS
```

Nondestructive Read (Device-Driver Function 05h) returns the next character from the input buffer without removing it from the buffer; subsequent read operations should return the same character.

This function is required for character-device drivers only.

Fields

nrrLength   Specifies the length, in bytes, of the **NDREADREQUEST** structure.

nrrUnit   Not used.

nrrFunction   Specifies the Nondestructive Read function: 05h.

nrrStatus   Specifies the status of the completed function. If the device input buffer has at least one character, the busy bit (bit 9) must be zero, indicating that MS-DOS need not wait to read a character. If the input buffer has no characters, the driver must set the busy bit. In both cases, the driver must set the done bit (bit 8).

If the function is not successful, the driver must set both the error and done bits (bits 15 and 8) and copy an error value to the low-order byte.

nrrReserved   Reserved; do not use.

nrrChar   Receives the next character in the input buffer. The driver must copy the character without removing it from the input buffer.

See Also

Device-Driver Function 04h Read

■ Input Status (Device-Driver Function 06h)

```
STATUSREQUEST   STRUC
    srLength    db  ?           ;length of record, in bytes
    srUnit      db  ?           ;not used
    srFunction  db  06h         ;function number
    srStatus    dw  ?           ;status
    srReserved  db  8 dup(?)    ;reserved
STATUSREQUEST   ENDS
```

Input Status (Device-Driver Function 06h) specifies whether any characters are waiting in the device-input buffer.

This function is required for character-device drivers only.

Fields

srLength   Specifies the length, in bytes, of the **STATUSREQUEST** structure.

srUnit   Not used.

srFunction   Specifies the Input Status function: 06h.

srStatus   Specifies the status of the completed function. If the device-input buffer has waiting characters, the busy bit (bit 9) must be zero, indicating that MS-DOS need not wait to read a character. If the buffer has no characters, the driver must set the busy bit. In either case, the driver must set the done bit (bit 8).

If the function is not successful, the driver must set both the error and done bits (bits 15 and 8) and copy an error value to the low-order byte.

srReserved   Reserved; do not use.

Comments

If the device has no input buffer, the busy bit must be zero.

Before attempting to read a character, MS-DOS may wait for a device to return a not-busy status.

See Also

Device-Driver Function 0Ah Output Status
Interrupt 21h Function 4406h Check Device Input Status

■ Input Flush (Device-Driver Function 07h)

```
FLUSHREQUEST    STRUC
    frLength    db  ?           ;length of record, in bytes
    frUnit      db  ?           ;not used
    frFunction  db  07h         ;function number
    frStatus    dw  ?           ;status
    frReserved  db  8 dup(?)    ;reserved
FLUSHREQUEST    ENDS
```

Input Flush (Device-Driver Function 07h) terminates any read operation in progress and empties the device-input buffer.

This function is required for character-device drivers only.

Fields

frLength   Specifies the length, in bytes, of the **FLUSHREQUEST** structure.

frUnit   Not used.

frFunction   Specifies the Input Flush function: 07h.

frStatus   Specifies the status of the completed function. If the function is successful, the driver must set the done bit (bit 8). Otherwise, the driver must set both the error and done bits (bits 15 and 8) and copy an error value to the low-order byte.

frReserved   Reserved; do not use.

See Also

Device-Driver Function 0Bh Output Flush
Interrupt 21h Function 0Ch Flush Buffer, Read Keyboard

■ Write/Write with Verify (Device-Driver Functions 08h and 09h)

```
READWRITEREQUEST      STRUC
    rwrLength         db  ?            ;length of record, in bytes
    rwrUnit           db  ?            ;unit number
    rwrFunction       db  ?            ;function number
    rwrStatus         dw  ?            ;status
    rwrReserved       db  8 dup(?)     ;reserved
    rwrMediaID        db  ?            ;INPUT:   media descriptor
    rwrBuffer         dd  ?            ;INPUT:   buffer address
    rwrBytesSec       dw  ?            ;INPUT:   number bytes/sectors to write
                                       ;OUTPUT: number bytes/sectors written
    rwrStartSec       dw  ?            ;INPUT:   starting-sector number
    rwrVolumeID       dd  ?            ;OUTPUT: volume identifier
    rwrHugeStartSec   dd  ?            ;INPUT:   32-bit starting-sector number
READWRITEREQUEST      ENDS
```

Write (Device-Driver Function 08h) and Write with Verify (Device-Driver Function 09h) transfer data from the specified buffer to a device. Write with Verify also reads the data back from the device, if possible, to verify that the data has been transferred correctly.

This function is required for both block- and character-device drivers.

Fields

rwrLength　　Specifies the length, in bytes, of the **READWRITEREQUEST** structure.

rwrUnit　　Specifies the device to which data is to be written. This field is used for block-device drivers only.

rwrFunction　　Specifies the Write or Write with Verify function: either 08h or 09h.

rwrStatus　　Specifies the status of the completed function. If the function is successful, the driver must set the done bit (bit 8). Otherwise, the driver must set both the error and done bits (bits 15 and 8) and copy an error value to the low-order byte.

rwrReserved　　Reserved; do not use.

rwrMediaID　　Specifies the media descriptor for the medium that MS-DOS assumes is in the disk drive. This field can be any one of the media descriptor values specified in Media Check (Device-Driver Function 01h). This field is used for block-device drivers only.

rwrBuffer　　Contains the 32-bit address (segment:offset) of the buffer containing the data to write to the device.

rwrBytesSec　　Contains the number of bytes or sectors to write and receives the number of bytes or sectors written. The following table describes input and output:

Input/Output	Description
Input	Specifies the number of bytes to write to a character device, or the number of sectors to write to a block device.
Output	Specifies the number of bytes written to a character device, or the number of sectors written to the block device. The driver must set this field; if there is an error, the driver should return the number of bytes or sectors written before the error occurred.

rwrStartSec   Specifies the first logical sector to write. If the first sector is larger than 65,535 bytes, this field contains 0FFFFh and the **rwrHugeStartSec** field specifies the first sector. This field is used for block-device drivers only.

rwrVolumeID   Contains the 32-bit address (segment:offset) of a zero-terminated ASCII string specifying the volume identifier for the disk most recently accessed. If the driver also returns error value 0Fh (invalid disk change), MS-DOS uses the volume identifier to prompt the user to insert the appropriate disk. This field is used for block-device drivers only.

rwrHugeStartSec   Specifies the first logical sector to write. This field is used only if the **rwrStartSec** field contains 0FFFFh. This field is used for block-device drivers only.

Comments   The driver must translate the logical-sector number supplied in the **rwrStartSec** or **rwrHugeStartSec** field to the appropriate head, track, and sector numbers.

The **rwrHugeStartSec** field is used only if bit 1 is set in the **dhAttributes** field in the block-device driver's **DEVICEHEADER** structure. For a full description of the **DEVICEHEADER** structure, see Section 9.9, "Structures."

See Also   Device-Driver Function 01h Media Check
Device-Driver Function 04h Read
Interrupt 21h Function 40h Write File or Device

■ Output Status (Device-Driver Function 0Ah)

```
STATUSREQUEST    STRUC
    srLength     db ?            ;length of record, in bytes
    srUnit       db ?            ;not used
    srFunction   db 0Ah          ;function number
    srStatus     dw ?            ;status
    srReserved   db 8 dup(?)     ;reserved
STATUSREQUEST    ENDS
```

Output Status (Device-Driver Function 0Ah) specifies whether any characters are in the device-output buffer.

This function is required for character-device drivers only.

Fields

srLength   Specifies the length, in bytes, of the **STATUSREQUEST** structure.

srUnit   Not used.

srFunction   Specifies the Output Status function: 0Ah.

srStatus   Specifies the status of the completed function. If the output buffer has any characters, the driver must set the busy bit (bit 9), indicating that the device is busy. If the output buffer has no characters, the busy bit must be zero. In both cases, the driver must set the done bit (bit 8).

If the function is not successful, the driver must set both the error and done bits (bits 15 and 8) and copy an error value to the low-order byte.

srReserved   Reserved; do not use.

See Also

Device-Driver Function 06h Input Status
Interrupt 21h Function 4407h Check Device Output Status

■ Output Flush (Device-Driver Function 0Bh)

```
FLUSHREQUEST    STRUC
    frLength    db ?            ;length of record, in bytes
    frUnit      db ?            ;not used
    frFunction  db 0Bh          ;function number
    frStatus    dw ?            ;status
    frReserved  db 8 dup(?)     ;reserved
FLUSHREQUEST    ENDS
```

Output Flush (Device-Driver Function 0Bh) terminates any write operation in progress and empties the device-output buffer.

This function is required for character-device drivers only.

Fields

frLength   Specifies the length, in bytes, of the **FLUSHREQUEST** structure.

frUnit   Not used.

frFunction   Specifies the Output Flush function: 0Bh.

frStatus   Specifies the status of the completed function. If the function is successful, the driver must set the done bit (bit 8). Otherwise, the driver must set both the error and done bits (bits 15 and 8) and copy an error value to the low-order byte.

frReserved   Reserved; do not use.

See Also

Device-Driver Function 07h Input Flush

■ IOCTL Write (Device-Driver Function 0Ch)

```
IOCTLRWREQUEST  STRUC
    irwrLength    db ?            ;length of record, in bytes
    irwrUnit      db ?            ;unit number
    irwrFunction  db 0Ch          ;function number
    irwrStatus    dw ?            ;status
    irwrReserved  db 8 dup(?)     ;reserved
    irwrData      db ?            ;not used
    irwrBuffer    dd ?            ;INPUT:   buffer address
    irwrBytes     dw ?            ;INPUT:   number of bytes requested
                                  ;OUTPUT:  number of bytes written
IOCTLRWREQUEST  ENDS
```

IOCTL Write (Device-Driver Function 0Ch) transfers data from a buffer to a device driver.

This function can be used for both block- and character-device drivers.

Fields   **irwrLength**   Specifies the length, in bytes, of the **IOCTLRWREQUEST** structure.

irwrUnit   Specifies the device to which data is to be written. This field is used for block-device drivers only.

irwrFunction   Specifies the IOCTL Write function: 0Ch.

irwrStatus   Specifies the status of the completed function. If the function is successful, the driver must set the done bit (bit 8). Otherwise, the driver must set both the error and done bits (bits 15 and 8) and copy an error value to the low-order byte.

irwrReserved   Reserved; do not use.

irwrData   Not used.

irwrBuffer   Contains the 32-bit address (segment:offset) of the buffer containing data to write to the device.

irwrBytes   Contains the number of bytes to write and receives the number of bytes written. The following table describes input and output:

Input/Output	Description
Input	Specifies the number of bytes to write. This number must not exceed the amount of data in the specified buffer.
Output	Specifies the number of bytes written. This number cannot exceed the requested number of bytes.

Comments   MS-DOS calls this function only if bit 14 is set in the **dhAttributes** field of the **DEVICEHEADER** structure for the driver. For a full description of the **DEVICEHEADER** structure, see Section 9.9, "Structures."

See Also   Device-Driver Function 03h IOCTL Read
Interrupt 21h Function 4403h Send Control Data to Character Device
Interrupt 21h Function 4405h Send Control Data to Block Device

Open Device (Device-Driver Function 0Dh)

```
OPENCLOSEREQUEST      STRUC
     ocrLength        db  ?            ;length of record, in bytes
     ocrUnit          db  ?            ;unit number (block device only)
     ocrFunction      db  0Dh          ;function number
     ocrStatus        dw  ?            ;status
     ocrReserved      db  8  dup(?)    ;reserved
OPENCLOSEREQUEST      ENDS
```

Open Device (Device-Driver Function 0Dh) informs the device driver that a file device or character device is being opened or created.

This function can be used for both block- and character-device drivers.

Fields

ocrLength   Specifies the length, in bytes, of the **OPENCLOSEREQUEST** structure.

ocrUnit   Specifies which device contains the file being opened or created. This field is used with block-device drivers only.

ocrFunction   Specifies the Open Device function: 0Dh.

ocrStatus   Specifies the status of the completed function. If the function is successful, the driver must set the done bit (bit 8). Otherwise, the driver must set both the error and done bits (bits 15 and 8) and copy an error value to the low-order byte.

ocrReserved   Reserved; do not use.

Comments

MS-DOS calls this function only if bit 11 is set in the **dhAttributes** field of the **DEVICEHEADER** structure for the driver. For a full description of the **DEVICEHEADER** structure, see Section 9.9, "Structures."

MS-DOS calls this function whenever an application opens or creates a file or opens a device. This function can be used in conjunction with Close Device (Device-Driver Function 0Eh) to manage internal buffers and device initialization. To manage internal buffers, this function, when used in a block-device driver, should increment the count of open files on the specified drive; Close Device decrements this count and flushes internal buffers when all files are closed. Keeping this count can also help the driver determine whether the medium in the drive has been removed before all files have been closed. To help manage device initialization, this function, when used in a character-device driver, can reset the device and send it control strings to prepare it for subsequent input. If a character-device driver offers this feature, it should also provide IOCTL Read and IOCTL Write (Device-Driver Functions 03h and 0Ch) to let programs get and set the current control strings.

See Also

Device-Driver Function 0Eh Close Device
Interrupt 21h Function 3Ch Create File with Handle
Interrupt 21h Function 3Dh Open File with Handle
Interrupt 21h Function 5Ah Create Temporary File
Interrupt 21h Function 5Bh Create New File
Interrupt 21h Function 6Ch Extended Open/Create

■ Close Device (Device-Driver Function 0Eh)

```
OPENCLOSEREQUEST    STRUC
    ocrLength       db ?            ;length of record, in bytes
    ocrUnit         db ?            ;unit number (block device only)
    ocrFunction     db 0Eh          ;function number
    ocrStatus       dw ?            ;status
    ocrReserved     db 8 dup(?)     ;reserved
OPENCLOSEREQUEST    ENDS
```

Close Device (Device-Driver Function 0Eh) informs the driver that a file device or character device is being closed.

This function can be used for both block- and character-device drivers.

Fields

ocrLength   Specifies the length, in bytes, of the **OPENCLOSEREQUEST** structure.

ocrUnit   Specifies the device on which the file is being closed. This field is used for block-device drivers only.

ocrFunction   Specifies the Close Device function: 0Eh.

ocrStatus   Specifies the status of the completed function. If the function is successful, the driver must set the done bit (bit 8). Otherwise, the driver must set both the error and done bits (bits 15 and 8) and copy an error value to the low-order byte.

ocrReserved   Reserved; do not use.

Comments

MS-DOS calls this function only if bit 11 is set in the **dhAttributes** field of the **DEVICEHEADER** structure for the driver. For a full description of the **DEVICEHEADER** structure, see Section 9.9, "Structures."

MS-DOS calls this function whenever an application closes a file or device. This function can be used in conjunction with Open Device (Device-Driver Function 0Dh) to manage internal buffers and device initialization.

See Also

Device-Driver Function 0Dh Open Device
Interrupt 21h Function 3Eh Close File with Handle

■ Removable Media (Device-Driver Function 0Fh)

```
REMOVEMEDIAREQUEST   STRUC
    rmrLength     db  ?          ;length of record, in bytes
    rmrUnit       db  ?          ;unit number
    rmrFunction   db  0Fh        ;function number
    rmrStatus     dw  ?          ;status
    rmrReserved   db  8 dup(?)   ;reserved
REMOVEMEDIAREQUEST   ENDS
```

Removable Media (Device-Driver Function 0Fh) specifies whether a drive contains a removable medium.

This function is used for block-device drivers only.

Fields

rmrLength   Specifies the length, in bytes, of the **REMOVEMEDIAREQUEST** structure.

rmrUnit   Specifies the device to check for removable media.

rmrFunction   Specifies the Removable Media function: 0Fh.

rmrStatus   Specifies the status of the completed function. If the disk in the specified drive is removable, the busy bit (bit 9) must be zero. If the disk is not removable, the driver must set the busy bit. In both cases, the driver must set the done bit (bit 8).

rmrReserved   Reserved; do not use.

Comments

MS-DOS calls this function only if bit 11 is set in the **dhAttributes** field of the **DEVICEHEADER** structure for the driver. For a full description of the **DEVICEHEADER** structure, see Section 9.9, "Structures."

Since MS-DOS assumes this function is always successful, it ignores any error value the function returns.

See Also

Interrupt 21h Function 4408h Does Device Use Removable Media

■ Output Until Busy (Device-Driver Function 10h)

```
OUTPUTREQUEST  STRUC
    orLength      db  ?            ;length of record, in bytes
    orUnit        db  ?            ;not used
    orFunction    db  10h          ;function number
    orStatus      dw  ?            ;status
    orReserved    db  8 dup(?)     ;reserved
    orData        db  ?            ;not used
    orBuffer      dd  ?            ;INPUT:   buffer address
    orBytes       dw  ?            ;INPUT:   number of bytes to write
                                   ;OUTPUT:  number of bytes written
OUTPUTREQUEST  ENDS
```

Output Until Busy (Device-Driver Function 10h) transfers data from the specified buffer to a device until the device signals that it cannot accept more input.

This function is used for character-device drivers only.

Fields

orLength   Specifies the length, in bytes, of the **OUTPUTREQUEST** structure.

orUnit   Not used.

orFunction   Specifies the Output Until Busy function: 10h.

orStatus   Specifies the status of the completed function. If the function is successful, the driver must set the done bit (bit 8). Otherwise, the driver must set both the error and done bits (bits 15 and 8) and copy an error value to the low-order byte.

orReserved   Reserved; do not use.

orData   Not used.

orBuffer   Contains the 32-bit address (segment:offset) of the buffer containing data to write to the device.

orBytes   Contains the number of bytes to write and receives the number of bytes written. The following table describes input and output:

Input/Output	Description
Input	Specifies the number of bytes to write. This number must not exceed the amount of data in the specified buffer.
Output	Specifies the number of bytes written. This number cannot exceed the requested number of bytes.

Comments

This function should write as much data to the device as possible until the device signals that it cannot accept more data, at which point the function should return immediately. The driver should not wait under any circumstances. It is not an error for the driver to transfer fewer bytes than MS-DOS requested, but the driver must return a value for the number of bytes transferred.

This function allows device drivers to take advantage of a printer's internal RAM buffers. The driver can send data to the printer until the printer's internal buffer is full and then return to MS-DOS immediately, rather than wait while data is printed. MS-DOS can then periodically check the printer's status and send more data only when the printer is ready.

See Also

Device-Driver Function 08h Write

■ Generic IOCTL (Device-Driver Function 13h)

```
IOCTLREQUEST    STRUC
    giLength    db ?              ;length of record, in bytes
    giUnit      db ?              ;unit number (block device only)
    giFunction  db 13h            ;function number
    giStatus    dw ?              ;status
    giReserved1 db 8 dup(?)       ;reserved
    giCategory  db ?              ;INPUT: device category
    giMinorCode db ?              ;INPUT: minor code
    giReserved2 dd ?              ;reserved
    giIOCTLData dd ?              ;INPUT: IOCTL data address
IOCTLREQUEST    ENDS
```

Generic IOCTL (Device-Driver Function 13h) directs the driver to carry out the generic input-and-output-control function specified by the **giCategory** and **giMinorCode** fields.

This function can be used for both block- and character-device drivers.

Fields

giLength   Specifies the length, in bytes, of the **IOCTLREQUEST** structure.

giUnit   Specifies the device number on which to carry out the IOCTL function. This field is used for block-device drivers only.

giFunction   Specifies the Generic IOCTL function: 13h.

giStatus   Specifies the status of the completed function. If the function is successful, the driver must set the done bit (bit 8). Otherwise, the driver must set both the error and done bits (bits 15 and 8) and copy an error value to the low-order byte.

giReserved1   Reserved; do not use.

giCategory   Specifies the device category. Serial, console, parallel, and disk drivers are represented by the following values:

Value	Meaning
01h	Serial device
03h	Console (display)
05h	Parallel printer
08h	Disk

If the driver supports a type of device not listed, the **giCategory** field must specify an 8-bit number that uniquely identifies the device. The driver must check this value.

giMinorCode   Specifies the minor code for Interrupt 21h Function 440Ch, Generic IOCTL for Character Devices. The meaning of the minor code depends on the device category. For serial, console, and parallel drivers, it can be one of the following:

Minor Code	Function
45h	Set Iteration Count
4Ah	Select Code Page
4Ch	Start Code-Page Prepare
4Dh	End Code-Page Prepare
65h	Get Iteration Count

Minor Code	Function
6Ah	Query Selected Code Page
6Bh	Query Code-Page Prepare List

For disk drivers, the value specifies the minor code for Interrupt 21h Function 440Dh, Generic IOCTL for Block Devices. It can be one of the following:

Minor Code	Function
40h	Set Device Parameters
41h	Write Track on Logical Drive
42h	Format Track on Logical Drive
46h	Set Media ID
60h	Get Device Parameters
61h	Read Track on Logical Drive
62h	Verify Track on Logical Drive
66h	Get Media ID
68h	Sense Media Type

Drivers can support additional minor codes as needed.

giReserved2   Reserved; do not use.

giIOCTLData   Contains a 32-bit address (segment:offset) of the structure associated with the specified IOCTL function. The structure type and contents depend on the minor code as specified by the **giMinorCode** field.

Comments

The driver must interpret the category and minor codes to determine which operation to carry out and then return any applicable information in the structure pointed to by the **giIOCTLData** field.

MS-DOS calls this function only if bit 6 is set in the **dhAttributes** field of the **DEVICEHEADER** structure for the driver. For a full description of the **DEVICEHEADER** structure, see Section 9.9, "Structures."

See Also

Device-Driver Function 19h Query IOCTL
Interrupt 21h Function 440Ch Generic IOCTL for Character Devices
Interrupt 21h Function 440Dh Generic IOCTL for Block Devices

■ Get Logical Device (Device-Driver Function 17h)

```
LOGDEVICEREQUEST      STRUC
    ldrLength    db  ?            ;length of record, in bytes
    ldrUnit      db  ?            ;INPUT:  unit number for drive to check
                                  ;OUTPUT: active drive number
    ldrFunction db 17h            ;function number
    ldrStatus    dw  ?            ;status
    ldrReserved db 8 dup(?)       ;reserved
LOGDEVICEREQUEST      ENDS
```

Get Logical Device (Device-Driver Function 17h) returns the active drive number for the specified drive.

This function is used for block-device drivers only.

Fields

ldrLength   Specifies the length, in bytes, of the **LOGDEVICEREQUEST** structure.

ldrUnit   Contains the device number to check and receives the active drive number. The following table describes input and output:

Input/Output	Description
Input	Specifies the drive number to check. The driver must determine whether the unit associated with this drive number has any other logical-drive numbers.
Output	Specifies the active drive number (1=A, 2=B, 3=C, etc.). The driver must set this field to the drive number set by the most recent call to Set Logical Device (Device-Driver Function 18h) or to zero if the specified drive has no other logical-drive numbers.

ldrFunction   Specifies the Get Logical Device function: 17h.

ldrStatus   Specifies the status of the completed function. If the function is successful, the driver must set the done bit (bit 8). Otherwise, the driver must set both the error and done bits (bits 15 and 8) and copy an error value to the low-order byte.

ldrReserved   Reserved. Do not use.

Comment

MS-DOS calls this function only if bit 6 is set in the **dhAttributes** field of the **DEVICEHEADER** structure for the driver. For a full description of the **DEVICEHEADER** structure, see Section 9.9, "Structures."

See Also

Device-Driver Function 18h Set Logical Device
Interrupt 21h Function 440Eh Get Logical Drive Map

■ Set Logical Device (Device-Driver Function 18h)

```
LOGDEVICEREQUEST    STRUC
    ldrLength       db ?            ;length of record, in bytes
    ldrUnit         db ?            ;unit number
    ldrFunction     db 18h          ;function number
    ldrStatus       dw ?            ;status
    ldrReserved     db 8 dup(?)     ;reserved
LOGDEVICEREQUEST    ENDS
```

Set Logical Device (Device-Driver Function 18h) sets the active drive number to the drive specified by the **ldrUnit** field.

This function is used for block-device drivers only.

Fields

ldrLength   Specifies the length, in bytes, of the **LOGDEVICEREQUEST** structure.

ldrUnit   Specifies the device to make active. This field contains a zero-based drive number.

ldrFunction   Specifies the Set Logical Device function: 18h.

ldrStatus   Specifies the status of the completed function. If the function is successful, the driver must set the done bit (bit 8). Otherwise, the driver must set both the error and done bits (bits 15 and 8) and copy an error value to the low-order byte.

Comment

MS-DOS calls this function only if bit 6 is set in the **dhAttributes** field of the **DEVICEHEADER** structure for the driver. For a full description of the **DEVICEHEADER** structure, see Section 9.9, "Structures."

See Also

Device-Driver Function 17h Get Logical Device
Interrupt 21h Function 440Fh Set Logical Drive Map

■ IOCTL Query (Device-Driver Function 19h)

```
IOCTLREQUEST    STRUC
    giLength        db  ?           ;length of record, in bytes
    giUnit          db  ?           ;unit number (block device only)
    giFunction      db  19h         ;function number
    giStatus        dw  ?           ;status
    giReserved1     db  8 dup(?)    ;reserved
    giCategory      db  ?           ;INPUT: device category
    giMinorCode     db  ?           ;INPUT: minor code
    giReserved2     dd  ?           ;reserved
    giIOCTLData     dd  ?           ;INPUT: IOCTL data address
IOCTLREQUEST    ENDS
```

IOCTL Query (Device-Driver Function 19h) determines whether a given generic IOCTL function (minor code) is supported by the driver.

This function can be used for both block- and character-device drivers.

Fields

giLength   Specifies the length, in bytes, of the **IOCTLREQUEST** structure.

giUnit   Specifies the device the request is for. This field is used for block-device drivers only.

giFunction   Specifies the IOCTL Query function: 19h.

giStatus   Receives the status of the query. If the driver does not support the given generic IOCTL function, it must set the error and done bits (bits 15 and 8) and set the low-order 8 bits to error value 03h (Unknown Function). Otherwise, it must set the done bit.

giReserved1   Reserved; do not use.

giCategory   Specifies the device category of the generic IOCTL function to be checked.

giMinorCode   Specifies the minor code of the generic IOCTL function to be checked.

giReserved2   Reserved; do not use.

giIOCTLData   This field is not used by this function and must not be changed.

Comments

MS-DOS calls this function only if bit 7 is set in the **dhAttributes** field of the **DEVICEHEADER** structure for the driver. For a full description of the **DEVICEHEADER** structure, see Section 9.9, "Structures."

See Also

Device-Driver Function 13h Generic IOCTL
Interrupt 21h Function 4410h Query IOCTL Handle
Interrupt 21h Function 4411h Query IOCTL Device

9.9 Structures

This section describes the structures MS-DOS uses with device-driver functions.

BPB

```
BPB     STRUC
    bpbBytesPerSec    dw    ?    ;bytes per sector
    bpbSecPerClust    db    ?    ;sectors per cluster
    bpbResSectors     dw    ?    ;number of reserved sectors
    bpbFATs           db    ?    ;number of file allocation tables
    bpbRootDirEnts    dw    ?    ;number of root-directory entries
    bpbSectors        dw    ?    ;total number of sectors
    bpbMedia          db    ?    ;media descriptor
    bpbFATsecs        dw    ?    ;number of sectors per FAT
    bpbSecPerTrack    dw    ?    ;sectors per track
    bpbHeads          dw    ?    ;number of heads
    bpbHiddenSecs     dd    ?    ;number of hidden sectors
    bpbHugeSectors    dd    ?    ;number of sectors if bpbSectors = 0
BPB     ENDS
```

The **BPB** structure contains information that defines the format of a disk or other storage medium.

Fields

bpbBytesPerSec   Specifies the number of bytes per sector.

bpbSecPerClust   Specifies the number of sectors per cluster. The sectors must be consecutive and a power of 2.

bpbResSectors   Specifies the number of reserved sectors on the drive, beginning with sector 0. Typically, this value is 1 (for the startup sector), unless the disk-drive manufacturer's software reserves additional sectors.

bpbFATs   Specifies the number of file allocation tables (FATs) following the reserved sectors. Most versions of MS-DOS maintain one or more additional copies of the FAT and use the extra copies to recover data on the disk if the first FAT is corrupted.

bpbRootDirEnts   Specifies the maximum number of entries in the root directory.

bpbSectors   Specifies the total number of sectors on the drive. If the size of the drive is greater than 32 MB, this field is zero and the number of sectors is specified by the **bpbHugeSectors** field.

bpbMedia   Specifies the media descriptor, a value in the range 00h through 0FFh that identifies the type of medium or disk in a drive. Some device drivers use the media descriptor to determine quickly whether the removable medium in a drive has changed. MS-DOS passes the media descriptor to the device driver so that programs can check the type of medium. Also, the first byte in the FAT is often (but not always) identical to the media descriptor.

Following are the most commonly used media descriptors and their corresponding media:

Value	Type of medium
0F0h	3.5-inch, 2 sides, 18 sectors/track (1.44 MB); 3.5-inch, 2 sides, 36 sectors/track (2.88 MB); 5.25-inch, 2 sides, 15 sectors/track (1.2 MB). This value is also used to describe other media types.
0F8h	Hard disk, any capacity.
0F9h	3.5-inch, 2 sides, 9 sectors/track, 80 tracks/side (720K); 5.25-inch, 2 sides, 15 sectors/track, 40 tracks/side (1.2 MB).
0FAh	5.25-inch, 1 side, 8 sectors/track, (320K).
0FBh	3.5-inch, 2 sides, 8 sectors/track (640K).

Value	Type of medium
0FCh	5.25-inch, 1 side, 9 sectors/track, 40 tracks/side (180K).
0FDh	5.25-inch, 2 sides, 9 sectors/track, 40 tracks/side (360K). This value is also used for 8-inch disks.
0FEh	5.25-inch, 1 side, 8 sectors/track, 40 tracks/side (160K). This value is also used for 8-inch disks.
0FFh	5.25-inch, 2 sides, 8 sectors/track, 40 tracks/side (320K).

bpbFATsecs   Specifies the number of sectors occupied by each FAT.

bpbSecPerTrack   Specifies the number of sectors per track.

bpbHeads   Specifies the number of read/write heads on the drive.

bpbHiddenSecs   Specifies the number of hidden sectors on the drive.

bpbHugeSectors   Specifies the number of sectors if the **bpbSectors** field is zero. This value supports drives larger than 32 MB.

■ DEVICEHEADER

```
DEVICEHEADER STRUC
    dhLink          dd  ?            ;link to next driver
    dhAttributes    dw  ?            ;device attributes
    dhStrategy      dw  ?            ;strategy-routine offset
    dhInterrupt     dw  ?            ;interrupt-routine offset
    dhNameOrUnits   db  '????????'   ;logical-device name
                                     ;(character device only)
                                     ;or number of units
                                     ;(block device only)
DEVICEHEADER ENDS
```

The **DEVICEHEADER** structure contains information about a device driver.

Fields

dhLink   Points to the next driver in the device-driver chain. For the last driver in the chain, this field is 0FFFFh.

dhAttributes   Specifies device attributes. The meaning of an individual bit in this field depends on the device type as specified by bit 15. Any bits in this field that are not used must be zero.

For character devices (bit 15 is 1), the field has the following attributes:

Bit	Description
0	1 = Standard input (STDIN) device.
1	1 = Standard output (STDOUT) device.
2	1 = NUL device.
3	1 = Clock device.
4	1 = Special device; fast character output.
5	Reserved; must be zero.
6	1 = Driver supports Generic IOCTL (Device-Driver Function 13h).
7	1 = Driver supports Query IOCTL (Device-Driver Function 19h).
8–10	Reserved; must be zero.

Bit	Description
11	1 = Device supports Open Device and Close Device (Device-Driver Functions 0Dh and 0Eh).
12	Reserved; must be zero.
13	1 = Driver supports Output Until Busy (Device-Driver Function 10h).
14	1 = Driver supports IOCTL Read and IOCTL Write (Device-Driver Functions 03h and 0Ch).
15	1 = Character device.

For block devices (bit 15 is 0), the field has the following attributes:

Bit	Description
0	Reserved; must be zero.
1	1 = Driver supports 32-bit sector addressing.
2–5	Reserved; must be zero.
6	1 = Driver supports Generic IOCTL, Get Logical Device, and Set Logical Device (Device-Driver Functions 13h, 17h, and 18h).
7	1 = Driver supports Query IOCTL (Device-Driver Function 19h).
8–10	Reserved; must be zero.
11	1 = Driver supports Open Device, Close Device, and Removable Media (Device-Driver Functions 0Dh, 0Eh, and 0Fh).
12	Reserved; must be zero.
13	1 = Driver requires MS-DOS to supply the first 512 bytes of the file allocation table (FAT) whenever it calls Build BPB (Device-Driver Function 02h).
14	1 = Driver supports IOCTL Read and IOCTL Write (Device-Driver Functions 03h and 0Ch).
15	0 = Block device.

dhStrategy   Specifies the offset of the strategy routine. The routine's segment address is the same as for the device header.

dhInterrupt   Specifies the offset of the interrupt routine. The routine's segment address is the same as for the device header.

dhNameOrUnits   Specifies the logical-device name or number of units, depending on the device type (as specified by bit 15 in the **dhAttributes** field).

For a character device (bit 15 is 1), all 8 bytes of this field specify the logical-device name. If the name has fewer than eight characters, the remaining bytes must be space characters (ASCII 20h).

For a block device (bit 15 is 0), the first byte of this field specifies the number of units (drives) this driver supports; the remaining bytes are reserved.

See Also   Interrupt 24h Critical-Error Handler
Interrupt 2Fh Function 0106h   Get Printer Device

■ REQUESTHEADER

```
REQUESTHEADER    STRUC
    rhLength     db ?              ;length of record, in bytes
    rhUnit       db ?              ;unit number (block device only)
    rhFunction   db ?              ;function number
    rhStatus     dw ?              ;status
    rhReserved   db 8 dup(?)       ;reserved
REQUESTHEADER    ENDS
```

The **REQUESTHEADER** structure contains information about a device-driver function.

Fields

rhLength   Specifies the length of the record, in bytes.

rhUnit   Identifies the device-driver function the request is for. For example, if the driver defines three functions, this field will contain 0, 1, or 2.

rhFunction   Specifies the action to be performed by the device driver. This field can be one of the following:

Value	Function
00h	Init
01h	Media Check
02h	Build BPB
03h	IOCTL Read
04h	Read
05h	Nondestructive Read
06h	Input Status
07h	Input Flush
08h	Write
09h	Write with Verify
0Ah	Output Status
0Bh	Output Flush
0Ch	IOCTL Write
0Dh	Open Device
0Eh	Close Device
0Fh	Removable Media
10h	Output Until Busy
13h	Generic IOCTL
17h	Get Logical Device
18h	Set Logical Device
19h	IOCTL Query

rhStatus   Specifies the status of the request when the device-driver interrupt routine returns control to MS-DOS. This field must be zero before MS-DOS calls the interrupt routine, which must set one or more bits in the field before returning to MS-DOS. The bits in this field have the following meanings:

Bit	Meaning
0–7	Specify an error value, but only if bit 15 is set. If an error occurs, the interrupt routine must set bit 15 and copy an error value to these bits. The error value can be one of the following:

Error	Meaning
00h	Write-protect violation
01h	Unknown unit
02h	Drive not ready
03h	Unknown command
04h	CRC error
05h	Incorrect length for drive-request structure
06h	Seek error
07h	Unknown media
08h	Sector not found
09h	Printer out of paper
0Ah	Write fault
0Bh	Read fault
0Ch	General failure
0Dh	Reserved
0Eh	Reserved
0Fh	Invalid disk change

Bit	Meaning
8	Specifies whether the operation has completed. If this bit is set, the operation is done.
9	Specifies whether the device is busy. If this bit is set, the device is busy. This bit is set only by Input Status, Output Status, and Removable Media (Device-Driver Functions 06h, 0Ah, and 0Fh).
15	Specifies whether an error occurred. If this bit is 1, bits 0 through 7 of the **rhStatus** field contain an error value.

rhReserved   Reserved; do not use.

All other bits are reserved and must be zero.

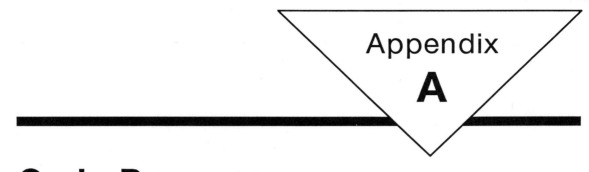

Appendix
A

Code Pages

This appendix contains code-page tables for the six code pages included with MS-DOS version 5.0.

437 United States

0		32		64	@	96	`	128	Ç	160	á	192	└	224	α
1	☺	33	!	65	A	97	a	129	ü	161	í	193	┴	225	ß
2	☻	34	"	66	B	98	b	130	é	162	ó	194	┬	226	Γ
3	♥	35	#	67	C	99	c	131	â	163	ú	195	├	227	π
4	♦	36	$	68	D	100	d	132	ä	164	ñ	196	─	228	Σ
5	♣	37	%	69	E	101	e	133	à	165	Ñ	197	┼	229	σ
6	♠	38	&	70	F	102	f	134	å	166	ª	198	╞	230	µ
7	•	39	'	71	G	103	g	135	ç	167	º	199	╟	231	τ
8	◘	40	(	72	H	104	h	136	ê	168	¿	200	╚	232	Φ
9	○	41	)	73	I	105	i	137	ë	169	⌐	201	╔	233	Θ
10	◙	42	*	74	J	106	j	138	è	170	¬	202	╩	234	Ω
11	♂	43	+	75	K	107	k	139	ï	171	½	203	╦	235	δ
12	♀	44	,	76	L	108	l	140	î	172	¼	204	╠	236	∞
13	♪	45	-	77	M	109	m	141	ì	173	¡	205	=	237	φ
14	♫	46	.	78	N	110	n	142	Ä	174	«	206	╬	238	ε
15	☼	47	/	79	O	111	o	143	Å	175	»	207	╧	239	∩
16	►	48	0	80	P	112	p	144	É	176	░	208	╨	240	≡
17	◄	49	1	81	Q	113	q	145	æ	177	▒	209	╤	241	±
18	↕	50	2	82	R	114	r	146	Æ	178	▓	210	╥	242	≥
19	‼	51	3	83	S	115	s	147	ô	179	│	211	╙	243	≤
20	¶	52	4	84	T	116	t	148	ö	180	┤	212	╘	244	⌠
21	§	53	5	85	U	117	u	149	ò	181	╡	213	╒	245	⌡
22	▬	54	6	86	V	118	v	150	û	182	╢	214	╓	246	÷
23	↨	55	7	87	W	119	w	151	ù	183	╖	215	╫	247	≈
24	↑	56	8	88	X	120	x	152	ÿ	184	╕	216	╪	248	°
25	↓	57	9	89	Y	121	y	153	Ö	185	╣	217	┘	249	·
26	→	58	:	90	Z	122	z	154	Ü	186	║	218	┌	250	·
27	←	59	;	91	[	123	{	155	¢	187	╗	219	█	251	√
28	∟	60	<	92	\	124	¦	156	£	188	╝	220	▄	252	ⁿ
29	↔	61	=	93	]	125	}	157	¥	189	╜	221	▌	253	²
30	▲	62	>	94	^	126	~	158	₧	190	╛	222	▐	254	■
31	▼	63	?	95	_	127	⌂	159	ƒ	191	┐	223	▀	255	

850 Multilingual (Latin I)

0		32		64	@	96	`	128	Ç	160	á	192	└	224	Ó
1	☺	33	!	65	A	97	a	129	ü	161	í	193	┴	225	ß
2	☻	34	"	66	B	98	b	130	é	162	ó	194	┬	226	Ô
3	♥	35	#	67	C	99	c	131	â	163	ú	195	├	227	Ò
4	♦	36	$	68	D	100	d	132	ä	164	ñ	196	—	228	õ
5	♣	37	%	69	E	101	e	133	à	165	Ñ	197	┼	229	Õ
6	♠	38	&	70	F	102	f	134	å	166	ª	198	ã	230	µ
7	•	39	'	71	G	103	g	135	ç	167	º	199	Ã	231	Þ
8	◘	40	(	72	H	104	h	136	ê	168	¿	200	╚	232	þ
9	○	41	)	73	I	105	i	137	ë	169	®	201	╔	233	Ú
10	◙	42	*	74	J	106	j	138	è	170	¬	202	╩	234	Û
11	♂	43	+	75	K	107	k	139	ï	171	½	203	╦	235	Ù
12	♀	44	,	76	L	108	l	140	î	172	¼	204	╠	236	ý
13	♪	45	-	77	M	109	m	141	ì	173	¡	205	=	237	Ý
14	♫	46	.	78	N	110	n	142	Ä	174	«	206	╬	238	¯
15	☼	47	/	79	O	111	o	143	Å	175	»	207	¤	239	´
16	►	48	0	80	P	112	p	144	É	176	░	208	ð	240	-
17	◄	49	1	81	Q	113	q	145	æ	177	▒	209	Ð	241	±
18	↕	50	2	82	R	114	r	146	Æ	178	▓	210	Ê	242	‗
19	‼	51	3	83	S	115	s	147	ô	179	│	211	Ë	243	¾
20	¶	52	4	84	T	116	t	148	ö	180	┤	212	È	244	¶
21	§	53	5	85	U	117	u	149	ò	181	Á	213	ı	245	§
22	▬	54	6	86	V	118	v	150	û	182	Â	214	Í	246	÷
23	↨	55	7	87	W	119	w	151	ù	183	À	215	Î	247	¸
24	↑	56	8	88	X	120	x	152	ÿ	184	©	216	Ï	248	°
25	↓	57	9	89	Y	121	y	153	Ö	185	╣	217	┘	249	¨
26	→	58	:	90	Z	122	z	154	Ü	186	║	218	┌	250	·
27	←	59	;	91	[	123	{	155	ø	187	╗	219	█	251	¹
28	∟	60	<	92	\	124	¦	156	£	188	╝	220	▄	252	³
29	↔	61	=	93	]	125	}	157	Ø	189	¢	221	¦	253	²
30	▲	62	>	94	^	126	~	158	×	190	¥	222	Ì	254	■
31	▼	63	?	95	_	127	⌂	159	ƒ	191	┐	223	▀	255	

852   Slavic (Latin II)

0		32		64	@	96	`	128	Ç	160	á	192	└	224	Ó
1	☺	33	!	65	A	97	a	129	ü	161	í	193	┴	225	ß
2	☻	34	"	66	B	98	b	130	é	162	ó	194	┬	226	Ô
3	♥	35	#	67	C	99	c	131	â	163	ú	195	├	227	Ń
4	♦	36	$	68	D	100	d	132	ä	164	Ą	196	─	228	ń
5	♣	37	%	69	E	101	e	133	ů	165	ą	197	┼	229	ň
6	♠	38	&	70	F	102	f	134	ć	166	Ž	198	Ă	230	Š
7	•	39	'	71	G	103	g	135	ç	167	ž	199	ă	231	š
8	◘	40	(	72	H	104	h	136	ł	168	Ę	200	╚	232	Ŕ
9	○	41	)	73	I	105	i	137	ë	169	ę	201	╔	233	Ú
10	◙	42	*	74	J	106	j	138	Ő	170		202	╩	234	ŕ
11	♂	43	+	75	K	107	k	139	ő	171	ź	203	╦	235	Ű
12	♀	44	,	76	L	108	l	140	î	172	Č	204	╠	236	ý
13	♪	45	-	77	M	109	m	141	Ź	173	ş	205	═	237	Ý
14	♫	46	.	78	N	110	n	142	Ä	174	«	206	╬	238	ţ
15	☼	47	/	79	O	111	o	143	Ć	175	»	207	¤	239	´
16	►	48	0	80	P	112	p	144	É	176	░	208	đ	240	-
17	◄	49	1	81	Q	113	q	145	Ĺ	177	▒	209	Đ	241	˝
18	↕	50	2	82	R	114	r	146	ĺ	178	▓	210	Ď	242	˛
19	‼	51	3	83	S	115	s	147	ô	179	│	211	Ë	243	ˇ
20	¶	52	4	84	T	116	t	148	ö	180	┤	212	ď	244	˘
21	§	53	5	85	U	117	u	149	Ľ	181	Á	213	Ň	245	§
22	▬	54	6	86	V	118	v	150	ľ	182	Â	214	Í	246	÷
23	↨	55	7	87	W	119	w	151	Ś	183	Ě	215	Î	247	¸
24	↑	56	8	88	X	120	x	152	ś	184	Ş	216	ě	248	°
25	↓	57	9	89	Y	121	y	153	Ö	185	╣	217	┘	249	¨
26	→	58	:	90	Z	122	z	154	Ü	186	║	218	┌	250	˙
27	←	59	;	91	[	123	{	155	Ť	187	╗	219	█	251	ű
28	∟	60	<	92	\	124	¦	156	ť	188	╝	220	▄	252	Ř
29	↔	61	=	93	]	125	}	157	Ł	189	Ż	221	Ţ	253	ř
30	▲	62	>	94	^	126	~	158	×	190	ż	222	Ů	254	■
31	▼	63	?	95	_	127	⌂	159	č	191	┐	223	▀	255	

860   Portuguese

0		32		64	@	96	`	128	Ç	160	á	192	L	224	α
1	☺	33	!	65	A	97	a	129	ü	161	í	193	⊥	225	ß
2	☻	34	"	66	B	98	b	130	é	162	ó	194	T	226	Γ
3	♥	35	#	67	C	99	c	131	â	163	ú	195	⊢	227	π
4	♦	36	$	68	D	100	d	132	ã	164	ñ	196	—	228	Σ
5	♣	37	%	69	E	101	e	133	à	165	Ñ	197	+	229	σ
6	♠	38	&	70	F	102	f	134	Á	166	ª	198	╞	230	μ
7	•	39	'	71	G	103	g	135	ç	167	º	199	╟	231	τ
8	◘	40	(	72	H	104	h	136	ê	168	¿	200	╚	232	Φ
9	○	41	)	73	I	105	i	137	Ê	169	Ò	201	╔	233	Θ
10	◙	42	*	74	J	106	j	138	è	170	¬	202	╩	234	Ω
11	♂	43	+	75	K	107	k	139	Í	171	½	203	╦	235	δ
12	♀	44	,	76	L	108	l	140	Ô	172	¼	204	╠	236	∞
13	♪	45	-	77	M	109	m	141	ì	173	¡	205	=	237	ø
14	♫	46	.	78	N	110	n	142	Ã	174	«	206	╬	238	ϵ
15	☼	47	/	79	O	111	o	143	Â	175	»	207	╧	239	∩
16	►	48	0	80	P	112	p	144	É	176	░	208	╨	240	≡
17	◄	49	1	81	Q	113	q	145	À	177	▒	209	╤	241	±
18	↕	50	2	82	R	114	r	146	È	178	▓	210	╥	242	≥
19	‼	51	3	83	S	115	s	147	Ô	179	│	211	╙	243	≤
20	¶	52	4	84	T	116	t	148	õ	180	┤	212	╘	244	⌠
21	§	53	5	85	U	117	u	149	ò	181	╡	213	╒	245	⌡
22	▬	54	6	86	V	118	v	150	Ú	182	╢	214	╓	246	÷
23	↨	55	7	87	W	119	w	151	ù	183	╖	215	╫	247	≈
24	↑	56	8	88	X	120	x	152	Ì	184	╕	216	╪	248	°
25	↓	57	9	89	Y	121	y	153	Õ	185	╣	217	┘	249	·
26	→	58	:	90	Z	122	z	154	Ü	186	║	218	┌	250	·
27	←	59	;	91	[	123	{	155	¢	187	╗	219	█	251	√
28	∟	60	<	92	\	124	¦	156	£	188	╝	220	▄	252	ⁿ
29	↔	61	=	93	]	125	}	157	Ù	189	╜	221	▌	253	²
30	▲	62	>	94	^	126	~	158	₨	190	╛	222	▐	254	■
31	▼	63	?	95	_	127	⌂	159	Ó	191	┐	223	▀	255	

863 Canadian-French

0		32		64	@	96	`	128	Ç	160	¦	192	L	224	α
1	☺	33	!	65	A	97	a	129	ü	161	´	193	⊥	225	ß
2	☻	34	"	66	B	98	b	130	é	162	ó	194	T	226	Γ
3	♥	35	#	67	C	99	c	131	â	163	ú	195	⊢	227	π
4	♦	36	$	68	D	100	d	132	Â	164	¨	196	—	228	Σ
5	♣	37	%	69	E	101	e	133	à	165	¸	197	+	229	σ
6	♠	38	&	70	F	102	f	134	¶	166	3	198	⊩	230	µ
7	•	39	'	71	G	103	g	135	ç	167	¯	199	‖	231	τ
8	◘	40	(	72	H	104	h	136	ê	168	î	200	╚	232	Φ
9	○	41	)	73	I	105	i	137	ë	169	⌐	201	╔	233	Θ
10	◙	42	*	74	J	106	j	138	è	170	¬	202	╩	234	Ω
11	♂	43	+	75	K	107	k	139	ï	171	½	203	╦	235	δ
12	♀	44	,	76	L	108	l	140	î	172	¼	204	╠	236	∞
13	♪	45	-	77	M	109	m	141	=	173	¾	205	=	237	ø
14	♫	46	.	78	N	110	n	142	À	174	«	206	╬	238	∈
15	☀	47	/	79	O	111	o	143	§	175	»	207	⊥	239	∩
16	►	48	0	80	P	112	p	144	É	176	░	208	╨	240	≡
17	◄	49	1	81	Q	113	q	145	È	177	▒	209	╤	241	±
18	↕	50	2	82	R	114	r	146	Ê	178	▓	210	╥	242	≥
19	‼	51	3	83	S	115	s	147	ô	179	│	211	╙	243	≤
20	¶	52	4	84	T	116	t	148	Ë	180	┤	212	╘	244	⌠
21	§	53	5	85	U	117	u	149	Ï	181	╡	213	╒	245	⌡
22	▬	54	6	86	V	118	v	150	û	182	╢	214	╓	246	÷
23	↨	55	7	87	W	119	w	151	ù	183	╖	215	╫	247	≈
24	↑	56	8	88	X	120	x	152	¤	184	╕	216	╪	248	°
25	↓	57	9	89	Y	121	y	153	Ô	185	╣	217	┘	249	·
26	→	58	:	90	Z	122	z	154	Ü	186	║	218	┌	250	·
27	←	59	;	91	[	123	{	155	¢	187	╗	219	█	251	√
28	∟	60	<	92	\	124	¦	156	£	188	╝	220	▄	252	ⁿ
29	↔	61	=	93	]	125	}	157	Ù	189	╜	221	▌	253	²
30	▲	62	>	94	^	126	~	158	Û	190	╛	222	▐	254	■
31	▼	63	?	95	_	127	⌂	159	ƒ	191	┐	223	▀	255	

865   Nordic

0	32	64 Ⓟ	96 `	128 Ç	160 á	192 L	224 α
1 ☺	33 !	65 A	97 a	129 ü	161 í	193 ⊥	225 ß
2 ☻	34 "	66 B	98 b	130 é	162 ó	194 T	226 Γ
3 ♥	35 #	67 C	99 c	131 â	163 ú	195 ├	227 π
4 ♦	36 $	68 D	100 d	132 ä	164 ñ	196 —	228 Σ
5 ♣	37 %	69 E	101 e	133 à	165 Ñ	197 +	229 σ
6 ♠	38 &	70 F	102 f	134 å	166 ª	198 ╞	230 µ
7 •	39 '	71 G	103 g	135 ç	167 º	199 ‖	231 τ
8 ◘	40 (	72 H	104 h	136 ê	168 ¿	200 ╚	232 Φ
9 ○	41)	73 I	105 i	137 ë	169 ⌐	201 ╔	233 Θ
10 ◙	42 *	74 J	106 j	138 è	170 ¬	202 ╩	234 Ω
11 ♂	43 +	75 K	107 k	139 ï	171 ½	203 ╦	235 δ
12 ♀	44 ,	76 L	108 l	140 î	172 ¼	204 ╠	236 ∞
13 ♪	45 -	77 M	109 m	141 ì	173 ¡	205 =	237 φ
14 ♫	46 .	78 N	110 n	142 Ä	174 «	206 ╬	238 ε
15 ☼	47 /	79 O	111 o	143 Å	175 ⌧	207 ⊥	239 ∩
16 ►	48 0	80 P	112 p	144 É	176 ░	208 ╨	240 ≡
17 ◄	49 1	81 Q	113 q	145 æ	177 ▒	209 T	241 ±
18 ↕	50 2	82 R	114 r	146 Æ	178 ▓	210 π	242 ≥
19 ‼	51 3	83 S	115 s	147 ô	179 │	211 ╙	243 ≤
20 ¶	52 4	84 T	116 t	148 ö	180 ┤	212 ╘	244 ⌠
21 §	53 5	85 U	117 u	149 ò	181 ╡	213 ╒	245 ⌡
22 ▬	54 6	86 V	118 v	150 û	182 ╢	214 π	246 ÷
23 ↨	55 7	87 W	119 w	151 ú	183 ╖	215 ╫	247 ≈
24 ↑	56 8	88 X	120 x	152 ÿ	184 ╕	216 ╪	248 °
25 ↓	57 9	89 Y	121 y	153 ö	185 ╣	217 ┘	249 ·
26 →	58 :	90 Z	122 z	154 Ü	186 ║	218 ┌	250 ·
27 ←	59 ;	91 [	123 {	155 ø	187 ╗	219 █	251 √
28 ∟	60 <	92 \	124 ¦	156 £	188 ╝	220 ▄	252 ⁿ
29 ↔	61 =	93]	125 }	157 Ø	189 ╜	221 ▌	253 ²
30 ▲	62 >	94 ^	126 ~	158 ₧	190 ┘	222 ▐	254 ■
31 ▼	63 ?	95 _	127 ⌂	159 ƒ	191 ┐	223 ▀	255

Appendix

B

Extended Key Codes

Extended key codes are 2-byte character values generated whenever the user presses certain keys and key combinations. MS-DOS system functions, such as Read File or Device (Interrupt 21h Function 3Fh), retrieve these extended key codes when reading from the keyboard. The following table lists the keys and key combinations that generate extended key codes:

Key	Alone	SHIFT+	CTRL+	ALT+
F1	0;59	0;84	0;94	0;104
F2	0;60	0;85	0;95	0;105
F3	0;61	0;86	0;96	0;106
F4	0;62	0;87	0;97	0;107
F5	0;63	0;88	0;98	0;108
F6	0;64	0;89	0;99	0;109
F7	0;65	0;90	0;100	0;110
F8	0;66	0;91	0;101	0;111
F9	0;67	0;92	0;102	0;112
F10	0;68	0;93	0;103	0;113
HOME	0;71	55	0;119	—
UP ARROW	0;72	56	—	—
PAGE UP	0;73	57	0;132	—
LEFT ARROW	0;75	52	0;115	—
RIGHT ARROW	0;77	54	0;116	—
END	0;79	49	0;117	—
DOWN ARROW	0;80	50	—	—
PAGE DOWN	0;81	51	0;118	—
INS	0;82	48	—	—
DEL	0;83	46	—	—
PRINT SCREEN	—	—	0;114	—
A	97	65	1	0;30
B	98	66	2	0;48
C	99	67	3	0;46
D	100	68	4	0;32
E	101	69	5	0;18
F	102	70	6	0;33
G	103	71	7	0;34

Key	Alone	SHIFT+	CTRL+	ALT+
H	104	72	8	0;35
I	105	73	9	0;23
J	106	74	10	0;36
K	107	75	11	0;37
L	108	76	12	0;38
M	109	77	13	0;50
N	110	78	14	0;49
O	111	79	15	0;24
P	112	80	16	0;25
Q	113	81	17	0;16
R	114	82	18	0;19
S	115	83	19	0;31
T	116	84	20	0;20
U	117	85	21	0;22
V	118	86	22	0;47
W	119	87	23	0;17
X	120	88	24	0;45
Y	121	89	25	0;21
Z	122	90	26	0;44
1	49	33	—	0;120
2	50	64	—	0;121
3	51	35	—	0;122
4	52	36	—	0;123
5	53	37	—	0;124
6	54	94	—	0;125
7	55	38	—	0;126
8	56	42	—	0;127
9	57	40	—	0;128
0	48	41	—	0;129
-	45	95	—	0;130
=	61	43	—	0;131
TAB	0	0;15	—	—
Null	0;3	—	—	—

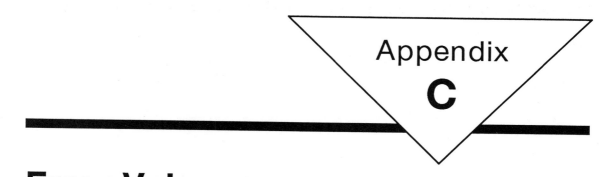

Error Values

Most of the Interrupt 21h function requests introduced with MS-DOS versions 2.0 and later set the carry flag if there is an error and identify the specific error by returning a number in the AX register. The following are the values that can be returned by functions, including Interrupt 21h Function 59h (Get Extended Error), and that are used in the ERROR structure in conjunction with Interrupt 21h Function 5D0Ah (Set Extended Error):

Value	Name
0001h	ERROR_INVALID_FUNCTION
0002h	ERROR_FILE_NOT_FOUND
0003h	ERROR_PATH_NOT_FOUND
0004h	ERROR_TOO_MANY_OPEN_FILES
0005h	ERROR_ACCESS_DENIED
0006h	ERROR_INVALID_HANDLE
0007h	ERROR_ARENA_TRASHED
0008h	ERROR_NOT_ENOUGH_MEMORY
0009h	ERROR_INVALID_BLOCK
000Ah	ERROR_BAD_ENVIRONMENT
000Bh	ERROR_BAD_FORMAT
000Ch	ERROR_INVALID_ACCESS
000Dh	ERROR_INVALID_DATA
000Fh	ERROR_INVALID_DRIVE
0010h	ERROR_CURRENT_DIRECTORY
0011h	ERROR_NOT_SAME_DEVICE
0012h	ERROR_NO_MORE_FILES
0013h	ERROR_WRITE_PROTECT
0014h	ERROR_BAD_UNIT
0015h	ERROR_NOT_READY
0016h	ERROR_BAD_COMMAND
0017h	ERROR_CRC
0018h	ERROR_BAD_LENGTH
0019h	ERROR_SEEK
001Ah	ERROR_NOT_DOS_DISK
001Bh	ERROR_SECTOR_NOT_FOUND
001Ch	ERROR_OUT_OF_PAPER
001Dh	ERROR_WRITE_FAULT

Value	Name
001Eh	ERROR_READ_FAULT
001Fh	ERROR_GEN_FAILURE
0020h	ERROR_SHARING_VIOLATION
0021h	ERROR_LOCK_VIOLATION
0022h	ERROR_WRONG_DISK
0023h	ERROR_FCB_UNAVAILABLE
0024h	ERROR_SHARING_BUFFER_EXCEEDED
0025h	ERROR_CODE_PAGE_MISMATCHED
0026h	ERROR_HANDLE_EOF
0027h	ERROR_HANDLE_DISK_FULL
0032h	ERROR_NOT_SUPPORTED
0033h	ERROR_REM_NOT_LIST
0034h	ERROR_DUP_NAME
0035h	ERROR_BAD_NETPATH
0036h	ERROR_NETWORK_BUSY
0037h	ERROR_DEV_NOT_EXIST
0038h	ERROR_TOO_MANY_CMDS
0039h	ERROR_ADAP_HDW_ERR
003Ah	ERROR_BAD_NET_RESP
003Bh	ERROR_UNEXP_NET_ERR
003Ch	ERROR_BAD_REM_ADAP
003Dh	ERROR_PRINTQ_FULL
003Eh	ERROR_NO_SPOOL_SPACE
003Fh	ERROR_PRINT_CANCELLED
0040h	ERROR_NETNAME_DELETED
0041h	ERROR_NETWORK_ACCESS_DENIED
0042h	ERROR_BAD_DEV_TYPE
0043h	ERROR_BAD_NET_NAME
0044h	ERROR_TOO_MANY_NAMES
0045h	ERROR_TOO_MANY_SESS
0046h	ERROR_SHARING_PAUSED
0047h	ERROR_REQ_NOT_ACCEP
0048h	ERROR_REDIR_PAUSED

Value	Name
0050h	ERROR_FILE_EXISTS
0051h	ERROR_DUP_FCB
0052h	ERROR_CANNOT_MAKE
0053h	ERROR_FAIL_I24
0054h	ERROR_OUT_OF_STRUCTURES
0055h	ERROR_ALREADY_ASSIGNED
0056h	ERROR_INVALID_PASSWORD
0057h	ERROR_INVALID_PARAMETER
0058h	ERROR_NET_WRITE_FAULT
005Ah	ERROR_SYS_COMP_NOT_LOADED

Index

G

H

I

T

U

V

W